Who's Who of the Horrors and Other Fantasy Films

THE INTERNATIONAL PERSONALITY ENCYCLOPEDIA
OF THE FANTASTIC FILM

David J. Hogan

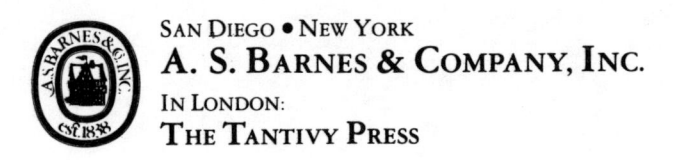

SAN DIEGO • NEW YORK
A. S. BARNES & COMPANY, INC.
IN LONDON:
THE TANTIVY PRESS

This book is dedicated to my parents
   for obvious reasons
To Kim
   for love,
And to Forrest J. Ackerman
   for making every Monster a Famous one.

Who's Who of the Horrors copyright © 1980

by David J. Hogan.

All rights reserved under International and Pan American Copyright Conventions. No part of this book may be reproduced in any manner whatsoever without written permission from the publisher, except in the case of brief quotations embodied in reviews and articles.

First Edition
Manufactured in the United States of America

For information write to:
A.S. Barnes & Company, Inc.
P.O. Box 3051
La Jolla, California 92038

The Tantivy Press
Magdalen House
136-148 Tooley Street
London, SE1 2TT, England

Library of Congress Cataloging in Publication Data

Hogan, David, 1953-
   Who's who of the horrors.

   1. Horror films — Dictionaries.   I.   Title.
PN1995.9.H6H6   791.43′0909′352   79-17606
ISBN 0-498-02475-X

1 2 3 4 5 6 7 8 9   84 83 82 81 80

Contents

Preface	4
Acknowledgments	6
Introduction	7
Who's Who of the Horrors	9
Index	257

Preface

My Mother, The Vampire Lady

This volume is the first reference book of its kind. It exists because there is a need for it, because the cineasts have for a long time ignored films that can be classed as horror, science fiction, or fantasy—the fantastic film. Serious works devoted to the genre comprise an unforgivably small portion of the great body of film literature. *Who's Who of the Horrors* is an alphabetical compendium of information about more than one thousand people who have made significant contributions to the fantastic film. It is hoped that the book will fill a gap in film reference; contained within its pages is a history of imaginative cinema.

Who's Who of the Horrors and other Fantasy Films is also a love letter.

In 1960 I was seven years old. That year my mother was featured as one Countess Battina in the pages of *Famous Monsters of Filmland* magazine. I was amazed. There she was, with a close family friend as Count Scalpela, dressed in black, looking cadaverous and starved, up to no good in a blood bank. I looked through the rest of the magazine, absorbing all the gruesome photographs and the punning but informative text, and I was hooked. I was the only kid in the neighborhood who saved all the old monster magazines. While my friends and I watched *The Unknown Terror* on television and they said, "That's not fungus, it's soap suds!", I would think, "Yeah, but what if it *was* fungus? What if the director *told* Mala Powers that it was fungus? Who can *blame* her for screaming so much?" What if? The question is at the core of the appeal and strength of the fantastic film; it can lead a person's mind anywhere, and it's a most satisfying trip.

As I grew older, I fell in love with Marilyn Monroe and learned who Godard is and why Raoul Walsh is a great director, but I still hung on to the old monster magazines. And bought new ones. I went to college and wrote lofty little essays on the significance of camera angles in *All the King's Men* and tried to pick apart *8½* with the rest of the world's undergraduates, but I'd still stay home Saturday afternoons to watch *King Kong* for the twenty-fifth time. I was terribly impressed by *Hiroshima, Mon Amour* and realized that Leni Riefenstahl is a genius, but still no film experience could make me shiver with awe and delight the way the climax of *Them!* could.

The first article I sold to a professional film magazine concerned *I Married a Monster from Outer Space.* I wrote it because the film is a good one that is little known. Such a consideration strikes me as being the overriding motivation behind this book. Not only are most people unaware of the artistic excellence of much of the fantastic film output, but they are unaware of the great value in *all* of it, and the distinctive way in which it speaks to us: as individuals, as members of a nation with a shared consciousness, and as human animals. Mala Powers may have screamed her head off when the fungus oozed down the walls of the cave and the fungus men were closing in, but she was rescued and, by golly, whether we knew it or not, we had just faced death and come out on top. And felt better. A bad little movie momentarily thrilled us and let us confront our most terrible fear and wring its neck. We asked "What if?" and found that, perhaps, it is a question with an answer that can make us feel better and braver.

Because the fantastic film speaks so pointedly to our fears, it may qualify as the most important of all movie genres. It asks the questions which, in more realistic contexts, might be intolerable. And the fantastic film, even at its worst, is also fun. At its best, it can be indescribably thrilling. This book is for film researchers and historians, but it is especially for everyone who has been thrilled by the giant ants of *Them!* as they trill in the storm drains of Los Angeles, for everyone who has wished that Barbara Steele would prowl around *their* house, for all the people who quiver with delicious terror when the Martian war machines of *The War of the Worlds* glide unharmed through the atomic haze, and for everyone who shares Colin Clive's frenzied excitement when, as *Frankenstein,* he cries, "It's alive! It's alive!"

Acknowledgments

The author would like to acknowledge the assistance and support of the following people in the preparation of this book:
  Frank Araca and Count Scalpela
  Mark Frank
  Paula Klaw and *Movie Star News*
  Wilma and Ellis Christian Lenz
  Paul Anthony Parla
  Stephen Sally
  Don and Maggie Thompson

Introduction

Entries are arranged alphabetically. Names in small caps in the body of an entry indicate a cross-reference. Years given for films are U.S. release dates; many films were actually shot the preceding year.

Birth and death dates are as accurate as possible. In a number of cases I have had to make a reasonable guess at a year of birth—this is indicated in the entry by "ca. (circa) 19-". In most instances these estimations have been based on quotes from other sources, which may read, for instance, ". . . he was eighteen years old at the time of his first feature in 1918." The birth entry would thus be "ca. 1900". I have hesitated to be more definite in such cases because the subject's year of birth could be 1899 or the source could be inexact. Overall, I have been pleased to record vital statistics and compile filmographies of many people for whom no such information has been recorded before in book form.

In a very few instances, birth dates given here differ from information given in other sources. At times in the course of research I became suspicious of certain information and did further research. A case in point involves birth dates for the Three Stooges. I was not satisfied with the dates supplied by an established source and consulted the respective autobiographies of Larry Fine and Moe Howard, two of the Stooges. There I found dates of birth which, I feel sure, are more reliable.

Finally, there is the matter of choosing the people to be included. Unavoidably, this is a highly subjective option. Some of them, like Karloff and the Chaneys, are of such obvious importance to the genre that there could be no question about their inclusion. The credentials of others demanded closer scrutiny. By and large, my rule has been to include people who in my judgment have made significant contributions to the fantastic film or whose involvement in a fantastic film is itself somehow significant. Most familiar names from the thirties, forties, and fifties appear here, as well as names new to the fantastic film. Some readers may be surprised to encounter the likes of Humphrey Bogart and Lenny Bruce. It is my hope that few readers will wonder why their particular favorite is missing. With the exception of Walt Disney, people active in cartoon animation have been excluded. Much as I love and respect the work of Max Fleischer, Chuck Jones, Bob Clampett, *et al*, to number them all would have swollen the book to unmanageable size. The cartoon men and women deserve a book of their own.

My cast of characters ranges from the crassly commercial to the avant-garde, from filmmakers active in the 1890s to those working in 1980. Prominent makeup artists, set designers, composers, and special effects technicians are represented along with performers, scenarists, producers, and directors. Due to considerations of individual importance and interest, not all filmographies are intended to be complete; only films with fantastic content are considered, and of those I have in some cases chosen titles that will best give an accurate picture of the progression of the subject's career. However, when a period follows the last film listed, the filmography may be considered to include all relevant films. Among the abbreviations used: d=director; p=producer; w=writer; co-w=co-writer; ph=photography; b/o=based on.

The reader may wish to refer to a number of other books for additional information. Walt Lee's three-volume *Reference Guide to Fantastic Films* (published 1972–74; Chelsea-Lee Books) is indispensable to the fantastic film enthusiast; it lists all films in the genre. Along broader lines, Leslie Halliwell's lively and informative *The Filmgoer's Companion* (latest, revised edition 1977; Hill and Wang) is recommended. Others: *Movie Magic* (1974; St. Martin's Press) and *The Horror People* (1976; St. Martin's Press), both by John Brosnan; *Dark Dreams* by Charles Derry (1977; A.S. Barnes); *Kings of the Bs* by Todd McCarthy and Charles Flynn (1975; E.P. Dutton); *Tarzan of the Movies* by Gabe Essoe (1968; Citadel); Calvin Beck's *Heroes of the Horrors* (1975; Collier); and *An Illustrated History of the Horror Film*, by Carlos Clarens (1967; Putnam).

Useful periodicals include Frederick S. Clarke's *Cinefantastique*, *Famous Monsters of Filmland*, *Castle of Frankenstein*, Sam Irvin's *Bizarre*, *Starlog*, and Mark Frank's *Photon*. My debt to all the above is gratefully acknowledged.

A

ABBOTT, BUD (1895–1974). Slender, acerbic American comedian who, with partner LOU COSTELLO, kept Universal Studios solvent during the first half of the forties. By the end of that decade their popularity had slipped badly, and their later films (with the notable exception of *Abbott and Costello Meet Frankenstein*, 1948) are dismal. Abbott was perhaps the finest straight man of his time, but his screen persona often borders on the unnecessarily cruel. For list of films see COSTELLO.

ACKERMAN, FORREST J (1916–). American science fiction and film authority, editor of *Famous Monsters of Filmland* magazine since its inception in 1958. Looking something like a stocky version of VINCENT PRICE, Ackerman has had cameo roles in *The Time Travelers*, 1964; *Queen of Blood*, 1966; *Dracula vs. Frankenstein*, 1971; *Schlock*, 1973; and *Kentucky Fried Movie*, 1978.

ACQUANETTA, (BURNU) (1921–). Mysterious-seeming American Indian actress and one time "Venezuelan Volcano," popular in exotic thrillers. *The Arabian Nights*, 1942; *Captive Wild Woman*, 1943; *Jungle Woman*, 1944; *Dead Man's Eyes*, 1944; *Tarzan and the Leopard Woman*, 1946. *Lost Continent*, 1951.

Bud Abbott *(top)* and Lou Costello, at the peak of their success in the 1940s.

Acquanetta leads her minions to the attack in *Tarzan and the Leopard Woman* (1946).

ADAM, KEN (1921–). British set designer who has done some spectacular work for the James Bond films, most notably the impressive rocket base in *You Only Live Twice*, 1967. *Dr. Strangelove* or: *How I Learned to Stop Worrying and Love the Bomb*, 1964; *Goldfinger*, 1964. *Thunderball*, 1965; *Chitty Chitty Bang Bang*, 1968; *Live and Let Die*, 1973; *Moonraker*, 1979; etc.

ADAMS, BEVERLY (1945–). Canadian leading lady in American films, most familiar as a good-looking mannequin in the brainless Matt Helm comedy-fantasies of the sixties. *Birds Do It*, 1966; *The Silencers*, 1966; *Murderer's Row*, 1966; *The Ambushers*, 1967; *Torture Garden*, 1968.

Julie Adams with Richard Carlson in *The Creature from the Black Lagoon* (1954).

Nick Adams amidst the panic in *Frankenstein Conquers the World* (1966).

ADAMS, JULIE (1927–). American leading lady who was a mainstay of Universal Studios during the fifties. She is most fetching in a white bathing suit in *The Creature from the Black Lagoon*, 1954; one can readily understand why the poor Gill-Man got so worked up. *Underwater City*, 1962; *Psychic Killer*, 1976. Married to actor/director RAY DANTON.

ADAMS, NICK (1932–68). Talented American character lead whose unorthodox looks and manner restricted his range of roles. Moviegoers were ready for Adams' type in the sixties, but by then his career had faded. *Die Monster Die!* 1965; *Monster Zero*, 1965; *Frankenstein Conquers the World*, 1966; *Mission Mars*, 1968.

ADAMSON, AL. American producer/director of hopelessly inept nudies and monster pictures. *Blood of Dracula's Castle*, 1969; *Blood of Ghastly Horror*, 1971; *Horror of the Blood Monsters* (an incoherent pastiche of dreadful Filipino films with new footage added), 1971; *Dracula vs. Frankenstein*, 1971; *Cinderella 2000*, 1977, etc.

ADDAMS, CHARLES (1913–). Macabre American cartoonist, noted for his ghoulish characters and fiendish wit. He designed the titles for *The Old Dark House*, 1963, and *Murder by Death*, 1976.

ADDAMS, DAWN (1930–). British leading lady active on the continent. *The Two Faces of Dr. Jekyll*, 1960; *The Vampire Lovers*, 1970; *The Vault of Horror*, 1973; *Star Maidens* (British TV), 1975.

AGAR, JOHN (1921–). American leading man of second features, first husband of Shirley Temple. Agar met and defeated all manner of beasts in his film career and was steadily active throughout the fifties and early sixties despite having been a bit on the dull side. He retired from films in the early seventies to sell insurance. *The Rocket Man*, 1954; *Revenge of the Creature*, 1955; *Tarantula*, 1955; *Daugher of Dr. Jekyll*, 1957; *The Brain from Planet Arous*, 1958; *Invisible Invaders*, 1959; *Hand of Death*, 1961; *Journey to the 7th Planet*, 1962; *Curse of the Swamp Creature*, 1967; *Zontar: The Thing From Venus*, 1968; *King Kong* (cameo), 1976.

ALDRICH, ROBERT (1918–). American director whose penchant for dense characterization led him to create heavy-handed but good-humored horror thrillers. His *Whatever Happened to Baby Jane?* 1962 is a genuine piece of kitschy Americana and helped legitimize the grotesque. *Hush, Hush Sweet Charlott*, 1964; *The Legend of Lylah Clare*, 1968.

ALLAND, WILLIAM (1916–). American producer associated with Universal during the fifties, former actor. Films as producer: *The Black Castle*, 1952; *It Came from Outer Space*, 1953; *The Creature from the Black Lagoon*, 1954; *Revenge of the Creature*, 1955; *This Island Earth*, 1955; *Tarantula*, 1955; *The Creature Walks among Us*, 1956; *The Deadly Mantis* (& story) 1957; *The Land Unknown*, 1957.

Tiny couple: John Agar and June Kenney in *Attack of the Puppet People* (1958).

ALLEN, DAVID. Talented young American stop-motion animator of the seventies, from television. *When Dinosaurs Ruled the Earth* (chasmasaurus sequence only) 1971; *Equinox*, 1971; *Flesh Gordon*, 1972; *The Crater Lake Monster*, 1977; *Laserblast*, 1977. *Witches Brew*, 1980.

ALLEN, IRWIN (1916–). Enterprising American producer/director whose films are characterized by splashy visuals and brainless scenarios. *The Animal World* (with dinosaur sequences by RAY HARRYHAUSEN) 1956; *The Story of Mankind*, 1957; *The Lost World*, 1960; *Voyage to the Bottom of the Sea*, 1961; *Five Weeks in a Balloon*, 1962; *One Hour to Doomsday*, 1968; *City Beneath the Sea*, 1971; *Swarm*, 1978; *When Time Ran Out*, 1980.

ALLEN, WOODY (1935–). Gifted American comedy writer/actor/director who found millions of fans with his persona of a red-haired and bespectacled neurotic nebbish. *What's Up Tiger Lily?* (a hilarious redubbing of an imitation-James Bond thriller from Japan), 1969; *Everything You Always Wanted to Know About Sex But Were Afraid to Ask*, 1972; *Sleeper*, 1973; *Love and Death*, 1975.

ALTMAN, ROBERT (1922–). Significant and prolific American director/screenwriter whose talent seems matched only by an unfortunate inclination toward the glib and facile. Altman's films, at their best, show a judicious understanding of human nature and a grudging fondness for the follies of the American heart and mind. Films with fantastic content: *Countdown*, 1968; *Brewster McCloud*, 1971; *Images*, 1972; *Quintet* (post-holocaust drama), 1979; *Popeye* (from the comic strip), 1980.

ALYN, KIRK (1915–). Stalwart and handsome American serial star of the forties, winning as "The Man of Steel" in *Superman*, 1948 and *Atom Man vs. Superman*, 1950. Also: *The Girl Who Dared*, 1944; *Radar Patrol vs. Spy King*, 1950; *Blackhawk*, 1952. In recent years Alyn has become popular on the nostalgia circuit and was cast as Lois Lane's father in *Superman*, 1978. Unfortunately, his footage was cut before the film's release, and all that remains is a shot of the back of his head.

Kirk Alyn as Superman in *Superman* (1948).

Merry Anders.

ANDERS, LUANA (1940–). Offbeat American leading lady whose relative obscurity conceals a considerable talent. *The Pit and the Pendulum*, 1961; *Dementia 13*, 1963; *Night Tide*, 1963; *The Killing Kind*, 1973.

ANDERS, MERRY (1932–). Pretty heroine of minor American films. *The Hypnotic Eye*, 1960; *20,000 Eyes*, 1961; *House of the Damned*, 1963; *Beauty and the Beast*, 1963; *Women of the Prehistoric Planet*, 1965; *Legacy of Blood*, 1972.

ANDERSON, LEONA. American actress whose brief bit as a blind witch-woman in WILLIAM CASTLE'S *House on Haunted Hill*, 1958, is the only genuinely frightening moment in an otherwise gimmicked film. Kids have been known to wet their pants when Anderson, leering and with clawlike hands outstretched, floats past the heroine in a dark basement.

ANDERSON, MICHAEL (1920–). British director who has displayed a competent touch on overblown projects. *Will Any Gentleman?...* 1956; *1984* (razor-sharp and his best work) 1956; *Doc Savage—Man of Bronze*, 1975; *Logan's Run*, 1976; *Dominique*, 1978.

Leona Anderson puts on her best face for the benefit of Carolyn Craig in *House on Haunted Hill* (1958).

Poster art from Michael Anderson's 1956 interpretation of George Orwell's *1984*.

14 ANDERSON

ANDERSON, RICHARD (1926–). Tall, quiet American supporting actor, familiar as Oscar Goldman on television's the "Six Million Dollar Man," 73–78. Films: *Forbidden Planet*, 1956; *Curse of the Faceless Man* (lead), 1958; *Seconds*, 1966.

ANDRESS, URSULA (1936–). Spectacularly endowed Swiss leading lady active on both sides of the Atlantic. She is a limited actress, but one is usually out of the theater and halfway home before noticing. *Dr. No* (as Honey), 1962; *She* (title role), 1965; *The Tenth Victim*, 1965; *Casino Royale*, 1967; *Clash of the Titans* (as Aphrodite), 1981.

ANDREWS, DANA (1909–). American leading man, a tough hero in the forties and later a determined character actor. *Curse of the Demon*, 1958; *Crack in the World*, 1965; *The Satan Bug*, 1965; *Spy in Your Eye*, 1966; *The Frozen Dead*, 1967.

Ursula Andress.

ANKERS, EVELYN (1918—). American leading lady of striking appearance who remained unruffled in confrontation with monsters and some improbable scripts. *Hold That Ghost*, 1941; *The Wolf Man*, 1941; *The Ghost of Frankenstein*, 1942; *The Mad Ghoul*, 1943; *Captive Wild Woman*, 1943; *Weird Woman*, 1944; *The Frozen Ghost*, 1945.

ANKRUM, MORRIS (1897—1964). American character actor whose authoritative voice and stern manner brought him many roles as general, scientist, and high-ranking politician. *Invaders from Mars*, 1953; *Half Human* (U.S.-release version only), 1955; *Earth vs. the Flying Saucers*, 1956; *The Giant Claw*, 1957; *Kronos*, 1957; *How to Make a Monster*, 1958; *Giant from the Unknown*, 1958; *The Most Dangerous Man Alive*, 1958. *X–The Man with the X-ray Eyes*, 1963; many others.

ARGENTO DARIO. Italian writer/director of stylish horror thrillers. *The Bird with the Crystal Plumage*, 1970; *Four Flies on Grey Velvet*, 1972; *Deep Red*, 1976; *Suspiria*, 1978.

Morris Ankrum *(left)* with Ed Kemmer and Sally Fraser in *Giant from the Unknown* (1958).

Evelyn Ankers menaced by Lon Chaney, Jr., in *The Wolf Man* (1941).

Jean Arless in a characteristic pose from William Castle's *Homicidal* (1961).

ARLEN, HAROLD (1905—   ). American songwriter who composed the lovely melodies heard in *The Wizard of Oz*, 1939. (See also E.Y. HARBURG). Arlen also scored *Cabin in the Sky*, 1943.

ARLEN, RICHARD (1898—1976). Tough, square-jawed American leading man, active from the twenties until his death. *Island of Lost Souls*, 1933; *Alice in Wonderland*, 1933; *The Lady and the Monster*, 1944; *The Phantom Speaks*, 1945; *The Crawling Hand*, 1963; *The Human Duplicators*, 1965.

ARLESS, JEAN (ca. 1940—   ). American actress whose debut in *Homicidal*, 1961, a murder thriller that hints at transsexuality, had a purposely ambiguous aspect; producer WILIAM CASTLE alluded to the possibility that she was in reality a he and admitted in interviews that the name was a *nom de plume*. Arless has not been seen on the screen again.

ARMSTRONG, ROBERT (1890—1973). American actor, usually cast as an aggressive fast talker. As Carl Denham, he brought back *King Kong*, 1933, and discovered *Son of Kong*, 1933. *The Mad Ghoul*, 1943; *Mighty Joe Young* (as Max O'Hara), 1949.

ARNESS, JAMES (1923—   ). Tall, amiable American actor who gained prominence as television's Marshal Matt Dillon ("Gunsmoke" 1955—75). *Two Lost Worlds*, 1950; *The Thing* (title role), 1951; *Them!* 1954.

Robert Armstrong.

ARNOLD, JACK (1916–). American director of ambitious science fiction thrillers whose reputation has become a bit inflated. Though usually thoughtful, a typical Arnold film works better in moments than as a whole. He is characteristically conscious of the frame and has explored its visual limits interestingly. Several critics have written of Arnold's fascination with the desert, but this may be simply a chance of script assignments. His *The Incredible Shrinking Man*, 1957, is one of the best science fiction films of the fifties and, despite its sensational subject matter, projects a quiet dignity. *It Came from Outer Space*, 1953; *The Creature from the Black Lagoon*, 1954; *Revenge of the Creature*, 1955; *Tarantula*, 1955; *This Island Earth* (part; uncredited), 1955; *The Monolith Monsters* (story only), 1957; *The Space Children*, 1958; *Monster on the Campus*, 1958.

ASHLEY, JOHN. American actor, a baby-faced teen type who ascended from second leads in Annette Funicello and Frankie Avalon beach movies to star status in low budget horror and science fiction films. He turned producer in the seventies. *How to Make a Monster*, 1958; *Frankenstein's Daughter*, 1959; *The Eye Creatures*, 1968; *Beast of Blood*, 1970; *Beast of the Yellow Night* (and co-p; w/EDDIE ROMERO), 1971; *Twilight People* (and co-p; w/EDDIE ROMERO), 1972; *The Womanhunt* (and p), 1972; *Blood Demon*, 1973; others.

ASHTON, ROY. Australian makeup artist, a longtime contributor to Hammer horror films, more recently with Amicus Films. *The Mummy*, 1959; *The Man Who Could Cheat Death*, 1959; *Brides of Dracula*, 1960; *The Curse of the Werewolf*, 1961; *The Evil of Frankenstein*, 1964; *The Gorgon*, 1964; *Dracula, Prince of Darkness*, 1966; *Asylum*, 1972; *Tales from the Crypt*, 1972; *The Vault of Horror*, 1973;

The Gill Man attacks in Jack Arnold's *The Creature from the Black Lagoon* (1954). Julie Adams is at the left.

Roy Ashton's brilliant makeup job on Oliver Reed for *Curse of the Werewolf* (1961).

James Arness and Joan Weldon discuss what to do about the giant ants in *Them!* (1954).

ASTHER, NILS (1897–). Swedish leading man in Hollywood during the forties. As *The Man in Half Moon Street*, 1944, he dreams of immortality and retains his youth with glandular transplants. When the implants fail, the predictable happens. *Night Monster*, 1942; *Bluebeard*, 1944.

ATWILL, LIONEL (1885–1946). Sinister-seeming British character actor who became Hollywood's greatest mad scientist. Often coming to a bad end, Atwill has an arm torn off by BORIS KARLOFF in *Son of Frankenstein*, 1939, and is decapitated by CLAUDE RAINS in *The Man Who Reclaimed His Head*, 1935. Also *Dr. X*, 1932; *The Vampire Bat*, 1933; *The Mystery of the Wax Museum*, 1933; *Mark of the Vampire*, 1935; *Man Made Monster*, 1941; *The Mad Doctor of Market Street*, 1942; *The Ghost of Frankenstein*, 1942; *Frankenstein Meets the Wolf Man*, 1943; *House of Frankenstein*, 1945; *House of Dracula*, 1945; others.

AUBERT, LENORE (ca. 1918–). Hollywood actress of Yugoslavian origin, usually seen as a darkly seductive schemer. *The Catman of Paris*, 1946; *Abbott and Costello Meet Frankenstein*, 1948; *Abbott and Costello Meet the Killer, Boris Karloff*, 1949.

AUER, MISCHA (1905–67). Eccentric Russian comic actor, in Hollywood from the late twenties. *Just Imagine*, 1930; *Drums of Jeopardy*, 1931; *The Monster Walks*, 1932; *Sinister Hands*, 1932; *Rasputin and the Empress*, 1933; *Tarzan the Fearless*, 1933; *Condemned to Live*, 1935; *Hold That Ghost*, 1941; *Hellzapoppin'*, 1942; *A Dog, a Mouse and a Sputnik*, 1960; *The Christmas That Almost Wasn't*, 1966.

AVALON, FRANKIE (1939–). American singer/actor, popular as hero of many beach party movies of the mid-sixties. *Voyage to the Bottom of the Sea*, 1961; *Panic in Year Zero*, 1962; *Ghost in the Invisible Bikini*, 1966; *Horror House*, 1970.

Lionel Atwill.

Roy Barcroft in a publicity still for *The Purple Monster Strikes* (1945).

B

BACLANOVA, OLGA (1899–1974). Russian dancer memorable as the supremely heartless high wire artist in *Freaks*, 1932. *The Man Who Laughs*, 1928.

BAKALEINIKOFF, MISCHA. Prolific Russian film composer active throughout the forties and fifties for Columbia's B-picture unit. His scores are effective but have a tendency to sound alike, heavy with blaring horns and mock-urban rhythms. *The Spiral Staircase*, 1945; *Voice of the Whistler*, 1945; *The Secret of the Whistler*, 1947; *Atom Man vs. Superman*, 1950; *Creature with the Atom Brain*, 1955; *It Came from Beneath the Sea*, 1955; *Earth vs. the Flying Saucers*, 1956; *The Werewolf*, 1956; *The Giant Claw*, 1957; *The 27th Day*, 1957; *Twenty Million Miles to Earth*, 1957; *Have Rocket, Will Travel*, 1959; many others.

BAKER, RICK (1950–). Talented young American makeup artist and costume maker with a fondness for apes. *The Octoman*, 1971; *Schlock*, 1973; *The Exorcist*, 1973; *It's Alive*, 1974; *King Kong* (as Kong, in a costume of his design), 1976; *Star Wars*, 1977; *The Incredible Melting Man*, 1978; *Kentucky Fried Movie*, 1978; *The Fury*, 1978; *Tanya's Island* (designs only), 1980.

BAKER, ROY WARD (1916–). Slick British director with Hammer and Amicus Films. *Five Million Years to Earth*, 1967; *The Anniversary*, 1968; *Moon Zero Two*, 1969; *The Vampire Lovers*, 1970; *Scars of Dracula*, 1970; *Dr. Jekyll and Sister Hyde*, 1972; *The Vault of Horror*, 1973; *The Legend of the Seven Golden Vampires*, 1974; etc.

BANKHEAD, TALLULAH (1902–68). Raspy, self-destructive American stage and screen star who followed BETTE DAVIS and JOAN CRAWFORD into psychological horror thrillers with *Die, Die My Darling*, 1965. This, her final film, seems to suit her penchant for theatricality.

BANKS, LESLIE (1890–1952). British character actor in Hollywood films, memorable as the mad Count Zaroff in *The Most Dangerous Game*, 1932. *The Trans-Atlantic Tunnel*, 1935; *Chamber of Horrors*, 1940.

BARCROFT, ROY (1902–69). American actor, everybody's favorite serial villain. In scores of films from 1932, including *Haunted Harbor*, 1944; *The Vampire's Ghost*, 1945; *The Purple Monster Strikes* (as leader of the Martians), 1945; *Flying Disc Man from Mars*, 1950, *Superman vs. the Gorilla Gang* (amateur), 1965; *Radar Men from the Moon*, 1952; *Billy the Kid vs. Dracula*, 1966; *Destination Inner Space*, 1966.

Demon racer Mathilda the Hun sets her sights in Paul Bartel's *Death Race 2000* (1975).

Gene Barry reaches for the alien capsule that could destroy the world in *The 27th Day* (1957).

BARKER, LEX (1919–73). American actor who in 1949 succeeded JOHNNY WEISMULLER as Hollywood's Tarzan and played the role in five films until 1953. Although Barker's interpretation of the character was the favorite of Tarzan creator EDGAR RICE BURROUGHS, he strikes one as being too urbane for the role. The films remain good fun, however, and gave Barker the exposure necessary to become a major star in Europe during the sixties. *Tarzan's Magic Fountain*, 1949; *Tarzan and the Slave Girl*, 1950; *Tarzan's Peril*, 1951; *Tarzan's Savage Fury*, 1952; *Tarzan and the She-Devil*, 1954; *The Blood Demon*, 1967.

BARR, TIM. American special effects technician, often in association with WAH CHANG and GENE WARREN. *The Time Machine* (Academy Award), 1960; *Atlantis, the Lost Continent*, 1961; *The Wonderful World of the Brothers Grimm*, 1962; others.

BARRON, LOUIS and BEBE. American husband and wife composer team whose most famous work is the "Electronic Tonalities" score for *Forbidden Planet*, 1956. Also *The Very Eye of the Night*, 1959; *Spaceboy*, 1972.

BARRY, GENE (1921–). Smooth American leading man, often cast as an urbane fellow with a sense of humor. As hero of *The War of the Worlds*, 1953, Barry more than holds his own against the special effects. Also seen in *The 27th Day*, 1957.

BARRY, JOHN (1933–). British composer who wrote excellent scores for a number of the James Bond thrillers. His score for the 1976 remake of *King Kong*, however, is a major disappointment. *Goldfinger*, 1964; *Thunderball*, 1965; *You Only Live Twice*, 1967; *On Her Majesty's Secret Service*, 1969: *Diamonds Are Forever*, 1971; *Moonraker*, 1979; *The Black Hole*, 1979; *Night Games*, 1980.

BARRYMORE, JOHN (1882–1942). American star actor, a brilliant talent whose self-destructiveness has become a Hollywood legend. *Dr. Jekyll and Mr. Hyde*, 1920; *Svengali*, 1931; *The Mad Genius*, 1931; *The Invisible Woman*, 1940.

BARRYMORE, LIONEL (1878–1954). Respected and much-liked American star character actor, often seen as a growly grump with a good heart. Brother of JOHN BARRYMORE. *The Devil's Garden*, 1920; *The Bells*, 1926; *Mysterious Island*, 1929; *The Unholy Night* (d only), 1929; *Rasputin and the Empress* (as Rasputin), 1933; *Mark of the Vampire*, 1935; *The Devil Doll*, 1936.

BARTEL, PAUL. Talented American director who made a promising commercial debut with *Private Parts*, 1972, but seemed to have forgotten everything by the time he directed *Death Race 2000*, 1975. *The Secret Cinema* (in which a young woman discovers she exists only in someone's film), ca. 70; *Hollywood Boulevard* (actor only), 1976; *Piranha* (actor only), 1978.

BARTON, CHARLES T. (1902–). American director who specialized in wartime fluff and later guided *Abbott and Costello Meet Frankenstein*, 1948, to delightful success. His direction deftly balances horror with comedy and coaxed the last outstanding performance from an aging but enthusiastic BELA LUGOSI. *The Time of Their Lives*, 1946; *Abbott and Costello Meet the Killer, Boris Karloff*, 1949; *Africa Screams*, 1949; *The Shaggy Dog*, 1959.

BASEHART, RICHARD (1915–). Soft-spoken American leading actor, most-widely familiar as Admiral Nelson on television's "Voyage to the Bottom of the Sea", 1964–68. *The Satan Bug*, 1965; *One Hour to Doomsday*, 1968; *Mansion of the Doomed*, 1976; *The Island of Dr. Moreau* (as the Sayer of the Law), 1977.

Charles T. Barton's delightful blend of horror and comedy, *Abbott and Costello Meet Frankenstein* (1948). Menacing our heroes are Bela Lugosi and Glenn Strange.

BATES, RALPH (1940–). Youthful British actor who found success in Hammer horror films of the early seventies. *The Horror of Frankenstein*, 1970; *Lust for a Vampire*, 1971; *Dr. Jekyll and Sister Hyde* (as Jekyll), 1972; *Fear in the Night*, 1975; *Devil Within Her*, 1976.

BAU, GEORGE (1905–74). American makeup artist who innovated new methods of constructing plastic and foam prosthetic appliances. *The Hunchback Of Notre Dame*, 1939; *Arsenic and Old Lace*, 1944; *House of Wax*, 1953; *The Black Sleep*, 1956.

BAU, GORDON (1907–75). American makeup artist whose elegant body designs transformed ROD STEIGER into *The Illustrated Man*, 1969. Brother of GEORGE BAU.

BAUR, HARRY (1881–1943). Accomplished French actor who played the alchemist in *Le Golem*, 1937. He made the mistake in 1942 of going to Nazi Germany to star in a splashy musical, and when it was discovered that he was a Jew, Goebbels ordered the actor's internment in a concentration camp where he was later executed. *Raspoutine* (as Rasputin), 1939.

BAVA, MARIO (1914–1980). Italian director of moody, often grisly horror thrillers. A former cinematographer, Bava retained a keen feel for the visual, although in recent years the scripts he interpreted had been substandard. He made his directorial debut in 1960 with *Black Sunday*, an atmospheric and elegantly disquieting work which has the added distinction of being the first starring vehicle for BARBARA STEELE. Soon afterward, Bava fell prey to self-indulgence and overuse of the zoom lens. Bava was perhaps the world's foremost creator of beautifully shot "bad" movies. *Caltiki, the Immortal Monster*, (ph only; credited as "John Foam"), 1961; *The Evil Eye*, 1962; *Black Sabbath*, 1963; *Blood and Black Lace*, 1964; *Planet of the Vampires*, 1965; *What!* (credited as John M. Old), 1965; *Dr. Goldfoot and the Girl Bombs*, 1966; *Kill Baby Kill*, 1967; *A Hatchet for the Honeymoon*, 1970: *Curse of the Living Dead*, 1974; *The House of Exorcism*, 1976; *Beyond the Door II*, 1979; others.

Beautiful Barbara Steele eyes the corpse of her father in Mario Bava's brilliant *Black Sunday* (1960).

John Beal as *The Vampire* (1957) with Coleen Gray.

BAXT, GEORGE. British screenwriter whose scenario for JOHN MOXEY'S *Horror Hotel*, 1960, is a real shocker. Also *Circus of Horrors*, 1960; *The Shadow of the Cat*, 1961; *Burn Witch Burn* (co-w; w/RICHARD MATHESON and CHARLES BEAUMONT), 1962; *Horror on Snape Island* (story only), 1972; etc.

BAXTER, LES (1922–). American composer who scored many of ROGER CORMAN'S POE films in the early sixties. *Macabre*, 1958; *The Bride and the Beast*, 1958; *House of Usher*, 1960; *The Pit and the Pendulum*, 1961; *Tales of Terror*, 1962; *Panic in Year Zero*, 1962; *The Raven*, 1962; *X—The Man with the X-ray Eyes*, 1963; *Cry of the Banshee*, 1970; *Frogs*, 1972; many others.

BAY, SARA (ca. 1952–). Spanish leading lady in low budget sex-horror films of the seventies. She has undulated through *Lady Frankenstein* (title role), 1973, and *The Devil's Wedding Night* (as Countess Dracula), 1973.

BEACHAM, STEPHANIE (1949–). Statuesque British leading lady. *The Nightcomers*, 1971; *The Devil's Widow*, 1972; *Dracula A.D.1972*, 1972; *And Now the Screaming Starts*, 1973.

BEAL, JOHN (1909–). American actor whose role as *The Vampire*, 1957, provides the most sympathetic filmic view of vampirism. As a small-town doctor, Beal's bloodlust is caused by pills he unwittingly takes; only in death does he revert to his true self. *The Cat and the Canary*, 1939.

BEATTY, CLYDE (1903–65). Intrepid American lion tamer and circus personality who starred in a few gaudy but amusing films. *The Lost Jungle*, 1934; *Darkest Africa* aka *Batmen of Africa*, 1936; *Africa Screams*, 1949.

Stephanie Beacham.

BEAUDINE, WILLIAM (1890–1970). American director of scores of programmers ranging from juvenile comedy to sexploitation. Possibly the most prolific director in the history of western cinema. *The Living Ghost*, 1942; *Voodoo Man*, 1944; *Ghost Chasers*, 1951; *Bela Lugosi Meets a Brooklyn Gorilla*, 1952; *Billy the Kid vs. Dracula*, 1966; *Jesse James Meets Frankenstein's Daugther*, 1966.

BEAUMONT, CHARLES (1929–67). Talented and active American science fiction and fantasy writer. *Queen of Outer Space*, 1958; *Burn Witch Burn* (co-w; w/RICHARD MATHESON and GEORGE BAXT), 1962; *The Haunted Palace*, 1963; *The Masque of the Red Death* (co-w; w/R. Wright Campbell), 1964; *The Seven Faces of Dr. Lao*, 1964.

BEEBE, FORD (1888–). Prolific American director of serials and B-films. *Shadow of the Eagle*, 1932; *Flash Gordon's Trip to Mars* (co-d; w/Robert F. Hill), 1938; *Flash Gordon Conquers the Universe* (co-d; w/Ray Taylor), 1940; *Night Monster*, 1942; *The Invisible Man's Revenge* (and p), 1944; many others.

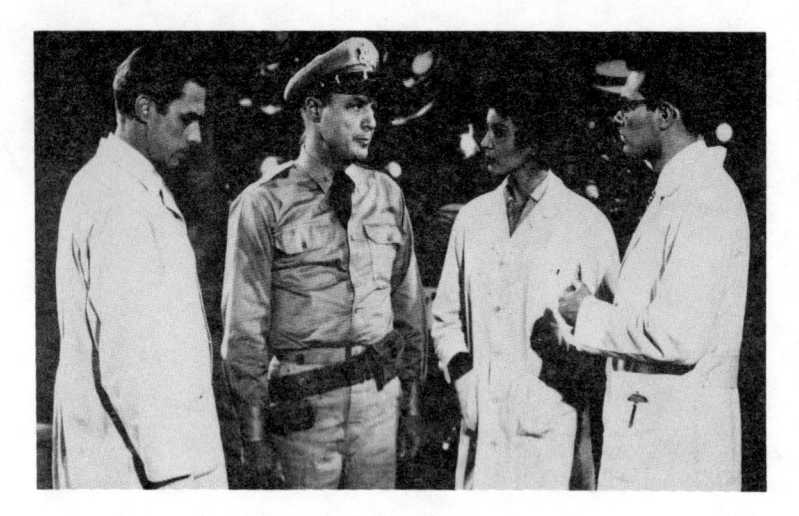

Russ Bender (in uniform) taking charge in Roger Corman's *It Conquered the World* (1956).

Bruce Bennett *(center)* inspects a victim of *The Cosmic Man* (1959).

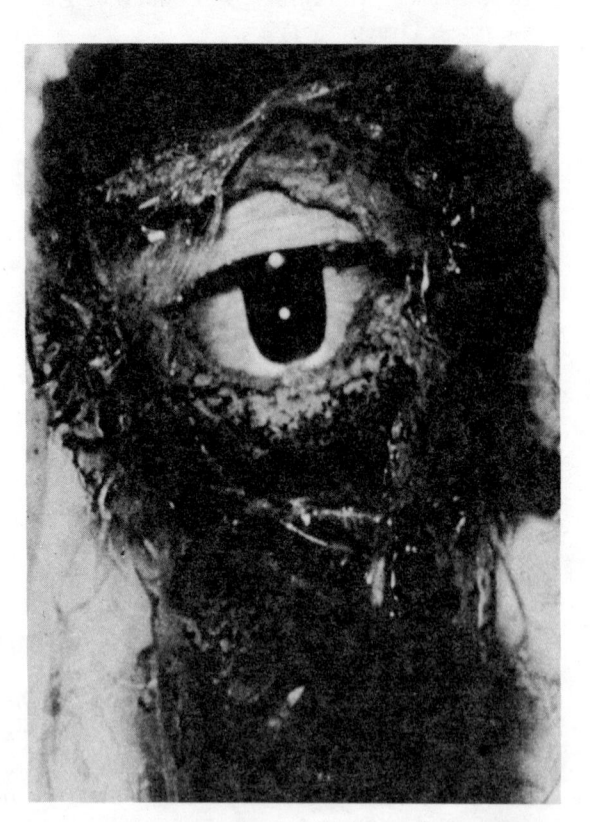

BEERY, WALLACE (1885–1949). Bulky, gravel-voiced American star character actor, beloved throughout the thirties, and a fine symbol of the good-hearted common man. In *The Lost World*, 1925, he plays the bearded, intrepid Professor Challenger and brings a brontosaurus to London. Best line: "My brontosaurus is loose!"

BELLAMY, RALPH (1904–). American character actor best known for his impersonation of Franklin Roosevelt. *The Ghost of Frankenstein*, 1942; *Rosemary's Baby*, 1968.

BENDER, RUSS (1910–69). American supporting actor in dozens of B-films throughout the fifties, usually as a sympathetic authority figure or friend to the hero. *It Conquered the World*, 1956; *Invasion of The Saucermen*, 1957; *The Amazing Colossal Man*, 1957; *War of the Colossal Beast*, 1958; *I Bury the Living*, 1958; *The Ghost of Dragstrip Hollow* (lead), 1959; *Panic in Year Zero*, 1962; *Space Monster* (lead), 1965; *The Satan Bug*, 1965; *The Navy vs. the Night Monsters*, 1966; many more.

BENNETT, BRUCE (1909–). Lithe American leading man and later supporting player, an Olympic athlete originally named Herman Brix who starred in *The New Adventures of Tarzan* in 1935. He shed the Tarzan image as well as his name and returned to the screen in 1940 as Bruce Bennett. *Shadow of Chinatown*, 1936; *Daredevils of the Red Circle*, 1939; *Before I Hang*, 1940; *The Cosmic Man*, 1958; *The Alligator People*, 1959.

BENNETT, SPENCER GORDON (1893–). American serial director. *The Midnight Warning*, 1932; *Spy Smasher*, 1943; *The Masked Marvel*, 1943; *The Purple Monster Strikes*, 1945; *Superman* (co-d; w/TOMMY CARR), 1948; *Batman and Robin*, 1949; *Atom Man vs. Superman*, 1950; *The Atomic Submarine*, 1960.

The fuzzy alien eyeball says hello in *The Atomic Submarine* (1960), directed by Spencer Gordon Bennett.

Ady Berber, blind but dangerous in *Dead Eyes of London* (1961).

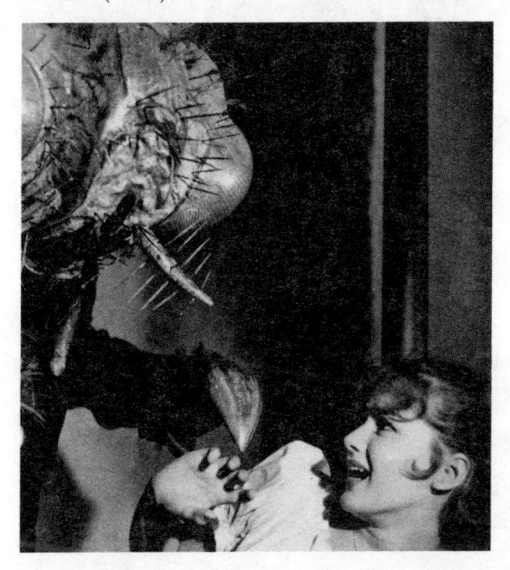

BERBER, ADY (ca. 1915–). Fleshy German actor, Europe's answer to TOR JOHNSON. Berber played the fiend in *Dead Eyes of London*, 1961.

BERGMAN, INGMAR (1918–). Highly regarded Swedish writer/director whose films are extremely personal and filled with complex imagery and symbolism. Bergman is fascinated by death, religion, superstition, and tricks of the mind, and his films often have fantastic content. *The Seventh Seal*, 1956; *The Magician*, 1958; *The Devil's Eye* (a comedy in which Don Juan is sent to seduce a virgin who has caused a sty in Satan's eye), 1961; *Hour of the Wolf*, 1967; *Shame*, 1968.

BERNARD, JAMES (1925–). Accomplished and prolific British composer who has scored most of the Hammer horror films. *The Creeping Unknown*, 1956; *Curse of Frankenstein*, 1957; *Horror of Dracula*, 1958; *The Hound of the Baskervilles*, 1959; *She*, 1965; *Frankenstein Created Woman*, 1967; *Torture Garden*, 1968; *The Devil's Bride*, 1968; *Taste the Blood of Dracula*, 1970; *The Legend of the Seven Golden Vampires*, 1974; many others.

BERNDS, EDWARD L. (1911–). American writer/director of co-features, long associated with Columbia's two-reel department and THE THREE STOOGES. *The Bowery Boys Meet the Monsters*, 1954; *World without End*, 1956; *Space Master X-7*, 1958; *Queen of Outer Space* (d only), 1958; *Return of the Fly*, 1959; *The Three Stooges in Orbit*, 1962; *The Three Stooges Meet Hercules*, 1962; etc.

Screams in the night: Edward L. Bernds's *Return of the Fly* (1959).

Nils Poppe *(left)* as Jof, the gentle juggler who sees life triumph over death in Ingmar Bergman's *The Seventh Seal* (1956).

BEROVA, OLINKA (ca.1945–). Czech actress introduced in *The Vengeance of She*, 1965; she made little impression and subsequently vanished from the screen.

BEST, WILLIE (1916–62). Black American comic actor, the funniest exponent of the bulging-eyes-and-quavering-voice school of racial humor. He is a fine foil for BOB HOPE in *The Ghost Breakers*, 1940. *The Monster Walks* (billed as *Sleep 'n' Eat*), 1932; *The Smiling Ghost*, 1941; *The Body Disappears*, 1941; *A-Haunting We Will Go*, 1942; *Face of Marble*, 1946; numerous others.

BESWICK, MARTINE (1941–). British leading lady in the BARBARA STEELE mold, former model. *Thunderball*, 1965; *One Million Years B.C.*, 1967; *Slave Girls*, 1968; *Dr. Jekyll and Sister Hyde* (as Sister Hyde), 1972; *Seizure* (as the Queen of Evil), 1974.

BEY, TURHAN (1920–). Turkish-Czech leading man in exotic Hollywood B-films; notable in *The Mummy's Tomb*, 1942. *The Mad Ghoul*, 1943.

BIRCH, PAUL (?–1969). Beefy, imposing American character actor whose extraterrestrial vampire in ROGER CORMAN's *Not of This Earth*, 1957, is surely one of the fantastic cinema's most incongruous images. Wearing a Brooks Brothers suit, sunglasses, and carrying a briefcase, Birch looks more like an insurance salesman than a bloodthirsty fiend. His theatrically trained voice is turned to a steady, menacing monotone as he calmly instructs his victims to gaze into his perfectly white eyes so that he may burn out their brains and feed. *The War of the Worlds*, 1953; *The Beast with 1,000,000 Eyes*, 1955; *The Day The World Ended*, 1956; *The 27th Day*, 1957; *Queen of Outer Space*, 1958.

BISSELL, WHIT (1914–). American general-purpose actor, frequently as smooth-talking authority figure or weak-willed lackey. *Lost Continent*, 1951; *Target—Earth*, 1954; *The Atomic Kid*, 1954; *I Was a Teenage Frankenstein* (as a modern-day descendant of Dr. Frankenstein), 1957; *I Was A Teenage Werewolf*, 1957; *The Time Machine*, 1960; *Soylent Green*, 1973; *Physic Killer*, 1976.

Martine Beswick.

Paul Birch as the extraterrestrial vampire in Roger Corman's *Not of This Earth* (1957).

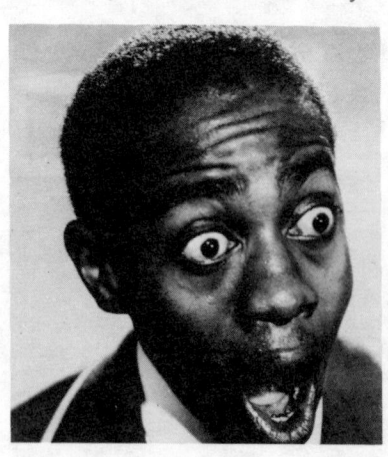

Willie Best.

Whit Bissell.

Rude alien: Jerome Bixby's *It!—The Terror from Beyond Space* (1958).

Honor Blackman with Sean Connery in *Goldfinger* (1964).

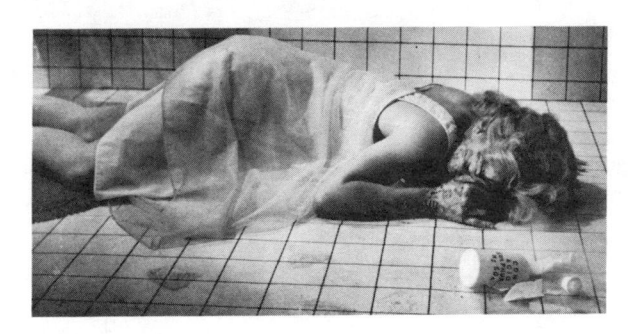

Household horror in George Blair's grisly *The Hypnotic Eye* (1960).

BIXBY, JEROME (1923–). American science fiction and horror author, justly famous for his brilliant short story "It's a *Good* Life." *Curse of the Faceless Man*, 1958; *It!—The Terror From Beyond Space*, 1958; *Fantastic Voyage* (story only; co-w; w/Ott. Klement), 1966; etc.

BLACKMAN, HONOR (1926–). Statuesque British leading lady who gained notoriety in Britain as karate-chopping Cathy Gale on television's "The Avengers" and worldwide fame as Pussy Galore in *Goldfinger*, 1964. *Jason and the Argonauts* (as Hera), 1963; *The Secret of My Success*, 1965; *Fright*, 1971; *To the Devil... A Daugther*, 1976.

BLACKMER, SIDNEY (1895–1973). Distinguished American character actor, often seen as a self-assured authority figure. He is the last man on Earth after the *Deluge*, 1933. *House of Secrets*, 1936; *The Lady and the Monster*, 1944; *Rosemary's Baby*, 1968.

BLAIR, GEORGE (1906–70). American second-feature director responsible for *The Hypnotic Eye*, 1960, surely one of the more disagreeable American films of the last twenty years. The picture concerns an unscrupulous hypnotist and is filled with tasteless closeups of mesmerized women washing their faces with acid and setting their hair afire at kitchen stoves. The heroine (MERRY ANDERS) is rescued moments after being commanded to step into a scalding shower. Exploitative but cheaply effective, *The Hypnotic Eye* makes its point despite itself. *The Ghost Goes Wild*, 1947 and *Sabu and the Magic Ring*, 1957.

BLAIR, LINDA (1959–). American juvenile actress who created quite a stir as the possessed child in *The Exorcist*, 1973, but scarcely a ripple after the 1977 sequel, *Exorcist II: The Heretic*. Much of the credit for her first performance, said doubters, was owed to veteran actress Mercedes McCambridge, who did overdubbing of many rude grunts and screams.

Linda Blair.

Paul Blaisdell's lumbering costume design for *The She Creature* (1956).

Mari Blanchard.

BLAISDELL, PAUL (ca. 1930–). American makeup artist, mask, and costume-builder associated with American-International Pictures during the fifties. A former magazine illustrator, Blaisdell created designs which are heavy-handed and obvious but loaded with vulgar personality. He is seen briefly out of costume at the conclusion of *The Ghost of Dragstrip Hollow*, 1959. *The She Creature*, 1956; *The Day the World Ended*, 1956; *It Conquered the World* (as the famous Cucumber Creature), 1956; *Invasion of the Saucermen*, 1957; *From Hell It Came* (as the ambulatory tree), 1957; *How to Make a Monster*, 1958; *It!—The Terror from beyond Space*, 1958; *The Cliff Monster* (and d), 1962.

BLANCHARD, MARI (1927–70). American leading lady of second features. *Abbott and Costello Go to Mars*, 1953; *Son of Sinbad*, 1955; *She-Devil*, 1957; *Twice-Told Tales*, 1964.

BLOCH, ROBERT (1917–). Popular American fictionist, remembered on the covers of innumerable pocket books as "the author of *Psycho*." Prolific and facile, Bloch is a bit overrated, but the enthusiasm evident in his work is a compensation. *The Cabinet of Caligari*, 1962; *Strait-Jacket*, 1964; *The Night Walker*, 1964; *The Psychopath*, 1966; *Torture Garden*, 1968 ; *The House That Dripped Blood*, 1970; *Asylum*, 1972 (1978 rerelease as *House of Crazies*), etc.

BLOCK, IRVING. American special-effects technician and matte artist who, often in tandem with JACK RABIN, has added gaudy luster to many low-budget science fiction films. *Rocketship X-M*, 1950; *Unknown World*, 1950; *Flight to Mars*, 1951; *Captive Women*, 1951; *Forbidden Planet*, 1956; *The Saga of the Viking Women and Their Voyage to the Waters of the Great Sea Serpent* (and story), 1957; *The Invisible Boy*, 1957; *Kronos* (and co-p), 1957; *Macabre*, 1958; *War of the Satellites*, 1958; many others.

BLOOM, CLAIRE (1931–). British leading actress, often in melodramatic roles. *The Wonderful World of the Brothers Grimm*, 1962; *The Haunting* (as the Lesbian medium), 1963; *Charly*, 1968; *The Illustrated Man*, 1969; *Clash of the Titans* (as Hera), 1981.

BLUE DEMON. Mexican masked wrestler in lurid science-horror thrillers. *El Demonio Azul*, 1963; *Blue Demon Contra el Poder Satanico*, 1964; *Blue Demon vs. Cerebros Infernales*, 1968; *Blue Demon vs. Las Diobolicas*, 1968; *Santo y Blue Demon Contra Los Monstruos* (see: SANTO), 1970; *Santo y Blue Demon Contra Dracula y El Hombre Lobo*, 1973; others.

BOEHM, KARL (1928–). Youthful German leading man whose portrayal of the psychosexually disturbed young photographer in *Peeping Tom*, 1960, is a judiciously crafted and genuinely sympathetic portrait. Also *The Wonderful World of the Brothers Grimm*, 1962.

Ray Bolger as the loveable Scarecrow in *The Wizard of Oz* (1939).

BOGART, HUMPHREY (1899–1957). American leading actor whose tough cynicism summed up Warner Brothers and the nineteen-forties and whose films continue to speak to millions of fans around the world. Best remembered as gangster or independent tough guy, Bogart played a pasty-faced vampire in *The Return of Dr. X*, 1939.

BOGDANOVICH, PETER (1939–). Prominent American director, former critic. Most of his seventies films have been only partially successful reworkings of familiar genres, but his *Targets*, 1968, remains fresh and involving and provided BORIS KARLOFF with his last important role. Bogdanovich also directed (and narrated) *Voyage to the Planet of Prehistoric Women* (credited as Derek Thomas), 1968.

BOLGER, RAY (1904–). Inventive American dancer and actor who played the Scarecrow in *The Wizard of Oz*, 1939.

BONESTELL, CHESLEY (1888–). American artist, best known for his carefully researched and highly dramatic depictions of other planets. Bonestell went to Hollywood in 1938 and worked on a variety of films as matte painter and designer. For *The Hunchback of Notre Dame*, 1939, he created a flawless matte painting of the great cathedral as it looked centuries ago, and designed the lunar surface and graceful rocketship seen in *Destination Moon*, 1950. *When Worlds Collide* (the spaceship and matte paintings of planets Bellus and Zyra), 1951; *The War of the Worlds* (the opening views of other worlds in our solar system), 1953; *Conquest of Space*, 1955. Bonestell remained active into his nineties.

The graceful spaceship designed by Chesley Bonestell for George Pal's *When Worlds Collide* (1951).

Sean Connery (as Zed) and Charlotte Rampling in John Boorman's *Zardoz* (1974).

BOORMAN, JOHN (1933–). Ambitious British writer/director whose *Zardoz*, 1974, is a near-brilliant allegory about our tangled society. He is less successful with *Exorcist II: The Heretic*, 1977.

BOOTH, WALTER R. (18?–19?). British trick film pioneer, onetime magician, active in motion pictures until the end of the first world war. Included in his scores of titles are *Upside Down* or *The Human Flies*, 1899; *The Haunted Curiosity Shop*, 1901; *The Famous Illusion of De Kolta*, 1901; *The Haunted Scene Painter*, 1904; *Tropical Tricks* (and actor), 1904; *The £1000 Spook*, 1907; *The Quick Change Mesmerist*, 1908; *The Bewitched Boxing Gloves*, 1910; *The Cap of Invisibility*, 1911; *In Gollywog Land*, 1912; *The Magical Mystic*, 1914; *The Portrait of Dolly Gray*, 1916.

BORG, VEDA ANN (1915–73). Hard-boiled American supporting actress of the forties. A serious automobile accident interrupted her career in 1939, but she returned to become a brassy staple of dozens of further films. *The Shadow* (serial), 1940; *Revenge of the Zombies* (as a rather fetching zombie), 1943; *The Girl Who Dared*, 1944; *The Big Noise*, 1944; etc.

Veda Ann Borg.

Carroll Borland and Bela Lugosi in *Mark of the Vampire* (1935).

BORGNINE, ERNEST (1915–). Beefy American star character actor, a notable heavy until cast as the gentle butcher *Marty* in 1955. Since then, his roles have become sympathetic and more varied. *The Legend of Lylah Clare*, 1968; *Willard* (in which he is eaten by rats), 1971; *The Neptune Factor*, 1973; *The Devil's Rain*, 1975; *The Black Hole*, 1979; *When Time Ran Out*, 1980.

BORLAND, CARROLL (1914–). American actress, protege of BELA LUGOSI, who came to prominence as the vampire girl Luna in *Mark of The Vampire*, 1935.

BOTTIN, ROB. American makeup artist specializing in grue who emerged in the late seventies. *King Kong*, 1976; *Star Wars*, 1977; *The Fury*, 1978; *The Incredible Melting Man* (also played title role), 1978; *Piranha*, 1978; *Tanya's Island*, 1980; *The Fog*, 1980; *Humanoids From the Deep*, 1980.

BOULLE, PIERRE (1912–). French novelist whose *Monkey Planet* reached the screen in 1968 as *Planet of the Apes*. There were four sequels: *Beneath the Planet of the Apes*, 1970; *Escape from the Planet of the Apes*, 1971; *Conquest of the Planet of the Apes*, 1972; *Battle for the Planet of the Apes*, 1973.

BOWIE, DAVID (ca. 1949–). Androgynous-seeming British pop singer who became popular in the early seventies by exploiting a bizarre persona. He gives an interesting performance as the alien in NICOLAS ROEG's *The Man Who Fell to Earth*, 1976.

BOWIE, LES (ca. 1920–79). British special effects expert who has managed to create a lot from a little. *The Creeping Unknown*, 1956; *The Crawling Eye*, 1958; *The Day the Earth Caught Fire*, 1961; *Curse of the Werewolf*, 1961; *Kiss of the Vampire*, 1963; *Dracula, Prince of Darkness*, 1966; *One Million Years B.C.*, 1967; *Dracula A.D. 1972*, 1972; *Frankenstein and the Monster from Hell*, 1973; many others.

BOYLE, PETER (1933–). Loud American character actor who specializes in vulgar, outspoken lowbrows. His zipper-headed, comic interpretation of the Monster in MEL BROOKS' *Young Frankenstein*, 1974, is highly effective.

BRADBURY, RAY (1920–). Important American writer of science fiction and fantasy who has created a body of work that is poetic, imaginative, and moving. Bradbury's gentle and evocative prose is not easy to translate into film; few attempts have been made. His best known work, *The Martian Chronicles*, intrigued moviemakers for years and finally appeared as a TV movie in 1980. *It Came from Outer Space* (treatment only), 1953; *The Beast from 20,000 Fathoms* (b/o his short story "The Foghorn"), 1953; *Fahrenheit 451* (b/o his novel), 1966; *The Illustrated Man* (b/o his short story collection), 1969.

BRADLEY, DAVID (1919–). American director of formula Bs who began by directing interesting amateur films, most notably an ambitious version of *Julius Caesar*, 1950. *Peer Gynt* (with sixteen-year-old CHARLTON HESTON in the title role), 1941; *12 to the Moon*, 1960; *Madmen of Mandoras*, 1964.

BRADY, SCOTT (1924–). Tough American leading man of the fifties who got puffy and gruff in middle age and slipped into cheap horror films. *Destination Inner Space*, 1966; *Castle of Evil*, 1968; *Nightmare in Wax*, 1969.

Peter Boyle as the Monster in Mel Brooks's *Young Frankenstein* (1974).

BRAKHAGE, STAN (1933–). Influential American underground filmmaker whose highly visual style led the way to more personalized filmic statements from his contemporaries. *Reflections in Black*, 1955; *The Way to Shadow Garden*, 1955; *Dog-Star Man*, 1959–64; others.

BRANDO, MARLON (1924–). Controversial American leading actor who surprised the film industry by accepting the role of the Kryptonian scientist Jor-el in *Superman*, 1978. An actor whose technique gets in the way of his talent, Brando is somewhat overrated.

BRANDON, HENRY (1910–). Fierce-looking American character actor, memorable as evil Silas Barnaby opposite LAUREL AND HARDY in *Babes in Toyland* aka *March of the Wooden Soldiers*, 1934; *Buck Rogers*, 1939; *Drums of Fu Manchu* (as Fu Manchu), 1940; *Scared Stiff*, 1953; *The Land Unknown*, 1957.

BRANDT, CAROLYN (ca. 1940–). American leading lady in absurd low-budget films for producer/director RAY DENNIS STECKLER. *The Incredibly Strange Creatures Who Stopped Living and Became Mixed-up Zombies*, 1963; *The Thrill Killers*, 1965; *Rat Pfink and Boo Boo*, 1966; *The Lemon Grove Kids Meet the Green Grasshopper and the Vampire Lady from Outer Space*, ca. 1967; *Blood Monster*, 1972.

BRANNON, FRED C. American director of lively Republic serials. *The Crimson Ghost* (co-d; w/WILLIAM WITNEY), 1946; *King of the Rocketmen*, 1949; *Radar Patrol vs. Spy King*, 1949; *The Invisible Monster*, 1950; *Flying Disc Man from Mars*, 1950; *Zombies of the Stratosphere*, 1952; etc.

BRIANT, SHANE (1946–). Young British leading man of Hammer horror films. *Demons of the Mind*, 1972; *Captain Kronos, Vampire Hunter*, 1973; *Frankenstein and the Monster from Hell*, 1973.

BRIDGES, LLOYD (1913–). Rugged American star actor of film and television. *Here Comes Mr. Jordan*, 1941; *Strange Confession*, 1945; *Rocketship X-M*, 1950; *Around the World Under the Sea*, 1966; *The Love War* (TV), 1970; *Haunts of the Very Rich* (TV), 1972.

BROCCOLI, ALBERT R. (1909–). American producer long active in Britain, partnered with HARRY SALTZMAN on the James Bond films since 1962. Produced as solo: *Chitty Chitty Bang Bang*, 1968.

BROLIN, JAMES (1940–). Rugged American leading man with television experience. *The Car*, 1977; *Capricorn One*, 1978; *The Amityville Horror*, 1979.

BRONSON, CHARLES (1922–). Craggy American actor who played assorted hoods and crazies until becoming a major international star in the seventies. When Bronson was still using his real name, Charles Buchinski, he appeared as the violent deaf-mute Igor in *House of Wax* 1953. *Master of the World*, 1961; *Telefon* (which involves devious post-hypnotic suggestion), 1977.

Commando Cody (probably George Wallace) and Aline Towne in a publicity still from Fred C. Brannon's *Radar Men from the Moon* (1952).

Mel Brooks is garroted in a typically hilarious scene from his *High Anxiety* (1978).

David Bruce, as *The Mad Ghoul* (1943), is about to get the drop on Robert Armstrong. George Zucco looks on.

Tod Browning with the cast of *Freaks* (1932).

BROOKS, MEL (1928–). Erratic, sometimes tasteless American comedy writer/director/actor whose *Young Frankenstein*, 1974, is a generally successful send-up of the Universal horrors. *High Anxiety*, 1978, is Brooks' homage to ALFRED HITCHCOCK and has many clever moments. A scene inspired by the famous shower sequence in *Psycho*, 1960, is hilariously inventive. He also played a cameo role in *The Muppet Movie*, 1979.

BROWNING, RICOU (1930–). American underwater expert who donned a rubber suit to play *The Creature from the Black Lagoon*, 1954, a physically demanding role. Browning repeated it in the first sequel, *Revenge of the Creature*, 1955.

BROWNING, TOD (1882–1962). American director whose flair for exploiting the grotesque overcomes his often stale visual style. *Dracula*, 1931, has some fine moments but has dated badly. Browning's best work remains *Freaks*, 1932, a film thought quite shocking at the time of its release though it is actually a touching story of human love and loyalty. *The Unholy Three*, 1925; *London after Midnight*, 1927; *The Unholy Three*, (sound remake), 1930; *Mark of the Vampire*, 1935; *Devil Doll*, 1936; *Miracles for Sale*, 1939.

BRUCE DAVID (1914–76). Sandy American actor who played the title role in *The Mad Ghoul*, 1943. *The Body Disappears*, 1941; *Jungle Hell*, 1956.

BRUCE, LENNY (1926–66). Biting and sporadically brilliant American comic who cowrote (with Jack Henley) the screenplay for *The Rocket Man*, a mild science fiction film of 1954.

BRUCE, NIGEL (1895–1953). British character actor in Hollywood, perfectly adorable as the perpetually befuddled Dr. Watson in the Universal Sherlock Holmes series 1939–46. *She*, 1935; *The Hound of the Baskervilles*, 1939; *The Blue Bird*, 1940; *Spider Woman*, 1944; *The Scarlet Claw*, 1944; *Pearl of Death*, 1944.

Nigel Bruce.

36 BRYNNER

BRYNNER, YUL (1915–). Russian character actor in Hollywood, a dominant personality whose signature is his bald head. *The Testament of Orpheus*, 1960; *Westworld* (as the killer android gunslinger), 1973; *The Ultimate Warrior*, 1975; *Futureworld* (cameo as the android gunslinger), 1976.

BUCHANAN, LARRY. American producer/director who in the late sixties made a series of uncredited remakes of American-International films of the fifties. The remakes are listless and flat and were designed for immediate release through AIP-TV. *Creature of Destruction* (from *The She Creature*, 1956), 1967; *The Eye Creatures* (from *Invasion of the Saucermen*, 1957), 1968; *In the Year 2889* (from *The Day the World Ended*, 1956), 1968; *It's Alive!* (original, but suspiciously similar to RICHARD MATHESON's short story, "Being."), 1968; *Zontar: The Thing from Venus* (from *It Conquered the World*, 1956), 1968.

BUJOLD, GENEVIEVE (1942–). French leading lady active in Europe and Hollywood who seemed at one time on the verge of major American stardom. Her rather boyish beauty contributes to a vulnerable appeal. *King of Hearts* (as the Queen of Hearts), 1967; *Obsession*, 1976; *Coma*, 1978.

BUÑUEL, LUIS (1900–). Spanish writer/director of avant-garde films, active in France and later Mexico, whose *Un Chien Andalou* (make with SALVADOR DALI), 1928 remains a startling excursion into bizarre surrealism. *L'Age D'Or*, 1930; *Los Olidados*, 1950; *The Exterminating Angel*, 1963; *Simon of the Desert*, 1969; *The Milky Way*, 1969.

BUONO, VICTOR (1938–). Immense American character actor, beared, and of theatrical intonation, who can project refined menace or slobbery dementia. *Whatever Happened to Baby Jane?*, 1962; *Hush, Hush Sweet Charlotte*, 1964; *The Strangler* (title role), 1964; *Beneath the Planet of the Apes*, 1970; *The Mad Butcher* (title role), 1972; *Moonchild*, 1972; *The Evil*, 1978.

Yul Brynner as the deadly android gunslinger malfunctions in *Westworld* (1973).

Genevieve Bujold.

Is it ambulatory puffed rice? No, just Larry Buchanan's *The Eye Creatures* (1968).

BURKE, BILLIE (1885-1970). American stage star and film actress, married to Flo Ziegfeld and notable as the good witch Glinda in *The Wizard of Oz*, 1939; *Topper*, 1937; *Topper Takes a Trip*, 1939; *Topper Returns*, 1941.

BURKE, KATHLEEN (ca. 1913-). American leading lady who won the role of the panther girl in *Island of Lost Souls*, 1933, in a contest. *Murders in the Zoo*, 1933.

BURNS, GEORGE (1896-). Indefatigable American comic who earned great success on radio with wife Gracie Allen during the thirties and who became a movie star in the nineteen-seventies. His mischievous face, his cigar, and his sharp one-liners are perfect for the title role in *Oh, God*, 1977.

BURR, RAYMOND (1917-). Canadian-born star character actor, typecast as a thick-set villain until finding fame as television's Perry Mason, 1957-66. *Bride of the Gorilla* (as the unfortunate who nightly frustrates wife BARBARA PAYTON by growing furry and loping off into the jungle), 1952; *Tarzan and the She Devil*, 1954; *Godzilla* (American-release prints only), 1954; *Godzilla at Large*, 1954; *Rear Window* (as the silver-haired murderer), 1954; *The Curse of King Tut* (TV), 1980.

Victor Buono.

Billie Burke as good witch Glinda, with Judy Garland and the Munchkins in *The Wizard of Oz* (1939).

BURROUGHS, EDGAR RICE (1875-1950). Prolific American author who earned public renown as creator of Tarzan, the British infant raised by apes. The character is among the most popular figures of modern world folklore and has appeared on the screen many times since 1918. The most familiar film Tarzan is JOHNNY WEISMULLER; Burroughs' favorite was LEX BARKER, whose civilized interpretation is nearer the original concept than Weismuller's childlike one. Many unauthorized Tarzan films have been made, in China, Italy, Turkey, Russia, Jamaica, Czechoslovakia, and India, the last nation producing an entire series intended primarily for distribution in Nigeria. For listings of American films see: RON ELY, MIKE HENRY, ELMO LINCOLN, JOCK MAHONEY, FRANK MERRILL, DENNY MILLER, GLENN MORRIS, JIM PIERCE, GENE POLLAR, GORDON SCOTT, P. DEMPSEY TABLER.

BUSHMAN, FRANCIS X. (1883-1966). American leading actor, a major star of silent films. *Dick Tracy*, 1937; *Peer Gynt* (amateur; voice only), 1941; *The Story of Mankind*, 1957; *12 to the Moon*, 1960; *The Phantom Planet*, 1962; *The Ghost in the Invisible Bikini*, 1966.

BYRD, RALPH (1909-52). Smiling, square-jawed American leading man in serials and second features, best remembered as *Dick Tracy*, 1937. Also *Dick Tracy's G-Men*, 1939; *Dick Tracy vs. Crime Inc.*, 1941; *The Jungle Book*, 1942; *Dick Tracy Meets Gruesome*, 1947; *Radar Secret Service*, 1950.

BYRON, JEAN (ca. 1930-). Poised American leading lady of minor films, remembered as the mother on televison's the "Patty Duke Show," 1963-66. *The Magnetic Monster*, 1953; *Jungle Moon Men*, 1955; *Invisible Invaders*, 1959.

Jean Byron.

Bruce Cabot.

Susan Cabot.

C

CABOT, BRUCE (1904–72). American actor who saved FAY WRAY from *King Kong* in 1933. He later became an effective screen villain.

CABOT, SUSAN (1927–). Dark-eyed leading lady of a few Hollywood films of the fifties, associated mainly with producer/director ROGER CORMAN. *The Saga of the Viking Women and Their Voyage to the Waters of the Great Sea Serpent*, 1957; *War of the Satellites*, 1958; *Wasp Woman* (title role), 1959.

CAGNEY, JAMES (1899–). Aggressive American star actor who epitomized much of the urban spirit of the thirties and forties. The self-assured cockiness of his persona made him legend; his mannerisms have inspired hosts of imitators. Cagney's versatility is respected but insufficiently mentioned; in 1957 he created a marvelous portrait of LON CHANEY, SR. in *Man of a Thousand Faces*, probably the finest of Hollywood's biopics on one of its own. Also: *A Midsummer Night's Dream* (as Bottom), 1935.

CAHN, EDWARD L. (1899–1963). American programmer director whose flat, documentarylike style is oddly suited to the hysterical subject matter of *Creature with the Atom Brain*, 1955. The film is structured like a traditional murder mystery and works up quite a bit of perverse horror as atomically resurrected dead men shamble about the city, indulging in an orgy of neck-breaking and spine snapping. Most are dressed in ordinary business suits and, as with PAUL BIRCH in ROGER CORMAN's *Not of This Earth*, 1957, the *true* horror is that of incongruity. *The She Creature*, 1956; *Voodoo Woman*, 1957; *Zombies of Mora Tau*, 1957; *Invasion of the Saucermen*, 1957; *It!—The Terror from Beyond Space*, 1958; *Curse of the Faceless Man*, 1958; *Invisible Invaders*, 1959.

CAMPBELL, WILLIAM (1926–). Tough-seeming American second lead, often seen as a greasy hood. *Dementia 13* (lead), 1963; *Hush, Hush Sweet Charlotte* (as the newspaper photographer), 1964; *Blood Bath* (lead), 1966.

CAPRA, FRANK (1897–). Accomplished American director, noted for his honest sentiment and faith in the common man. Never mawkish, Capra created films which probably would not appeal to today's movie goers. *It's A Wonderful Life*, 1946, concerns a despondent man who, with the help of a guardian angel, is shown how much worse the lives of his friends might have been had he never lived. *Lost Horizon* (the definitive version of the Shangri-La story), 1937; *Arsenic and Old Lace* (highly amusing but stagey and loud and atypical of Capra's output), 1944.

Aliens animate dead bodies in Edward L. Cahn's enjoyable 1959 quickie *Invisible Invaders*.

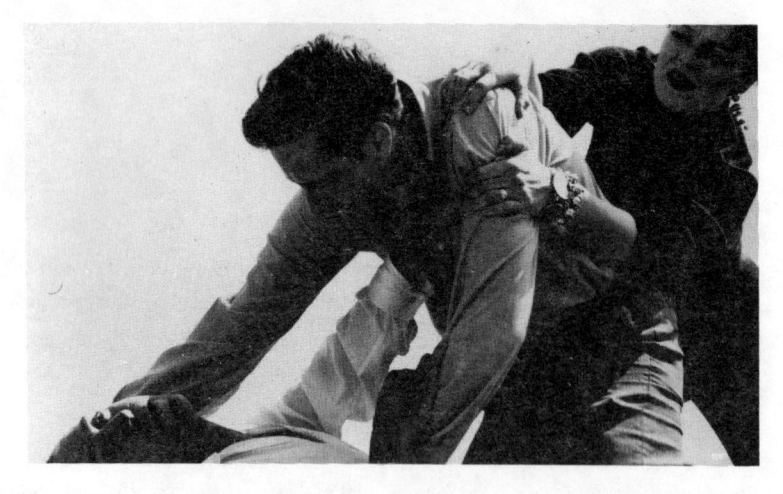

Anthony Carbone *(left)* losing his battle for Betsy Jones-Moreland, *The Last Woman on Earth* (1960). Carbone's attacker is Edward Wain.

CARBONE, ANTHONY (ca.1930–). American actor, best cast as a laughing, hedonistic Italians. A *Bucket of Blood*, 1959; *The Last Woman on Earth*, 1960; *Creature from the Haunted Sea* (lead, doing an enjoyable BOGART take-off), 1961; *The Pit and the Pendulum*, 1961.

CARDONA, RENE. Mexican director of sexy horror thrillers, former actor. *El Baul Macabro* (as actor only), 1936; *The Living Idol* (associate d), 1957; *Doctor of Doom*, 1964; *Wrestling Women vs. the Aztec Mummy*, 1965; *Las Mujeres Panteras*, 1967; *Las Luchadoras contra el Robot Asesino*, 1969; *El Vampiro y el Sexo*, 1969; *Capulina contra los Vampiros*, 1972; *Night of 1000 Cats*, 1972; others.

CARLSON, RICHARD (1912–77). Capable American leading man of the fifties who began by playing light love interests. *Hold That Ghost*, 1941; *It Came from Outer Space*, 1953; *The Magnetic Monster*, 1953; *The Maze*, 1953; *The Creature from the Black Lagoon*, 1954; *Riders to the Stars* (and d), 1954; *Tormented*, 1960; *The Power*, 1968; *The Valley of Gwangi*, 1969.

Richard Carlson.

CARLSON, VERONICA (1945–). Statuesque, blonde British leading lady in Hammer films. *Dracula Has Risen from the Grave*, 1968; *Frankenstein Must Be Destroyed*, 1969; *The Horror of Frankenstein*, 1970; *Old Dracula* aka *Vampira*, 1975.

CARNERA, PRIMO (1906–67). Giant-sized Italian wrestler, circus performer, actor, and world heavyweight boxing champion. Carnera played tug-of-war with *Mighty Joe Young* in 1949 and lost. *Hercules Unchained*, 1960.

CARPENTER, JOHN (CA. 1948–). Talented American writer-director whose enjoyably derivative *Halloween*, 1979, was one of the big horror hits of the seventies. *Dark Star*, 1974; *Eyes of Laura Mars* (sc only), 1978; *The Fog*, 1980.

CARR, TOMMY (1907–). American second feature and serial director who codirected (with SPENCER GORDON BENNETT) *Superman* in 1948 and successfully brought the character to the long-running television series, 1951–58. *Brick Bradford* (with co-director Spencer Bennett), 1947.

CASTLE 41

John Carradine is *The Cosmic Man* (1959).

Peggie Castle goes berserk in *Back from the Dead* (1957). Arthur Franz *(right)* attempts to restrain her.

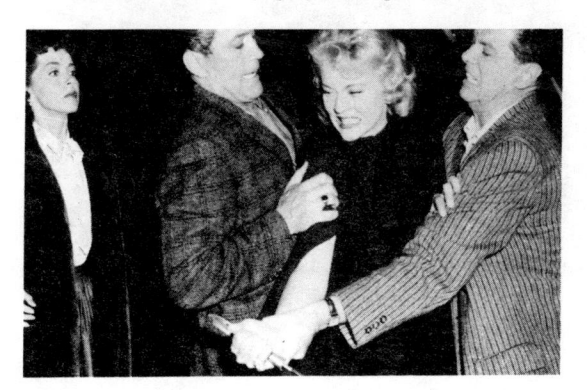

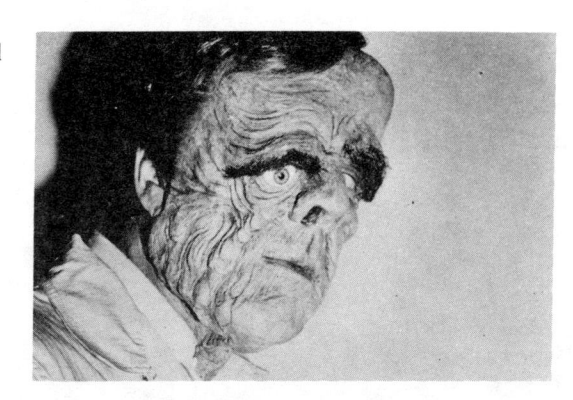

Leo G. Carroll, twisted by acromegaly in *Tarantula* (1955). Makeup by Bud Westmore.

CARRADINE, JOHN (1906–). Gaunt American character actor who filled good roles until the 1950s but since then has been doing hammy self-parodies in dozens of inferior films. His interpretation of Dracula, however, is gentlemanly and interesting. *Bride of Frankenstein*, 1935; *Whispering Ghosts*, 1942; *The Invisible Man's Revenge*, 1944; *Bluebeard* (title role), 1944; *House of Frankenstein* (as Dracula), 1945; *House of Dracula* (as Dracula), 1945; *Half Human* (U.S.-release version only), 1955; *The Unearthly*, 1957; *The Cosmic Man*, 1959; *Invisible Invaders*, 1959; *Invasion of the Animal People* (U.S.-release version only), 1962; *House of the Black Death*, 1965; *Billy The Kid vs. Dracula* (as Dracula), 1966; *The Astro-Zombies*, 1969; *Everything You Always Wanted to Know about Sex but Were Afraid to Ask* (as the crazed scientist who creates a giant, marauding breast), 1972; *The House of the Seven Corpses*, 1973; *Satan's Cheerleaders*, 1976; *The Sentinel*, 1977; many more.

CARRERAS, SIR JAMES (1910–). British producer and head of Hammer Films who led his studio and the world film industry to a revival of period horror with *Curse of Frankenstein*, 1957. Retired in 1972.

CARRERAS, MICHAEL (1927–). British producer/director who became head of Hammer Films in 1971. Son of SIR JAMES CARRERAS. As director: *Maniac*, 1963; *The Curse of the Mummy's Tomb*, 1964; *Prehistoric Women*, 1968; *The Lost Continent*, 1968; *Blood from the Mummy's Tomb* (last few days only, after death of director SETH HOLT), 1971.

CARROLL, LEO G. (1892–1972). British character actor in Hollywood, often seen as a stuffy but basically decent fellow. Notable as the hideously acromegalic scientist in *Tarantula*, 1955. Also *The Spy with My Face* (this and the following are theatrical-release versions of television's the "Man From U.N.C.L.E.," 1964–68), 1966. *One Spy Too Many*, 1966; *The Venetian Affair*, 1967; *The Helicopter Spies*, 1967.

CASTLE, PEGGIE (1926–73). American leading lady of the fifties, a brittle blonde who seemed ideally suited to B-pictures. *Invasion U.S.A.*, 1953; *Back from the Dead*, 1957; *Beginning of the End*, 1957.

42 CASTLE

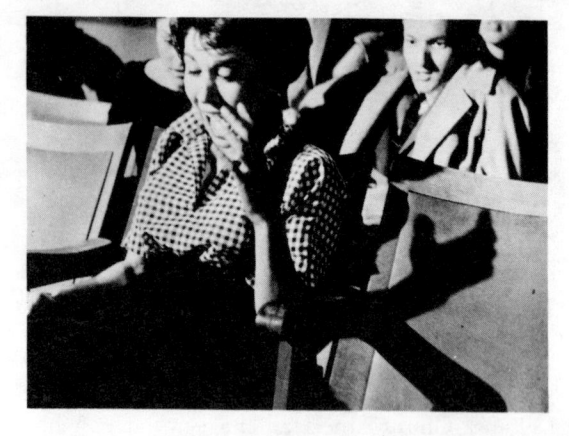

CASTLE, WILLIAM (1914–77). Enterprising American producer/director of gimmicky, imitative horror films who made a name for himself in the fifties and sixties with some outlandish promotional ideas, such as stringing a luminous skeleton over the heads of his audiences. At their best, Castle's films are spooky, if derivative. *The Whistler* (d only), 1944; *Mark of the Whistler* (d only), 1944; *Voice of the Whistler* (d only), 1945; *The Mysterious Intruder* (d only), 1946; *House on Haunted Hill*, 1958; *The Tingler*, 1959; *13 Ghosts* (3-D), 1960; *Homicidal*, 1961; *The Old Dark House*, 1963; *Strait-Jacket*, 1964; *The Night Walker*, 1965; *I Saw What You Did*, 1965; *Rosemary's Baby* (p only; directed by ROMAN POLANSKI), 1968; *Shanks*, 1974; others.

Horror in the aisles in *The Tingler* (1959), directed by William Castle.

CAVANAGH, PAUL (1895–1964). Tall, thin, British character actor in Hollywood from the twenties. *Tarzan and His Mate*, 1934; *The Strange Case of Dr. Rx*, 1942; *The Scarlet Claw*, 1944; *The Man in Half Moon Street*, 1944; *Port Sinister*, 1953; *House of Wax*, 1953; *Francis in the Haunted House*, 1956; *The Man Who Turned to Stone* (title role), 1957; *The Four Skulls of Jonathan Drake*, 1959.

Skeletal thrills as Carol Ohmart meets the acid bath in William Castle's *House on Haunted Hill* (1958).

CHAFFEY, DON (1917–). British director whose luck with script assignments seems to be either very good or very bad. His *Jason and the Argonauts*, 1963 (and 1978 rerelease) is at once intelligent and thoroughly delightful, and Chaffey's hand is not overwhelmed by RAY HARRYHAUSEN's magical special effects. Other films: *One Million Years B.C.*, 1967; *Creatures the World Forgot*, 1971.

CHAMBERS, JOHN (1924–). American makeup artist who specializes in amazingly mobile facial prosthetics. *Planet of the Apes*, 1968; *Beneath the Planet of the Apes*, 1970; *Escape from the Planet of the Apes*, 1971; *Conquest of the Planet of the Apes*, 1972; *Battle for the Planet of the Apes*, 1973; *The Island of Dr. Moreau*, 1977.

CHANDLER, HELEN (1906–65). American leading lady of the thirties, notable as Mina in *Dracula*, 1931. Married and divorced actor BRAMWELL FLETCHER and screenwriter CYRIL HUME.

The sea god Neptune aids the sailors in Don Chaffey's splendid *Jason and the Argonauts* (1963).

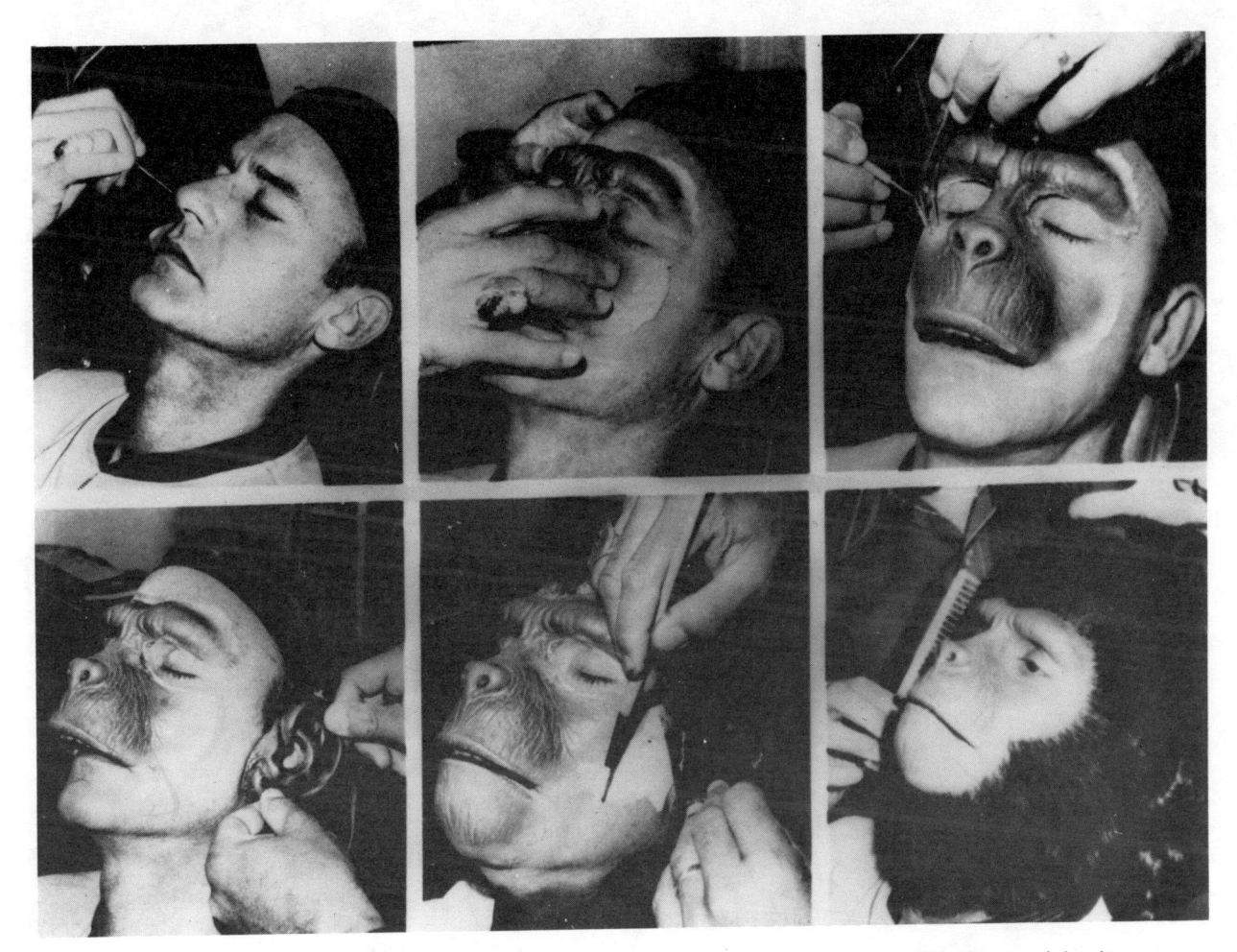

Roddy McDowall is transformed from man to ape by makeup wizard John Chambers for 1968's *Planet of the Apes*.

Lon Chaney in *London after Midnight* (1927).

CHANEY, LON (1883–1930). American star character actor of the twenties, outstanding for his gift of mime and skill with makeup; he was known as "The Man of a Thousand Faces." The son of deaf mutes, Chaney grew up with an understanding of nonverbal communication and brought a unique quality to Hollywood after leaving the stage in 1914. His willingness to contort his face and body, often painfully, to give credibility to a characterization led to grotesque roles, but even the most bizarre reveal humanity and sympathy. His 1923 interpretation of *The Hunchback of Notre Dame*, in particular, conveys a fine sensitivity. Chaney's most widely acclaimed performance: Eric, the scarred and demented *Phantom of the Opera*, 1925. To achieve the effect of a fireravaged face Chaney pulled up his nose with fish hooks, jammed discs beneath his lips to suggest thrusting cheekbones, and wore painful false teeth. In *London after Midnight*, 1927, he impersonated a shark-toothed vampire to fascinating effect, but his finest role was probably as the criminal ventriloquist Echo in the sound remake

Lon Chaney as the criminal ventriloquist in *The Unholy Three* (1930).

of *The Unholy Three*, 1930, a story Chaney had done in a silent version five years before. In the remake, he displayed a remarkable vocal facility and for much of the film was disguised as an old woman. Hailed for his unexpected talent, Chaney seemed assured of stardom in talkies, but was hospitalized in the summer of 1930 for what was officially "acute anemia." In August of that year he died, a victim of cancer of the throat. At the end, he could not speak. Not strictly a horror star, Lon Chaney was the quintessential character actor and an artist of almost unlimited talent. Of special interest: a fine biographical film from 1957, *Man of a Thousand Faces*, which starred JAMES CAGNEY. *The Miracle Man*, 1919; *The Penalty*, 1920; *A Blind Bargain*, 1922; *The Monster*, 1925; *Mr. Wu*, 1927; *The Unknown*, 1927; *Mockery*, 1927.

CHANEY

CHANEY, LON JR. (1906–73). Ursine and craggy American character actor, son of LON CHANEY, whose attempt to follow in his father's footsteps was only in part successful. An actor of limited range but considerable strength, Chaney, Jr. enjoyed a few good roles early in his career, *e.g.* as Lennie in *Of Mice and Men*, 1939, but soon sank to grunting parodies of KARLOFF and finally to hideous Z-films in the sixties and seventies. His attempt to trade on the Chaney name maintained him as a minor box office draw, but paradoxically restricted him to fruitless roles. In his last years, Chaney, Jr. was plagued by a variety of illnesses but continued working. His finest performance in the horror genre was as the tormented Larry Talbot in *The Wolf Man*, 1941. *One Million B.C.*, 1940; *Man Made Monster*, 1941; *The Ghost of Frankenstein* (as the Monster), 1942; *The Mummy's Tomb* (as the Mummy), 1942; *Frankenstein Meets the Wolf Man*, 1943; *Son of Dracula* (as Alucard), 1943; *Calling Dr. Death*, 1943; *Weird Woman*, 1944; *Cobra Woman*, 1944; *The Mummy's Curse*, 1944; *House of Dracula* (as the Wolf Man), 1945; *House of Frankenstein* (as the Wolf Man), 1945; *The Frozen Ghost*, 1945; *Abbott and Costello Meet Frankenstein* (his best reprisal of the Talbot role), 1948; *Bride of the Gorilla*, 1952; *The Black Castle*, 1952; *The Black Sleep*, 1956; *The Indestructible Man* (particularly well-cast as The Butcher, a vicious criminal resurrected after his execution), 1956; *The Cyclops*, 1957; *La Casa del Terror* (Mexican; cast as a werewolf), 1959; *The Alligator People*, 1959; *The Haunted Palace*, 1963; *Witchcraft*, 1964; *House of the Black Death*, 1965; *Dr. Terror's Gallery of Horrors*, 1967; *Hillbillys* [sic] *in a Haunted House*, 1967; *Spider Baby* or: *The Maddest Story Ever Told*, 1970; *Dracula vs. Frankenstein*, 1971.

The beginning of the end for resurrected killer Lon Chaney, Jr., in *The Indestructible Man* (1956).

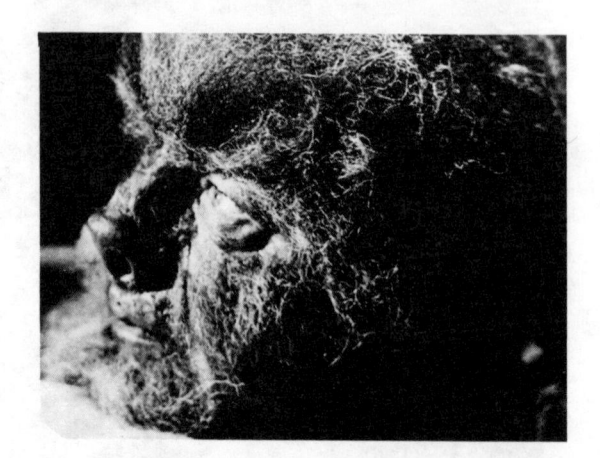

Lon Chaney, Jr., as the werewolf in this rare shot from *La Casa del Terror* (1959).

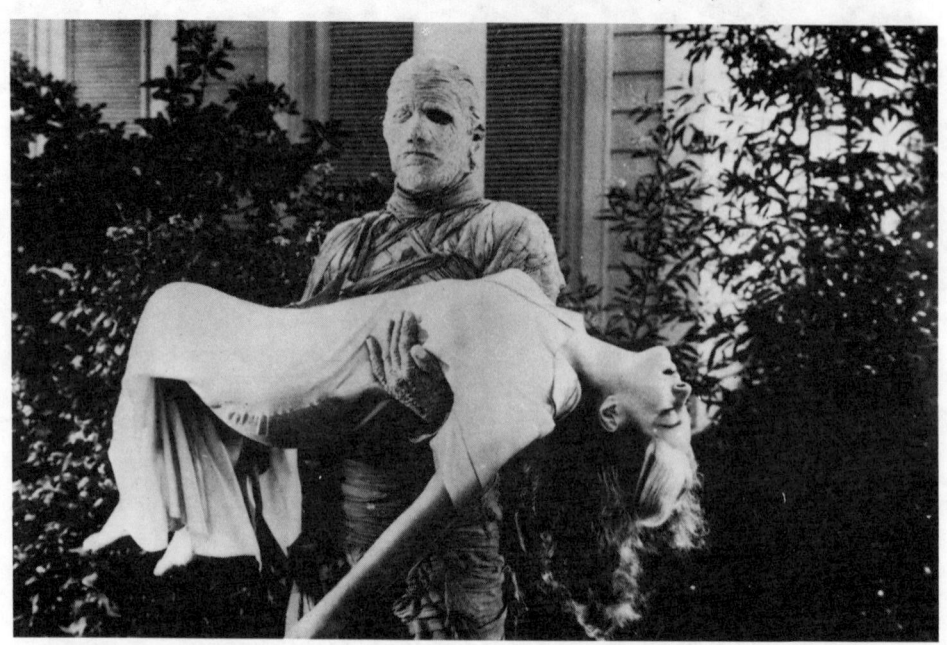

Lon Chaney, Jr., as Kharis in *The Mummy's Tomb* (1942).

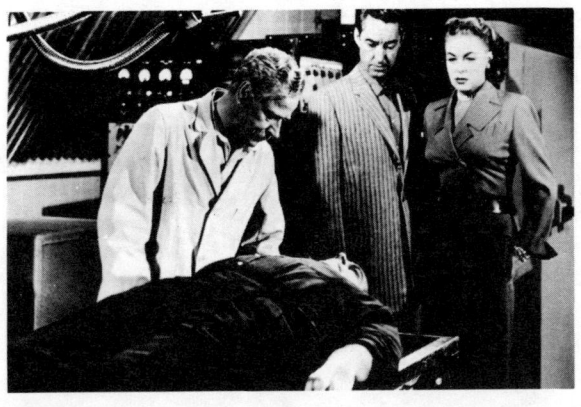

Marguerite Chapman, with James Griffith *(right)* in *The Amazing Transparent Man* (1960).

Julie Christie.

CHANG, WAH (CA. 1925–). Chinese-American model animator, associated with producer GEORGE PAL from the Puppetoon days, 1943–47. *The Monster from Green Hell*, 1958; *tom thumb* (creation of the Yawning Man), 1958; *The Time Machine* (Academy Award), 1960; *Dinosaurus*, 1960; *The Wonderful World of the Brothers Grimm*, 1962; *The Seven Faces of Dr. Lao*, 1964; *The Power*, 1968; *Dinosaurs, the Terrible Lizards*, 1970; others.

CHAPMAN, BEN. American underwater expert who played the monster in the underwater sequences of *The Creature Walks among Us*, 1956. See also: DON MEGOWAN.

CHAPMAN, MARGUERITE (1916–). American leading lady of the forties and fifties. *The Body Disappears*, 1941; *Spy Smasher*, 1942; *Flight to Mars*, 1951; *The Amazing Transparent Man*, 1961.

CHASE, CHARLEY (1893–1940). Dapper and mustachioed American comedian, popular in silent and sound two-reelers for Hal Roach. Much underrated, Chase usually played a harried husband; a number of his shorts have fantastic content. *Nature in the Wrong* (an amusing Tarzan spoof), 1933; *Now We'll Tell One*, 1933; *Another Wild Idea*, 1934; *Life Hesitates at 40*, 1935; *Okay, Toots!*, 1935; *Public Ghost No. 1*, 1935.

CHRISTIE, JULIE (1940–). Chic British leading lady, the screen's contemporary darling during the sixties. *Fahrenheit 451*, 1966; *Don't Look Now*, 1973; *Demon Seed* (as the woman who is imprisoned and violated by a computer), 1977.

48 CLARKE

CLARKE, ARTHUR C. (1917–). Leading British science fiction author who collaborated with STANLEY KUBRICK on the screenplay for *2001: A Space Odyssey*, 1968.

CLARKE, GARY (CA. 1935–). American juvenile lead of fifties B-films. *How to Make a Monster* (as the Teenage Werewolf), 1958; *Missile to the Moon*, 1959.

CLARKE, MAE (1910–). American leading lady of the thirties and forties, fated to be remembered as the girl who took the grapefruit in the face from JAMES CAGNEY in *Public Enemy*, 1931; *Frankenstein* (as Elizabeth), 1931; *King of the Rocketmen*, 1949.

CLARKE, ROBERT (CA. 1920–). American leading man who brought a fine enthusiasm to minor films. *Bedlam*, 1946; *The Man from Planet X*, 1950; *Captive Women*, 1952; *She-Monster*, 1958; *The Hideous Sun Demon* (title role; and p, story, co-d; w/Thomas Cassarino), 1959; *The Incredible Petrified World*, 1959; *Beyond the Time Barrier* (and p), 1960.

CLAYTON, JACK (1921–). British producer/director with a flair for heavy mood. *The Bespoke Overcoat* (directorial debut; a timid man returns from the grave), 1955; *The Innocents*, 1961; *Our Mother's House*, 1967.

CLEAVE, VAN. American composer. *The Conquest of Space*, 1955; *The Space Children*, 1958; *The Colossus of New York*, 1958; *Project X*, 1968; etc.

CLEMENS, BRIAN (1931–). British screenwriter whose golden touch, evident in television's "The Avengers," 1964–69, then turned to lead. *See No Evil*, 1971; *Dr. Jekyll and Sister Hyde*, 1972; *Captain Kronos, Vampire Hunter* (and d), 1972; *The Golden Voyage of Sinbad*, 1973; *The Watcher in the Woods*, 1980.

CLEMENTS, STANLEY (1926–). American actor of the forties and fifties who usually played tough kids and who succeeded LEO GORCEY as foil for HUNTZ HALL in Monogram/Allied Artists' long-running Bowery Boys series. The boys meet the Devil (BYRON FOULGER) in *Up in Smoke*, 1957. *Ghosts on the Loose*, 1943; *The Rocket Man*, 1954; *Dig That Uranium*, 1956; *Spook Chasers*, 1957.

Gary Clarke *(center)* and Gary Conway spend a pleasant evening with demented makeup artist Robert H. Harris in *How to Make a Monster* (1958).

Mae Clarke with Tristram Coffin in *King of the Rocketmen* (1949).

CLIVE, COLIN (1898–1937). British leading man who was brought to Hollywood from the stage. His Dr. Frankenstein (*Frankenstein*, 1931, and *Bride of Frankenstein*, 1935) remains the definitive (if twitchily neurotic) portrayal. *Mad Love*, 1935.

CLOUZOT, HENRI-GEORGES (1907–1977). French writer/director whose *Les Diaboliques*, 1955, is a much-celebrated study of psychological terror and murder.

COATES, PHYLLIS (CA. 1927–). American leading lady of forties and fifties co-features. *Superman and the Mole Men* (as Lois Lane; and as Lois, 1951–52, in the "Adventures of Superman," television series, 1951–58) 51; *Panther Girl of the Kongo* (title role), 1955; *I Was a Teenage Frankenstein*, 1957; *The Incredible Petrified World*, 1959.

Robert Clarke midway in his transformation to *The Hideous Sun Demon* (1959).

Colin Clive as Dr. Frankenstein, with Elsa Lanchester, *The Bride of Frankenstein* (1935).

Phyllis Coates as reporter Lois Lane, with George Reeves as Superman.

Beast (Jean Marais) strides with Beauty (Josette Day) along the corridor of human-arm candelabra in Jean Cocteau's haunting *The Beauty and The Beast* (1946).

COCTEAU, JEAN (1889–1963). Noted French writer/director who brought a peculiarly surreal elegance to the cinema. *The Beauty and the Beast*, 1946, must surely rank among the most lyrically beautiful films ever made. Also *Orpheus*, 1950; *Disorder* (as actor only), 1950; *The Testament of Orpheus*, 1960.

COFFIN, TRISTRAM. Mustachioed American actor in second features and serials, an effective villain who was occasionally cast as hero. *Spy Smasher*, 1942; *The Corpse Vanishes*, 1942; *King of the Rocketmen* (serial; title role), 1949; *Radar Secret Service*, 1950; *Creature with the Atom Brain*, 1955; *The Night the World Exploded*, 1957; *The Resurrection of Zachary Wheeler*, 1971; others.

COHEN, HERMAN (1928–). American producer who revolutionized the Hollywood film industry in the mid-fifties after he studied demographics and concluded that most box office money was clutched in the hands of kids. His *I Was a Teenage Frankenstein*, 1957, opened the teenage horror cycle and was widely imitated, especially by Cohen himself. *I Was a Teenage Werewolf*, 1957; *Blood of Dracula*, 1957; *How to Make a Monster* (which features *both* the teenage monsters), 1958; *Horrors of the Black Museum*, 1959; *Konga*, 1961; *Black Zoo*, 1963; *Berserk!*, 1968; *Trog*, 1970.

COHEN, LARRY. American writer/producer/director of modest but sometimes effective horror thrillers. *It's Alive*, 1974 (and 77 re-release); *Demon*, 1976; *It Lives Again*, 1978.

Tristram Coffin *(left)*, about to be strangled by an atomic zombie in Edward L. Cahn's *Creature with the Atom Brain* (1955).

A tense and moody moment from *I Was a Teenage Werewolf* (1957), produced by Herman Cohen and directed by Gene Fowler, Jr.

52 COLLINS

COLLINS, JOAN (1933–). Sultry, dark-eyed British leading lady who appeared in a variety of vampish roles in Britain and Hollywood until becoming something of a fixture in anthology horror films of the early seventies. Still a fine beauty, Collins has screamed in *Fear in the Night*, 1972; *Tales from the Crypt*, 1972; *Tales That Witness Madness*, 1973; *Quest for Love*, 1973; *Devil within Her*, 1976; *Empire of the Ants*, 1977.

COLLINSON, MADELEINE AND MARY (CA. 1952–) (CA. 1952–). American twin sister actresses who starred in *Twins of Evil*, 1971, for Hammer after appearing together in a *Playboy* magazine gatefold.

CONNERY, SEAN (1930–). Dark Scottish leading man active in Britain and Hollywood who gained world renown as superspy, superstud James Bond. His conception of the character is somewhat more brutish than that of creator IAN FLEMING, but Connery's film interpretation remains the best liked of the various movie Bonds. He finally tired of the role in the early seventies and has since proven himself in a variety of challenging dramatic roles. *Darby O'Gill and the Little People*, 1958; *Tarzan's Greatest Adventure*, 1959; *Dr. No* (first in the James Bond series), 1962; *Goldfinger*, 1964; *Thunderball*, 1965; *You Only Live Twice*, 1967; *Diamonds Are Forever* (his final turn as James Bond), 1971; *Zardoz* (as Zed), 1974; *Meteor*, 1979.

CONNOR, KEVIN. British director of the seventies. *From Beyond the Grave*, 1975; *The Land That Time Forgot*, 1975; *At the Earth's Core*, 1976; *Warlords of Atlantis*, 1978; *Arabian Adventure*, 1979.

Joan Collins.

Doug McClure leaps to save a comrade from a pterodactyl in Kevin Connor's *The Land That Time Forgot* (1975).

CONNORS, MIKE "TOUCH" (1925–). American television star ("Tightrope," 1959–60, "Mannix," 1968–76) whose career began in Hollywood cheapies; often cast as a greasy hood. *The Day the World Ended* (as the last greasy hood on Earth), 1956; *Voodoo Woman*, 1957.

CONREID, HANS (1917–). Eccentric American comic/character actor of histrionic voice and manner. *The 5000 Fingers of Dr. T* (as Dr. T), 1953; *The Twonky*, 1953; *The Monster That Challenged the World*, 1957; *The Shaggy D.A.*, 1976; *The Cat From Outer Space*, 1978.

CONSTANTINE, EDDIE (1917–). Pockmarked American actor in French films, effective as the grim hero Lemmy Caution in JEAN-LUC GODARD's *Alphaville*, 1965. *Attack of the Robots*, 1962; *It Lives Again*, 1978.

CONWAY, GARY (1938–). Athletic, boyish American leading man of second features and television. *The Saga of the Viking Women and Their Voyage to the Waters of the Great Sea Serpent*, 1957; *I Was a Teenage Frankenstein* (title role), 1957; *How to Make a Monster* (as the Teenage Frankenstein), 1958. TV series: "Land of the Giants," 1968–70.

CONWAY, TOM (1904–67). Russian-born British leading man, most active in Hollywood, where he found popularity as star of the Falcon series, 1942–46. Brother of GEORGE SANDERS. *Tarzan's Secret Treasure*, 1941; *The Cat People*, 1942; *I Walked with a Zombie*, 1943; *Bride of the Gorilla*, 1952; *Tarzan and the She-Devil*, 1953; *The She Creature*, 1956; *The Atomic Submarine*, 1960; *12 to the Moon*, 1960.

Hans Conreid *(center)* shows the embryonic beast to the military in *The Monster That Challenged the World* (1957).

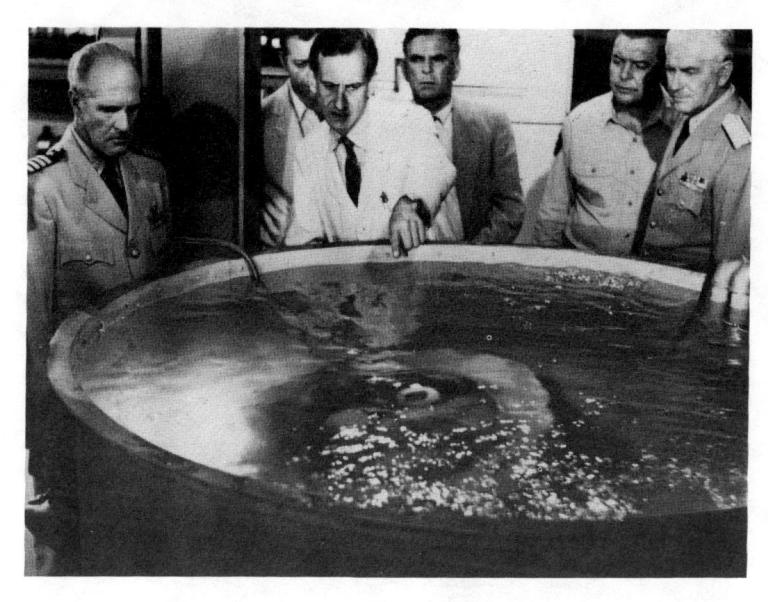

COOK, ELISHA JR. (1902–). American character actor, the sublime fall guy. *Stranger on the Third Floor*, 1940; *House on Haunted Hill*, 1958; *The Haunted Palace*, 1963; *Rosemary's Baby*, 1968; *Blacula*, 1972.

COOPER, MERIAN C. (1893–1973). Ambitious and imaginative American producer, associated with director ERNEST B. SCHOEDSACK and responsible for *King Kong*, 1933. *The Most Dangerous Game*, 1932; *Son of Kong*, 1933. *She*, 1935; *Mighty Joe Young*, 1949.

COPPOLLA, FRANCIS FORD (1939–). American director who came to prominence (*The Godfather*, 1972, et al.) after an apprenticeship with producer ROGER CORMAN. *Dementia 13*, 1963; *The Terror* (part; uncredited), 1963.

CORDAY, MARA (1932–). Dark-eyed American leading lady of the fifties. *Tarantula*, 1955; *The Black Scorpion*, 1957; *The Giant Claw*, 1957.

CORMAN, GENE. American independent producer, often in association with brother ROGER CORMAN. *Night of the Blood Beast* (and story), 1958; *Attack of the Giant Leeches*, 1959; *Beast from Haunted Cave*, 1959.

Mara Corday with Richard Denning *(left)* in a posed shot from *The Black Scorpion* (1957).

Crustacean terror: decapitation in Roger Corman's grisly but good-humored *Attack of the Crab Monsters* (1957).

CORMAN, ROGER (1926–). American producer/director whose prolific output during the fifties crowned him "King of the B's." He rose from messenger at Twentieth Century Fox to head of his own film corporation; in a single year (1957) he directed eight films and started two more. Cursed with small budgets but blessed with verve and humor, Corman's early films consistently showcase fine acting and deft pacing. *The Day the World Ended*, 1956, is the first of many science fiction films he directed and is a good example of his ability to wring believability from hackneyed concepts. *Not of This Earth*, 1957, is a darkly humorous science fiction-horror entry (see also: PAUL BIRCH), as is *Wasp Woman*, 1959. The most outstanding film from his early period is *The Little Shop of Horrors*, 1960, a mad and brilliant farce involving a young nebbish and his talking, man-eating plant. Shot in 2½ days for $34,000, it defies the Hollywood myth that a good film cannot be made on a shoestring. In 1960, Corman began a profitable association with the dark prose of EDGAR ALLAN POE and the talents of actor VINCENT PRICE. At this point his films become more richly visual; although the films of the Poe series vary in quality, they are evocative and immensely interesting. *The Masque of the Red Death*, 1964, is the most elegant, a marvelously perverse study of death and decadent nobility. Since the early seventies Corman has been a full-time producer and has devoted much of his energy to his New World Pictures, which imports many films for the art house circuit, as well as encouraging young and promising domestic talent. Always accessible to young filmmakers and actors, Corman has been mentor to such varied talents as Ellen Burstyn, FRANCIS FORD COPPOLLA, Monte Hellman, JACK HILL, PETER BOGDANOVICH, and JACK NICHOLSON. His generosity is common knowledge in Hollywood. Unpretentious, intensely involved with his projects, Corman is one of America's most significant film auteurs. *Monster from the Ocean Floor* (p only), 1954; *The Beast with 1,000,000 Eyes* (p only), 1955; *It Conquered the World*, 1956; *The Undead*, 1957; *Attack of the Crab Monsters*, 1957; *The Saga of the Viking Women and Their Voyage to the Waters of the Great Sea Serpent*, 1957; *War of the Satellites*, 1958; *Night of the Blood Beast* (p only), 1958; *A Bucket of Blood*, 1959; *House of Usher*, 1960; *The Last Woman on Earth*, 1960; *Creature from the Haunted Sea*, 1961; *The Pit and the Pendulum*, 1961; *The Premature Burial*, 1962; *Tales of Terror*, 1962; *Tower of London*, 1962; *The Raven*, 1963; *The Terror*, 1963; *X—The Man with the X-Ray Eyes*, 1963; *The Haunted Palace*, 1963; *Dementia 13* (p only), 1963; *The Tomb of Ligeia*, 1965; *The Trip*, 1967; *De Sade* (prepared by Corman, though he filmed only a few scenes with KEIR DULLEA; mainly directed by CYRIL ENDFIELD), 1969; *Gas-s-s-s*, 1970.

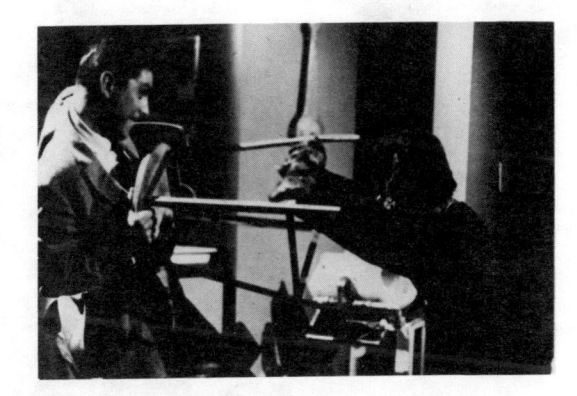

Roger Corman's *The Wasp Woman* (1959) on the rampage.

The extraterrestrial vampire (Paul Birch) confers with the planet Davanna in Roger Corman's *Not of This Earth* (1957).

Adrienne Corri in *Devil Girl from Mars* (1954).

Blissful ignorance: Lou Costello with Bela Lugosi and Glenn Strange in *Abbott and Costello Meet Frankenstein* (1948).

CORNTHWAITE, ROBERT (1917–). American supporting actor, convincing as the fanatically idealistic scientist in *The Thing*, 1951. *The War of the Worlds*, 1953.

CORRI, ADRIENNE (1930–). Good-looking leading lady of British B's. *Devil Girl from Mars*, 1954; *Corridors of Blood*, 1958; *The Hellfire Club*, 1961; *The Tell-Tale Heart* aka *Hidden Room of 1000 Horrors*, 1960; *The Anatomist*, 1961; *A Study in Terror*, 1966; *Moon Zero Two*, 1969; *A Clockwork Orange* (as Mrs. Alexander), 1971; *Vampire Circus*, 1972; *Madhouse*, 1973.

CORRIGAN, RAY "CRASH" (1907-76). Burly American cowboy and serial star of the thirties. *Dante's Inferno*, 1935; *Undersea Kingdom*, 1936; *The Monster and the Ape* (as the ape), 1945; *Killer Ape*, 1953; *It!—The Terror from beyond Space* (as It!, a decidedly foul-tempered Martian), 1958.

COSCARELLI, DON (1952–). Enthusiastic American filmmaker whose *Phantasm*, 1979, is a wildly inventive plunge into the milieu of sinister mortuaries, killer dwarfs, and the fourth dimension. If his narrative technique can catch up with his imagination, Coscarelli may become an important horror film auteur. See also WILLARD GREEN.

COSTELLO, LOU (1906-59). Chubby and innocent-seeming American comic, a much-underrated talent, half of the most popular comedy team of the nineteen-forties. With his ineptitude and basic sweetness, Costello skillfully offset the bitterness of partner BUD ABBOTT and became one of Hollywood's most lovable images. The Abbott and Costello films made a lot of money for Universal, but by the second half of the forties the quality of the pictures had declined, and the only worthwhile film the team made after 1945 was *Abbott and Costello Meet Frankenstein*, 1948. It succeeds admirably in being at once funny and genuinely spooky but unfortunately led to a series of inferior spinoffs, such as *Abbott and Costello Meet the Mummy*, 1955. *Hold That Ghost*, 1941; *The Time of Their Lives*, 1946; *Abbott and Costello Meet the Killer, Boris Karloff*, 1949; *Abbott and Costello Meet the Invisible Man*, 1951; *Jack and the Beanstalk*, 1952; *Abbott and Costello Go to Mars* (an intriguing title for what is probably the team's worst film), 1953; *Abbott and Costello Meet Dr. Jekyll and Mr. Hyde*, 1953. In addition, Lou Costello starred as a solo opposite Dorothy Provine in a mild 1959 fantasy-comedy entitled *The 30-Foot Bride of Candy Rock*.

COTTEN, JOSEPH (1905–). Powerful American star character actor, once associated with ORSON WELLES. Cotten's career, at its peak in the forties, has since declined, but he remains an impressive screen personality. *Shadow of a Doubt* (as the murderous Uncle Charlie), 1943; *Portrait of Jennie*, 1948; *From the Earth to the Moon*, 1958; *Hush, Hush Sweet Charlotte*, 1964; *Latitude Zero*, 1969; *The Abominable Dr. Phibes*, 1971; *Baron Blood*, 1972; *Lady Frankenstein*, 1973; *Soylent Green*, 1973; *The Hearse*, 1980.

COULOURIS, GEORGE (1903–). Forceful British character actor who has carried a determined personality into old age. *Womaneater*, 1957; *The Skull*, 1965; *Blood from the Mummy's Tomb*, 1971; *Horror on Snape Island*, 1972; *Antichristo*, 1974.

COURT, HAZEL (1926–). Lushly beautiful British leading lady who came to Hollywood in the early sixties and appeared in some films for director ROGER CORMAN. *Ghost Ship*, 1953; *Devil Girl from Mars*, 1954; *The Curse of Frankenstein*, 1957; *Dr. Blood's Coffin*, 1961; *The Premature Burial*, 1962; *The Raven*, 1963; *The Masque of the Red Death*, 1964.

Joseph Cotten.

Hazel Court in a publicity pose from *The Curse of Frankenstein* (1957).

58 CRABBE

Buster Crabbe.

Kim Parker is about to have her brain sucked from her head in this scene from *Fiend without a Face* (1958), directed by Arthur Crabtree.

CRABBE, LARRY "BUSTER" (1907–). Athletic and enthusiastic American serial star and former Olympic swimmer, best remembered as *Flash Gordon*, 1936, and as star of its sequels, *Flash Gordon's Trip to Mars*, 1938, and *Flash Gordon Conquers the Universe*, 1940. In 1979, Crabbe made a guest appearance as a veteran spaceship pilot on the Buck Rogers television series. *Tarzan the Fearless*, 1933; *Buck Rogers*, 1939.

CRABTREE, ARTHUR (1900–). British director of a pair of distasteful but effective horror thrillers, *Fiend without a Face*, 1958, and *Horrors of the Black Museum*, 1959.

CRANE, RICHARD (1918–69). American leading man of the fifties, popular as television's Rocky Jones, Space Ranger, 1953–55; episodes from the series were edited together in 1953–54 to make feature films distributed in Europe. *Forbidden Moon*, 1953; *Gypsy Moon*, 1953; *Silver Needle in the Sky*, 1954; *Out of This World*, 1954; *Robot of Regalio*, 1954; *Beyond the Moon*, 1954; *Blast Off*, 1954; *The Cold Sun*, 1954; *Crash of Moons*, 1954; *Duel in Space*, 1954; *Inferno in Space*, 1954; *The Magnetic Moon*, 1954; *Menace from Outer Space*, 1954; *Manhunt in Space*, 1954. In addition to the Rocky Jones films, Crane starred in the following: *Mysterious Island* (serial), 1951; *The Neanderthal Man*, 1953; *The Devil's Partner*, 1958; *The Alligator People*, 1959; *House of the Damned*, 1963.

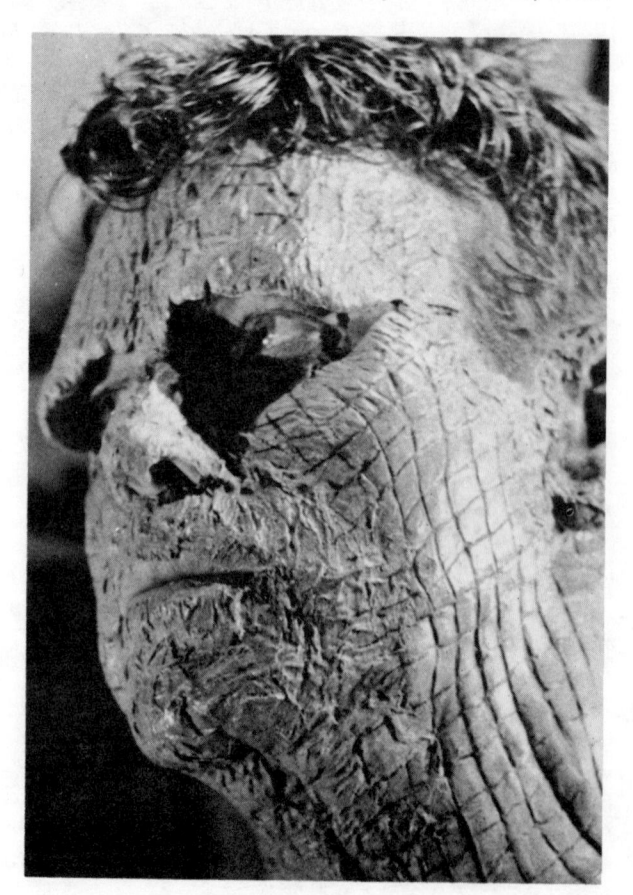

Scaly fellow: Richard Crane in *The Alligator People* (1959).

CRAWFORD, JOAN (1906–77). Popular American leading lady, a former chorine who, with her piercing eyes and large mouth, came to epitomize strong-willed women for four decades. She moved easily into character roles as she grew older, and followed BETTE DAVIS into the Grand Guignol revival of the early sixties. *The Unknown*, 1927; *Whatever Happened to Baby Jane?*, 1962; *Strait-Jacket*, 1964; *I Saw What You Did*, 1965; *Berserk!*, 1968; *Trog*, 1970.

CREGAR, LAIRD (1916–44). Heavyset American character lead who suggested a maturity beyond his years. At home in gaslit murder thrillers like *The Lodger* (as Jack the Ripper), 1944, and *Hangover Square*, 1945. *Heaven Can Wait* (as the Devil), 1943.

CRICHTON, MICHAEL (1942–). Successful American novelist turned director. His *Coma*, 1978, is a riveting combination of genres: science fiction, horror, suspense, and classic murder mystery. Despite a lot of technical jargon, the film rolls along to a thrilling climax. *The Andromeda Strain* (original story only, b/o his novel), 1971; *Westworld* (and w), 1973; *The Terminal Man* (original story only, b/o his novel), 1974.

CROFT, DOUGLAS. American juvenile actor of the forties who portrayed Batman's aide Robin in a 1943 serial, *The Batman*.

Axe murderess Joan Crawford returns home after twenty years in confinement in *Strait-Jacket* (1964).

CRONENBERG, DAVID (CA. 1948–). Young Canadian writer/director of the seventies who has shown a certain amount of unsubtle style. *Stereo*, 1969; *Crimes of the Future* (semiprofessional; science-fiction (sex satire), 1970; *They Came from Within*, 1976; *Rabid*, 1977; *The Brood*, 1978; *Scanners*, 1980.

CROSBY, FLOYD (1899–). American cinematographer who brought a crisp and economical visual style to many films for ROGER CORMAN. *Monster from the Ocean Floor*, 1954; *Attack of the Crab Monsters*, 1957; *War of the Satellites*, 1958; *House of Usher*, 1960; *The Pit and the Pendulum*, 1961; *The Premature Burial*, 1962; *Tower of London*, 1962; *Tales of Terror*, 1962; *The Raven*, 1963; *Black Zoo*, 1963; *X—The Man with the X-Ray Eyes*, 1963; *The Haunted Palace*, 1963; etc.

CUNHA, RICHARD. American director of second features. *She Demons*, 1958; *Giant from the Unknown* (and ph), 1958; *Frankenstein's Daughter*, 1959; *Missile to the Moon*, 1959; *Bloodlust* (ph only), 1961.

CUNNINGHAM, SEAN S. American producer/writer/director with a predilection for heavy-handed gore. *The Last House on the Left* (p & co-w only), 1973; *Friday the 13th* (p & d), 1980.

CURIEL, FEDERICO. Mexican director of outrageous thrillers which usually involve Nostrodamus or masked wrestlers and monsters. *The Curse of Nostrodamus*, 1961; *The Blood of Nostrodamus*, 1962; *Monster Demolisher*, 1962; *Genii of Darkness*, 1962; *Neutron Against the Death Robots*, 1962; *Neutron and the Black Mask*, 1962; *Santo Contra el Rey de Crimen*, 1963; *Las Vampiras*, 1968; *Santo en la Vengaza de las Mujeres Vampira*, 1969; *The Champions of Justice Return*, 1972; etc.

CURTIS, BILLY (CA. 1911–). American midget character actor with vaudeville experience who has played in numerous Hollywood fantasies. *The Wizard of Oz*, 1939; *The Thing* (doubling for JAMES ARNESS in the shrinking sequence), 1951; *Invaders From Mars*, 1953; *High Plains Drifter* (co-starring role as Mordecai), 1973.

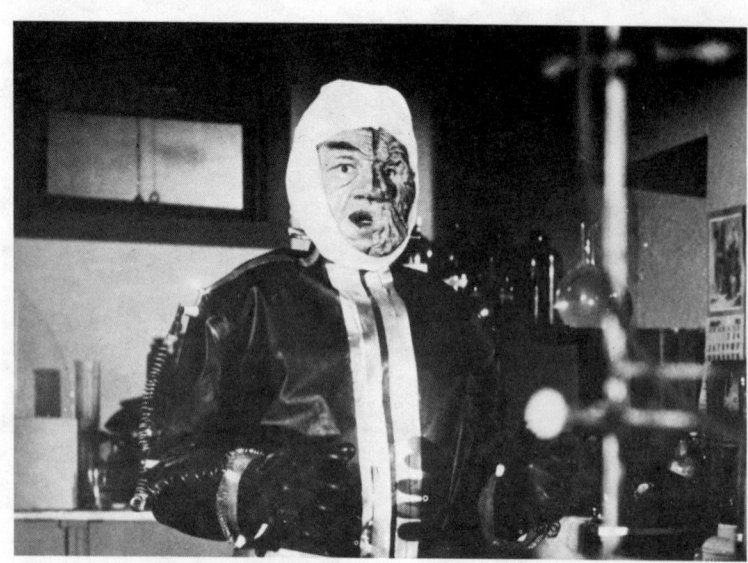

Harry Wilson as *Frankenstein's Daughter* (1959), directed by Richard Cunha.

CURTIS, DAN. American producer/director also active in television. His taste for occult shockers has been impaired by a predilection for the obvious, but he can usually be counted on to deliver more than a few good moments. *House of Dark Shadows* (b/o his successful television serial "Dark Shadows," 1966-71), 1970; *Night of Dark Shadows*, 1971; *The Night Stalker* (TV; p only; pilot for television series the "Night Stalker," 1974-75), 1972; *The Night Strangler* (TV), 1973; *Dracula* (TV; theatrical release in Britain), 1973; *Trilogy of Terror* (TV), 1975; *Burnt Offerings* (and co-w; w/William F. Nolan), 1976.

CURTIS, JAMIE LEE (CA. 1955-). American actress of the eighties, daughter of JANET LEIGH and Tony Curtis. *Halloween* (leading role), 1979; *The Fog*, 1980; *Prom Night*, (1980).

CURTIS, KEN (1916-). American actor, popular as Festus on television's "Gunsmoke," 1964-75. In the late fifties he produced for Southwest radio tycoon Gordon McLendon a pair of science fiction quickies, *The Giant Gila Monster*, 1959 and *The Killer Shrews*, 1959. In the latter, Curtis cast himself as the villain and at the climax falls off a roof and is gobbled up by the hungry shrews.

CURTIZ, MICHAEL (1888-1962). Energetic Hungarian director long in Hollywood with Warner Brothers and active until his death. Despite his European background, Curtiz's films capture an authentic American flavor. *Alraune*, 1918; *The Mad Genius*, 1931; *Dr. X*, 1932; *The Mystery of the Wax Museum*, 1933; *The Walking Dead*, 1936.

CUSHING, PETER (1913-). Courtly British character lead, active in films since the late thirties. He played Dr. Frankenstein in *Curse of Frankenstein*, 1957, and has since been typed, often as Frankenstein or never-say-die vampire hunter Van Helsing in Dracula films. *Horror of Dracula*, 1958; *The Mummy*, 1959; *The Hound of the Baskervilles* (as Sherlock Holmes), 1959; *Brides of Dracula*, 1960; *The Skull*, 1965; *Corruption*, 1968; *Frankenstein Must Be Destroyed*, 1969; *Tales from the Crypt*, 1972; *Frankenstein and the Monster from Hell*, 1973; *Star Wars* (as Governor Tarkin), 1977; *Land of the Minotaur*, 1977; many others.

A touch of class: Peter Cushing in *Creeping Flesh* (1972).

Dinosaur by model animator Jim Danforth in *When Dinosaurs Ruled the Earth* (1971).

D

D'AGOSTINO, ALBERT S. (1893–1970). American set designer who created a finely gothic atmosphere for many horror films of the thirties and forties, including some produced by VAL LEWTON. Notable among D'agostino's later projects is *The Thing*, 1951, for which he designed particularly stark and foreboding sets. *Werewolf of London*, 1935; *The Man Who Reclaimed His Head*, 1935; *The Raven*, 1935; *Dracula's Daughter*, 1936; *The Cat People*, 1942; *I Walked with a Zombie*, 1943; *Curse of the Cat People*, 1944; *The Body Snatcher*, 1945; *Isle of the Dead*, 1945; *The Spiral Staircase*, 1945; others.

DAGOVER, LIL (1897–1980). German leading actress in gothic/expressionist films of the teens and twenties. *The Cabinet of Dr. Caligari*, 1919; *Die Goldene See (The Spiders)*, 1919; *Destiny*, 1921; *Dr. Mabuse, The Gambler*, 1922; *The Phantom*, 1922; *The Chronicles of the Gray House*, 1925.

Henry Daniell as Dr. MacFarlane in *The Body Snatcher* (1945).

DAHL, ROALD (1916–). British author who has brought his whimsical imagination to a few films. Married to actress PATRICIA NEAL. *Chitty Chitty Bang Bang* (co-w; w/RICHARD MAIBAUM; b/o the book by IAN FLEMING), 1968; *You Only Live Twice* (b/o the novel by IAN FLEMING), 1969; *Willy Wonka and the Chocolate Factory* (b/o his book *Charlie and the Chocolate Factory*), 1971; *The Night Digger*, 1971.

DALI, SALVADOR (1904–). Spanish surrealist artist who has dabbled in film. A significant figure in twentieth-century art, Dali is also a shrewd self-promoter, and his film work is as much promotion as art. With LUIS BUÑUEL: *Un Chien Andalou*, 1929; *L'Age D'Or*, 1930. Also designed the dream sequence for ALFRED HITCHCOCK's *Spellbound*, 1945.

DALLESANDRO, JOE (1948–). Dull-eyed American actor, once active in Andy Warhol's underground cinema, who has been moving slowly into the mainstream. *Blood for Dracula*, 1974; *Andy Warhol's Frankenstein* (directed by PAUL MORRISSEY), 1974; *Black Moon*, 1975.

DAMON, MARK (1935–). American leading man who has worked in Europe as well as Hollywood. *House of Usher*, 1960; *Black Sabbath*, 1963; *Hannah, Queen of the Vampires*, 1972; *The Devil's Wedding Night*, 1973; *Crypt of the Living Dead*, 1973.

DANFORTH, JIM (CA. 1938–). American stop-motion animator who seems the logical successor to RAY HARRYHAUSEN. *The Wonderful World of the Brothers Grimm*, 1962; *Jack the Giant Killer*, 1962; *Journey to the 7th Planet* (post-production doctoring only), 1962; *The Seven Faces of Dr. Lao*, 1964; *When Dinosaurs Ruled the Earth*, 1971; *Flesh Gordon* (credited as Mij Htrofnad), 1972; etc.

DANIELL, HENRY (1894–1963). Cultured and seemingly passionless British character actor, a sinister Moriarty opposite BASIL RATHBONE's Sherlock Holmes, and notable as the ghoulish Dr. Macfarlane in *The Body Snatcher*, 1945. *The Thirteenth Chair*, 1937; *Castle in the Desert*, 1942; *Siren of Atlantis*, 1948; *The Story of Mankind*, 1957; *From the Earth to the Moon*, 1958; *The Four Skulls of Jonathan Drake*, 1959; *Voyage to the Bottom of the Sea*, 1961.

DANTON, RAY (1931–). Slick American leading man of the early sixties who later turned to direction. Long married to actress JULIE ADAMS. As director: *Hannah, Queen of the Vampires*, 1972; *The Deathmaster*, 1972; *Crypt of the Living Dead*, 1973; *Psychic Killer*, 1976.

Bette Davis in *Hush, Hush Sweet Charlotte* (1964), directed by Robert Aldrich.

DAVIS, BETTE (1908–). Versatile and powerful American leading actress, one of the screen's imperishable personalities. She opened the door to horror roles for aging leading ladies with a bravura performance in *Whatever Happened to Baby Jane?*, 1962. *Hush, Hush Sweet Charlotte*, 1964; *Dead Ringer*, 1964; *The Nanny*, 1965; *The Anniversary*, 1968; *Burnt Offerings*, 1976; *The Dark Secret of Harvest Home* (TV), 1978; *Return from Witch Mountain*, 1978; *The Watcher in the Woods*, 1980.

DAWN, JACK (1889–1956). American makeup artist with MGM who created the wondrous faces for many residents of the land of Oz in *The Wizard of Oz*, 1939. His makeup for BERT LAHR's Cowardly Lion is perhaps the most delightful element of a thoroughly delightful film.

Albert Dekker *(left)* looking deceptively benign as *Dr. Cyclops* (1939).

DAY, JOSETTE (1914–). Elegant French leading lady, an unforgettable Beauty opposite JEAN MARAIS's Beast in JEAN COCTEAU's *The Beauty and the Beast*, 1946.

DEARDEN, BASIL (1911–71). British writer/director, responsible for the "Hearse Driver" segment and linking story of the fine anthology horror film *Dead of Night*, 1946. Also directed *Man in the Moon*, 1961; *The Mind Benders*, 1963; *The Man Who Haunted Himself*, 1971.

DE CARLO, YVONNE (1922–). Canadian leading lady in Hollywood films, specializing in amusing costume productions until gaining wide populariy as Lily Munster in television's the "Munsters," 1964–66. She repeated the role in *Munster Go Home*, a 1966 film feature. *The Power*, 1968; *Silent Scream*, 1980.

DE CORDOBA, PEDRO (1881–1950). American character actor, usually cast as a villain. *The Devil Doll*, 1936; *Earthbound*, 1940; *Before I Hang*, 1940; *The Ghost Breakers*, 1940; *Tarzan Triumphs*, 1943; *The Picture of Dorian Gray*, 1945; *The Beast with Five Fingers*, 1946; *The Time of Their Lives*, 1946.

DE HAVILLAND, OLIVIA (1916–). Beautiful British-born leading lady in Hollywood, Warner Brothers' number one personification of demure desirability in the thirties and forties. Still lovely in middle age, De Havilland is one of a number of older leading ladies who spruced up hysterical horror thrillers of the early sixties. Sister of JOAN FONTAINE. *A Midsummer Night's Dream*, 1935; *Hush, Hush Sweet Charlotte* (as the villainess), 1964; *The Screaming Woman* (TV), 1972.

DEIN, EDWARD. American screenwriter. *Calling Dr. Death*, 1943; *Jungle Woman*, 1944; *The Soul of a Monster*, 1944; *The Cat Creeps* (co-w; w/Jerry Warner), 1946; *The Leech Woman* (d only), 1960.

DEKKER, ALBERT (1904–68). Imposing American character actor, memorable as the bald and fatally myopic *Dr. Cyclops*, 1939. *Among the Living*, 1941; *Tarzan's Magic Fountain*, 1949; *She-Devil*, 1957; *Gammera the Invincible*, 1966.

Jack Dawn's brilliant makeup for the Cowardly Lion (Bert Lahr) in *The Wizard of Oz* (1939).

Richard Denning.

Bruce Dern, looking atypically rational.

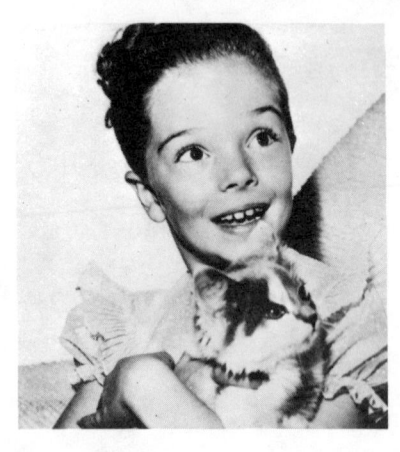

Sandy Descher.

DeLaurentiis, Dino (1919–). Internationally active Italian producer who has cultivated an aggressive image but has produced only a few memorable films. His *King Kong*, 1976, appeared after an avalanche of publicity and hoopla and turned out to be only slightly superior to Japanese assembly-line monster productions. John Guillerman's direction is leaden and unimaginative, acting and art direction indifferent, and the much-publicized budget ($25+ million) scarcely in evidence. Kong is played by RICK BAKER in a handsome ape suit. The effect is disappointing considering the big budget and the media buildup. The scene in which Kong battles a papier-mache serpent is only ludicrous. WILLIS O'BRIEN's 1933 *King Kong* remains one of the highest achievements of the genre, and one can only wonder what a good contemporary animator like RAY HARRYHAUSEN or JIM DANFORTH would have done with the film's generous budget. Despite this costly semi-failure, DeLaurentiis continues to enjoy high respect within the industry. *Ulysses*, 1952; *Barbarella*, 1968; *Flash Gordon*, 1980; others.

Delgado, Marcel (1900–76). American model maker who built *King Kong*, 1933, *Son of Kong*, 1933, *Mighty Joe Young*, 1949, and many other beasts and dinosaurs. Few of his constructions stood more than eighteen inches high.

Del Ruth, Roy (1895–1961). Workmanlike and versatile American director, active from the silent era until his death. *The Terror*, 1928; *Topper Returns*, 1941; *Phantom of the Rue Morgue*, 1954; *The Alligator People*, 1959.

Denberg, Susan (CA. 1945–). American model and *Playboy* playmate who went to England to star in *Frankenstein Created Woman*, 1967.

Deneuve, Catherine (1943–). French leading lady, frequently wooden on screen but effective as the sexually repressed girl in ROMAN POLANSKI's *Repulsion*, 1965. *Les Creatures*, 1966; *Peau D'Ane* aka *The Magic Donkey*, 1970.

Denning, Richard (1914–). Likeable American leading man with radio experience, a capable B-picture hero. Married to actress EVELYN ANKERS. *Television Spy*, 1939; *The Creature from the Black Lagoon*, 1954; *Target—Earth*, 1954; *Creature with the Atom Brain*, 1955; *The Day the World Ended*, 1956; *The Black Scorpion*, 1957; *Twice-Told Tales*, 1963.

Dent, Vernon (1900–63). Beefy American comic actor, a familiar antagonist of THE THREE STOOGES, sometimes cast as a friendly fellow. Dent is at his best playing irate fathers, mad scientists, or surly cops. *Soul of the Beast*, 1923; *Idle Roomers* (two-reeler), 1944; *A Bird in the Head* (two-reeler; as the crazy scientist who covets Curly's tiny bird brain), 1946; *Mummy's Dummies* (two-reeler), 1948; *Heavenly Daze* (two-reeler; as a big-shot angel), 1949; *Fuelin' Around* (two-reeler), 1949; *Three Arabian Nuts* (two-reeler), 1951; *Scrambled Brains* (two-reeler), 1951; *Bedlam in Paradise* (two-reeler), 1955.

DE PALMA, BRIAN (1944–). Derivative but highly talented American director, much influenced by ALFRED HITCHCOCK. His *Carrie*, 1976, is a minor masterpiece of Grand Guignol. *Dionysus in 69*, 1969; *Sisters*, 1973; *Phantom of the Paradise*, 1975; *Obsession*, 1976; *The Fury*, 1978. *Dressed to Kill*, 1980.

DEREN, MAYA (1917–61). Innovative Russian-born filmmaker active in America, regarded as the "mother of the underground film." She became a leading advocate of personal expression in experimental cinema. Her own works range from the profoundly disturbing to the sensuously elegant. An exceptionally beautiful woman, Deren is the central figure in *At Land*, 1944, and in the disconcerting and obsessive *Meshes of the Afternoon*, 1943. *Ritual in Transfigured Time*, 1946; *The Very Eye of the Night*, 1959.

DERN, BRUCE (1936–). Toothy, boyish American character actor who became a star in the seventies after long typecasting as an oddball. *Hush, Hush Sweet Charlotte*, 1964; *The Trip*, 1967; *The Incredible Two-headed Transplant*, 1970; *Silent Running*, 1972; *Family Plot*, 1976.

DERR, RICHARD (1917–). American leading man of second features. *The Man Who Wouldn't Die*, 1942; *Castle in the Desert*, 1942; *When Worlds Collide*, 1951; *Invisible Avenger* (as The Shadow), 1958; *Terror Is a Man*, 1959.

DESCHER, SANDY (1948–). Big-eyed American child actress, remembered as the catatonic little girl in *Them!*, 1954; *It Grows on Trees*, 1952; *Meet Mr. Kringle*, 1956; *The Space Children*, 1958.

DEVON, RICHARD (CA. 1920–). Lean American supporting actor, usually cast as a sinister hood. *Blood of Dracula*, 1957; *The Undead* (as Satan), 1957; *The Saga of the Viking Women and Their Voyage to the Waters of the Great Sea Serpent*, 1957; *War of the Satellites*, 1958; *The Silencers*, 1966.

Richard Devon *(foreground)* guides his men through the choppy process screen waters in this interesting production shot from *The Saga of The Viking Women and Their Voyage to The Waters of The Great Sea Serpent* (1957).

An unwary African about to blunder into the mandibles of a giant wasp. *The Monster from Green Hell* (1958), special effects created by Louis DeWitt.

DeWitt, Louis. American special-effects technician of the fifties. *The Beast of Hollow Mountain*, 1956; *The Invisible Boy*, 1957; *Kronos*, 1957; *War of the Satellites*, 1958; *Macabre*, 1958; *The Monster from Green Hell*, 1958; *The Atomic Submarine*, 1960; etc.

Dexter, Anthony (1919–). American leading man given a big buildup when he played *Valentino* in 1951. He never lived the role down; his career thereafter plummeted. *Fire Maidens of Outer Space*, 1956; *The Story of Mankind*, 1957; *12 to the Moon*, 1960; *The Phantom Planet*, 1962.

Dexter, Maury (ca. 1928–). American producer/director of second features. His *The Day Mars Invaded Earth*, 1963, has its share of good moments. *House of the Damned*, 1963; *Raiders from Beneath the Sea*, 1965.

Dexter, Von. American composer associated with producer William Castle. Scored *House on Haunted Hill*, 1958; *The Tingler*, 1959; *13 Ghosts*, 1960; *Mr. Sardonicus*, 1961.

Dickerson, Beech (ca. 1935–). American actor of the fifties, associated with director Roger Corman and often cast as a goonish young fellow. *Attack of the Crab Monsters*, 1957; *War of the Satellites*, 1958; *Teenage Caveman*, 1958; *Creature from the Haunted Sea*, 1961.

Dieterle, William (1893–1972). German director in Hollywood, former actor. *Three Wax Men*, 1924; *Faust*, 1926; *At Edge of World*, 1929. As a director, Dieterle developed an expansive visual style and applied it to a wide range of projects. His *Portrait of Jennie*, 1948, is among Hollywood's more successful excursions into pure fantasy. (See also: Jennifer Jones). *A Midsummer Night's Dream*, 1935; *The Hunchback of Notre Dame*, 1939.

Anton Diffring *(left)* in *Circus of Horrors* (1960).

DIFFRING, ANTON (1918–). Grim and pale-eyed German actor in Britain, effective as *The Man Who Could Cheat Death*, 1959. Also: *Tales of Frankenstein* (never released), 1957; *Circus of Horrors*, 1960; *Fahrenheit 451*, 1966; *The Beast Must Die*, 1974.

DISNEY, WALT (1901–66). American cartoon animator, later studio head, who built an empire by playing to the obvious limits of the American imagination. To his credit, Disney was blessed with a genuine artistic perception, and his early work is often vibrant and wonderfully alive. His contribution to the art of cartoon animation is inestimable. His personal enthusiasm never waned, but the spine seemed to go out of the Disney product as Mickey Mouse and Company grew into a multi-million-dollar business. By the late forties, much of the studio's output had become bland and sentimental. The technical level of the cartoons remained high, but the earlier verve was lost. Still, those films made during Disney's lifetime are consistently entertaining and have delighted millions. *Snow White and the Seven Dwarfs*, 1938, was the industry's first feature-length cartoon and is beautifully executed. *Fantasia*, 1940, is a deceptively cerebral film that masquerades as merely a visual feast for middlebrows; it has enjoyed a resurgence of popularity since the late sixties. *Pinocchio*, 1940; *Song of the South*, 1946; *Cinderella*, 1950; *Alice in Wonderland*, 1951; *Peter Pan*, 1953; *20,000 Leagues under the Sea*, 1954; *Darby O'Gill and the Little People*, 1958; *Sleeping Beauty*, 1959; *The Absent-Minded Professor*, 1961; *Babes in Toyland* (perhaps Disney's only out-and-out disaster), 1961; *Son of Flubber*, 1963; others.

Jiminy Cricket and, of course, Pinocchio in a scene from Walt Disney's 1940 production.

The leprechauns celebrate in Walt Disney's *Darby O'Gill and the Little People* (1958).

DIX, RICHARD (1894–1949). Sturdy American leading man of the twenties and thirties, popular in the Whistler series, 1944–48; the films characteristically have elements of horror. *The Trans-Atlantic Tunnel*, 1935; *The Ghost Ship*, 1943; *The Whistler*, 1944; *Mark of the Whistler*, 1944; *The Power of the Whistler*, 1945; *Voice of the Whistler*, 1945; *The Mysterious Intruder*, 1946; *The 13th Hour*, 1947; *The Secret of the Whistler*, 1947.

DIX, WILLIAM (1956–). British child actor of the sixties, infuriatingly bratty as the little boy opposite BETTE DAVIS in *The Nanny*, 1965. *Dr. Doolittle*, 1967.

DOMERGUE, FAITH (1925–). Sultry-looking American leading lady, a Howard Hughes discovery. She was the victim in 1950 of an overblown publicity campaign that promised more than was delivered; thereafter she slowly faded in popularity. *This Island Earth*, 1955; *Cult of the Cobra*, 1955; *It Came from Beneath the Sea*, 1955; *The Atomic Man*, 1956; *Voyage to the Prehistoric Planet*, 1965; *Legacy of Blood*, 1972; *The House of the Seven Corpses*, 1973.

DONLEVY, BRIAN (1899–1972). American leading actor, usually a burly but well-meaning tough guy. When his career began to falter in the mid-fifties, Donlevy went to England and found success as hero of the first two Quatermass thrillers, *The Creeping Unknown*, 1955, and *Enemy from Space*, 1956. *Curse of the Fly*, 1965; *Gammera the Invincible*, 1966.

Faith Domergue.

The monstrous ants from *Them!*, directed by Gordon Douglas in 1954.

Diana Dors early in her career.

DONNER, RICHARD. American director from television who had a big hit with *The Omen*, 1976, and was signed to direct *Superman*, 1978. The latter is a flawed but eye-filling gestalt of Fordian sentiment, noisy science fiction, and grand adventure. Donner's successful juggling of the disparate approaches is a feat in itself, but what will be remembered as his major accomplishment is his translation of the Superman character from pulp paper to thrilling reality. See also: CHRISTOPHER REEVE.

DONOVAN, KING (CA. 1919-). American supporting actor, remembered as the man in *Invasion of the Body Snatchers*, 1956, who discovers a duplicate of himself quietly forming on his pool table. *Angels in the Outfield*, 1951; *The Magnetic Monster*, 1953; *The Beast from 20,000 Fathoms*, 1953.

DORAN, ANN (1914-). American supporting actress. *The Man They Could Not Hang*, 1939; *The Green Hornet*, 1940; *Fear in the Night*, 1947; *The Man Who Turned to Stone*, 1957; *It!—The Terror from beyond Space*, 1958.

DORS, DIANA (1931-). British leading lady, England's answer to Marilyn Monroe in the fifties. Once typed in bad-girl roles, Dors has in recent years become pink and plump and now plays wives and over-the-hill teases. *Berserk!*, 1968; *The Amazing Mr. Blunden*, 1972; *Nothing but the Night*, 1972; *Theatre of Blood*, 1973; *From Beyond the Grave*, 1975.

DOUGLAS, GORDON (1909-). American director who progressed from "Our Gang" comedies of the thirties to slick crime thrillers of the sixties. His *Them!*, 1954, is a science fiction classic, a compelling work of uncompromising verisimilitude. Much-imitated (its giant ants inspiring hordes of similar mutations), it is Douglas' finest effort and among the best American films of the fifties. *Gildersleeve's Ghost*, 1944; *Zombies on Broadway*, 1945; *Way . . . Way Out*, 1966; *Skullduggery*, 1970.

DOUGLAS, HELEN GAHAGAN (CA. 1910-). American leading lady who starred in the first version of *She*, 1935, and later entered national politics as a United States Congresswoman from California.

DOYLE, SIR ARTHUR CONAN (1859-1930). British novelist and short-story writer famous as the creator of Sherlock Holmes. Doyle grew to resent Holmes' immense popularity and even tried to kill off his fictional detective, but an outraged public refused to stand for it. Fantastic films inspired by the Sherlock Holmes stories include *The Hound of the Baskervilles*, 1939 and 1959; *Spider Woman*, 1944; *The Scarlet Claw*, 1944; *Pearl of Death*, 1944. Doyle's novel *The Lost World* has inspired two film versions, a splendid one in 1925 which boasts trick effects by WILLIS O'BRIEN and a surprisingly tepid version in 1960.

DRACHE, HEINZ. German actor popular in European B-films, often in adaptations of EDGAR WALLACE novels. *The Avenger*, 1960; *The Door with Seven Locks*, 1962; *The Indian Scarf*, 1963; *The Mysterious Magician*, 1965; *The Brides of Fu Manchu*, 1966; etc.

DREYER, CARL (1889–1968). Renowned Danish director whose *Vampyr*, 1932, is a classic of understated horror. *Leaves from Satan's Book*, 1920; *The Witch Woman* (and w), 1920; *Day of Wrath*, 1947.

DREYFUSS, RICHARD (1949–). Ingenuous American leading man of the seventies. Short and verging on chubbiness, Dreyfuss is a movie hero for the common man. *Jaws*, 1975; *Close Encounters of the Third Kind*, 1977.

Richard Dreyfuss searches for the alien spacecraft in *Close Encounters of the Third Kind* (1977).

Kenne Duncan.

Pamela Duncan, in a publicity still from *The Undead* (1957).

DUBOV, PAUL (-1979). American actor of the fifties and sixties, later a screen and television writer. Seen to best advantage as nattily-dressed hoods in low-budget crime thrillers, Dubov is featured in a number of fantastic films. *The Mystery of Marie Roget*, 1942; *Voodoo Woman*, 1957; *The Day the World Ended* (as Radek), 1956; *The Atomic Submarine*, 1960; *The Underwater City*, 1962.

DULLEA, KEIR (1936-). Intense American leading man. *2001: A Space Odyssey*, 1968; *De Sade* (title role), 1969; *Black Christmas*, 1975; *Brave New World* (TV), 1980.

DUNCAN, DAVID (1913-). American screenwriter. *The Black Scorpion*, 1957; *The Thing That Couldn't Die*, 1958; *Monster on the Campus*, 1958; *The Leech Woman*, 1960; *The Time Machine*, 1960; *Fantastic Voyage* (adaptation only), 1966.

DUNCAN, JOHNNY (CA.1925-). American juvenile actor of the forties, onetime member of Monogram's East Side Kids group and Robin the teen-aged crimefighter in the 1949 serial *Batman and Robin*.

DUNCAN, KENNE (1902-72). American actor and stuntman, often a sneaky henchman in Republic serials of the forties. *Flash Gordon's Trip to Mars*, 1938; *Buck Rogers*, 1939; *The Adventures of Captain Marvel*, 1941; *The Man with Two Lives*, 1942; *Haunted Harbor*, 1944; *The Purple Monster Strikes*, 1945; *The Crimson Ghost*, 1946; *Radar Secret Service*, 1950; *The Astounding She Monster*, 1958; *Night of the Ghouls*, 1959; *Superman vs. the Gorilla Gang* (amateur), 1965.

DUNCAN, PAMELA (C. 1932-). Leading lady of American second features. *Attack of the Crab Monsters*, 1957; *The Undead*, 1957.

DUNLAP, PAUL. American composer of generally uninspired film scores, busiest during the fifties. *Lost Continent*, 1951; *Target—Earth*, 1954; *I Was a Teenage Frankenstein*, 1957; *I Was a Teenage Werewolf*, 1957; *How to Make a Monster*, 1958; *Frankenstein—1970*, 1958; *The Four Skulls of Jonathan Drake*, 1959; *The Three Stooges Meet Hercules*, 1962; *Black Zoo*, 1963; *The Destructors*, 1967; *Castle of Evil*, 1968; many others.

DUNN, MICHAEL (1934-73). Highly talented American dwarf actor, popular on television's the "Wild, Wild West" (1965-69) as the evil Dr. Loveless. *Murders in the Rue Morgue*, 1971; *House of Freaks*, 1973; *The Mutation*, 1973; *The Werewolf of Washington* (as Dr. Kiss), 1973.

DWAN, ALLAN (1885-). Prolific American director, active since the early silent era and lately the object of a minor cult. *The Gorilla*, 1939; *The Most Dangerous Man Alive* (last to date), 1958.

DYALL, VALENTINE (1908–). Imposing British character actor who has lent his sepulchral voice to a few horror films, notably *Horror Hotel*, 1960, as the sinister warlock Jethro Kane. *Corridor of Mirrors*, 1948; *Room to Let*, 1950; *The Haunting*, 1963; *The Horror of It All*, 1964; *The Slipper and the Rose*, 1976.

DYKSTRA, JOHN. American special effects technician. *Star Wars*, 1977; *Battlestar Galactica*, 1978; *Star Trek: The Motion Picture*, 1979.

Is it love? Harry Earles as Hans, the innocent circus midget who marries Olga Baclanova, the cruel high-wire artist in Tod Browning's *Freaks* (1932).

Anthony Eisley.

E

EARLES, HARRY (CA. 1900–?). American actor of the twenties and thirties, a baby-faced midget who convincingly projects evil in *The Unholy Three*, 1925 (and sound remake, 1930). Sympathetic as the gentle bridegroom Hans in TOD BROWNING's *Freaks*, 1932.

EASTWOOD, CLINT (1930–). Rugged American star actor who created in the mid-sixties a film persona of tough conviction and individuality. Condemned by some critics for the unrelenting violence of his movie vehicles, Eastwood is a versatile and committed filmmaker who projects a powerful star quaity. While a contract player with Universal Pictures in the early fifties, he napalmed *Tarantula*, 1955, and met the monster in *Revenge of the Creature*, 1955. Later films: *The Witches* (French-Italian anthology film), 1965; *The Beguiled* (Gothic Western), 1971; *Play Misty For Me* (& d), 1971; *High Plains Drifter* (& d), 1973. The amoral nihilism of Eastwood's horror films is in perfect, if disturbing, harmony with his screen persona, and assures him an important place in the cinema of the fantastic.

EDOUART, ALEXANDER FARCIOT (CA. 1895–1980). French special effects expert in Hollywood, responsible for the marvelous illusions in *Dr. Cyclops*, 1939, cleverly using rear projection and outsized sets and props. *The Space Children*, 1958.

EGE, JULIE (CA. 1947–). Norwegian glamour girl in Hammer films of the seventies. *Creatures the World Forgot*, 1971; *The Mutation*, 1973; *The Last Days of Man on Earth*, 1974; *Craze*, 1974; *The Legend of the Seven Golden Vampires*, 1974.

EISLEY, ANTHONY (CA. 1925–). Smooth American B-picture leading man and television actor. *Wasp Woman* (billed as Fred Eisley), 1959; *The Navy vs. the Night Monsters*, 1966; *Journey to the Center of Time*, 1968; *The Witchmaker*, 1969; *Dracula vs. Frankenstein*, 1971.

EKEROT, BENGT. Swedish actor who played Death with disturbing grim humor in INGMAR BERGMAN's *The Seventh Seal*, 1956.

EKLAND, BRITT (1942–). Big-eyed Swedish leading lady in Britain, roles mainly decorative. *Asylum*, 1972; *Night Hair Child*, 1972; *The Wicker Man* (unreleased in United States), 1973; *The Man with the Golden Gun* (as Mary Goodnight), 1974.

ELLENSHAW, HARRISON (PETER) (CA. 1947–). British matte artist in the U.S., son of special effects wizard PETER ELLENSHAW and head of DISNEY Studio's matte department since 1974. Films: *Star Wars*, 1977; *Return From Witch Mountain*, 1978; *The Cat From Outer Space*, 1978; *The Black Hole*, 1979; *The Empire Strikes Back*, 1980.

ELLENSHAW, PETER (1913–). British special effects designer and matte artist, associated with the DISNEY organization since the early fifties. *Things to Come*, 1936; *The Thief of Bagdad*, 1940; *20,000 Leagues Under the Sea*, 1954; *Darby O'Gill and the Little People*, 1958; *Mary Poppins* (Academy Award), 1964; *The Gnome-Mobile*, 1967; *The Love Bug*, 1969; *The Island at the Top of the World*, 1973; *The Black Hole*, 1979; others.

ELY, RON (1938–). Giant-sized American actor who was the television incarnation of Tarzan, 1966–69, and who appeared as pulp hero Doc Savage in GEORGE PAL's unsuccessful *Doc Savage, The Man of Bronze*, 1975. Ely is fine as the intrepid Doc, but the film's treatment is self-consciously campy. *Tarzan's Jungle Rebellion*, 1967 (reedited TV episodes); *Tarzan's Deadly Silence* (reedited TV episodes), 1970.

ENDFIELD, CYRIL (1914–). American director active in Britain since the early sixties. *Tarzan's Savage Fury*, 1952; *Mysterious Island*, 1961; *De Sade* (begun by ROGER CORMAN), 1969.

Marla English.

Richard Eyer and friend Robbie the Robot in *The Invisible Boy* (1957).

ENGLISH, JOHN. American serial director, often teamed with WILLIAM WITNEY. *Captain America* (co-d; w/Elmer Clifton), 1943–44. For more film titles see: WILLIAM WITNEY.

ENGLISH, MARLA (CA. 1930–). Feline American leading lady of the fifties. *The She Creature*, 1956; *Voodoo Woman*, 1957.

ENRICO, ROBERT (1931–). Sensitive French director of the short film *An Occurrence at Owl Creek Bridge*, 1961, which concerns a man about to be executed during the American Civil War. He apparently escapes the hangman's knot and flees to his home, only to be yanked back to reality by the noose as he imagines himself finally reaching his wife's arms. This haunting film is unusual in its tension and its success at winning viewer involvement. Based on the short story by Ambrose Bierce.

ERICSON, JOHN (1927–). Germany-born American leading man who never quite made it. *The Seven Faces of Dr. Lao*, 1964; *Operation Atlantis*, 1965; *The Destructors*, 1967; *The Bamboo Saucer*, 1968; *Bedknobs and Broomsticks*, 1971; *Crash!* (possessed car), 1976.

ESSEX, HARRY (1910–). American screenwriter, most active during the fifties. *Man Made Monster* (original story only), 1941; *It Came from Outer Space* (b/o "The Meteor," a screen treatment by RAY BRADBURY), 1953; *The Creature from the Black Lagoon*, 1954; *The Cremators* (and p, d), 1972.

EYER, RICHARD (CA. 1946–). American boy actor of the fifties. *The Invisible Boy*, 1957; *The 7th Voyage of Sinbad* (as the Genie), 1958.

EZEKIAN, HARRY. American small-part actor of the thirties who appears in *Island of Lost Souls*, 1933, as the repulsive Pig-Man Gola.

F

FAHEY, MYRNA (1939–73). American leading lady of a few minor films, notably as the female lead in ROGER CORMAN's *House of Usher*, 1960.

FARROW, MIA (1945–). Slender American leading lady, popular during the sixties, who played the lead in ROMAN POLANSKI's *Rosemary's Baby*, 1968. Her nervous demeanor is well suited to the role of the young woman who will bear the Devil's child. *See No Evil*, 1971.

78 FEIST

FEIST, FELIX (1906–65). American director whose *Donovan's Brain*, 1953, is an underplayed and intelligent study of a living, disembodied brain. *Deluge*, 1933; *Dreams*, 1940.

FELDMAN, MARTY (1933–). Google-eyed British comic who became a hit in America after an association with MEL BROOKS. *The Bed Sitting Room*, 1969; *Every Home Should Have One* (and co-w; cast as a vampire), 1970; *Young Frankenstein* (as Igor), 1974; *The Last Remake of Beau Geste* (many fantasy sequences), and d), 1977.

FELDSTEIN, ALBERT (1925–). American comic book writer/artist of the forties and fifties and later editor of WILLIAM GAINES' *Mad* magazine. Feldstein's grisly but good-humored stories for the legendary E.C. horror comics of the early 1950s inspired a pair of successful British films, *Tales from the Crypt*, 1972 and *The Vault of Horror*, 1973.

FIELD, SHIRLEY ANN (1938–). Decorative British leading lady of the fifties and sixties. *Horrors of the Black Museum*, 1959; *Peeping Tom*, 1960; *Man in the Moon*, 1961; *These Are the Damned*, 1961; *Dr. Maniac*, 1973.

FINCH, JON (1941–). British leading man of the seventies. *The Vampire Lovers*, 1970; *The Horror of Frankenstein*, 1970; *Macbeth* (title role), 1971; *Frenzy*, 1972; *The Final Program*, 1973; *The Last Days of Man on Earth*, 1974.

Jon Finch.

Lew Ayres, Gene Evans, and Nancy Davis observe *Donovan's Brain* (1953), directed by Felix Feist.

Invaders from another world resurrect the dead in Terence Fisher's *The Earth Dies Screaming* (1964).

FISHER, CARRIE (1956–). American actress, daughter of Debbie Reynolds and Eddie Fisher, who made her screen debut as spunky Princess Leia in *Star Wars*, 1977. She repeated the role for the 1980 sequel *The Empire Strikes Back:*

FISHER, TERENCE (1904–80). British director with Hammer Films who initiated the revival of classic horrors with *The Curse of Frankenstein*, 1957. Effective throughout the sixties, Fisher later appeared to have lost enthusiasm. *The Horror of Dracula*, 1958; *Brides of Dracula*, 1960; *The Two Faces of Dr. Jekyll*, 1960; *The Phantom of the Opera*, 1962; *Island of Terror*, 1966; *Frankenstein and the Monster from Hell*, 1973; others.

FLEISCHER, RICHARD (1916–). American director of big commercial films, son of cartoon animation pioneer Max Fleischer. *20,000 Leagues Under the Sea*, 1954; *Fantastic Voyage*, 1966; *See No Evil*, 1971; *Soylent Green*, 1973.

FLEMING, ERIC (1924–66). Purposeful American leading man, long popular as trail boss Gil Favor on television's "Rawhide," 1958–66. Drowned while filming in Peru. *Conquest of Space*, 1955; *Fright*, 1957; *Queen of Outer Space*, 1958; *Curse of the Undead*, 1959.

Eric Fleming *(right)* and Dave Willock wrest a blaster from the grip of Laurie Mitchell, the scarred *Queen of Outer Space* (1958).

80 FLEMING

FLEMING, IAN (1906–64). British novelist who created the lady-killing spy James Bond. *Dr. No* reached the screen in 1962 and opened the floodgates to Fleming's character, letting loose all manner of imitative spies, secret agents, and cloak-and-dagger operators. Fleming's own tongue-and-cheek approach is well suited to the cinema; the Bond films are uniformly delightful. *The Man with the Golden Gun*, 1974, is the last adaptation of a Fleming novel. Thenceforth, the rights of the producers include only his book titles. Other James Bond films with fantastic content: *Goldfinger* (the best of the series), 1964; *Thunderball*, 1965; *You Only Live Twice*, 1967; *On Her Majesty's Secret Service* (with GEORGE LAZENBY as Bond), 1969; *Diamonds Are Forever* (the last to star SEAN CONNERY), 1971; *Live and Let Die* (debut of ROGER MOORE as James Bond), 1973; *The Spy Who Loved Me*, 1977; *Moonraker*, 1979. Fleming's fanciful book for children, *Chitty Chitty Bang Bang*, reached the screen in 1968.

FLEMING, VICTOR (1883–1949). American director responsible for a perennial film classic, *The Wizard of Oz*, 1939. *Dr. Jekyll and Mr. Hyde*, 1941.

Cast of *The Wizard of Oz* (1939), directed by Victor Fleming. Left to right: Judy Garland, Frank Morgan, Charley Grapewin, Ray Bolger, Jack Haley, Bert Lahr, Clara Blandick.

A gallery of James Bond villains inspired by the novels of Ian Fleming. Left to right from the top they are Joseph Wiseman in *Dr. No* (1962), Harold Sakata in *Goldfinger* (1964), Lotte Lenya in *From Russia with Love* (1963), Telly Savalas in *On Her Majesty's Secret Service* (1969), Richard Kiel in *The Spy Who Loved Me* (1977), Curt Jurgens in *The Spy Who Loved Me*, Adolfo Celli in *Thunderball* (1965), Yaphet Kotto in *Live and Let Die* (1973), Christopher Lee in *The Man with the Golden Gun* (1974), and Donald Pleasence in *You Only Live Twice* (1967).

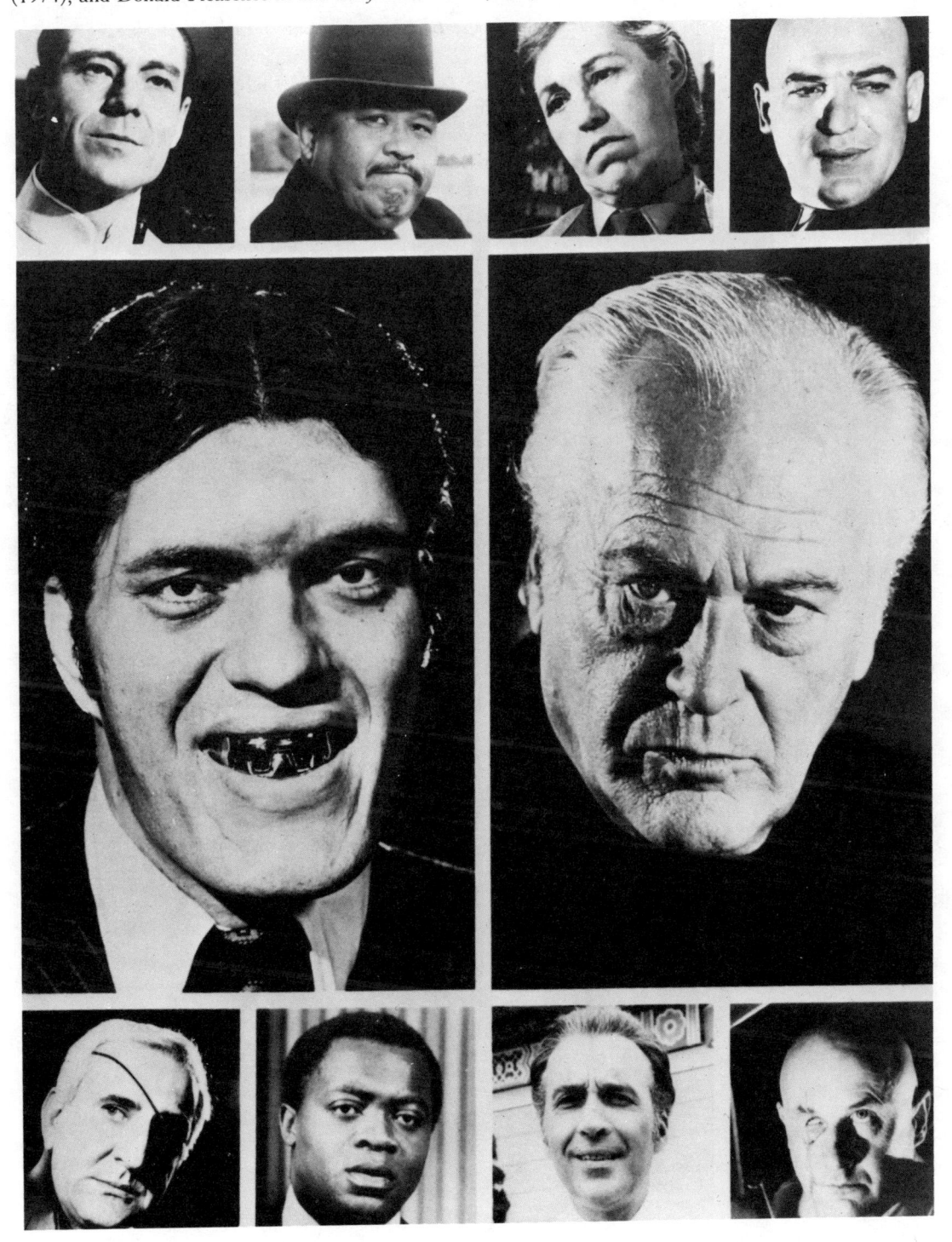

FLEMYNG, GORDON (1934-). British television director who has done film versions of the popular Dr. Who teleseries. *Dr. Who and the Daleks*, 1966; *Daleks—Invasion Earth 2150 A.D.*, 1968.

FLEMYNG, ROBERT (1912-). Cool British leading actor who is uncomfortably convincing as the murderous and necrophilic physician in *The Horrible Dr. Hichcock*, 1962. *The Blood Beast Terror*, 1967; *Invasion of the Body Stealers* aka *Thin Air*, 1970.

FLETCHER, BRAMWELL (1904-). British leading man active in Hollywood during the thirties and forties. In *The Mummy*, 1932, he is Norton, the young archeologist driven insane by the sight of the living mummy. "He went for a little walk," he titters when asked of the mummy's whereabouts. "You should have seen his face..." Once married to actress HELEN CHANDLER. *Daughter of the Dragon*, 1931; *Svengali*, 1931; *The Undying Monster*, 1942.

FLOREY, ROBERT (1900-). French-born director of Hollywood programmers capable of considerable mood and atmosphere. *The Life and Death of 9413—A Hollywood Extra* (amateur; expressionist satire), 1928; *The Loves of Zero* (experimental), 1928; *Murders in the Rue Morgue*, 1932; *The Florentine Dagger*, 1935; *The Face Behind the Mask* (sensitive treatment of rather distasteful subject matter; see: PETER LORRE), 1941; *The Beast with Five Fingers*, 1946.

FOCH, NINA (1924-). American leading actress of the forties, later character player. *Cry of the Werewolf* (as the werewoman), 1944; *The Return of the Vampire*, 1944; *Escape in the Fog*, 1945.

FONDA, JANE (1937-). Gifted American leading actress, a onetime Hollywood glamour girl who became a controversial political activist in the late sixties. Daughter of actor Henry Fonda, sister of actor Peter Fonda. *Barbarella*, 1968. Also seen in the "Metzengerstein" segment of *Spirits of the Dead*, 1969; *The Blue Bird* (as Night), 1976; *The China Syndrome*, 1979.

FONTAINE, JOAN (1917-). Soft-spoken British leading lady in Hollywood, sister of OLIVIA DE HAVILLAND. As Fontaine grew older, good roles in traditional films became harder to find, and she took work in thrillers. *Voyage to the Bottom of the Sea*, 1961; *The Devil's Own* (last film to date), 1967.

FORAN, DICK (1910-). Hearty and good-natured American leading man of the thirties and forties. *The Mummy's Hand*, 1940; *Horror Island*, 1941; *The Mummy's Tomb*, 1942; *The Atomic Submarine*, 1960.

Jane Fonda as *Barbarella* (1968).

FORBES, BRYAN (1926–). British writer/director who began his career in the late forties as an actor. In 1974 he directed *The Stepford Wives* and created a film that is slick and glossy but with an unrealized potential. IRA LEVIN's potboiler novel could have become a marvelous film, but Forbes avoids developing the basic premise, so the "shock" that men of an affluent bedroom community are replacing their wives with androids is left at that. The film is barely a springboard, and the shame is that the picture was acclaimed in some quarters as outstanding science fiction. Films as actor: *The Creeping Unknown*, 1956; *Satellite in the Sky*, 1956; *Enemy from Space*, 1956. As writer-director: *Man in the Moon* (w only), 1961; *Seance on a Wet Afternoon*, 1964; *The Slipper and the Rose*, 1976.

FORD, GRACE (CA. 1910–). American actress with a notable performance as the miniature murderess Lachna in *The Devil Doll*, 1936.

FORD, WALLACE (1897–1966). Likeable British actor in Hollywood from 1930. *Freaks* (as the good clown Bozo), 1932; *The Mysterious Mr. Wong*, 1935; *The Man Who Reclaimed His Head*, 1935; *The Mummy's Hand*, 1940; *The Mummy's Tomb*, 1942; *The Ape Man*, 1943; *Shadow of a Doubt*, 1943; *Harvey*, 1950.

FOREST, MARK (1933–). American athlete popular in Italy as the mythic superman Maciste. To suit American taste, a more familiar name is usually substituted in English-dubbed prints, often Samson or Hercules. *Son of Samson*, 1960; *Goliath and the Dragon*, 1960; *Molemen vs. the Son of Hercules*, 1961; *Death in the Arena*, 1962; *Maciste, Spartan Gladiator*, 1964; *Goliath and the Sins of Babylon*, 1964; many others.

FOSTER, BARRY (1931–). Red-haired British actor, marvelous as the perverted necktie murderer who loves his mother in ALFRED HITCHCOCK's *Frenzy*, 1972. *Twisted Nerve*, 1969.

FOSTER, JODIE (1962–). Husky-voiced American juvenile lead of the seventies who has attracted much critical acclaim, particularly for her role as the child prostitute in Martin Scorsese's urban horror film *Taxi Driver*, 1976. *The Little Girl Who Lived Down the Lane*, 1977; *Freaky Friday*, 1977.

FOSTER, PRESTON (1900–70). Tough American leading man of the thirties and forties, often cast as a gangster and chilling as the one-armed, cannibalistic *Dr. X*, 1932. *The Time Travelers*, 1964.

FOULGER, BYRON (1900–70). American small-part actor, usually seen as a timid bookkeeper, assistant, or sniveling lackey. *Dick Tracy*, 1937; *The Man They Could Not Hang*, 1939; *Television Spy*, 1939; *The Man with Nine Lives*, 1940; *Man Made Monster*, 1941; *The Whistler*, 1944; *The Magnetic Monster*, 1953; *Up in Smoke* (as the Devil), 1957; *The Devil's Partner*, 1958; *The Gnome-Mobile*, 1967. Television series: "Captain Nice," 1967.

Byron Foulger, obviously ready for anything.

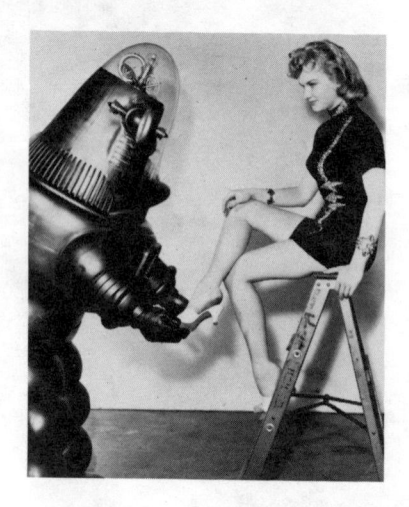

Anne Francis and Robby the Robot in a charming publicity still from *Forbidden Planet* (1956).

The captive humans in *I Married a Monster from Outer Space* (1958), directed by Gene Fowler, Jr.

FOWLER, GENE JR. American director who brought a crisp visual style and sharp pacing to B-pictures of the fifties. A onetime editor for FRITZ LANG. *I Was a Teenage Werewolf*, 1957; *I Married a Monster from Outer Space* (a moody gem), 1958.

FOX, WALLACE (1895–1958). American programmer director of the forties. *The Corpse Vanishes*, 1942; *Bowery at Midnight*, 1942; *Pillow of Death*, 1945.

FRANCIS, ANNE (1932–). Blonde American leading lady, usually playing a pretty girl with a sharp tongue, but all sugar as naive Altaira in *Forbidden Planet*, 1956. *Portrait of Jennie* (bit), 1948; *The Rocket Man*, 1954; *The Satan Bug*, 1965; *Haunts of the Very Rich* (TV), 1972.

Insanity runs riot in Freddie Francis's *Paranoiac* (1963).

FRANCIS, FREDDIE (1917–). British director who scored greater success as a cinematographer. At his best as director, Francis possesses a discerning eye for detail; at his worst, he is unimaginative and plodding. *The Innocents* (ph only), 1961; *Paranoic*, 1963; *The Day of the Triffids* (lighthouse sequence only; uncredited), 1963; *The Evil of Frankenstein*, 1964; *Night Must Fall* (ph only), 1964; *The Skull*, 1965; *Torture Garden*, 1968; *Dracula Has Risen from the Grave*, 1968; *Tales That Witness Madness*, 1973, others.

Arthur Franz.

FRANCIS, KEVIN (CA. 1948–). British independent producer, son of director FREDDIE FRANCIS. *Persecution*, 1974; *Legend of the Werewolf*, 1974; *The Terror of Sheba*, 1974.

FRANCISCUS, JAMES (1934–). Blonde, good-looking American television star ("Mr. Novak," 1963–65, "Longstreet," 1971–72) whose film career never got off the ground. *The Valley of Gwangi*, 1969; *Marooned*, 1969; *Beneath the Planet of the Apes*, 1970; *When Time Ran Out*, 1980.

FRANCO, JESUS. Spanish director of heavy-handed period horror thrillers. *Eugenie—The Story of Her Journey into Perversion*, 1970; *Vampyros Lesbos*, 1970; *El Conde Dracula*, 1970; *Venus in Furs*, 1970; *El Dr. Mabuse*, 1971; *La Hua de Dracula*, 1972; others.

FRANJU, GEORGES (1912–). French director who moved from graphically shocking documentaries (*Le Sang des Betes*, 1948, is a harrowing look at a charnel house) to graphically shocking but thoughtful horror features. *Eyes without a Face* aka *The Horror Chamber of Dr. Faustus*, 1959; *Spotlight on a Murderer*, 1960; *Shadowman*, 1976.

FRANKENHEIMER, JOHN (1930–). Ambitious, uneven American director, a major talent with a predilection for faintly overblown projects. His *Seconds*, 1966, concerning an aging man who wants a second helping of life, is chillingly plausible. *The Manchurian Candidate*, 1962; *Prophecy*, 1979.

FRANKLIN, PAMELA (1949–). British child acress of considerable talent who has found modest success as an adult. *The Innocents*, 1960; *The Nanny*, 1965; *Our Mother's House*, 1967; *Necromancy*, 1971; *The Legend of Hell House*, 1973; *Food of the Gods*, 1976.

FRANKS, CHLOE (1963–). British child actress in horror films. *Trog*, 1970; *Whoever Slew Auntie Roo?*, 1971; *The House That Dripped Blood*, 1971; *Tales from the Crypt*, 1972; *I, Monster*, 1973.

FRANZ, ARTHUR (1920–). American leading man of cofeatures. *Abbott and Costello Meet the Invisible Man* (as the Invisible Man), 1951; *Invaders from Mars*, 1953; *Back from the Dead*, 1957; *Monster on the Campus*, 1958; *The Atomic Submarine*, 1960.

88 FREDA

Freda, Riccardo (1909–). Highly visual Italian director of gothic horror films; former art critic. *I Vampiri*, 1957; *The Witch's Curse*, 1960; *The Horrible Dr. Hichcock*, 1962; *The Ghost* (credited as Robert Hampton), 1965; *The Exterminators*, 1965; many others.

Freeborn, Stuart (1914–). Inventive British makeup artist, active since the mid-thirties. *Dr. Strangelove*, 1964; *2001: A Space Odyssey* (the ape-men), 1968; *The Omen*, 1976; *Star Wars* (notably the design for Chewbacca), 1977; *The Empire Strikes Back*, 1980.

Frees, Paul (ca. 1925–). American voice artist and actor, active in all media since the early fifties. His introductory narration for George Pal's *The War of the Worlds*, 1953, effectively sets that picture's frantic tone. *The Thing*, 1951; *Earth vs. the Flying Saucers* (as the voice of the alien invaders), 1956; *The Cyclops* (voice effects), 1957; *Space Master X-7*, 1958; *Eyes in Outer Space*, 1959; *The H-Man* (dubbing), 1959; *The Time Machine* (as voice of the talking rings), 1960; *Atlantis, The Lost Continent* (narrator), 1961; many others.

The victim is squeezed and slowly digested by *Caltiki, the Immortal Monster* (1961), directed by Riccardo Freda.

Jonathan Frid's vampiric Barnabas Collins in *House of Dark Shadows* (1970).

FREUND, KARL (1890–1969). Distinguished German cameraman who came to Hollywood in the early thirties and tried a hand at directing. His horror films are keenly atmospheric and show a flair for the grotesque. Freund was lured from retirement by Desi Arnaz in the early fifties and revamped television-shooting technique with a three-camera system. *Metropolis* (ph only; directed by FRITZ LANG), 1926; *The Mummy*, 1932; *Mad Love*, 1935.

FRID, JONATHAN. American actor who had huge success as Barnabas the vampire on television's "Dark Shadows," 1966–71 and who played the role in a 1970 film feature, *House of Dark Shadows*. *Seizure*, 1974.

FRIEDKIN, WILLIAM (1939–). Major American director of slick, commercial thrillers. His *The Exorcist*, 1973, was one of the most controversial films of the seventies and triggered a trend in occult shockers.

FRIEDMAN, DAVID. American independent producer, initially associated with HERSCHELL GORDON LEWIS. *Blood Feast*, 1963; *Two Thousand Maniacs* (and art-directed), 1964; *She Freak* (and w), 1966; *Space Thing*, 1968.

FROBE, GERT (1912–). Heavyset German character actor in Europe and Hollywood, memorable as the maniacal villain *Goldfinger*, 1964. *The Testament of Dr. Mabuse*, 1962; *Those Fantastic Flying Fools* aka *Blast Off!; Rocket to the Moon*, 1967; *Chitty Chitty Bang Bang*, 1968.

FRYE, DWIGHT (1899–1943). American character actor who specialized in grotesques. He grovels grandly as Renfield in *Dracula*, 1931. *Frankenstein* (as Fritz, the hunchback), 1931; *Strange Adventure*, 1932; *The Vampire Bat*, 1933; *The Invisible Man*, 1933; *Bride of Frankenstein* (as Karl), 1935; *The Crime of Dr. Crespi*, 1935; *The Cat and the Canary*, 1939; *Drums of Fu Manchu*, 1940; *The Ghost of Frankenstein*, 1942; *Frankenstein Meets the Wolf Man*, 1943; *Dead Men Walk*, 1943.

FUEST, ROBERT (1927–). British director of the art deco *The Abominable Dr. Phibes*, 1971, and its campy sequel, *Dr. Phibes Rises Again*, 1973. *The Last Days of Man on Earth*, 1974; *The Devil's Rain*, 1975.

FUKUDA, JUN. Japanese director of monster fantasies for Toho films. *Godzilla vs. the Sea Monster* aka *Ebirah, Horror of the Deep*, 1966; *Son of Godzilla*, 1968; *Godzilla Tai Giagan* (*Godzilla vs. Gigan*), 1971; *Godzilla vs. Megalon* (and w), 1973; others.

FULTON, JOHN P. (1902–). American special-effects wizard, expert in process photography and miniatures. Fulton's most celebrated effect is the parting of the Red Sea for *The Ten Commandments*, 1956; also worth noting is his work on *The Invisible Man*, 1933. *The Invisible Man Returns*, 1940; *Invisible Agent*, 1942; *Son of Dracula*, 1943; *The Invisible Man's Revenge*, 1944; *Conquest of Space*, 1955; *I Married a Monster from Outer Space*, 1958; *The Colossus of New York*, 1958; *The Bamboo Saucer*, 1968; many others.

FURIE, SIDNEY J. (1933–). Variably talented, often topical Canadian director active in the United States and Britain. *The Snake Woman*, 1961; *Dr. Blood's Coffin*, 1961. He has since moved on to projects that are bigger but no weightier.

FURNEAUX, YVONNE (1928–). French leading lady in Hammer films during the fifties and sixties. *The Mummy*, 1959; *Repulsion*, 1965.

Dwight Frye pricks his finger and Dracula (Bela Lugosi) is extremely interested in this moment from *Dracula* (1931).

G

GABOR, ZSA ZSA (1919–). Hungarian actress of dubious skill, painfully noticeable in *Queen of Outer Space*, 1958; critic Joe Kane has rather dryly described her as "the only Venusian with a Hungarian accent." *The Girl in the Kremlin* (which involves the faked death of Stalin and his continued life after plastic surgery), 1957; *Picture Mommy Dead*, 1966.

GAINES, WILLIAM M. (1922–). American comic book and later magazine (*MAD*) publisher whose popular E.C. horror comics of the early 1950s provided the basis for two British thrillers, *Tales from the Crypt*, 1972, and *The Vault of Horror*, 1973.

GARLAND, BEVERLY (1926–). Hardboiled, good-looking American leading lady of the fifties, usually cast as a strong-willed heroine with plenty of moxie. *The Rocket Man*, 1954; *Curucu, Beast of the Amazon*, 1956; *It Conquered the World*, 1956; *Not of This Earth*, 1957; *The Alligator People*, 1959; *Twice Told Tales*, 1963; *Pretty Poison*, 1968; *The Mad Room*, 1969.

Beverly Garland in the grip of Paul Birch, the fiendish vampire from another world in *Not of This Earth* (1957).

92 GARLAND

Eternal innocence: Judy Garland as Dorothy in *The Wizard of Oz* (1939).

Richard Garland *(right)* in *Attack of The Crab Monsters* (1957). Russell Johnson is at the far left.

Valerie Gaunt.

GARLAND, JUDY (1922–69). American singer and actress, a supremely talented entertainer whose real life was a tormented rollercoaster ride. Much-married and unstable, Garland made tabloid headlines throughout her life, but her brilliant gifts will survive them. When Shirley Temple was unavailable, MGM chose Garland to play the Kansas girl Dorothy in *The Wizard of Oz*, 1939; the result is firmly entrenched in millions of hearts.

GARLAND, RICHARD (?–1969). American B-picture leading man of the fifties, once married to actress BEVERLY GARLAND. *The Undead*, 1957; *Attack of the Crab Monsters*, 1957; *Panic in Year Zero*, 1962; *Mutiny in Outer Space*, 1965.

GATES, TUDOR. British screenwriter with an apparent taste for Lesbian vampires. *Barbarella* (co-w), 1968; *The Vampire Lovers*, 1970; *Lust for a Vampire*, 1971; *Twins of Evil*, 1972.

GAUNT, VALERIE (CA. 1933–). Attractive British actress associated with Hammer Films. *The Curse of Frankenstein*, 1957; *The Horror of Dracula* (arresting as a seductive vampiress), 1958.

GAY, RAMON (1917–60). Mexican leading man, popular in the late fifties. *Yambao* aka *Cry of the Bewitched*, 1956; *The Aztec Mummy*, 1957; *The Robot vs. the Aztec Mummy*, 1959; *The Curse of the Doll People*, 1960; *The Curse of the Aztec Mummy*, 1961.

GEESON, JUDY (1948–). British leading lady of the sixties and seventies, often in seductive roles. *Berserk!*, 1968; *Goodbye Gemini*, 1970; *Doomwatch*, 1972; *Fear in the Night*, 1972; *Star Maidens* (British TV), 1975; *Dominique*, 1978.

GEMORA, CHARLES (1903–61). Diminutive Manila-born mask and costume maker who played gorillas in innumerable Hollywood thrillers and comedies of the thirties, forties, and fifties. *Ingagi*, 1930; *The Gorilla*, 1939; *The War of the Worlds* (as the Martian), 1953; *Phantom of the Rue Morgue*, 1954; *I Married a Monster from Outer Space* (as the alien invader), 1958; *Jack the Giant Killer*, 1962.

GERSHENSON, JOSEPH (1904–). Russian composer in Hollywood, associated with Universal during the forties and fifties. *The Time of Their Lives* (p only), 1946; *Cult of the Cobra*, 1955; *The Mole People*, 1956; *The Creature Walks among Us*, 1956; *The Monolith Monsters*, 1957; *The Land Unknown*, 1957; *The Deadly Mantis*, 1957; *The Thing That Couldn't Die*, 1958; *Monster on the Campus* (and p), 1958; *The Leech Woman* (p only), 1960.

GIBBONS, CEDRIC (1895–1960). American art director, winner of seven Oscars (he designed the statuette) whose best work was done on *The Wizard of Oz*, 1939. Gibbons codirected *Tarzan and His Mate*, 1934, with Jack Conway, who is uncredited. *The Devil Doll*, 1936; *Dr. Jekyll and Mr. Hyde*, 1941; *Forbidden Planet*, 1956.

Charles Gemora's fine alien makeup as seen in *I Married a Monster from Outer Space* (1958).

The magical splendor of Munchkinland, designed by Cedric Gibbons for *The Wizard of Oz* (1939). At the center of attention are Judy Garland and Billie Burke.

GIBSON, ALAN (1938–). Canadian director active in Britain for Hammer. *Crescendo*, 1969; *Goodbye Gemini*, 1970; *Dracula* A.D. *1972*, 1972; *The Satanic Rites of Dracula*, 1974.

GILBERT, LEWIS (1920–). British director of two of the more entertaining and certainly noisier James Bond thrillers, *You Only Live Twice*, 1967, and *The Spy Who Loved Me*, 1977. *Moonraker*, 1979.

GILLESPIE, ARNOLD (1889–1978). American special-effects expert and head of MGM's special-effects department, 1936–1966. He created, among other things, the terrifying twister in *The Wizard of Oz*, 1939, Robby the Robot from *Forbidden Plant*, 1956, and the destruction of *Atlantis, The Lost Continent*, 1961.

GILLING, JOHN (1912–). Prolific British writer/director who progressed from a routine early output to some interesting films of the sixties. *Horror Maniacs* (w only), 1948; *Old Mother Riley Meets the Vampire* aka *Vampire over London; My Son, The Vampire* (p & d), 1952; *A Ghost for Sale* (w only), 1952; *The Gamma People*, 1956; *Mania*, 1960; *The Shadow of the Cat* (d only), 1961; *The Plague of the Zombies* (d only), 1966; *The Reptile* (d only), 1966; *The Mummy's Shroud*, 1967.

GIRDLER, WILLIAM (1947–78). American producer/director of imitative but effective shockers; killed in a freak helicopter crash. *Asylum of Satan*, 1971; *Three on a Meathook*, 1973; *Abby*, 1974; *Grizzly* (d only), 1976; *The Manitou*, 1978.

The dead live again in John Gilling's atmospheric *The Plague of The Zombies* (1966).

GLASSER, ALBERT. American composer who brought the electronic music of the theramin to many science fiction Bs of the fifties. *The Monster Maker*, 1944; *Rocketship X-M* (orchestrations only), 1950; *Port Sinister*, 1953; *The Indestructible Man*, 1956; *The Amazing Colossal Man*, 1957; *Beginning of the End*, 1957; *War of the Colossal Beast*, 1958; *Attack of the Puppet People*, 1958; *Earth vs. the Spider*, 1958; *Giant from the Unknown*, 1958; *Teenage Caveman*, 1958; *Confessions of an Opium Eater*, 1962; many more.

GLUT, DON (CA. 1943–). Prolific and enthusiastic American amateur filmmaker who has worked with B-western and horror actors KENNE DUNCAN, ROY BARCROFT, and GLENN STRANGE. *Return of the Wolf Man*, 1957; *Frankenstein Meets Dracula*, 1957; *The Frankenstein Story*, 1958; *The Teenage Werewolf*, 1959; *The Adventures of the Spirit* (featuring Glenn Strange as Frankenstein's Monster), 1963; *Spy Smasher vs. the Purple Monster*, 1964; *Superman vs. the Gorilla Gang*, 1965; *Rocketman Flies Again*, 1966; many others.

GODARD, JEAN-LUC (1930–). Ambitious but often rambling French director who stands at the forefront of avant-garde filmmaking in Europe. His *Alphaville*, 1965, is a mad and garish science-fantasy about a computer-ruled planet and the efforts of one Earthman to liberate it. Filled with outrageous pop art images and absurd situations, *Alphaville* remains somehow apt and evocative of contemporary concerns. Also: *RoGoPaG* ("Le Nouveau Monde" [The New World] segment), 1962.

Eddie Constantine *(right)* breaches the computer stronghold in Jean-Luc Godard's fascinating *Alphaville* (1965).

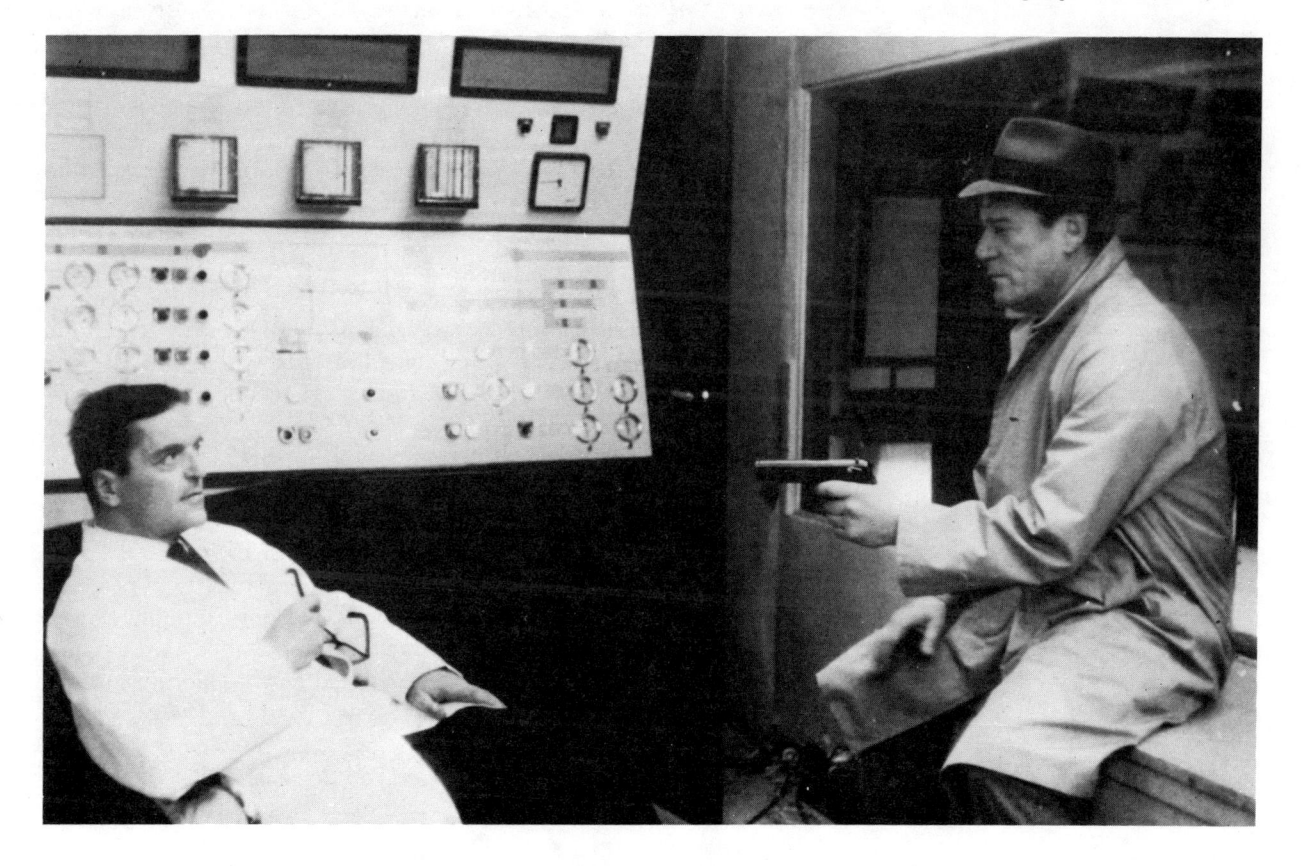

Leo Gorcey *(left)* and Huntz Hall in a typically serene moment from *The Bowery Boys Meet The Monsters* (1954).

GODDARD, PAULETTE (1911–). Vivacious American leading lady of the forties, once married to Charlie Chaplin. *The Cat and the Canary*, 1939; *The Ghost Breakers*, 1940.

GOETHE, JOHANN WOLFGANG VON (1749–1832). German poet, dramatist, novelist, and scientist whose dramatic poem *Faust, eine Tragödie* inspired Charles Gounod's opera *Faust* and later twenty-seven film versions from 1897. Variations on the theme number in the dozens. *Faust*, 1897, 1906, 1909, 1910, 1915, 1921, 1926 (with EMIL JANNINGS as Mephistopheles), 1960, etc. *Faust and Marguerite*, 1897; *Faust and the Lily*, 1913; *Fountain of Youth*, 1921; *Faust Fantasy*, 1935; *Faust and the Devil*, 1950; *Faustina*, 1956; *Faust XX*, 1966; *Bedazzled*, 1967; many others.

GOLDONI, LEILA (CA. 1938–). American leading actress who has made impressive film appearances. *Hysteria*, 1965; *Blood Fiend*, 1968. *Invasion of the Body Snatchers*, 1978.

GORCEY, BERNARD (1888–1955). Swiss-born Hollywood character actor, most familiar as sweet shop proprietor Louie Dumbrowski in the Bowery Boys comedies. Father of Bowery Boys David and LEO GORCEY. *Spook Busters*, 1946; *Mr. Hex*, 1949; *Mr. Hex*, 1946; *Master Minds*, 1949; *Ghost Chasers*, 1951; *The Bowery Boys Meet the Monsters*, 1954; others.

GORCEY, LEO (1915–69). Aggressive, low-brow American comic actor, brought to Hollywood from the stage in 1937 for a dramatic role in *Dead End* and was thereafter permanently typed as a Brooklynesque tough. He starred in the long-running Bowery Boys series for Monogram (which became Allied Artists) and, with foil HUNTZ HALL, met an occasional gorilla, monster, or mad scientist. *Spooks Run Wild*, 1941; *Spook Busters*, 1946; *Mr. Hex*, 1949; *Master Minds*, 1949; *Ghost Chasers*, 1951; *The Bowery Boys Meet the Monsters*, 1954; *Bowery to Bagdad*, 1955; *The Phynx* (cameo), 1970; others.

Voodoo Woman (1957), produced by Alex Gordon.

GORDON, ALEX (CA. 1925–). British independent B-picture producer and promoter in Hollywood who helped a fading BELA LUGOSI find stage and film work in the mid-fifties. *Bride of the Monster* (w only), 1956; *The She Creature*, 1956; *Voodoo Woman*, 1957; *The Atomic Submarine*, 1960; *The Underwater City*, 1962.

GORDON, BERT I. (1922–). American producer/director/writer of shoddy trick films with miserable special effects. Gordon's budgets have expanded over the years, but his talent remains smaller than his ambition. *Serpent Island*, 1954; *King Dinosaur*, 1955; *The Cyclops*, 1957; *The Amazing Colossal Man*, 1957; *Beginning of the End* (p and d only), 1957; *War of the Colossal Beast*, 1958; *Earth vs. the Spider*, 1958; *The Boy and the Pirates*, 1960; *Tormented*, 1960; *The Magic Sword* (an agreeable juvenile fantasy), 1962; *Village of the Giants*, 1965; *Picture Mommy Dead*, 1966; *Necromancy*, 1971; *Food of the Gods*, 1976; *Empire of the Ants*, 1977; *The Coming*, 1980.

GORDON, LEO (1922–). Cold-eyed American character actor and screenwriter, usually cast as a brutal tough guy. *Attack of the Giant Leeches* (w only), 1959; *Wasp Woman* (w only), 1959; *Tarzan Goes to India* (actor only), 1962; *Tower of London* (co-w only; w/F. Amos Powell and James B. Gordon), 1962; *The Terror* (co-w only; w/ JACK HILL), 1963; *The Haunted Palace* (actor only), 1963.

Dean Parkin in Bert I. Gordon's *War of The Colossal Beast* (1958).

GORDON, MARY (1882–1963). Stocky Scottish character actress in Hollywood. *Bride of Frankenstein*, 1935; *The Hound of the Baskervilles* (as Sherlock Holmes' landlady, Mrs. Hudson), 1939; *The Invisible Woman*, 1940; *The Mummy's Tomb*, 1942; *Pearl of Death*, 1944; *Spider Woman*, 1944; *The Body Snatcher*, 1945.

GORDON, RUTH (1896–). American actress and screenwriter (usually in collaboration with husband Garson Kanin) who won popular notice and an Academy Award as the saucy but dangerous devil-worshipping old lady in *Rosemary's Baby*, 1968. *Whatever Happened to Aunt Alice?*, 1969; *The Big Bus*, 1976.

GORSHIN, FRANK (1935–). Energetic and talented American impressionist and actor, familiar as the Riddler on television's "Batman," 1966–68. He took the role in a 1966 theatrical film, *Batman. Invasion of the Saucermen*, 1957.

GOUGH, MICHAEL (1917–). British character actor whose fierce scowl and exaggerated manner make him ideal as a crazy scientist and similar roles. *Horror of Dracula*, 1958; *Horrors of the Black Museum* (lead), 1959; *Konga* (lead), 1961; *The Black Zoo* (lead), 1963; *Berserk!*, 1968; *Trog*, 1970; *Horror Hospital*, 1973; many others.

GRAHAME, GLORIA (1925–). Singular American leading lady, at home as the quirkily seductive female in many crime thrillers of the fifties. With her curiously pinched mouth, sibilant consonants, and haunted eyes, Grahame is a natural for the horror films of her later years. *It's Wonderful Life*, 1946; *Blood and Lace*, 1971; *Mansion of the Doomed*, 1976.

GRANT, CARY (1904–). Indestructible British leading man in Hollywood whose charm, good humor, and elan kept his star shining for more than thirty years. *Alice in Wonderland* (as the Mock Turtle), 1933; *Topper* (as the ghost), 1937; *Arsenic and Old Lace*, 1944.

GRANT, KATHRYN (1933–). American leading lady in second features of the fifties, later wife of Bing Crosby. Grant is a sweet heroine in *The 7th Voyage of Sinbad*, 1958. *The Night the World Exploded*, 1957.

GRAVES, PETER (1925–). American leading man of a few fifties Bs who failed to project much personality until finding success on television's "Mission: Impossible," 1967–73. Brother of JAMES ARNESS. *Red Planet Mars*, 1952; *Killers from Space*, 1954; *It Conquered the World*, 1956; *Beginning of the End*, 1957; *Parts-the Clonus Horror*, 1979.

GRAY, CAROLE (1940–). Sensual South African–British leading lady of the sixties. *Curse of the Fly*, 1965; *Island of Terror*, 1965; *The Brides of Fu Manchu*, 1966; *Devils of Darkness*, 1966.

Frank Gorshin as the Riddler in *Batman* (1966).

Michael Gough *(right)* in *Horrors of The Black Museum* (1959).

Gloria Grahame.

An unusual publicity shot from *Beginning of The End* (1957), featuring Peter Graves and Peggie Castle.

GRAY, CHARLES (1928–). Regular-featured British actor, an uninteresting Blofeld opposite SEAN CONNERY's James Bond in *Diamonds are Forever*, 1971. *Man in the Moon*, 1961; *The Devil's Bride*, 1968; *The Beast Must Die*, 1974; *The Rocky Horror Picture Show* (as the narrator), 1975; *The Legacy*, 1979.

GRAY, COLEEN (1922–). American leading lady who made a strong impression in crime thrillers of the late forties; her promise quickly faded, and she spent the fifties in mostly minor films. *The Vampire*, 1957; *The Leech Woman* (title role), 1960.

GREEN, NIGEL (1924–72). Handsome and forthright British star character actor, a fine Nayland Smith opposite CHRISTOPHER LEE's Fu Manchu in *The Face of Fu Manchu*, 1965. *Corridors of Blood*, 1958; *Mysterious Island*, 1961; *Jason and the Argonauts* (zestful and spirited as Hercules), 1963; *The Masque of the Red Death*, 1964; *The Skull*, 1965; *The Wrecking Crew*, 1968; *Countess Dracula*, 1972.

GREEN, WILLARD (?–1978). American mechanical engineer who designed and built the malevolent silver sphere seen in DON COSCARELLI's *Phantasm*, 1979. Flesh-boring and bloodsucking, the sphere is among the most appallingly ingenious inventions in horror film history.

GREENWAY, LEE. Unsung American makeup artist who created the chilling face and hands of *The Thing*, 1951.

GREER, DABBS (CA. 1920–). Sandy American character actor who often plays weak-willed fall guys. In *The Vampire*, 1957, he meets a particularly ignominious end as JOHN BEAL stuffs him headfirst into an incinerator. Most active on television since the sixties. *House of Wax*, 1953; *Invasion of the Body Snatchers*, 1956; *It!—The Terror from Beyond Space*, 1958; others.

Edmund Gwenn.

GREFE, WILLIAM. American director of independent low-budget movies, often filmed in swamps. *Death Curse of Tartu* (and w), 1966; *Sting of Death*, 1967; *Stanley* (and p; story), 1972; *Impulse*, 1975.

GRIFFITH, CHARLES B. American screenwriter associated with producer ROGER CORMAN. His script for *The Little Shop of Horrors*, 1960, is mad and brilliant. *It Conquered the World* (actor only), 1956; *Attack of the Crab Monsters* (and associate p), 1957; *Not of This Earth* (co-w; w/MARK HANNA), 1957; *The Undead* (co-w; w/MARK HANNA), 1957; *A Bucket of Blood*, 1959; *Beast from Haunted Cave*, 1959; *Creature from the Haunted Sea*, 1961; *Death Race 2000* (co-w; w/Robert Thom), 1975; *Hollywood Boulevard* (actor only), 1976; *Dr. Heckyl And Mr. Hype* (and d), 1980.

GRIFFITH, D.W. (1874–1948). Pioneering American filmmaker who established the ground rules for narrative technique, montage, crosscutting, and editing. His best films are eminently watchable today; his relegation to obscurity after the mid-twenties is inexcusable. Some sources credit Griffith with direction of Hal Roach's *One Million B.C.*, 1940, others with supervision of process shots involving dinosaurs. Griffith films with fantastic content (often of the religious sort): *Rescued from an Eagle's Nest* (actor only; directed by EDWIN S. PORTER), 1908; *Edgar Allan Poe*, 1909; *The Sealed Room*, 1909; *Man's Genesis*, 1912; *The Avenging Conscience* (b/o "The Tell-Tale Heart" and "Annabel Lee," by EDGAR ALLAN POE), 1914; *Intolerance*, 1916; *Macbeth* (p only), 1916; *The Fall of Babylon* (includes footage from *Intolerance*, 1916), 1919; *Dream Street*, 1921; *The Sorrows of Satan*, 1926.

GRIMALDI, HUGO. American programmer director. *Gigantis, the Fire Monster* (American footage only), 1959; *The Human Duplicators*, 1965; *Mutiny in Outer Space*, 1965.

GRINDE, NICK (1893–). Energetic and often imaginative American B-film director, most active in the thirties. *The Man They Could Not Hang*, 1939; *The Man with Nine Lives*, 1940; *Before I Hang*, 1940.

GRIPPO, JAN. American cheapies producer with Monogram. *Spook Busters*, 1946; *Mr. Hex*, 1946; *Ghost Chasers*, 1951; others.

GROSS, JERRY. American producer of low-budget films whose name fits his work. *I Drink Your Blood*, 1971; *From Ear to Ear*, 1971.

GUEST, VAL (1911–). British writer/director who began his career with comedy in the thirties and wound up in melodrama. *The Creeping Unknown* (d only), 1955; *Enemy from Space*, 1956; *The Day the Earth Caught Fire*, 1961; *When Dinosaurs Ruled the Earth*, 1971; others.

GUFFEY, CARY (1973–). American child actor of the seventies, impressively convincing as the little boy fascinated by the pretty lights in *Close Encounters of the Third Kind*, 1977.

GUINNESS, SIR ALEC (1914–). Superbly talented and invariably delightful British star character actor, noted for his gift of characterization and fine-honed wit. In 1977 he gave us the Force as Ben (Obi-Wan) Kenobi in *Star Wars*. *The Man in the White Suit* (as the inventor of an indestructible fabric), 1952; *Scrooge* (as Marley's Ghost), 1970.

GWENN, EDMUND (1875–1959). British star character actor in Hollywood who specialized in likeably gruff old men. An Oscar winner for his memorable performance as Kris Kringle in *Miracle on 34th Street*, 1947. *The Walking Dead*, 1936; *Between Two Worlds*, 1944; *Bewitched*, 1945; *Them!* (as the blustery entomologist), 1954; *It's a Dog's Life* (comedy involving dogs with human intelligence), 1955.

GWYNNE, ANNE (1918–). Pretty American leading lady of minor films of the forties, chiefly for Universal. *Black Friday*, 1940; *Flash Gordon Conquers The Universe*, 1940; *The Black Cat*, 1941; *The Strange Case of Dr. Rx*, 1942; *Weird Woman*, 1944; *Murder In The Blue Room*, 1944; *House of Frankenstein*, 1945; *The Ghost Goes Wild*, 1947; *Dick Tracy Meets Gruesome*, 1947; *Teenage Monster*, 1957.

GWYNNE, MICHAEL (1916–76). British actor who played the palsied Monster in TERENCE FISHER's *Revenge of Frankenstein*, 1958. *Village of the Damned*, 1960; *Scars of Dracula*, 1970.

Jack Haley's Tin Man in *The Wizard of Oz* (1939).

H

HALEY, JACK (1899–1979). Likeable American light actor, best remembered as the Tin Man in *The Wizard of Oz*, 1939.

HALL, HUNTZ (1920–). Long-faced, dopey American comic actor, a mainstay of the Bowery Boys and constant aggravation to partner LEO GORCEY. In addition to fantastic films listed under GORCEY, Hall is featured in *The Return of Dr. X*, 1939; *The Love Bug Rides Again*, 1973.

HALL, JON (1913–). American beefcake star of the forties, often seen in South Sea settings. Hall is a successful manufacturer of camera equipment. *The Amazing Exploits of the Clutching Hand* (billed as Charles Locher), 1936. *Invisible Agent* (title role), 1942; *The Arabian Nights*, 1942; *Ali Baba and the Forty Thieves*, 1944; *Cobra Woman*, 1944; *The Invisible Man's Revenge* (as the Invisible Man), 1944; *Zamba, The Gorilla*, 1949; *The Beach Girls and the Monster* aka *Monster from the Surf* (and d), 1965.

An interesting shot from Victor Hugo Halperin's *White Zombie* (1932).

HALLER, DANIEL (1928–). American set designer associated with ROGER CORMAN in the early sixties; later a director. As designer: *The Devil's Partner*, 1958; *Night of the Blood Beast*, 1958; *The Ghost of Dragstrip Hollow*, 1959; *A Bucket of Blood*, 1959; *The Little Shop of Horrors*, 1960; *The Atomic Submarine*, 1960; *House of Usher*, 1960; *The Pit and the Pendulum*, 1961; *The Premature Burial*, 1962; *Tower of London*, 1962; *Tales of Terror*, 1962; *The Comedy of Terrors*, 1963; *The Terror*, 1963; *The Raven*, 1963; *X—The Man with the X-Ray Eyes*, 1963; *The Haunted Palace*, 1963; etc. As director: *Die Monster Die!*, 1965; *War-Gods of the Deep* (p only), 1965; *The Dunwich Horror*, 1970; *Buck Rogers in the 25th Century*, 1979.

HALLER, ERNEST (1896–1970). Oscar-winning American cinematographer who gave a hard edge to ROBERT ALDRICH's *Whatever Happened to Baby Jane?*, 1962. *The House of Horror* (w-Sol Polito), 1929; *King of the Jungle*, 1933; *Murders in the Zoo*, 1933; *Back from the Dead*, 1957; *The Boy and the Pirates*, 1960; *Dead Ringer*, 1964.

HALLIDAY, BRYANT. Thin-faced British leading actor in sharp little B-films. *Devil Doll*, 1964; *Curse of the Voodoo*, 1964; *The Projected Man*, 1967; *Horror on Snape Island*, 1972.

HALPERIN, VICTOR HUGO (1895–). American second-feature director of the thirties, whose *White Zombie*, 1932, is a triumph of style over content. *Supernatural* (and p), 1933; *Revolt of the Zombies* (and co-w), 1936; *Torture Ship*, 1939.

HALSEY, BRETT (CA. 1935–). Youthful American leading man of the fifties and sixties. *Return of the Fly* (as the Fly), 1959; *The Atomic Submarine*, 1960; *Twice Told Tales*, 1963; *Spy in Your Eye*, 1966; etc.

An unusual pre-production shot of Margaret Hamilton as the Wicked Witch in *The Wizard of Oz* (1939); note the long hair.

HAMA, MIE (CA. 1945–). Japanese leading lady of the sixties. *King Kong vs. Godzilla*, 1963; *You Only Live Twice* (as Kissy Suzuki), 1967; *King Kong Escapes*, 1968; etc.

HAMILTON, GUY (1922–). British director who favors breakneck pacing and splashy visuals. His *Goldfinger*, 1964, brims with zesty razzle-dazzle and remains the quintessential James Bond thriller. *Diamonds Are Forever*, 1971; *Live and Let Die*, 1973; *The Man with the Golden Gun*, 1974.

HAMILTON, MARGARET (1902–). Spinsterish American character actress, a onetime schoolteacher from Cleveland, Ohio, who became famous as the Wicked Witch of the West in *The Wizard of Oz*, 1939. *13 Ghosts*, 1960; *Brewster McCloud*, 1971.

104 HAMMILL

HAMMILL, MARK (1952–). American juvenile lead featured in GEORGE LUCAS' *Star Wars*, 1977, as young hero Luke Skywalker. He repeated the role in the 1980 sequel *The Empire Strikes Back*.

HANNA, MARK. American screenwriter active in fantastic cinema during the fifties. *Not of This Earth* (co-w; w-CHARLES B. GRIFFITH, 1957; *The Undead* (co-w; w-CHARLES B. GRIFFITH), 1957; *The Amazing Colossal Man* (co-w; w-BERT I. GORDON), 1957; *Attack of the Fifty-Foot Woman*, 1958; *Terror from the Year 5000* (production coordinator), 1958.

HANSEN, GUNNAR. Bearlike American actor, delightfully grotesque as the bizarre Leatherface in *The Texas Chain Saw Massacre*, 1974. *The Demon Lover*, 1976.

HARBURG, E.Y. "YIP" (CA. 1898–). American song lyricist who wrote the delightful and often affecting lyrics for HAROLD ARLEN's melodies in *The Wizard of Oz*, 1939, notably "Over the Rainbow." *Cabin in the Sky*, 1943.

HARDWICKE, SIR CEDRIC (1893–1964). British star character actor, long active in theater and film. His cultured voice provides fine narration for *The War of the Worlds*, 1953, and serves as an effective link to the besieged England of WELLS' novel. *The Ghoul*, 1934; *Things to Come* (replacing ERNEST THESIGER), 1936; *The Hunchback of Notre Dame*, 1939; *The Invisible Man Returns*, 1940; *The Ghost of Frankenstein* (as Ludwig Frankenstein), 1942; *Invisible Agent*, 1942; *The Lodger*, 1944; *The Picture of Dorian Gray* (narration), 1945; *Bait* (as the Devil), 1954; *The Story of Mankind*, 1957; *The Magic Fountain*, 1961; *Five Weeks in a Balloon*, 1962.

HARDY, OLIVER (1892–1957). Rotund American comic whose tie-twiddling, slow burn, and unending exasperation with partner STAN LAUREL endeared him to millions. Before this teaming in 1927, Hardy played the Tin Woodsman in Larry Semon's *The Wizard of Oz*, 1925. For a listing of Laurel and Hardy's fantastic films, see: LAUREL.

HARRINGTON, CURTIS (1928–). American director of promising avant-garde films of the forties and fifties who has spent most of his commercial career valiantly straining to rise above his material. *The Wormwood Star*, 1955; *Night Tide*, 1963; *Voyage to the Prehistoric Planet* (credited as John Sebastian; and w), 1965; *Queen of Blood*, 1966; *Games*, 1967; *How Awful about Allan* (TV), 1970; *What's the Matter with Helen?*, 1971; *Whoever Slew Auntie Roo?*, 1971; *The Killing Kind*, 1973; *Ruby*, 1977.

Tie-twiddling as art: the one and only Oliver Hardy.

Stan Laurel, Oliver Hardy, and convivial friend in *A Chump at Oxford* (1940).

106 HARRIS

HARRIS, JACK H. (CA. 1929–). American independent producer of science fiction films who in 1959 offered one million dollars to anyone who could duplicate the feats of *The 4-D Man*, 1959, i.e., walk through walls. Harris did not have to pay. *The Blob* (which has become a minor cult film, only partly because of the presence of a young STEVE MCQUEEN), 1958; *Dinosaurus*, 1960; *The Oldest Profession*, 1968; *Equinox* (supervised new footage shot for theatrical release), 1971; *Beware! The Blob*, 1972; *The Legend of Hillbilly John*, 1973; *Eyes of Laura Mars* (exec p), 1978.

HARRIS, JULIE (1925–). Leading American stage actress who plays with distinction as the repressed medium in *The Haunting*, 1963. *How Awful about Allan* (TV), 1970.

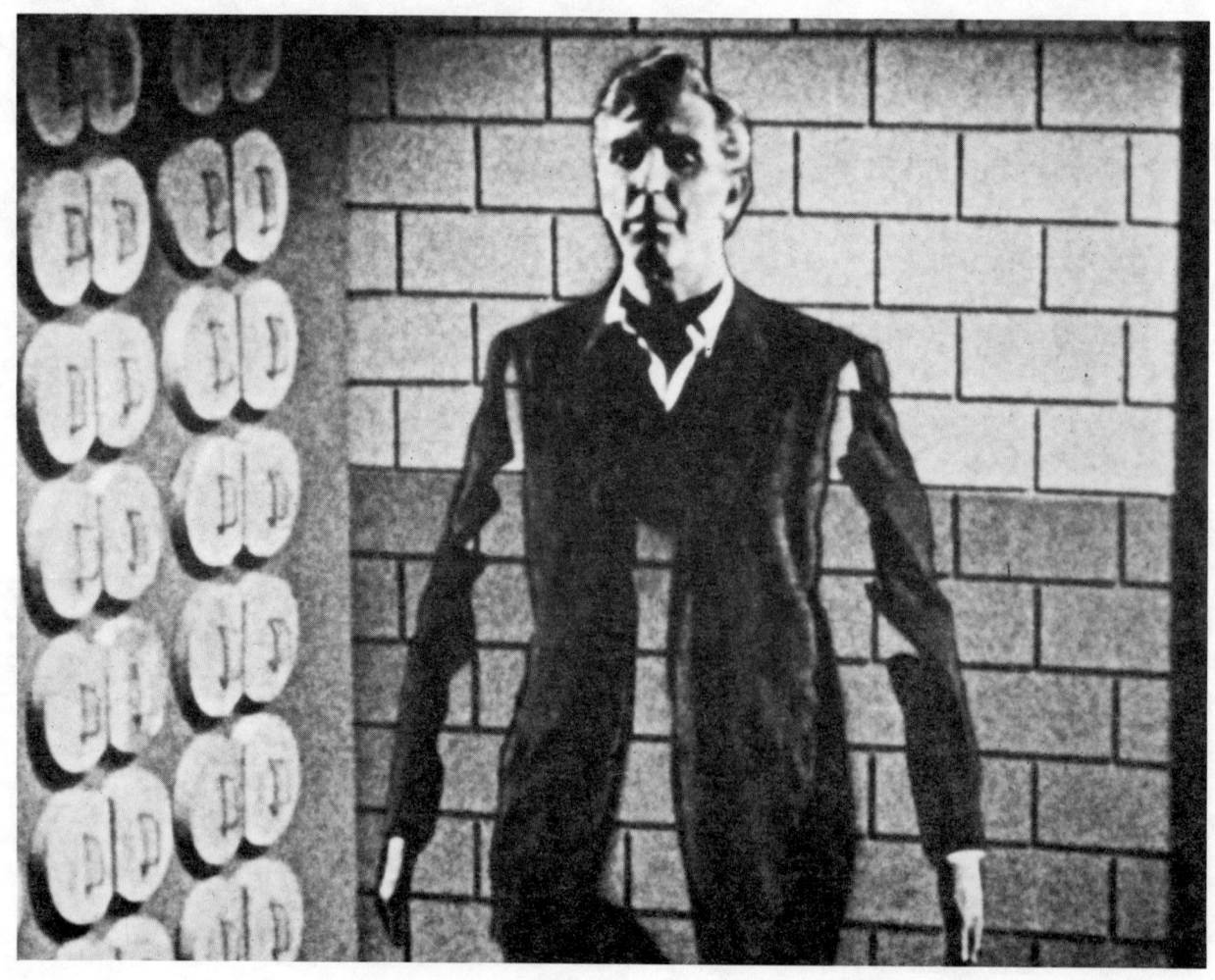

Jack H. Harris's *The 4-D Man* (1959) makes walking through walls look easy. The actor is Robert Lansing.

HARRIS, MARILYN (CA. 1923–). American child actress remembered as the little girl in *Frankenstein*, 1931, who could not float like her daisies.

HARRIS, ROBERT H. (CA. 1909–). American character actor, often cast as a pudgy, sweaty schemer. His notable foray into the fantastic comes in *How to Make a Monster*, 1958, as a Hollywood makeup artist who turns homicidal after new studio chiefs fire him. *The Invisible Boy*, 1957.

HARRISON, SANDRA (CA. 1938–). American adolescent lead of a few American-International quickies of the fifties, notable as the vampire girl in *Blood of Dracula*, 1957.

Marilyn Harris as the little girl who is unlucky enough to befriend the Monster (Boris Karloff) in *Frankenstein* (1931).

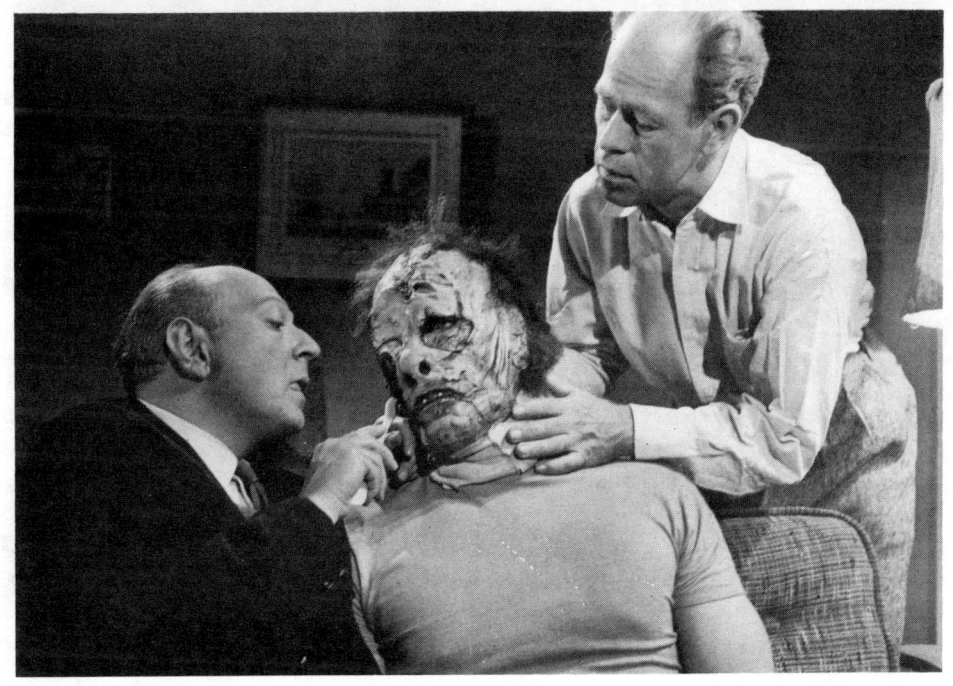

Mad makeup artist Robert H. Harris *(left)* and assistant Paul Brinegar inspect their latest creation in *How to Make a Monster* (1958).

The Cyclops, animated by Ray Harryhausen for *The Seventh Voyage of Sinbad* (1958).

HARRYHAUSEN, RAY (1920–). American stop-motion animator, protégé of WILLIS O'BRIEN. A brilliant technician, Harryhausen falls short of his mentor's skill in expressing personality; his films are breathtaking, but they appeal more to the mind than to the heart. Lately, Harryhausen has been hampered by bad scripts. When the screenplay is a good one, e.g. *Jason and the Argonauts* (Jan Read and Beverly Cross), 1963 and 1978 rerelease, and *First Men in the Moon* (NIGEL KNEALE and Jan Read), 1964, the result is wonderful. *Mighty Joe Young* (with O'Brien), 1949. *The Beast from 20,000 Fathoms*, 1953; *It Came from Beneath the Sea* (due to budgetary considerations, Harryhausen's giant octopus sports only six tentacles), 1955; *Earth vs. the Flying Saucers*, 1956; *The Animal World*, 1956; *Twenty Million Miles to Earth* (featuring the fabulous Venusian Ymir), 1957; *The 7th Voyage of Sinbad*, 1958; *The Three Worlds of Gulliver*, 1960; *Mysterious Island*, 1961; *One Million Years B.C.*, 1967; *The Valley of Gwangi*, 1969; *The Golden Voyage of Sinbad*, 1973; *Sinbad and the Eye of the Tiger*, 1977; *Clash of the Titans*, 1981. In addition, Harryhausen worked on numerous fantasy shorts from the forties, including some of GEORGE PAL's Puppetoons.

The awesome battle with the skeletal victims of the Hydra at the climax of *Jason and The Argonauts* (1963), special effects by Ray Harryhausen.

Ray Harryhausen's Venusian Ymir faces off with an elephant in *Twenty Million Miles to Earth* (1957).

Rondo Hatten *(left)* with Tom Neal and Jane Adams in *The Brute Man* (1946).

HART, FERDINAND. French actor of the thirties, a particularly glowering Golem in *Le Golem*, 1937.

HART, SUSAN (CA. 1935–). Dark, soft-spoken American leading lady of the sixties, widow of American-International chief JAMES H. NICHOLSON. *The Slime People*, 1963; *War-Gods of the Deep*, 1965; *Dr. Goldfoot and the Bikini Machine*, 1965; *The Ghost in the Invisible Bikini* (title role), 1966.

HARTL, KARL. German director of lavish science fiction films of the thirties. His *Gold*, 1934, caused Allied scientists some concern after World War II: its depiction of atomic reactors was accurate enough to support the suspicion that the Nazis had unlocked the secrets of the atom. All prints were confiscated in 1945 and carefully studied. The suspicions proved baseless; the canny atomic "scientists" were Hartl and set designer Otto Hunte. Footage from *Gold* was incorporated into a 1953 American film, *The Magnetic Monster*. *F.P. 1* aka *Floating Platform 1 Does Not Answer*, 1933.

HARVEY, HERK. American independent producer/director responsible for *Carnival of Souls*, 1962, an excellent little film about a young woman haunted by apparitions after being involved in an auto accident. The key sequence takes place at an amusement park, where the girl witnesses a mad ballroom dance and faceless merrymakers. Ultimately, it is revealed that the girl died in the car crash and that the apparitions are simply her fellow spirits. Shot in stark black-and-white and often with a suggestion of fast motion, *Carnival of Souls* creates disquiet by disclosing the strange beauty of horror.

HASKIN, BYRON (1899–). American director, former special-effects man, often in association with producer GEORGE PAL. Lacking a recognizable visual style, Haskin is a practiced technician whose primary problem has been the insertion of actors around splashy special effects. He created moments of almost unbearable suspense in *The War of the Worlds*, 1953, but achieved his finest cinema for numerous episodes of television's "The Outer Limits," 1963–64. *Tarzan's Peril*, 1951; *Conquest of Space*, 1955; *From the Earth to the Moon*, 1958; *Captain Sinbad*, 1963; *Robinson Crusoe on Mars*, 1964; *The Power*, 1968.

HATFIELD, HURD (1918–). American leading man whose good looks served him well when he played the debauched young-old man in *The Picture of Dorian Gray*, 1945. *Tarzan and the Slave Girl*, 1950.

HATTEN, RONDO (1894–1946). Acromegalic American character actor whose grotesque features were exploited in a series of low-budget melodramas of the forties. *The Hunchback of Notre Dame*, 1939; *Pearl of Death*, 1944; *Jungle Captive*, 1945; *House of Horrors*, 1946; *The Spider Woman Strikes Back*, 1946; *The Brute Man*, 1946.

HAWKINS, JACK (1910–73). Thick-set British star character actor, a powerful presence in films for more than forty years. He lost his voice to cancer in the late sixties but relied on post-production dubbing and continued to work. *The Lodger*, 1932; *Theatre of Blood*, 1973; *Tales That Witness Madness*, 1973.

HAWKS, HOWARD (1896–1977). Iconoclastic and tough-minded American director who built his reputation on determined heroes, independent heroines, and celebrations of the professional attitude. He ventured into science fiction in 1951 with *The Thing*, for which he is credited as producer. Although Christian Nyby is listed as director, the film is quite obviously the work of Hawks, carrying such trademarks as overlapping dialogue, male camaraderie, and a heroine good for something more than screaming. Various sources, among them star KENNETH TOBEY, confirm that Hawks directed. *The Thing*, a tightly constructed masterpiece of isolation and steadily mounting terror, initiated a flood of similar (and usually inferior) films.

HAYDEN, LINDA (1954–). British leading lady of the baby-doll type who came to horror films after exposure in a nudie movie. *Taste the Blood of Dracula*, 1970; *Blood on Satan's Claw*, 1971; *Madhouse*, 1973; *Night Watch*, 1973; *Old Dracula* aka *Vampira*, 1975; *The Boys from Brazil*, 1978.

HAYES, ALLISON (1930–77). Sensual American leading lady of fifties B-pictures. *The Unearthly*, 1957; *The Disembodied*, 1957; *The Undead*, 1957; *Zombies of Mora-Tau*, 1957; *Attack of the Fifty-Foot Woman* (she played the lead in this film, which has become a kitsch classic), 1958; *The Hypnotic Eye*, 1960; *The Crawling Hand*, 1963.

Allison Hayes.

John Carradine has Allison Hayes looking twice in *The Unearthly* (1957).

112 HAYWARD

HAYWARD, LOUIS (1909–). Amiable American leading man, often in costume movies. He took the title role in *Son of Dr. Jekyll*, 1951. *The Search for Bridey Murphy*, 1956; *Terror in the Wax Museum*, 1973.

HAZE, JONATHAN (CA. 1935–). Immature-seeming American actor, usually a quirky loser and often for director ROGER CORMAN. *The Day the World Ended*, 1956; *It Conquered the World*, 1956; *Not of This Earth* (as Jeremy, the chauffer), 1957; *The Saga of the Viking Women and Their Voyage to the Waters of the Great Sea Serpent*, 1957; *The Little Shop of Horrors* (the lead, as zany florist shop assistant Seymour Krelboing), 1960; *Invasion of the Star Creatures* (w only), 1962; *X—The Man with the X-Ray Eyes*, 1963; *The Terror*, 1963; others.

Jonathan Haze as klutzy but well-meaning Seymour Krelboing in Roger Corman's cult favorite *The Little Shop of Horrors* (1960).

HEDISON, DAVID (formerly Al) (1928–). American leading man of films and television ("Voyage to the Bottom of the Sea," 1964–68) who took the title role in *The Fly*, 1958. *The Lost World*, 1960; *Live and Let Die*, 1973.

HEGGIE, O.P. (1879–1936). Australian-born character actor in Hollywood, fondly remembered by horror fans as the kindly, blind hermit who befriends the Monster in *Bride of Frankenstein*, 1935. *The Mysterious Dr. Fu Manchu*, 1929; *The Return of Dr. Fu Manchu*, 1930.

HEINLEIN, ROBERT (1907–). Popular American science fiction writer whose imagination is sometimes harnessed to somewhat simple-minded socio-political philosophies. He has dabbled in Hollywood screenwriting. *Destination Moon* (co-w; w/Rip Van Ronkel and James O'Hanlon; b/o Heinlein's novel, *Rocket Ship Galileo*), 1950; *Project Moonbase* (co-w; w/Jack Seaman), 1953.

O. P. Heggie as the blind hermit who befriends the Monster (Boris Karloff) in *The Bride of Frankenstein* (1935).

Brigitte Helm.

HELM, BRIGITTE (1906–). German leading actress of the twenties and thirties, enchanting as the robot-woman Maria in FRITZ LANG's *Metropolis*, 1926; her carnal dance before an audience of lustful men is unforgettable. Helm married a Jew in 1933 and later exiled herself in Paris. *Alraune*, 1928; *At Edge of World*, 1929; *Daughter of Evil* (remake of *Alraune*, 1928), 1930; *L'Atlantide*, 1931; *Gold*, 1934.

HELTON, PERCY (1894–1971). Unappealing American character actor who specialized in whiny, scheming old men. *Miracle on 34th Street*, 1947; *Abbott and Costello Meet the Killer, Boris Karloff*, 1949; *Scared Stiff*, 1953; *20,000 Leagues under the Sea*, 1954; *Spook Chasers*, 1957; *Hush, Hush Sweet Charlotte*, 1964; *Head*, 1968.

HENNESY, DALE. Imaginative American set designer who won an Oscar for his work on *Fantastic Voyage*, 1966. *Sleeper*, 1973; *Young Frankenstein* (except the laboratory set; see: KENNETH STRICKFADEN), 1974; etc.

HENRY, CHARLOTTE (1916–). American adolescent lead of the thirties, whose fresh good looks and enthusiastic manner made her an ideal *Alice in Wonderland*, 1933. Equally delightful as Bo-Peep in LAUREL and HARDY's much-underrated *Babes in Toyland* aka *The March of the Wooden Soldiers*, 1934. *Rasputin and the Empress*, 1933.

HENRY, MIKE (1937–). Muscular American actor and onetime professional footballer who makes an agreeable Tarzan in *Tarzan and the Valley of Gold*, 1966; *Tarzan and the Great River*, 1967; and *Tarzan and the Jungle Boy*, 1968. Legal entanglements prevented Henry from bringing the character to television (see: RON ELY), and he became a successful producer of television commercials. Briefly seen in *Soylent Green*, 1973.

Charlotte Henry *(far left)* as Bo-Peep in *Babes in Toyland* (1934); her friends are Felix Knight, Oliver Hardy, and Stan Laurel. The unhappy villain is Henry Brandon.

HENRY, THOMAS B. Sharp-featured American supporting actor, almost invariably cast as the general in charge of what to do about the rampaging monster. *Earth vs. the Flying Saucers*, 1956; *Beginning of the End*, 1957; *Twenty Million Miles to Earth*, 1957; *Blood of Dracula* (as the unfeeling father), 1957; *Space Master X-7*, 1958; others.

HERBERT, HOLMES (1882-1953). British character actor, active in Hollywood from the early twenties. Circus and minstrel experience. *The Terror*, 1928; *Daughter of the Dragon*, 1931; *The Mystery of the Wax Museum*, 1933; *The Invisible Man*, 1933; *Mark of the Vampire*, 1935; *House of Secrets*, 1936; *The Ghost of Frankenstein*, 1942; *Calling Dr. Death*, 1944; *The Mummy's Curse*, 1945.

HERBERT, HUGH (1887-1952). American comic actor, known for his perpetually addled state of mind and "woo woo" sound. *A Midsummer Night's Dream* (as Snout), 1935; *Sh! The Octopus*, 1938; *The Black Cat*, 1941; *Hellzapoppin'*, 1942.

HERRMANN, BERNARD (1911-75). Brilliant and evocative film composer, always fresh and exciting even as he perpetuated a recognizable style. An artist of great integrity and conviction, Herrmann refused to give less than his best to any project, no matter how inconsequential. His score for HITCHCOCK's *Psycho*, 1960, is one of the most memorable in the history of cinema. *The Devil and Daniel Webster*, 1941; *Hangover Square*, 1945; *The Ghost and Mrs. Muir*, 1947; *The Day the Earth Stood Still*, 1951; *The 7th Voyage of Sinbad*, 1958; *Journey to the Center of the Earth*, 1959; *The Three Worlds of Gulliver*, 1960; *Mysterious Island*, 1961; *Jason and the Argonauts*, 1963; *The Birds* (sound consultant, as no actual music is heard), 1963; *Fahrenheit 451*, 1966; *Twisted Nerve*, 1969; *The Night Digger*, 1971; *Sisters*, 1973; *It's Alive*, 1974; *Obsession*, 1976; *It Lives Again*, 1978.

Thomas B. Henry and Joyce Meadows search for *The Brain from Planet Arous* (1958).

Charlton Heston in *Planet of The Apes* (1968).

HESSLER, GORDON (1930–). American producer/director who has been successful in England. *The Oblong Box*, 1969; *Scream and Scream Again*, 1970; *Cry of the Banshee*, 1970; *Murders in the Rue Morgue*, 1971; *The Golden Voyage of Sinbad*, 1973; others.

HESTON, CHARLTON (1924–). American leading man, often in epic roles, who has lately appeared in some routine science fiction. *Peer Gynt* (amateur; title role), 1941; *Planet of the Apes*, 1968; *Beneath the Planet of the Apes*, 1970; *The Omega Man*, 1971; *Soylent Green*, 1973.

HILL, JACK. Talented but sluggish American director, formerly associated with producer/director ROGER CORMAN. *The Terror* (part; uncredited; and co-w; w/LEO GORDON), 1963; *Blood Bath* (and p; co-w; w/STEPHANIE ROTHMAN), 1966; *The Fear Chamber* aka *The Incredible Invasion* (American scenes only; and w), 1968; *The House of Evil* aka *The Snake People* (American scenes only; and w), 1968; *Spider Baby or: The Maddest Story Ever Told*, 1970; *Death Ship* (story only), 1980.

HILLYER, LAMBERT (1889–). American B-western director of the forties who tried a few fantastic films. *Superspeed*, 1935; *The Invisible Ray*, 1936; *Dracula's Daughter*, 1936.

HINDS, ANTHONY (1922–). British producer associated with Hammer Films. He has also written screenplays under the name John Elder. *The Curse of Frankenstein*, 1957; *The Horror of Dracula*, 1958; *Brides of Dracula*, 1960; *Curse of the Werewolf* (and w), 1961; *Kiss of the Vampire* (and w), 1963; *The Evil of Frankenstein* (and w), 1964; *Scars of Dracula* (w only), 1970; *Frankenstein and the Monster from Hell* (w only), 1973.

HITCHCOCK, ALFRED (1899–1980). Portly British director long active in Hollywood whose face and manner were familiar the world over. The only director whose name has been a marquee selling point, Hitchcock was also one of the finest artists in cinema history, a brilliant technician, and a deft manipulator of audience expectations. Condemned by some critics for his dogged commercialism, he was always fresh, innovative, and unique. His often tasteless subject matter was made delightful by a fine sense of the absurd as well as a cheery vulgarity and a gift for black humor. Hitchcock's most effective films exploit paranoia, often with an "innocent man wrongly accused" motif. Perhaps the most influential of modern directors, Hitchcock set the tone for much of the world film output of the sixties and seventies with *Psycho*, 1960, the blackest of black comedies, and possibly among the finest films ever made. With its devious plotting, camerawork and finely calculated shock effects, *Psycho* is not only an unparalleled study in horror but a challenging and amusing intellectual exercise. Hitchcock remained active until the end of his life. *The Lodger*, 1926; *Shadow of a Doubt*, 1943; *Spellbound*, 1945; *Rear Window*, 1954; *Vertigo*, 1958; *The Birds*, 1963; *Frenzy*, 1972; *Family Plot*, 1976.

Alfred Hitchcock, of course.

Inoshiro Honda's Rodan devastates Tokyo in 1957.

HOBSON, VALERIE (1917–). Dark-eyed and beautiful British actress, a leading lady while still in her teens. *Bride of Frankenstein* (as Elizabeth), 1935; *Werewolf of London*, 1935; *The Mystery of Edwin Drood*, 1935.

HOEY, DENNIS (1893–1960). British character actor in Hollywood, best remembered as the thick, faintly pompous Inspector Lestrade in the BASIL RATHBONE Sherlock Holmes films. *Murder in the Red Barn*, 1935; *Frankenstein Meets the Wolf Man*, 1943; *Spider Woman*, 1944; *Pearl of Death*, 1944; *A Thousand and One Nights*, 1945; *Tarzan and the Leopard Woman*, 1946; *She-Wolf of London*, 1946.

HOLDEN, GLORIA (1909–). Dark British character actress who has the title role in *Dracula's Daughter*, 1936; *Miracles for Sale*, 1939.

HOLDREN, JUDD (1915–74). American serial star of the fifties, associated with Republic Pictures. *Captain Video*, 1951; *Zombies of the Stratosphere*, 1952; *Commando Cody, Sky Marshal of the Universe*, 1953; *The Lost Planet*, 1953; *The Amazing Colossal Man*, 1957.

HOLE, WILLIAM J. JR. Talentless American director of the fifties. *The Devil's Hand*, 1958; *The Ghost of Dragstrip Hollow*, 1959.

HOLT, SETH (1923-71). British director of Hammer horror films. *Scream of Fear*, 1961; *The Nanny*, 1965; *Blood from the Mummy's Tomb* (died during filming and replaced by MICHAEL CARRERAS), 1971.

HOMOLKA, OSCAR (1899-1978). Thickset Viennese character actor, often cast as a spy or foreign heavy and notable as GUY ROLFE's hideously scarred aide in *Mr. Sardonicus*, 1961.

HONDA, INOSHIRO. Japanese director with Toho Studios who specializes in noisy monster epics. His *Godzilla*, 1954, has enough gritty realism to make it a good film of its kind, but Honda's touch has become broader as the quality of scripts given him has declined. The more recent Godzilla films are juvenile comedies, full of obnoxious children and slapstick rubber monsters. *Rodan*, 1957; *The Mysterians*, 1959; *The H-Man*, 1959; *Mothra*, 1961; *King Kong vs. Godzilla*, 1963; *Godzilla vs. the Thing*, 1964; *Ghidrah, The Three-Headed Monster*, 1965; *Frankenstein Conquers the World*, 1966; *King Kong Escapes*, 1968; *War of the Gargantuas*, 1970; *Godzilla's Revenge*, 1971; others.

HOOPER, TOBE (1946-). American independent filmmaker whose grisly but good-humored *The Texas Chain Saw Massacre*, 1974, brought him immediate notoriety. Also directed *Eaten Alive* aka *Death Trap*, 1975; *Starlight Slaughter*, 1976; *Salem's Lot* (TV; theatrical distribution in Europe), 1979; *Fun House*, 1980.

HOPE, BOB (1903-). Indestructible British-born comedian and film actor, in America from early childhood. Seemingly ageless, Hope has been cracking one-liners since the thirties and remains enormously popular. Two of his films, *The Cat and the Canary*, 1939 and *The Ghost Breakers*, 1940, are genuinely spooky and are regarded with special fondness. In addition, many of the popular *Road to* ———— films he made with Bing Crosby have fanciful sequences. He also made a cameo appearance in *The Muppet Movie*, 1979.

HOPPER, WILLIAM (1915-70). Husky American actor, popular as Paul Drake on television's "Perry Mason," 1957-66, who could not overcome a basically dull persona. Son of actress/columnist Hedda Hopper. *The Return of Dr. X*, 1939; *Conquest of Space*, 1955; *The Bad Seed*, 1956; *The Deadly Mantis*, 1957; *Twenty Million Miles to Earth*, 1957.

HORTON, EDWARD EVERETT (1886-1970). Eccentric American character actor who played all manner of comic oddballs. *The Terror*, 1928; *Alice in Wonderland*, 1933; *Here Comes Mr. Jordan*, 1941; *The Body Disappears*, 1941; *I Married an Angel*, 1942; *Arsenic and Old Lace*, 1944; *Down to Earth*, 1947; *The Story of Mankind*, 1957.

Olin Howlin is nibbled by *The Blob* (1958).

HOUCK, JOY N. JR. American director of low-budget films who moved from sexploitation to horror. *Night of Bloody Horror* (and p), 1969; *Night of the Strangler*, 1975; *The Creature from Black Lake*, 1976.

HOUDINI, HARRY (1874–1926). Legendary American escape artist, at his height in the twenties and still the subject of much wonder and speculation. He made a number of film appearances, notably as *The Man from Beyond*, 1922, who revives after being encased in ice for one hundred years and who marries his reincarnated fiancee. Also: *The Master Mystery*, 1919; *Terror Island*, 1920. A 1953 biopic stars Tony Curtis, and an outstanding one starring Paul Michael Glaser was made for television in 1976.

HOUGH, JAN (1941–). Uneven British director whose *The Legend of Hell House*, 1973, is an intelligent treatment of ghosts and the para-normal. *Twins of Evil*, 1971; *Escape to Witch Mountain*, 1975.

HOWLIN, OLIN (1896–1959). Skinny American comic actor, often appearing as a rubber-limbed eccentric. In films from 1918, Howlin is noted for his final two appearances: in *Them!*, 1954, as the patient in the alchoholic ward who has seen the giant ants in the Los Angeles storm drains and as the unhappy old man who is the first victim of *The Blob*, 1958. *The Return of Dr. X*, 1939; *The Man Who Wouldn't Die*, 1942; *Return of the Whistler*, 1948.

HOYT, JOHN (1905–). Gray-haired American character actor, usually a sour or scheming authority figure. *Lost Continent*, 1951; *When Worlds Collide* (as ruthless millionaire Sydney Stanton), 1951; *Attack of the Puppet People* (as the insane scientist), 1958; *X—The Man with the X-Ray Eyes*, 1963; *Two on a Guillotine*, 1965; *Flesh Gordon*, 1972.

HUGO, VICTOR (1802–85). French poet and novelist whose *Notre Dame de Paris* has inspired ten versions since 1911, the three best known being *The Hunchback of Notre Dame* in 1923 (LON CHANEY, SR.), 1939 (CHARLES LAUGHTON), and 1957 (ANTHONY QUINN). Also *Notre Dame de Paris*, 1911; *Notre Dame*, 1913; *The Darling of Paris*, 1916; *Badshah Dampati* (Indian), 1953; etc. Hugo's hunchback has appeared in numerous filmic variations, *e.g.* The Hunchback of the Morgue, 1972.

HULL, HENRY (1890–1977). American character actor who played the title role in *Werewolf of London*, 1935. Because Hull would not tolerate elaborate makeup, JACK PIERCE created a light, easily applied design which is among his most interesting images. *Miracles for Sale*, 1939; *Master of the World*, 1961.

HUMBERSTONE, H. BRUCE (1903–). Prolific American second feature director responsible for a number of the amusing Charlie Chan mysteries, many of which have spooky or fantastic elements. *The Crooked Circle*, 1932; *Charlie Chan at the Opera*, 1936; *Charlie Chan at the Olympics*, 1937; *Wonder Man*, 1944; *Tarzan and the Lost Safari*, 1957.

HUME, CYRIL. American screenwriter with MGM who went to Shakespeare's the *Tempest* as inspiration for *Forbidden Planet*, 1956. Once married to actress HELEN CHANDLER. *Tarzan Escapes*, 1936; *Jungle Princess*, 1936; *Tarzan Finds a Son!*, 1939; *Tarzan's Savage Fury* (co-w; w/Hans Jacoby and Shirley White), 1952; *The Invisible Boy*, 1957.

HUNNICUT, GAYLE (1943–). Willowy American leading lady of the sixties and seventies who brought her striking beauty to *Eye of the Cat*, 1969; *Fragment of Fear*, 1971; *The Legend of Hell House*, 1973; *The Martian Chronicles* (TV; theatrical release in Britain), 1980.

HUNT, PETER (1928–). British editor involved with the James Bond fantasies and director of *On Her Majesty's Secret Service*, 1969, in many ways the most intelligent film of the Bond series. Significantly, it did the least business and took some years to earn back its considerable cost. As editor: *Dr. No*, 1962; *Goldfinger*, 1964; *Thunderball*, 1965. As second unit director: *You Only Live Twice*, 1967.

HUTTON, ROBERT (1920–). Smooth, mustachioed American actor who can play both sympathetic and conniving roles. *The Man without a Body*, 1958; *Invisible Invaders*, 1959; *The Slime People* (and d), 1963; *They Came from Beyond Space*, 1967; *The Vulture*, 1967; *Cry of the Banshee*, 1970; *The Crypt*, 1972.

HYAMS, LEILA (1905–). Blonde, down-to-earth American leading lady of the twenties and thirties, notable as Venus, the sharp heroine of TOD BROWNING's *Freaks*, 1932. *The Wizard*, 1927; *The Phantom of Paris*, 1931; *Island of Lost Souls*, 1933.

HYER, MARTHA (1929–). Blonde American leading lady of the fifties and sixties who has not fulfilled her early promise. *Abbott and Costello Go to Mars*, 1953; *Riders to the Stars*, 1954; *First Men in the Moon* (charming as the spunky Victorian heroine), 1964; *Pyro*, 1964; *Picture Mommy Dead*, 1966; *House of 1000 Dolls*, 1967.

John Hoyt.

Leila Hyams.

Henry Hull.

Martha Hyer, looking remarkably calm in the face of moon men: *First Men in The Moon* (1964).

I

IFUKUBE, AKIRA. Japanese film composer who has written heavy but effective scores for many Toho and Daiei Studio monster epics. *Godzilla*, 1954; *Varan the Unbelievable*, 1958; *The Mysterians*, 1959; *Godzilla vs. the Thing*, 1964; *Monster Zero*, 1965; *Ghidrah the Three-Headed Monster*, 1965; *King Kong Escapes*, 1968; *Destroy All Monsters*, 1969; others.

INESCORT, FRIEDA (1901–76). Scottish actress in Hollywood. *Tarzan Finds a Son!*, 1939; *The Return of the Vampire*, 1944; *The She Creature*, 1956; *The Alligator People*, 1959.

INGRAM, REX (1895–1969). Hearty black American actor who specialized in larger-than-life roles, a lively genie in *The Thief of Bagdad*, 1940. *Tarzan of the Apes*, 1918; *Green Pastures* (as De Lawd), 1936; *Cabin in the Sky* (as the Devil), 1943; *A Thousand and One Nights*, 1945; *Tarzan's Hidden Jungle*, 1955.

Genie Rex Ingram ponders the presence of tiny Sabu in *The Thief of Bagdad* (1940).

IRVING, AMY (1954–). Striking young American leading actress of the seventies. *Carrie*, 1976; *The Fury* (as Gillian), 1978.

IWERKS, UB (1900–71). American cartoon animator and special effects technician, long associated with WALT DISNEY. Iwerks was instrumental in the creation of the multiplane camera (which achieves a three-dimensional, layered look in cartoon animation) and in the development of complex matte systems which allowed convincing blending of different elements within the frame, *e.g.*, actors with animated dinosaurs. *20,000 Leagues Under the Sea*, 1954; *The Absent-Minded Professor*, 1961; *Son of Flubber*, 1963; *The Birds*, 1963; many others.

J

JACKSON, FREDA (1909–). British character actress, often cast as a sharp lady with a lot to say. *Brides of Dracula*, 1960; *The Shadow of the Cat*, 1961; *Die Monster Die!*, 1965; *The Valley of Gwangi*, 1969.

JAFFE, SAM (1897–). Soft-spoken American character actor, memorable as the High Lama in FRANK CAPRA's *Lost Horizon*, 1937. *The Day the Earth Stood Still* (as Professor Barnhardt, a character modeled after Albert Einstein), 1951; *The Dunwich Horror*, 1970; *The Tell-Tale Heart* (short), 1971.

JAGGER, DEAN (1903–). American character lead, usually cast as a mature man with a level head. *Revolt of the Zombies*, 1936; *It Grows on Trees*, 1952; *It's a Dog's Life*, 1955; *X—The Unknown*, 1957; *End of the World*, 1977.

JANNINGS, EMIL (1884–1950). German star character actor, perhaps the most popular film personality in Europe during the twenties, who frittered away his career and reputation on brainlessly overblown Nazi-sponsored projects during the thirties and forties. Before a tendency to overact got the better of him, Jannings starred effectively in a number of horror thrillers. *The Eyes of the Mummy*, 1918; *Waxworks* (as Haroun-al-Raschid), 1924; *Faust* (as Mephistopheles), 1926.

JAY, GRIFFIN. American screenwriter of the forties. *The Mummy's Hand* (co-w; w/Maxwell Shane), 1940; *The Mummy's Tomb* (co-w; w/HENRY SUCHER), 1942; *Captive Wild Woman* (co-w; w/ HENRY SUCHER), 1943; *The Return of the Vampire*, 1944; *The Mummy's Ghost* (co-w; w/HENRY SUCHER), 1944; *Cry of the Werewolf* (co-w; w/Charles O'Neil), 1944; others.

JAYNE, JENNIFER (CA. 1935–). British leading lady of the sixties. *The Crawling Eye*, 1958; *Dr. Terror's House of Horrors*, 1964; *Hysteria*, 1965; *They Came from beyond Space*, 1967; etc.

JEFFRIES, LIONEL (1926–). Energetic British character actor, the epitome of good-humored eccentricity; his Professor Cavor in *First Men in the Moon*, 1964, is a stitch. *The Revenge of Frankenstein*, 1958; *Those Fantastic Flying Fools* aka *Blast Off; Rocket to the Moon*, 1967; *Chitty Chitty Bang Bang*, 1968; *Whoever Slew Auntie Roo?*, 1971; *The Amazing Mr. Blunden* (w and d only), 1972.

JENNINGS, GORDON (CA. 1900–53). American special effects technician long associated with Paramount who supervised the mind-boggling visuals for GEORGE PAL's *The War of the Worlds*, 1953. He died unexpectedly and never knew of his richly-deserved 1953 Academy Award. Also worked on *The Mad Doctor*, 1941; *When Worlds Collide* (Academy Award), 1951.

JESSEL, PATRICIA (1921–68). Handsome and imposing British character actress, magnificently evil as the witch Elizabeth Selwyn in *Horror Hotel*, 1960. *They All Died Laughing*, 1964.

JODOROWSKY, ALEXANDRO (1930–). Mexican director of the seventies whose pretentious and muddled films have earned him a cult reputation. *El Topo*, 1971, is a metaphysical western that fails by attempting to say too much. Full of violence and quasi-religious images, it mystifies rather than enlightens. *The Holy Mountain*, 1974.

JOHANN, ZITA (1904–). Hungarian-born, exotic American leading lady of the thirties seen to good advantage in *The Mummy*, 1932.

Lionel Jeffries as Cavor, the man who brings to the moon and its insectoid dwellers the common cold, in *First Men in The Moon* (1964).

Glynis Johns *(right)* with Diana Dors in *The Weak and The Wicked*, a suspense film from 1954.

JOHNS, GLYNIS (1923–). British leading actress, a most fetching mermaid in *Miranda*, 1948. *Mad about Men* (double role: as Miranda the mermaid, and human look-alike), 1954; *The Cabinet of Caligari*, 1962; *The Vault of Horror*, 1973.

JOHNSON, NOBLE (1897–). Imposing American black actor and producer of early black films who is remembered as the glowering native chief in *King Kong*, 1933; and its sequel, *Son of Kong*, 1933. *The Thief of Bagdad*, 1924; *Murders in the Rue Morgue*, 1932; *The Most Dangerous Game*, 1932; *The Mummy*, 1932; *She*, 1935; *The Ghost Breakers* (as the zombie), 1940; *The Mad Doctor of Market Street*, 1942; *The Jungle Book*, 1942.

Vengeful witch Patricia Jessel is led to the stake in *Horror Hotel* (1960).

Los Angeles ablaze in *The War of The Worlds* (1953); special effects supervised by Gordon Jennings.

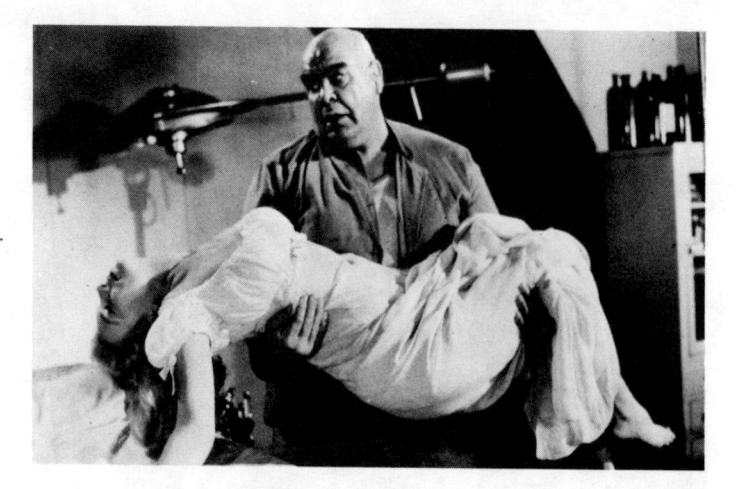

Tor Johnson carries on in *The Unearthly* (1957).

JOHNSON, RUSSELL (CA. 1920–). Regular-featured American general purpose actor, best-known as the Professor on television's "Gilligan's Island." 1964–67. *It Came from Outer Space*, 1953; *This Island Earth*, 1955; *Attack of the Crab Monsters*, 1957; *The Space Children*, 1958.

JOHNSON, TOR (1903–71). Towering Swedish character actor, a professional wrestler before going to work in Hollywood cheapies. Massive, bald, and fleshy, Johnson specialized in grunting maniacs. *The Ghost Catchers*, 1944; *The Canterville Ghost*, 1944; *Plan 9 from Outer Space*, 1956; *Bride of the Monster*, 1956; *The Black Sleep*, 1956; *The Unearthly*, 1957; *Night of the Ghouls*, 1959; *The Beast of Yucca Flats* (title role), 1961.

JONES, CAROLYN (1929–). Big-eyed, faintly eccentric American leading lady, best known as Morticia on television's the "Addams Family," 1964–66. *House of Wax* (as the murdered girl who is coated in wax and displayed as Joan of Arc), 1953; *The War of the Worlds* (bit), 1953; *Invasion of the Body Snatchers*, 1956.

JONES, DARBY. Tall, impossibly thin American black actor of the forties, splendidly eerie as the undead slave in *I Walked with a Zombie*, 1943. *Tarzan the Fearless*, 1933; *Tarzan Escapes*, 1936; *Zombies on Broadway*, 1945; *Zamba, the Gorilla*, 1949.

JONES, DEAN (1933–). Bland American leading man, familiar as the wholesome hero of many tepid DISNEY studio fantasies. *Two on a Guillotine*, 1965; *The Love Bug*, 1969; *Million Dollar Duck*, 1971; *Mr. Superinvisible*, 1976; *Herbie Goes to Monte Carlo*, 1977.

JONES, DUANE (CA. 1940–). American black actor who gained wide exposure as the hero in *Night of the Living Dead*, 1968, but who has done little since. *Ganja and Hess* (vampirism), 1973.

JONES, FREDDIE (1927–). British character actor who appears as the vengeful but bald and dumpy monster in *Frankenstein Must Be Destroyed*, 1970. *The Satanic Rites of Dracula*, 1974.

Duane Jones *(center)* with Judith O'Dea in George Romero's *Night of The Living Dead* (1968).

JONES, JENNIFER (1919–). Sensitive American leading lady of the forties and fifties, a dark-haired beauty who acted under the name Phyllis Isley until meeting producer David Selznick in 1942, who changed her name to Jennifer Jones and later married her. Jones relied heavily upon Selznick's judgment, and while he chose a number of good vehicles for her, others were overblown and empty. Perhaps the finest was *Portrait of Jennie*, 1948, a delicate and lyrical fantasy about an artist (JOSEPH COTTEN) obsessed with a lovely little girl (Jones) who seems years older each time he sees her. It becomes apparent that the girl, Jennie, is somehow displaced in time and that the artist can have no hope of possessing her. At one point Jennie sings, "Where I come from/Nobody knows,/And where I'm going/Everything goes./The wind blows,/The sea flows—/Where I come from/Nobody knows." Despite a rather contrived climax, *Portrait of Jennie* is a rare instance of Hollywood's attempting mature fantasy; the film was not a commercial success and was briefly reissued in 1950 as *Tidal Wave*. *Dick Tracy's G-Men* (serial; billed as Phyllis Isley), 1939; *The Song of Bernadette*, 1943; *Angel, Angel, Down We Go*, 1969, (rereleased in 1971 as *Cult of the Damned*).

JONES, L.Q. (1936–). American actor, familiar as the villain in many westerns, partnered with actor ALVY MOORE to produce modest but interesting horror thrillers. *The Devil's Bedroom* (also as actor), 1963; *The Witchmaker*, 1969; *The Brotherhood of Satan* (also as actor), 1971; *A Boy and His Dog* (and d; b/o the prizewinning novella by Harlan Ellison), 1976.

JONES-MORELAND, BETSY. American actress associated with director ROGER CORMAN. *The Saga of the Viking Women and Their Voyage to the Waters of the Great Sea Serpent*, 1957; *The Last Woman on Earth* (title role), 1960; *Creature from the Haunted Sea*, 1961.

JORDAN, BOBBY (1923–65). American juvenile actor who came to Hollywood to repeat his stage role from *Dead End*, 1937, and later became one of the Bowery Boys with *Dead End* costars LEO GORCEY and HUNTZ HALL. *Spooks Run Wild*, 1941; *Ghosts on the Loose*, 1943; *Mr. Hex*, 1946; *Spook Busters*, 1946.

Jennifer Jones and Joseph Cotten in a quiet moment from *Portrait of Jennie* (1948).

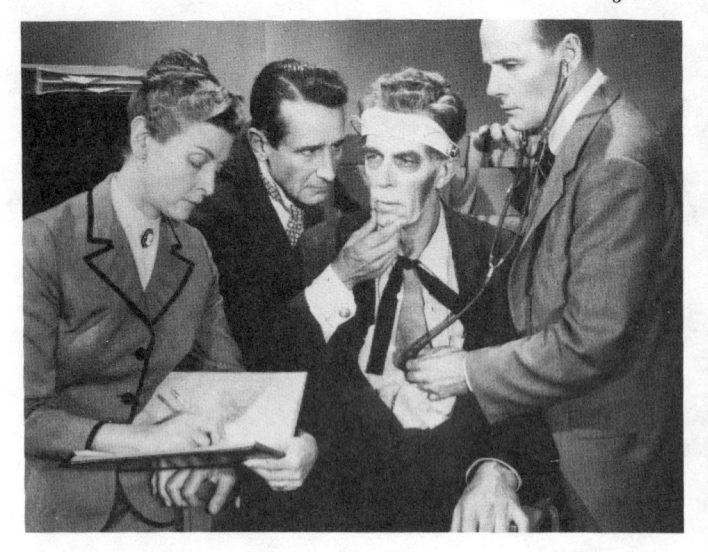

Victor Jory *(left)* examines Paul Cavanagh, *The Man Who Turned to Stone* (1957).

Cult favorite Allison Hayes meets an alien in Nathan Juran's *Attack of The Fifty-Foot Woman* (1958).

JORY, VICTOR (1902–). Menacing Canadian character actor in Hollywood, best cast as a cynical and smooth-talking villain. *The Shadow* (title role), 1940; *Cat Women of the Moon*, 1953; *The Man Who Turned to Stone*, 1957; etc.

JUDD, EDWARD (1932–). British leading man of the sixties, an engaging hero in *First Men in the Moon*, 1964. *X—The Unknown*, 1957; *The Day the Earth Caught Fire*, 1962; *Island of Terror*, 1966; *The Vault of Horror*, 1973; etcetera.

JURAN, NATHAN (HERTZ) (1907–). Austrian director of Hollywood second features who is most successful when backed by big doses of special effects; former art director (Academy Award for *How Green Was My Valley*, 1942). *The Black Castle*, 1952; *The Deadly Mantis*, 1957; *Twenty Million Miles to Earth*, 1957; *The 7th Voyage of Sinbad*, 1958; *Attack of the Fifty-Foot Woman*, 1958; *Flight of the Lost Balloon*, 1961; *Jack the Giant Killer* (and co-w; w/Orville H. Hampton), 1962; *First Men in the Moon* (his best, a charming bit of mock Victoriana), 1964; *The Boy Who Cried Werewolf*, 1973.

JURGENS, CURT (1912–). German star caracter actor, often seen as a cultured heel. *April 1, 2000*, 1950; *The Vault of Horror*, 1973;. *The Spy Who Loved Me*, 1977.

Boris Karloff, ca. 1961.

K

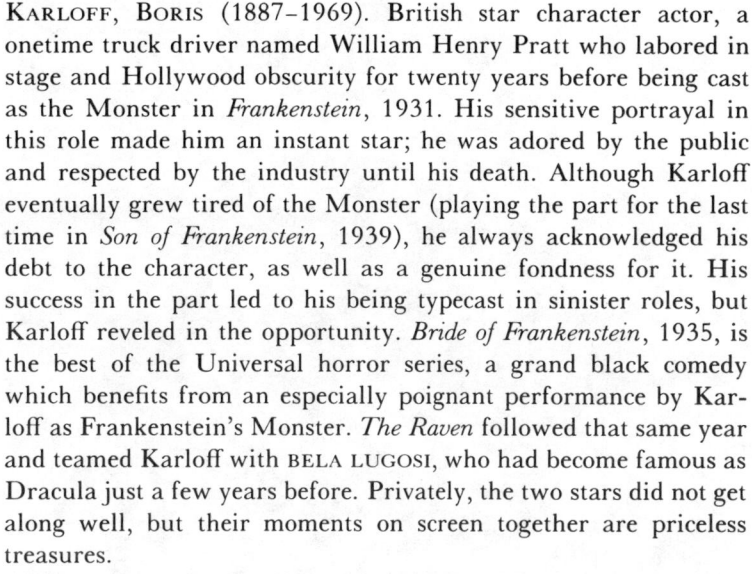

KARLOFF, BORIS (1887–1969). British star character actor, a onetime truck driver named William Henry Pratt who labored in stage and Hollywood obscurity for twenty years before being cast as the Monster in *Frankenstein*, 1931. His sensitive portrayal in this role made him an instant star; he was adored by the public and respected by the industry until his death. Although Karloff eventually grew tired of the Monster (playing the part for the last time in *Son of Frankenstein*, 1939), he always acknowledged his debt to the character, as well as a genuine fondness for it. His success in the part led to his being typecast in sinister roles, but Karloff reveled in the opportunity. *Bride of Frankenstein*, 1935, is the best of the Universal horror series, a grand black comedy which benefits from an especially poignant performance by Karloff as Frankenstein's Monster. *The Raven* followed that same year and teamed Karloff with BELA LUGOSI, who had become famous as Dracula just a few years before. Privately, the two stars did not get along well, but their moments on screen together are priceless treasures.

Throughout the thirties and forties, Karloff played a broad variety of roles: a resurrected dead man (*The Walking Dead*, 1936), an Oriental sleuth (*Mr. Wong, Detective*, 1938, and two sequels), a bald executioner in old England (*Tower of London*, 1939), a mad doctor (*Black Friday*, 1940), a grave robber (*The Body Snatcher*, 1945), and even an Indian chief (*The Unconquered*, 1947). Horror films waned in popularity as the fifties approached, and Karloff's screen appearances became less frequent. He did radio and stage work (notable in the latter as Captain Hook in a 1950 production of *Peter Pan*) and also made appearances on television, most prominently as host of "Thriller," 1960–62. Ironically, it was television that brought him a great burst of film work during the last decade of his life. His older films had been telecast on local stations for years and won him an entirely new generation of fans. Karloff worked for director ROGER CORMAN on *The Raven*, 1963, a whimsical story about warring wizards which costarred VINCENT PRICE and PETER LORRE. Other films for Corman followed, usually with verteran supporting casts. In 1968, Karloff filled one of his finest roles as aging horror film star Byron Orlock in *Targets*. Directed by a talented newcomer named PETER BOGDANOVICH, the film provided Karloff with an opportunity to look at his own career; it is also a serious comment on our violent society.

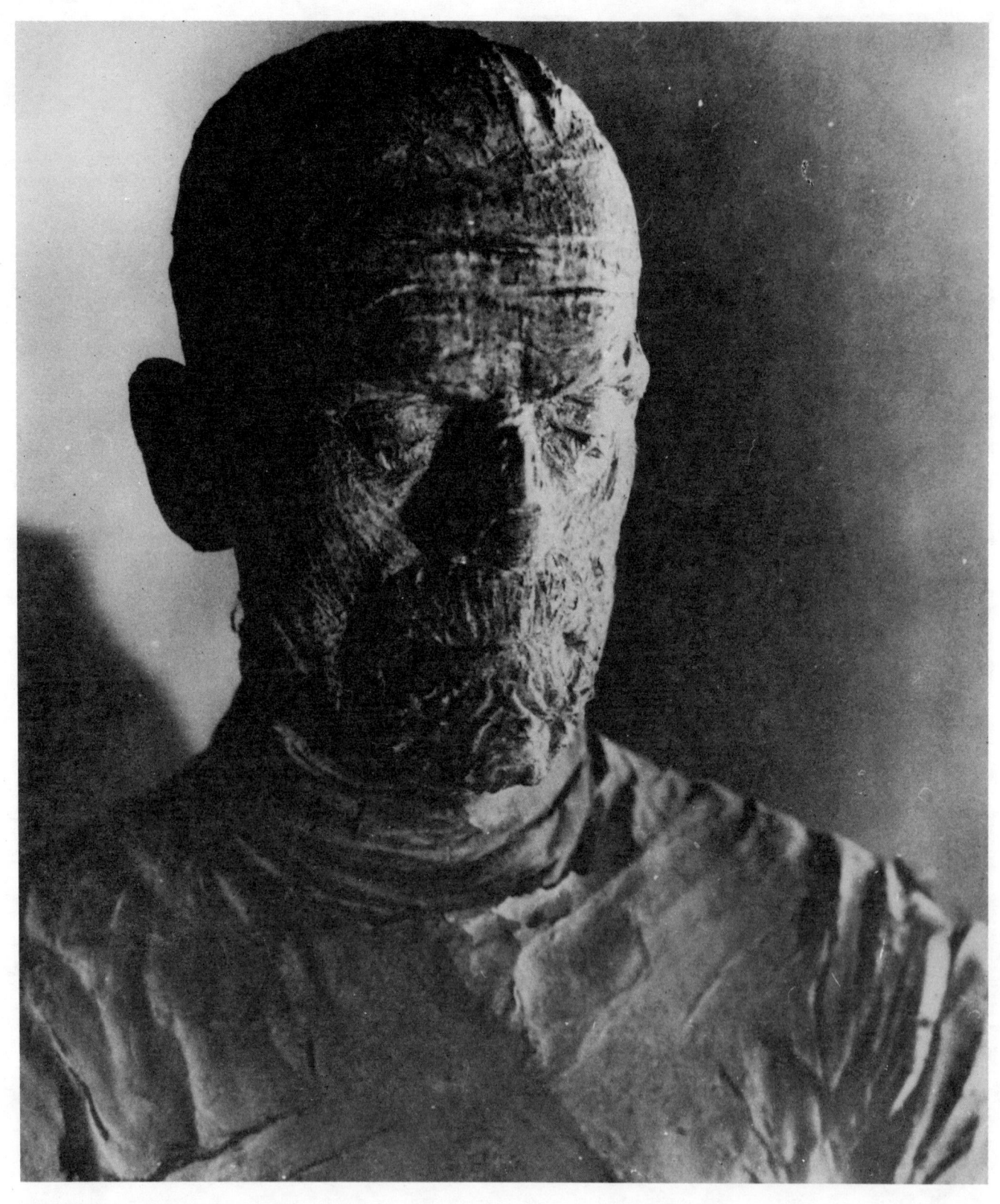

Boris Karloff as *The Mummy* (1932).

By then Karloff was past eighty and in failing health. Respiratory difficulties and crippling arthritis limited his movement, but he refused to let his fans down. More popular at the time than ever before, he negotiated a four-picture deal with a Mexican producer, arranging to shoot his scenes with an American crew in Hollywood. The work tired him, and on top of it came more television appearances and a trip to England. There, in late 1968, Karloff was badly stricken by the respiratory ailment. He was hospitalized for three months and died in February 1969. With his death, the world of entertainment suffered an irreparable loss, Karloff was *sui generis*. But his star has not dimmed; the gentle voice and menacing manner live on. *The Bells* (as the mesmerist), 1926; *Tarzan and the Golden Lion* (as chief of the Waziris), 1927; *The Unholy Night* (as a Hindu servant), 1929; *The Mad Genius*, 1931; *King of the Wild*, 1931; *The Old Dark House*, 1932; *The Mask of Fu Manchu*, 1932; *The Mummy*, 1932; *The Ghoul*, 1934; *The Black Cat*, 1934; *The Black Room*, 1935; *The Invisible Ray*, 1936; *The Man Who Lived Again*, 1936; *Charlie Chan at the Opera*, 1936; *Night Key*, 1937; *The Man They Could Not Hang*, 1939; *The Man with Nine Lives*, 1940; *Before I Hang*, 1940; *The Ape*, 1940; *You'll Find Out*, 1940; *The Devil Commands*, 1941; *The Boogie Man Will Get You*, 1942; *The Climax*, 1944; *House of Frankenstein*, 1945; *Isle of the Dead*, 1945; *Bedlam*, 1946; *The Secret Life of Walter Mitty* (as Dr. Hollingshead), 1947; *Dick Tracy Meets Gruesome* (as Gruesome), 1947; *Abbott and Costello Meet the Killer, Boris Karloff* (as Swami Talpur), 1949; *The Strange Door*, 1951; *The Black Castle*, 1952; *Abbott and Costello Meet Dr. Jekyll and Mr. Hyde* (as Jekyll; most Hyde scenes played by stuntman EDDIE PARKER), 1953; *The Hindu aka Sabaka*, 1953; *Voodoo Island*, 1957; *The Haunted Strangler*, 1958; *Frankenstein—1970*, 1958; *Corridors of Blood*, 1958; *The Terror*, 1963; *The Comedy of Terrors*, 1963; *Black Sabbath*, 1963; *Die Monster Die!*, 1965; *The Ghost in the Invisible Bikini*, 1966; *The Venetian Affair*, 1967; *The Sorcerers*, 1967; *The Crimson Cult*, 1968; *The Fear Chamber* aka *The Incredible Invasion*, 1968; *The House of Evil* aka *The Snake People*, 1968; *Cauldron of Blood*, 1968.

KARLSON, PHIL (1908–). American director of well-made, often brutal crime thrillers. *The Silencers*, 1966, and *The Wrecking Crew*, 1968, are Matt Helm fantasies and not very good, but Karlson's *Ben*, 1972, is great fun.

KATZ, FRED. American composer who created quirky yet evocative scores for a number of films directed by ROGER CORMAN. *A Bucket of Blood*, 1959; *Wasp Woman*, 1959; *The Little Shop of Horrors*, 1960; *Creature from the Haunted Sea*, 1961.

Allison Hayes meets the undead in Sam Katzman's *The Zombies of Mora Tau* (1957).

KATZMAN, SAM (1901–73). Amazingly energetic American producer who cranked out profitable low-budgeters for forty years. His success with the shoddy Jungle Jim series won him the nickname "Jungle Sam." *Voodoo Man*, 1944; *The Lost Tribe*, 1949; *Fury of the Congo*, 1951; *Jungle Jim in the Forbidden Land*, 1952; *Killer Ape*, 1953; *Jungle Moon Men*, 1955; *Earth vs. the Flying Saucers*, 1956; *The Werewolf*, 1956; *The Man Who Turned to Stone*, 1957; *Zombies of Mora Tau*, 1957; *The Giant Claw*, 1957; *The Night the World Exploded*, 1957; many others.

KEIR, ANDREW (1926–). Scottish character lead in British films, an intrepid Dr. Quatermass in *Five Million Years to Earth*, 1967. Also *Dracula, Prince of Darkness*, 1966; *Daleks—Invasion Earth 2150 A.D.*, 1968; *Blood from the Mummy's Tomb*, 1971; etc.

KELLJAN, BOB. American writer/director of tight little horror thrillers. *Count Yorga, Vampire*, 1970; *The Return of Count Yorga*, 1971; *Scream, Blacula, Scream* (d only), 1973.

KELLOGG, RAY. American special effects man (*The Day the Earth Stood Still*, 1951) who prepared himself for a later association with JOHN WAYNE by directing *The Giant Gila Monster* (and co-w; w/ Jay Sims), 1959, and *The Killer Shrews*, 1959.

KEMMER, ED. American leading man of a few B-films of the fifties, star of television's "Space Patrol," 1950–56. *World Beyond the Moon* (several episodes of Space Patrol edited together to make a feature), 1953; *Earth vs. the Spider*, 1958; *Giant from the Unknown*, 1958; others.

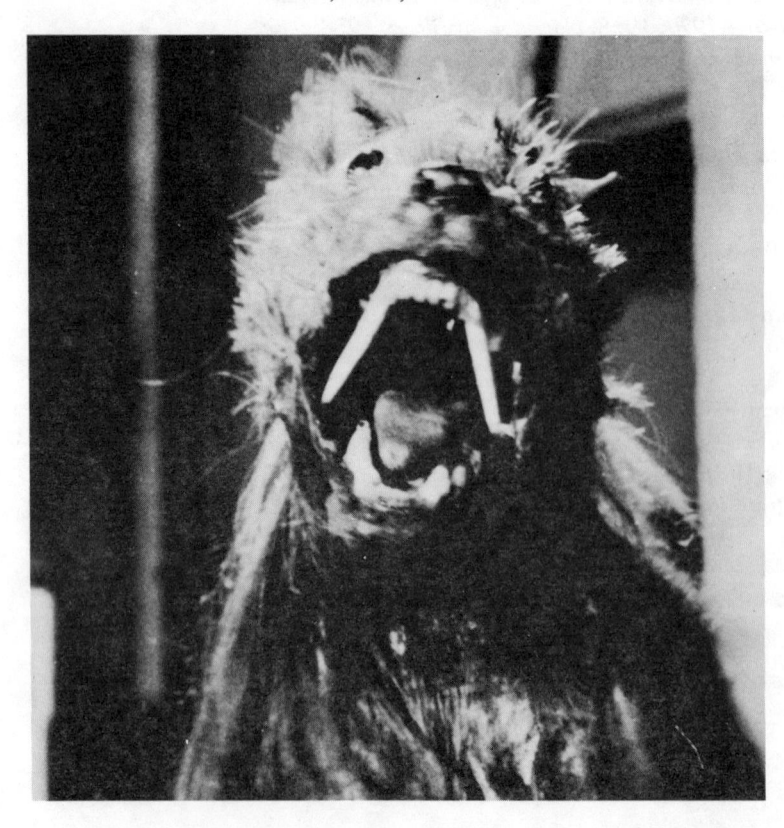

Mutant carnivores run wild in Ray Kellogg's *The Killer Shrews* (1959).

Kenney, June (ca. 1938–). Blonde adolescent lead of the fifties. *The Saga of the Viking Women and Their Voyage to the Waters of the Great Sea Serpent*, 1957; *Attack of the Puppet People*, 1958; *Earth vs. the Spider*, 1958; *Bloodlust*, 1961.

Kenton, Earle C. (1896–1980). American director of B-pictures who displayed a talent for making sense of implausible scripts and whose *Island of Lost Souls*, 1933, is perhaps the most atmospheric and purely frightening Hollywood film of the thirties. *The Ghost of Frankenstein*, 1942; *House of Frankenstein*, 1945; *House of Dracula*, 1945; *The Cat Creeps*, 1946.

Kerr, Deborah (1921–). Highly attractive British leading lady of intelligent appeal, notable as the disturbed governess in *The Innocents*, 1961. *Eye of the Devil*, 1967.

Ygor (Bela Lugosi) leads the monster (Lon Chaney, Jr.) through a graveyard in *The Ghost of Frankenstein* (1942), directed by Erle C. Kenton.

KEVAN, JACK. American makeup artist associated with BUD WESTMORE and Universal Studios in the fifties. *The Wizard of Oz* (designs for the Munchkins and miscellaneous residents of Oz; see also: JACK DAWN), 1939; *The Picture of Dorian Gray*, 1945; *Abbott and Costello Meet Dr. Jekyll and Mr. Hyde*, 1953; *The Creature from the Black Lagoon*, 1954; *Man of a Thousand Faces* (the LON CHANEY, SR. story), 1957; *Monster on the Campus*, 1958; *The Monster of Piedras Blancas* (and p), 1959; many others.

KIDDER, MARGOT (1948–). Slightly offbeat Canadian leading actress in Hollywood films of the seventies. *Sisters*, 1973; *The Reincarnation of Peter Proud*, 1975; *Superman* (as Lois Lane), 1978.

Jack Kevan's magnificent *Monster of Piedras Blancas* (1959).

KIEL, RICHARD (1939–). Giant American character actor who played monsters in low-budget quickies before finding modest fame as the villain Jaws in *The Spy Who Loved Me*, 1977. *Phantom Planet*, 1962; *The Magic Sword*, 1962; *Eegah!*, 1962; *House of the Damned*, 1963; *The Human Duplicators*, 1965; *A Man Called Dagger*, 1967; *Moonraker* (as Jaws), 1979; *The Humanoid* (title role), 1979; *The Phoenix*, 1979.

KIER, UDO (1944–). German actor associated with director PAUL MORRISSEY. *Mark of the Devil*, 1972; *Blood for Dracula* (as Dracula), 1974; *Andy Warhol's Frankenstein* (as Frankenstein), 1974; *Suspiria*, 1978.

KING, STEPHEN (1947–). Highly popular American horror novelist and short story writer who emerged in the early seventies. An outstanding talent, King has become a significant literary figure while maintaining a commitment to the horror genre. Works filmed: *Carrie* (from the novel), 1976; *Salem's Lot* (TV; from the novel; theatrical distribution in Europe), 1979; *The Shining* (from the novel), 1980.

Richard Kiel.

Udo Kier as Dracula in *Blood for Dracula* (1974).

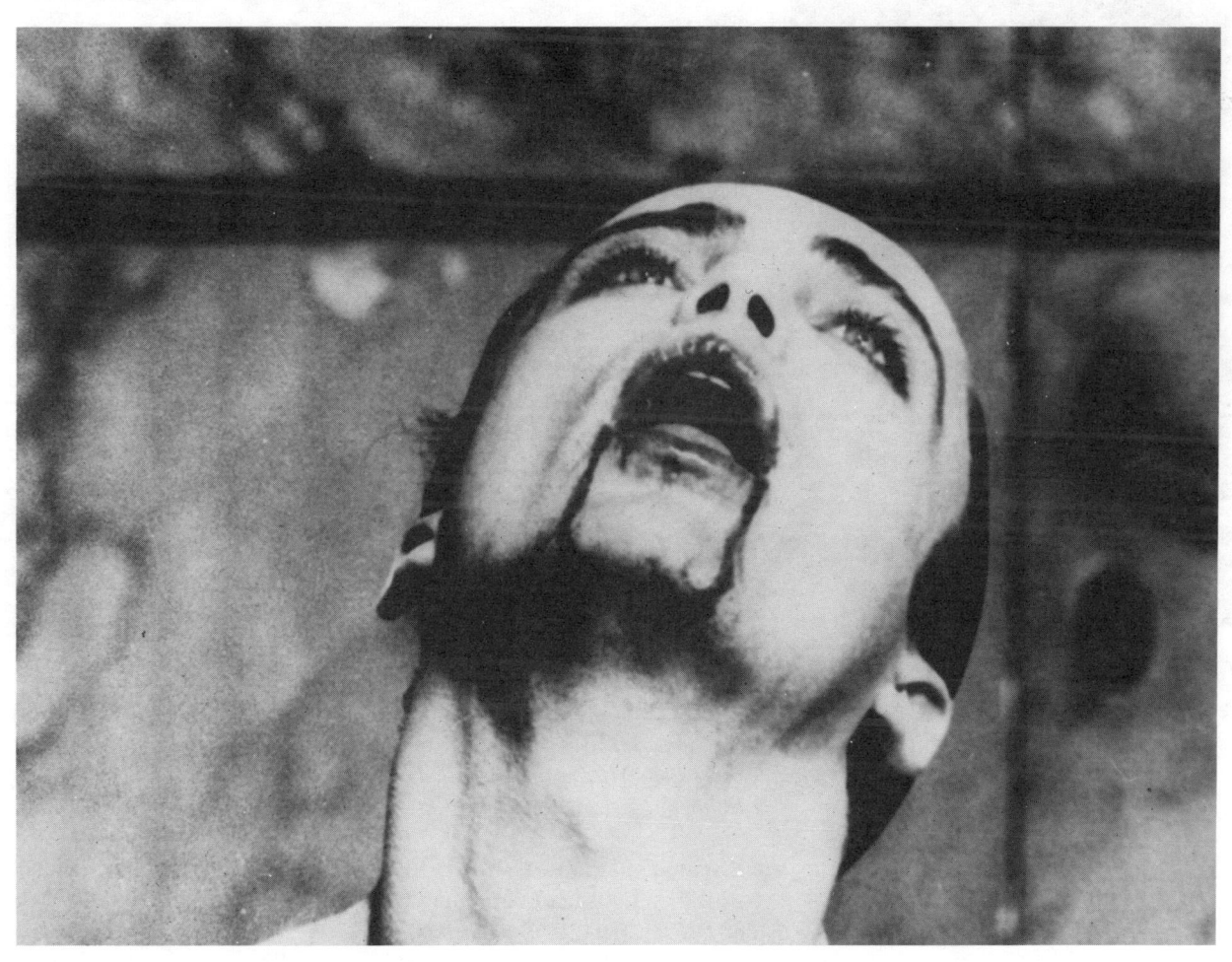

Sandra Knight *(right)* screams at the sight of *Frankenstein's Daughter* (1959). Harry Wilson plays the monster, and Donald Murphy *(far right)* the descendant of the original Dr. Frankenstein.

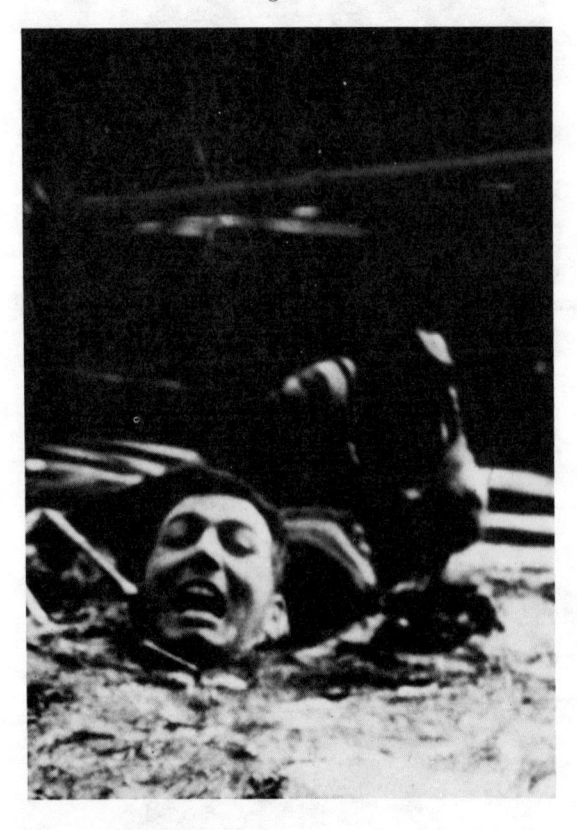

Michael Emmet is dragged to a watery grave in Bernard L. Kowalski's *Attack of The Giant Leeches* (1959).

KINGSTON, KIWI. Towering Australian wrestler who played the Monster in Hammer's *The Evil of Frankenstein*, 1964. Despite clownish makeup by ROY ASHTON, Kingston's performance successfully earns audience sympathy. *Hysteria*, 1965.

KIRK, TOMMY (1941–). American juvenile actor of the fifties, a onetime mainstay of WALT DISNEY movies who, after losing his youthful charm, appeared in a number of low-budget horror thrillers. *The Shaggy Dog*, 1959; *Babes in Toyland*, 1961; *Moon Pilot*, 1962; *Pajama Party* (SF-comedy), 1964; *The Misadventures of Merlin Jones*, 1964; *The Monkey's Uncle*, 1965; *Village of the Giants*, 1965; *It's Alive!*, 1968; *Blood of Ghastly Horror*, 1971.

KLEIN-ROGGE, RUDOLF (1889–1955). Commanding German character actor in silent films, outstanding as the demented genius Rotwang in FRITZ LANG's *Metropolis*, 1926. *Dr. Mabuse, The Gambler* (as Mabuse), 1922; *The Testament of Dr. Mabuse*, 1933.

KLIMOVSKY, LEON. Spanish director of gruesome, derivative vampire thrillers. *La Noche de Walpurgys*, 1970; *Revolt of the Dead Ones*, 1973; *The Vampires' Night Orgy*, 1974; *The Werewolf vs. the Vampire Woman*, 1974; *Vengeance of the Zombies*, 1975; numerous others.

KNAGGS, SKELTON (1911–55). Skinny British character actor in Hollywood Bs of the forties, usually cast as a myopic little weirdo. *The Ghost Ship*, 1943; *Isle of the Dead*, 1945; *House of Dracula*, 1945; *Dick Tracy Meets Gruesome*, 1947; *Master Minds*, 1949.

KNEALE, NIGEL (1922–). Talented British screenwriter who created the Quatermass serial for British television. *The Creeping Unknown* (from the Quatermass serial; original story only), 1956; *Enemy from Space* (co-w; w/VAL GUEST; b/o the television serial), 1957; *The Abominable Snowman of the Himalayas* (b/o Kneale's play, *The Creature*), 1957; *First Men in the Moon* (co-w; w/Jan Read), 1964; *The Devil's Own*, 1967; *Five Million Years to Earth*, 1967.

KNIGHT, SANDRA (CA. 1938–). Quiet American leading lady of the fifties and sixties, associated with American-International. *Frankenstein's Daughter*, 1959; *Tower of London*, 1962; *The Terror*, 1963; *Blood Bath*, 1966.

KNOTTS, DON (1924–). Skinny, hyper American comic actor, briefly a box office draw in the sixties after television success ("Andy Griffith Show," 1960–68; as Deputy Barney Fife). *The Incredible Mr. Limpet*, 1964; *The Ghost and Mr. Chicken*, 1966; *The Reluctant Astronaut*, 1967; *Gus*, 1976.

KNOWLES, PATRIC (1911–). Likeable British actor in Hollywood, usually a light leading man. *The Wolf Man*, 1941; *The Strange Case of Dr. Rx*, 1942; *Frankenstein Meets the Wolf Man*, 1943; *Dream Girl*, 1947; *Terror in the Wax Museum*, 1973.

KOMAI, TETSU (1894-1970). Japanese actor in Hollywood who played the obedient Dog-Man M'Ling in *Island of Lost Souls*, 1933. *The Return of Dr. Fu Manchu*, 1930; *Daughter of the Dragon*, 1931; *The Adventures of Captain Marvel*, 1941; *The Night Walker*, 1964.

KOSLECK, MARTIN (1907-). Russian character actor in American films, well cast as Nazis (especially Goebbels) during the war years. In his horror films, Kosleck is usually a brilliant but evil genius. *Daughter of Evil*, 1930; *The Mad Doctor*, 1941; *The Frozen Ghost*, 1945; *The Great Alaskan Mystery* (serial), 1944; *The Mummy's Curse*, 1945; *House of Horrors*, 1946; *The Flesh Eaters*, 1964.

KOVACK, NANCY (1935-). Fine-boned American leading lady of the sixties. *Diary of a Madman*, 1962; *Jason and the Argonauts* (as Medea), 1963; *The Silencers*, 1966; *Tarzan and the Valley of Gold*, 1966; *Marooned*, 1969.

KOWALSKI, BERNARD L. (1931-). American director most successful in television. *Night of the Blood Beast*, 1958; *Attack of the Giant Leeches*, 1959; *Sssssss*, 1973.

KRAMER, STANLEY (1913-). American producer/director whose projects have been marred by pretentious liberalism. *The 5000 Fingers of Dr. T* (p only), 1953; *On the Beach*, 1959.

KRAUSS, WERNER (1884-1959). Versatile German star character actor who played multiple roles in the infamous 1940 Nazi film *Jud Süss* and sowed the seeds of the postwar destruction of his career. He is memorable as the black-souled mesmerist Caligari in *The Cabinet of Dr. Caligari*, 1919. *Nacht Des Grauens*, 1916; *Waxworks*, 1924; *Secrets of a Soul*, 1925; *The Student of Prague*, 1926.

KRUGER, OTTO (1885-1974). American star character actor, often cast as a gentlemanly European. *Dracula's Daughter*, 1936; *Tarzan's Desert Mystery*, 1943; *Wonder Man*, 1945; *Jungle Captive*, 1945; *Escape in the Fog*, 1945; *The Woman Who Came Back*, 1945; *The Colossus of New York*, 1958; *The Wonderful World of the Brothers Grimm*, 1962.

Otto Kruger.

Werner Krauss *(left)*, with Conrad Veidt and Lil Dagover in *The Cabinet of Dr. Caligari* (1919).

The droogies rumble in *A Clockwork Orange*, Stanley Kubrick's stylized *tour de force* of 1971.

KUBRICK, STANLEY (1928–). Innovative and important American director active on both sides of the Atlantic. A highly diversified talent, Kubrick has defied pigeonholing, remaining an individualistic and highly committed artist. His *Dr. Strangelove or: How I Learned to Stop Worrying and Love the Bomb*, 1964, is perhaps the keenest black comedy ever filmed and surely the maddest look at man's gift for self-destruction. *2001: A Space Odyssey*, 1968, is Kubrick's best-known work and certainly his most ambitious; despite its lofty theme, it is sterile and lacking in humanity, though it provides an unparalleled visual feast. Kubrick's masterpiece is *A Clockwork Orange*, 1971, a stinging look at human violence and the deterioration of the quality of modern life, and an indictment of those whose solution is to make mind-slaves of offenders and victims alike. Cruelly funny, it is also one of the most sobering films of our time. *The Shining*, 1980.

The humans prepare to face the secret of the universe in Stanley Kubrick's *2001: A Space Odyssey* (1968).

KULKY, HENRY (1911–65). Bulky professional wrestler (known as Bomber Kulkavich) and actor, usually seen as a surly tough guy. *Tarzan's Magic Fountain*, 1948; *Mighty Joe Young* (as himself; in the tug-of-war sequence, with PRIMO CARNERA, The Swedish Angel, et al), 1949; *The 5000 Fingers of Dr. T*, 1953; *Tobor the Great*, 1954. Kulky later became a regular on television's "Voyage to the Bottom of the Sea," 1964–65.

L

LACHMAN, HARRY (1886–1975). British director in Hollywood from 1933. *Dante's Inferno*, 1935; *The Man Who Lived Twice*, 1936; *Castle in the Desert*, 1942; *The Loves of Edgar Allan Poe*, 1942; *Dr. Renault's Secret*, 1942.

LACKTEEN, FRANK (1894–1968). Cadaverously gaunt Hollywood character actor of Asian birth, familiarly cast as Orientals, jungle chieftains, and sinister hoods. *Jungle Mystery*, 1932; *Tarzan the*

Henry Kulky.

The man who made lowbrow comedy high art: Bert Lahr as the Cowardly Lion in *The Wizard of Oz* (1939).

138 LADD

Fearless, 1933; *Mummy's Boys*, 1936; *The Mummy's Hand*, 1940; *A Bird in the Head* (two-reeler), 1946; *The Underwater City*, 1962; others.

LADD, ALAN (1913–64). Blonde and aloof American leading man, a popular tough hero throughout the forties and fifties. Early in his career, Ladd appeared in *Island of Lost Souls* (unbilled; as a Manimal), 1933; *The Green Hornet*, 1940; *The Black Cat*, 1941; *The Reluctant Dragon*, 1941.

LAHR, BERT (1895–1968). Delightfully lowbrow American vaudeville and film entertainer whose endearing Cowardly Lion in *The Wizard of Oz*, 1939, is film folklore.

LAKE, VERONICA (1919–73). Seductive and engaging American leading lady of the forties, famous for her downswept blonde hair and come-hither look. A delight in *I Married a Witch*, 1942, Lake lost vogue soon after and slipped into obscurity. Her final film (which she produced) is *Flesh Feast*, 1970, which trade ads trumpeted as "Winner of the Golden Maggot Award for Boxoffice Excellence."

LAMONT, CHARLES (1898–). American director who specialized in unimaginative, lowbrow comedies. *Techno-Crazy* (short), 1933; *Abbott and Costello Meet the Invisible Man*, 1951; *Abbott and Costello Go to Mars*, 1953; *Abbott and Costello Meet Dr. Jekyll and Mr. Hyde*, 1953; *Abbott and Costello Meet the Mummy*, 1955; *Francis in the Haunted House*, 1956.

LANCASTER, BURT (1913–). Rugged American leading man who moved into character roles in middle age. In 1977 he took the title role in the competent but uninspired *Island of Dr. Moreau*, a remake of *Island of Lost Souls*, 1933.

LANCELOT, SIR. American black actor of the forties and fifties. *I Walked with a Zombie*, 1943; *The Ghost Ship*, 1943; *The Curse of the Cat People*, 1944; *The Unknown Terror*, 1957.

LANCHESTER, ELSA (1902–). Eccentric and unique British character actress active in Hollywood, widow of CHARLES LAUGHTON. Horror fans are still fascinated by Lanchester's twitchy and screamy *Bride of Frankenstein* (in which she also played MARY SHELLEY), 1935. *The Ghost Goes West*, 1936; *Bell, Book and Candle* (delightful as a fluttery Greenwich Village witch), 1958; *Pajama Party* (sf-comedy), 1964; *Willard*, 1971; *Terror in the Wax Museum*, 1973.

LANDERS, LEW (1901–62). Prolific American director of low-budget westerns and thrillers. *The Raven* (credited as Louis Friedlander), 1935; *The Boogie Man Will Get You*, 1942; *The Return of the Vampire*, 1944; *The Enchanted Forest*, 1945; *Shadow of Terror*, 1945; *The Power of the Whistler*, 1945; *Hurricane Island*, 1951; *Aladdin and His Lamp*, 1952; *Terrified*, 1963.

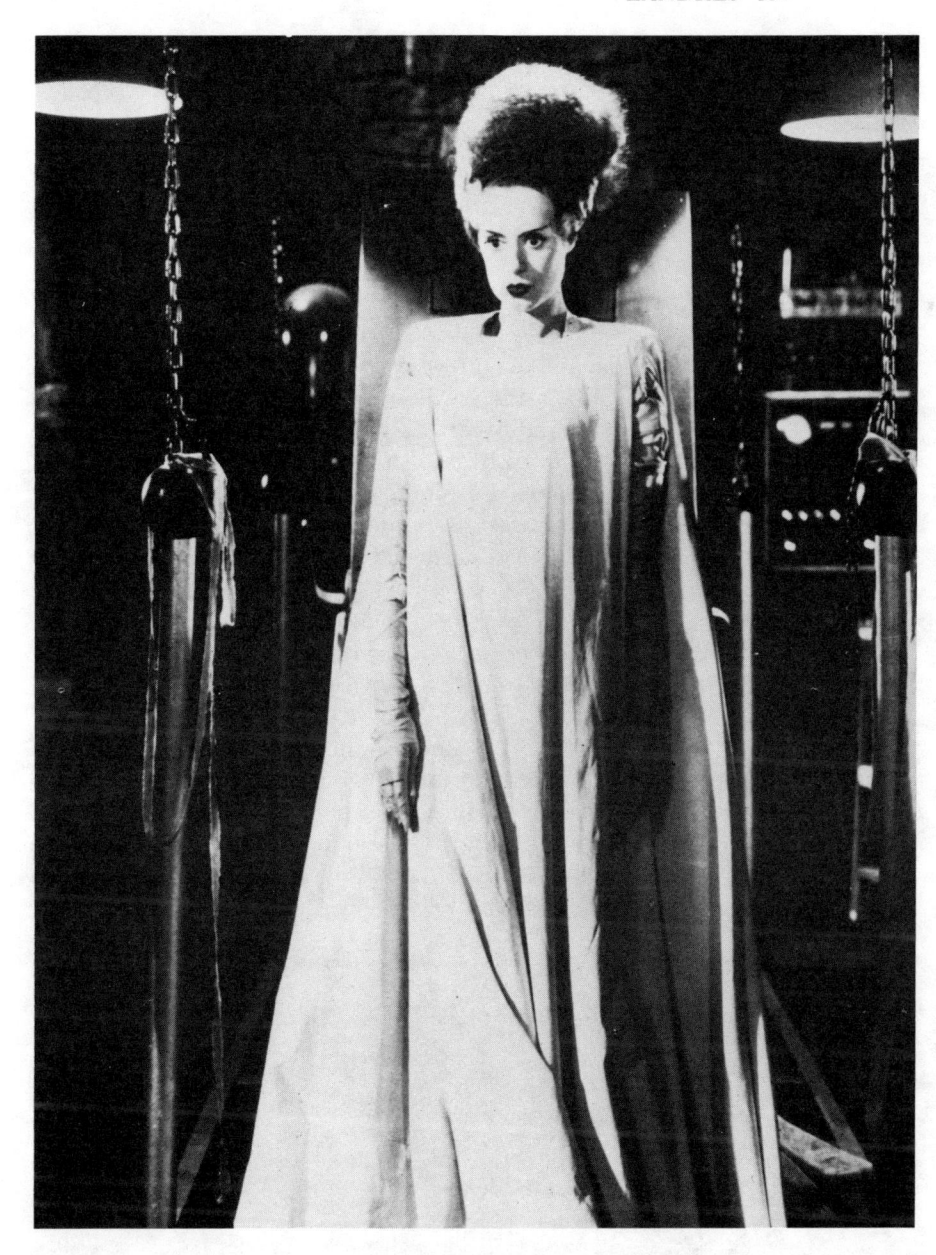

Elsa Lanchester as *The Bride of Frankenstein* (1935).

LANDIS, JOHN (CA. 1951–). American filmmaker who wrote, directed, and starred in *Schlock 73*, an amusing spoof of movie clichés which involves a resurrected ape-man. *Kentucky Fried Movie*, 1978. *The Incredible Shrinking Woman*, 1980.

LANDON, MICHAEL (1937–). Youthful American actor who did some film work before leaving for the bigger and better bonanzas offered by television. Remembered as the title unfortunate in *I Was a Teenage Werewolf*, 1957.

LANDRES, PAUL (1912–). American director who brought some style to B-films of the fifties. *The Vampire*, 1957; *Return of Dracula*, 1958; *The Flame Barrier*, 1958.

The first plutonium bomb claims its first victim: Glenn Langan as *The Amazing Colossal Man* (1957).

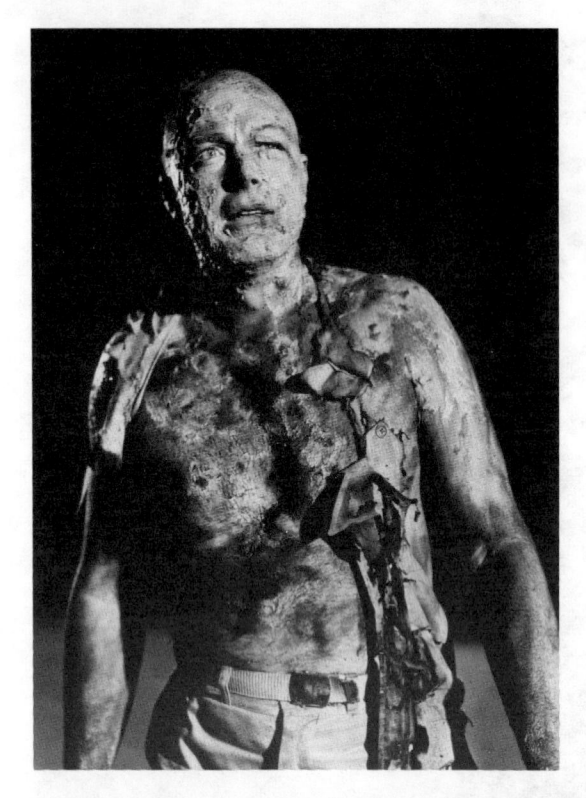

LANE, BEN. American makeup artist most active in television who created GUY ROLFE's hideous rictus grin for *Mr. Sardonicus*, 1961. *Homicidal*, 1961.

LANE, VICKY. Tall American actress who played the ape woman in *Jungle Captive*, 1945, after ACQUANETTA grew tired of such unladylike roles.

LANG, FRITZ (1890–1976). German director who enjoyed success in the United States as well as Germany. His films are taut and uncompromising and often reveal a cynical view of human nature. In *Metropolis*, 1926, Lang created unforgettable images of dispirited workers toiling beneath a great city, and with *M*, 1931, a brilliant and multilevel story of a child murderer (PETER LORRE), he offered one of the finest filmic studies of psychomania. Recurring themes in Lang's works include revenge, lynch law, and responsibility for one's misdeeds. *Hilda Warren and Death* (actor only; cast as Death), 1916; *Die Goldene See* (*The Spiders*), 1919; *Destiny*, 1921; *Dr. Mabuse, the Gambler*, 1922; *Siegfried*, 1925; *Die Frau im Mond* (*The Girl in the Moon*), 1929; *The Testament of Dr. Mabuse*, 1933; *The Thousand Eyes of Dr. Mabuse*, 1960.

LANGAN, GLENN (1917–). American juvenile actor and light leading man of the thirties and forties who, after maturity, slid into inferior second features. He gives a notable and thoughtful performance in BERT I. GORDON's overambitious but interesting *The Amazing Colossal Man*, 1957. *The Return of Dr. X*, 1939; *Mutiny in Outer Space*, 1965.

Charles Laughton is taken to the House of Pain by the Manimals he has created in *Island of Lost Souls* (1933).

LANSING, JOI (1930–72). Baby-faced blonde bombshell of the fifties, one of the more appealing Marilyn Monroe acolytes. *The Atomic Submarine*, 1960; *Hillbillys in a Haunted House*, 1967; *Bigfoot*, 1971.

LA PLANTE, LAURA (1904–). American leading lady of the twenties, notable as the girl menaced by the fiend in *The Cat and the Canary*, 1928. *The Last Warning*, 1929.

LAUGHTON, CHARLES (1899–1962). Gifted British star character actor, a unique personality who was at his best playing plump prigs. His Dr. Moreau in *Island of Lost Souls*, 1933, is among the most repulsively evil characters in screen history. Long married to actress ELSA LANCHESTER. *The Old Dark House*, 1932; *The Hunchback of Notre Dame* (title role), 1939; *The Canterville Ghost*, 1944; *The Strange Door*, 1951.

LAUREL, STAN (1890–1965). Reedy, long-faced British comic who teamed with OLIVER HARDY in Hollywood and entered legend. Always the creative thrust behind the team, Laurel elevated slapstick to high art. His whimpering, chronically confused persona is remembered with affection the world over. Unsurpassed in their era or any other, Stan and Ollie made gem after gem, many with fantastic content. *Flying Elephants*, 1927; *Habeas Corpus*, 1928; *Brats*, 1930; *The Laurel and Hardy Murder Case*, 1930; *Babes in Toyland* aka *March of the Wooden Soldiers*, 1934; *A Chump at Oxford* (the team's last great feature; Stanley cracks his head against a window and becomes Oxford's long-lost genius, Lord Paddington), 1940; *A-Haunting We Will Go*, 1942; *Atoll K* aka *Utopia*; *Robinson Crusoeland* (their final film), 1951.

The pure wonderfulness of Stan Laurel.

Stan Laurel, Oliver Hardy, and a very large pussycat in a scene from *Babes in Toyland* (1934).

LAURIE, PIPER (1932–). American leading lady of the fifties who had an unrewarding time of it, *e.g. Son of Ali Baba*, 1952, but who came back in the seventies as a good-looking character actress. She makes a stunning impression as the fanatically religious mother of *Carrie*, 1976, and took the title role in *Ruby*, 1977.

LAUTER, HARRY (1925–). American general purpose actor of the fifties, star of the last (and non-fantastic) Republic serial, *King of the Carnival*, 1955. *Zamba, The Gorilla*, 1949; *Flying Disc Man from Mars*, 1950; *The Day the Earth Stood Still*, 1951; *It Came from Beneath the Sea*, 1955; *Earth vs. the Flying Saucers*, 1956; *Tarzan's Fight for Life*, 1958; many others.

LAW, JOHN PHILIP (1936–). Woodenly handsome American leading man of the sixties and seventies. *Barbarella* (as the Angel), 1968; *Danger: Diabolik* (as Diabolik), 1968; *The Golden Voyage of Sinbad* (as Sinbad), 1973.

LAWRENCE, MARC (1910–). Pockmarked and dark-eyed American character actor, cast since the early thirties as sinister hoods. *Trapped by Television*, 1936; *Beware, Spooks*, 1939; *Charlie Chan at the Wax Museum* (in his element among the figures of infamous criminal fiends), 1940; *The Monster and the Girl*, 1941; *Hold That Ghost*, 1941; *Krakatoa East of Java*, 1969; *Diamonds Are Forever*, 1971; *The Man with the Golden Gun*, 1974; others.

LAZENBY, GEORGE (1939–). Australian leading man given much publicity as the new James Bond when SEAN CONNERY temporarily bowed out in 1969. Lazenby's conception of the spy in *On Her Majesty's Secret Service* is agreeable. He and film were rather unfairly trounced by critics; Lazenby's career has been all but dormant since. *Kentucky Fried Movie*, 1978.

LEAKEY, PHIL. British makeup artist who created the mangled face of the Monster in *The Curse of Frankenstein*, 1957. Garish-seeming in photographs, the design works well on film, due in large part to the playing of CHRISTOPHER LEE, the actor obscured beneath the latex scar tissue. *Room to Let*, 1950; *The Creeping Unknown*, 1956; *The Revenge of Frankenstein*, 1958; *The Horror of Dracula*, 1958; *The Eyes of Annie Jones*, 1964; *Old Dracula* aka *Vampira*, 1975; others.

LE BORG, REGINALD (1902–). American second feature director. *Calling Dr. Death*, 1943; *Weird Woman*, 1944; *The Mummy's Ghost*, 1944; *The Black Sleep*, 1956; *Voodoo Island*, 1957; *Diary of a Madman*, 1963; *The Eyes of Annie Jones*, 1964; *House of the Black Death* (second unit director), 1965; etc.

LEDERER, FRANCIS (1906–). Character actor of Czechoslovakian extraction, in American films from 1933. In *Return of Dracula*, 1958, Lederer pursues his victims in modern-day California; with his padded overcoat, sly smile, and slicked hair, his Dracula resembles a fanged Tony Curtis. Also *Terror Is a Man*, 1959.

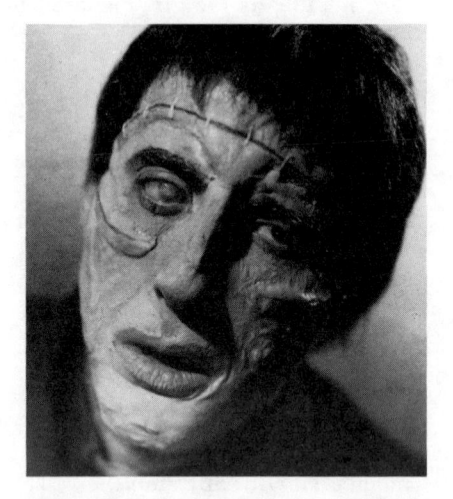

Christopher Lee as the Monster in *The Curse of Frankenstein* (1957); makeup by Phil Leakey.

Francis Lederer and the shocking conclusion of *The Return of Dracula* (1958).

LEE, BERNARD (1909–). British character actor, familiar in every James Bond thriller since *Dr. No*, 1962, as M, Bond's uncommonly patient superior. *The Terror*, 1938; *Dr. Terror's House of Horrors*, 1964; *Frankenstein and the Monster from Hell*, 1973.

LEE, CHRISTOPHER (1922–). Lean, towering British character actor, well known as Dracula in numerous films from 1958. His conception of the vampire count in *The Horror of Dracula*, 1958, is the first to stress the character's inherent sexuality, and Lee has become the only horror actor since BELA LUGOSI to have a fervent female following. After finally tiring of Dracula and similar roles in the early seventies, Lee began turning his talents to mainstream roles. An actor of great capability and presence, he is on the verge of fully realizing his talent. *Corridor of Mirrors*, 1948; *The Curse of Frankenstein* (as the Monster), 1957; *Corridors of Blood*, 1958; *The Hound of the Baskervilles* (as Sir Henry Baskerville), 1959; *The Mummy* (as Kharis, the Mummy), 1959; *The Man Who Could Cheat Death*, 1959; *Horror Hotel* (as Professor Driscoll), 1960; *The Two Faces of Dr. Jekyll*, 1960; *Les Mains d'Orlac* (*The Hands of Orlac*), 1960; *Uncle Was a Vampire*, 1960; *Scream of Fear*, 1961; *Hercules in the Haunted World*, 1961; *Terror in the Crypt*, 1963; *Castle of the Living Dead*, 1964; *The Gorgon*, 1964; *Dr. Terror's House of Horrors*, 1964; *She*, 1965; *What!*, 1965; *Horror Castle*, 1965; *The Face of Fu Manchu* (as Fu Manchu), 1965; *The Skull*, 1965; *Dracula, Prince of Darkness*, 1966; *Rasputin, The Mad Monk* (title role), 1966; *The Brides of Fu Manchu*, 1966; *Psycho-Circus*, 1967; *Blood Demon*, 1967; *Island of the Burning Damned*, 1967; *Blood Fiend*, 1968; *Vengeance of Fu Manchu*, 1968; *The Devil's Bride*, 1968; *The Castle of Fu Manchu*, 1968; *The Crimson Cult*, 1968; *Kiss and Kill* (as Fu Manchu), 1969; *The Oblong Box*, 1969; *Dracula Has Risen from the Grave*, 1969; *Eugenie—The Story of Her Journey into Perversion*, 1970; *Scream and Scream Again*, 1970; *Scars of Dracula*, 1970; *Count Dracula*, 1970; *Taste the Blood of Dracula*, 1970; *The House That Dripped Blood*, 1971; *I, Monster*, 1971; *In Search of Dracula* (TV; as Vlad the Impaler), 1971; *Night of the Blood Monster*, 1972; *Dracula A.D. 1972*, 1972; *Horror Express*, 1972; *The Creeping Flesh*, 1972; *Nothing but the Night* (and executive p), 1972; *The Wicker Man*, 1973; *The Satanic Rites of Dracula*, 1973; *Raw Meat*, 1973; *Poor Devil* (TV; as Lucifer), 1973; *The Man with The Golden Gun* (as Scaramanga), 1974; *To the Devil . . . A Daughter*, 1976; *End of the World*, 1977; *Hollywood Meatcleaver Massacre* (an inexplicable prologue appearance), 1977; *Starship Invasions*, 1977; *Return from Witch Mountain*, 1978; *Arabian Adventure*, 1979.

LEE, ROWLAND V. (1891–1975). American director whose *Son of Frankenstein*, 1939, is the most heavily Germanic film of the Universal Frankenstein series. *The Mysterious Dr. Fu Manchu*, 1929; *The Return of Dr. Fu Manchu*, 1930; *Tower of London* (and p), 1939.

Christopher Lee as Dracula, the role that made him world famous; *The Horror of Dracula* (1958).

Christopher Lee as Dracula rings in a new victim in *Dracula Has Risen from the Grave* (1969).

LEIGH, JANET (1927–). American leading lady of the fifties and sixties whose grisly fate in *Psycho*, 1960, kept theater-goers out of the shower stall. *Night of the Lepus*, 1972; *The Fog*, 1980.

LENI, PAUL (1885–1929). German expressionist director. *Three Wax Men*, 1924; *The Chinese Parrot*, 1927; *The Cat and the Canary*, 1928; *The Man Who Laughs*, 1928; *The Last Warning*, 1929.

LESSER, SOL (1890–). American executive who produced the Hollywood Tarzan films from 1943 to 1958. *Tarzan Triumphs*, 1943; *Tarzan and the Leopard Woman*, 1946; *Tarzan's Peril*, 1951; *Tarzan and the She-Devil*, 1954; *Tarzan's Hidden Jungle*, 1955; *Tarzan and the Trappers*, 1958; others. See also: LEX BARKER, GORDON SCOTT, JOHNNY WEISMULLER.

LESTER, MARK (1958–). British child actor of the sixties, sometimes just too saccharine. *Spaceflight IC-1*, 1965; *Our Mother's House*, 1967; *Night Hair Child* (as the young sexual psychopath), 1971; *Whoever Slew Auntie Roo?*, 1971.

LEVIN, HENRY (1909–). Slick American director who brought bright charm to *The Wonderful World of the Brothers Grimm* (co-d; w/GEORGE PAL), 1962. *Cry of the Werewolf*, 1944; *Journey to the Center of the Earth*, 1959; *Murderer's Row*, 1966; *The Ambushers*, 1967.

Will the policeman see the parcel of stolen money? Janet Leigh and Mort Mills in a brilliant but little-discussed scene from Alfred Hitchcock's *Psycho* (1960).

LEVIN, IRA (1929–). American potboiler novelist whose *Rosemary's Baby* was beautifully filmed by ROMAN POLANSKI in 1968. Levin's rather simplistic themes are broadened and expanded, creating a riveting chronicle of the vulnerable girl who is carrying Satan's child. BRYAN FORBES' *The Stepford Wives*, 1974, concerns a town in which the men are replacing their wives with androids. It is an adaptation of another Levin novel and fails by exploiting only the most obvious aspects of the book and distorting them into clownish leitmotifs. Forbes' film is structurally similar to Polanski's, but it is more absurd than chilling. *The Boys from Brazil* (b/o his novel), 1978.

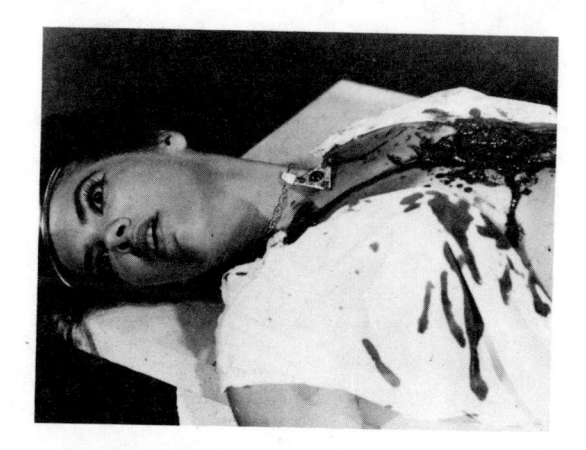

LEWIS, HERSCHELL GORDON (1926–). American producer/director/screenwriter and full-time ad man who progressed from innocuous nudies to horror shockers featuring dismemberment, eye gouging, impalement, and cannibalism. A former professor of English, Lewis makes his films on infinitesimal budgets and with buckets of blood. His *Blood Feast*, 1963, is perhaps the most infamous American film of the sixties. *Two Thousand Maniacs*, 1964; *Monster a Go-Go*, 1965; *Color Me Blood Red*, 1965; *The Gruesome Twosome*, 1967; *A Taste of Blood*, 1967; *Something Weird*, 1968; *She-Devils on Wheels*, 1968; *The Wizard of Gore* (p and d only), 1971; *The Gore-Gore Girls*, 1972.

One of the calmer moments from Herschell Gordon Lewis's amazing gore film *Blood Feast* (1963).

LEWIS, JERRY (1926–). Mugging American comic actor and director, a onetime partner of DEAN MARTIN who dissipated his considerable talent in increasingly undisciplined vehicles. In his early films, Lewis is nicely offset by Martin but as a solo he descends into mawkishness and embarrassing self-indulgence. The pity is that Lewis possesses a fine comic mind and an often-outstanding flair for visual humor, and that with strong direction, could have become as great as the French always said he was. Among his funniest (and least uneven) films is *The Nutty Professor*, 1964, a spoof of the Jekyll/Hyde story in which Hyde is incarnated as supercool swinger Buddy Love. Egotistical and self-centered, the character suggests the elements of Lewis' own decline. *Scared Stiff*, 1953; *Visit to a Small Planet* (as a visitor from outer space), 1960.

Dean Martin and Jerry Lewis in a publicity shot from *Scared Stiff* (1953).

Herbert Lom.

LEWIS, JOSEPH H. (1900–). Talented American second feature director, best known for a tight and thoughtful crime thriller from 1950, *Gun Crazy*. He brought his flair for evocative visuals to *The Invisible Ghost*, 1941, and *The Mad Doctor of Market Street*, 1942.

LEWIS, SHELDON (1869–1958). American character actor of the teens and twenties who took the title role in *Dr. Jekyll and Mr. Hyde*, 1916. *The Iron Claw*, 1916; *The Hidden Hand* (serial), 1917–18; *Seven Footprints to Satan*, 1929; *The Monster Walks*, 1932.

LEWTON, VAL (1904–51). American producer active at RKO throughout the forties, whose good taste and canny business sense led him to success with a series of modest but effective horror thrillers, many directed by JACQUES TOURNEUR. *The Cat People*, 1942; *The Leopard Man*, 1943; *The Curse of the Cat People*, 1944; *The Body Snatcher*, 1945; *Isle of the Dead*, 1945; *Bedlam*, 1946.

LILJEDAHL, MARIE (CA. 1952–). Swedish actress in fanciful skin films of the early seventies. *Eugenie—The Story of Her Journey into Perversion*, 1970; *The Secret of Dorian Gray*, 1971; *Grimm's Fairy Tales for Adults*, 1971.

LINCOLN, ELMO (1889–1952). Barrel-chested American actor of the silent era who was the first screen incarnation of EDGAR RICE BURROUGH'S *Tarzan of the Apes*, 1918. *The Romance of Tarzan*, 1918; *The Flaming Disk*, 1920; *The Adventures of Tarzan*, 1921; *The Hunchback of Notre Dame* (bit part), 1923; *King of the Jungle* (not a Tarzan film), 1927.

LIPPERT, ROBERT L. (1909–). American independent producer and distributor. *Rocketship X-M*, 1950; *Radar Secret Service*, 1950; *Lost Continent*, 1951; *Unknown World*, 1951; *Superman and the Mole Men*, 1951; *Highly Dangerous*, 1951; *Project Moonbase*, 1953; *Ghost Ship*, 1953; *King Dinosaur*, 1955; others.

LOCKWOOD, GARY (1937–). American leading man of film and television. *The Magic Sword*, 1962; *2001: A Space Odyssey*, 1968.

LOM, HERBERT (1917–). Accomplished British actor of Czech extraction whose best roles have been as grotesque eccentrics. He is as skilled at depicting dark villainy as with humor. *Mysterious Island* (as Nemo), 1961; *The Phantom of the Opera* (title role), 1962; *Journey to the Far Side of the Sun*, 1969; *Vampyr*, 1970; *Count Dracula*, 1970; *Murders in the Rue Morgue*, 1971; *Asylum*, 1972; *And Now the Screaming Starts*, 1973; *The Pink Panther Strikes Again* (as Dreyfus), 1976.

LONG, RICHARD (1927–74). Suave and smiling American leading man, popular on television. Married to actress MARA CORDAY. *Cult of the Cobra*, 1955; *House on Haunted Hill*, 1958.

LOOMIS, NANCY (CA. 1955–). Dark-haired American actress of the eighties, associated with director JOHN CARPENTER and best seen as cheeky adolescents. *Halloween*, 1979; *The Fog*, 1980.

LORRE, PETER (1904–64). Unique Hungarian star character actor whose silky, accented voice, small stature, and soft, jaded eyes kept him in demand for more than thirty years. Usually appearing as a man with something to hide when not an out-and-out villain, Lorre possessed a commanding screen presence and could steal scenes from even the likes of BORIS KARLOFF. After triumphing as the psychotic child killer in FRITZ LANG's *M* in 1931, Lorre filmed in Germany and Britain and came to Hollywood in 1935, where he played a variety of roles, gaining popularity as star of the fast-moving Mr. Moto series, 1937–39. A sensitive performance in ROBERT FLOREY's *The Face behind the Mask*, 1941, as a hideously-scarred but good-hearted immigrant who becomes involved with criminals, led to an appearance as the prissy but dangerous Joel Cairo in John Huston's *The Maltese Falcon*, 1941. Lorre subsequently joined the stable of Warners stars and for the next half-dozen years played sadistic Nazis, comic crazies, and unorthodox heroes. Illness in the early fifties precipitated a weight problem, and his film roles became routine. ROGER CORMAN's POE adaptations of the early sixties gave Lorre an opportunity to reaffirm his affinity with the macabre. His popularity was steadily gaining when he died in early 1964 of complications caused by high blood pressure. One of Hollywood's truly irreplaceable personalities, Lorre continues to be a popular star. *F.P. 1* aka *Floating Platform 1 Does Not Answer*, 1933; *Mad Love*, 1935; *Island of Doomed Men*, 1940; *Stranger on the Third Floor*, 1940; *You'll Find Out*, 1940; *Invisible Agent*, 1942; *The Boogie Man Will Get You*, 1942; *Arsenic and Old Lace* (as Dr. Einstein), 1944; *The Beast with Five Fingers*, 1946; *Der Verlorene* (*The Lost One*; and d), 1951; *20,000 Leagues under the Sea*, 1954; *The Story of Mankind*, 1957; *Voyage to the Bottom of the Sea*, 1961; *Five Weeks in a Balloon*, 1962; *Tales of Terror*, 1962; *The Raven*, 1963; *The Comedy of Terrors*, 1963.

The irreplaceable Peter Lorre in character as Mr. Moto, 1939.

Peter Lorre in 1964, near the end of his life.

Eugene Lourie's *Gorgo* (1961).

LOURIE, EUGENE (CA. 1905–). French set designer who turned to direction in the United States and Britain. *The Beast from 20,000 Fathoms*, 1953; *The Colossus of New York*, 1958; *The Giant Behemoth* (co-d; w/Douglas Hickok; and w), 1959; *Gorgo*, 1961.

LOVECRAFT, HOWARD PHILLIPS (1890–1937). Reclusive and somewhat mysterious American writer whose stories of cosmic horror have tempted filmmakers for years without inspiring many actual films. His florid writing style is difficult to adapt, and the visualization of the more horrific elements in his works may not make for convincing drama. Television has adapted stories like "Pickman's Model" and "Cool Air" with some success, but only two notable theatrical films have been based on Lovecraft's work. *Die Monster Die!*, 1965, is based on *The Colour Out of Space* and has its moments, but 1970's *The Dunwich Horror* falls flat. ROGER CORMAN'S *The Haunted Palace*, 1963, was, in part, inspired by Lovecraft's *The Case of Charles Dexter Ward*.

LOWERY, ROBERT (1914–71). Heavy-eyed American actor who appears as a rather baggy Batman in *Batman and Robin*, 1949, a lackluster Columbia serial. *Tarzan's Desert Mystery*, 1943; *Revenge of the Zombies*, 1943; *The Mummy's Ghost*, 1944; *The Monster and the Ape*, 1945; *House of Horrors*, 1946; *The Undertaker and His Pals*, 1967.

LUBIN, ARTHUR (1901–). Prolific American director of broad comedy and heavy melodrama, active since the thirties. *Black Friday*, 1940; *Hold That Ghost*, 1941; *The Phantom of the Opera*, 1943; *Ali Baba and the Forty Thieves*, 1944; *The Spider Woman Strikes Back*, 1946; *Francis* (the talking mule), 1949; *Francis Goes to the Races*, 1951; *Francis Goes to West Point*, 1952; *It Grows on Trees*, 1952; *Francis in the Navy*, 1955; *Il Ladro di Bagdad* (*The Thief of Bagdad*), 1960; *The Incredible Mr. Limpet*, 1964.

An Imperial Stormtrooper attacks in George Lucas's epic *Star Wars* (1977).

LUCAN, ARTHUR (1887–1954). Lowbrow British comic actor and music hall entertainer, long popular in the provinces as Old Mother Riley, a vulgar Irish washerwoman. *Old Mother Riley Meets the Vampire*, 1952, is a shambles but features BELA LUGOSI and was distributed in the United States in 1964 as *My Son, The Vampire*. *Old Mother Riley's Ghosts*, 1941; *Jungle Treasure*, 1951. Appearing in the films as Old Mother Riley's daughter was Lucan's wife, Kitty McShane (1898–1964).

LUCAS, GEORGE (1945–). American director whose *Star Wars*, 1977, was one of the big pop hits of the seventies. *Thx 1138*, 1971; *The Empire Strikes Back* (executive p only), 1980.

Bela Lugosi in the early 1940s.

LUGOSI, BELA (1882-1956). Hungarian star character actor in Hollywood from 1923, whose 1931 interpretation of Dracula has become one of the screen world's most familiar and popular personae. The role of the elegant vampire count made Lugosi a star in America after his reign as a matinee idol of the Hungarian stage. But it was his undoing as well. His unwillingness to perfect his command of English and a marked carelessness with money led him to dubious roles in many minor films, often as a mere red herring in bland murder mysteries. To the public, Lugosi and Dracula were synonymous, and the resultant typecasting depressed him. Outside the horror genre, his roles were noticeable but small (e.g. *Ninotchka*, 1939), and even these dried up in the forties. A proud and jealous man, Lugosi struggled through rocky marriages and a steady chipping at his ego. A splendid appearance as Dracula in *Abbott and Costello Meet Frankenstein*, 1948, bolstered his badly sagging career (his agent had to plead to secure the part for him), but only temporarily. In 1955, Lugosi voluntarily hospitalized himself for treatment of drug addiction; great pain in his legs had led him to take morphine, and his dependence on it lasted for two decades. A sickly skeleton when committed (photographs from this period are truly shocking), Lugosi emerged in good shape four months later. Then seventy-two, he was anxious to resume his career and secured roles in a number of wretched, low-budget films that, if nothing else, put his name and image back before the public. The sale of his older films to television had produced a new generation of fans, and he was finding some success in personal appearances. Gratified and hopeful, Lugosi was on the verge of regaining his enormous popularity when he died at his modest Hollywood apartment in August 1956. Lugosi is now secure in his position as one of Hollywood's immortal star images. *Az Elet Kiralya* (*The Royal Life* aka *The Picture of Dorian Gray*), 1917; *Der Januskopf* (b/o STEVENSON's *Dr. Jekyll and Mr. Hyde*; Lugosi cast as Jekyll's butler), 1920; *The Thirteenth Chair*, 1929; *Murders in the Re Morgue*, 1932; *White Zombie*, 1932; *Chandu, The Magician* (as Roxor), 1932; *Island of Lost Souls* (as the Sayer of the Law), 1933; *The Whispering Shadow* (serial), 1933; *International House*, 1933; *Night of Terror*, 1933; *The Black Cat*, 1934; *The Return of Chandu* (serial; cast as Chandu), 1934; *The Mysterious Mr. Wong* (as Wong), 1935; *Murder by Television*, 1935; *Mark of the Vampire*, 1935; *The Raven* (as Dr. Vollin), 1935; *The Invisible Ray*, 1936; *Shadow of Chinatown* (serial), 1936; *The Phantom Ship* aka *The Mystery of the Marie Celeste*, 1937; *Son of Frankenstein* (as Ygor), 1939; *The Gorilla*, 1939; *The Phantom Creeps* (serial), 1939; *Human Monster*, 1940; *Black Friday*, 1940; *The Devil Bat*, 1940; *The Invisible Ghost*, 1941; *The Black Cat*, 1941; *Spooks Run Wild*, 1941; *The Wolf Man* (as Bela, the fortune-teller), 1941; *Black Dragons*, 1942; *The Ghost of Frankenstein* (as Ygor), 1942; *The Corpse Vanishes*, 1942; *Night Monster*, 1942; *Bowery at Midnight*, 1942; *Frankenstein Meets the Wolf Man* (miscast as

Bela Lugosi as Ygor in *Son of Frankenstein* (1939).

Frankenstein's Monster), 1943; *The Ape Man*, 1943; *Ghosts on the Loose*, 1943; *The Return of the Vampire*, 1944; *Voodoo Man*, 1944; *Return of the Ape Man*, 1944; *The Body Snatcher* (as Joseph), 1945; *Zombies on Broadway*, 1945; *Genius at Work*, 1946; *Scared to Death*, 1947; *Old Mother Riley Meets the Vampire* aka *Vampire over London; My Son, The Vampire*, 1952; *Bela Lugosi Meets a Brooklyn Gorilla*, 1952; *Glen or Glenda?* aka *I Changed My Sex* and *I Led Two Lives* and *The Transvestite* (magical sex-change; Lugosi plays The Spirit), 1953; *Bride of the Monster* (as Dr. Eric Vornoff), 1956; *The Black Sleep*, 1956; *Plan 9 from Outer Space* aka *Grave Robbers from Outer Space* (Lugosi died during filming; most of his footage is disconnected from the main narrative, and much is done by a none-too-convincing "double"), 1956.

LUPINO, IDA (1914–). British leading lady in Hollywood since the thirties, a canny urban type who held her own against the likes of HUMPHREY BOGART and George Raft. She moved easily into character roles later in her career and also became a successful director. *The Devil's Rain*, 1975; *Food of the Gods*, 1976.

LUPO, ALBERTO. Italian actor who is appropriately awful as the scarred and fiendish *Atom Age Vampire*, 1960. *Le Baccanti*, 1960; *Night of Violence*, 1965.

LYDECKER, HOWARD AND THEODORE (1911–69) (1908–). Immensely talented American special effects team, brothers who created stunningly convincing miniatures for innumerable Republic serials and action films. *Dick Tracy*, 1937; *The Adventures of Captain Marvel*, 1941; *Spy Smasher*, 1942; *Captain America*, 1943; *Haunted Harbor*, 1944; *The Purple Monster Strikes*, 1945; *King of the Rocketmen*, 1949; *Flying Disc Man from Mars*, 1950; *Radar Men from the Moon*, 1952; *Zombies of the Stratosphere*, 1952; *Commando Cody, Sky Marshal of the Universe*, 1953; *Tobor the Great*, 1954; many others.

LYNDON, BARRÉ (1896–1972). British playwright who went to Hollywood in the thirties and became a successful screenwriter. *The Lodger*, 1944; *The Man in Half Moon Street* (original story only, b/o his play), 1944; *The War of the Worlds* (from the novel by H.G. WELLS), 1953; *Man in the Attic*, 1953; *Conquest of Space* (co-w; w/Philip Yordan and GOERGE WORTHING YATES), 1955; *The Man Who Could Cheat Death* (original story only, b/o his play *The Man In Half Moon Street*), 1959; *Dark Intruder*, 1965.

LYON, FRANCIS D. (1905–). American second feature director who made some competent thrillers in the fifties but became deadly dull in the sixties. *Cult of the Cobra*, 1955; *Destination Inner Space*, 1966; *The Destructors*, 1967; *Castle of Evil*, 1968.

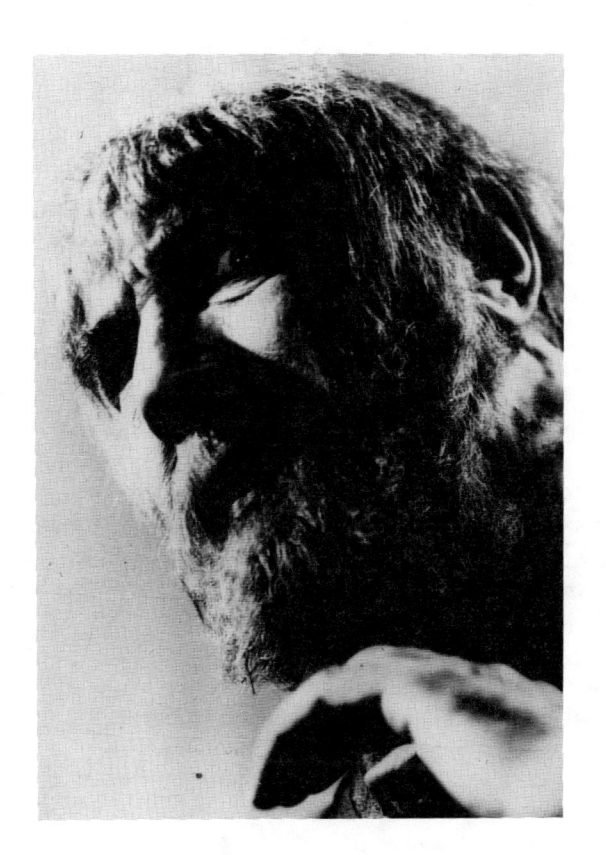

Alberto Lupo as the *The Atom Age Vampire* (1960).

George Macready.

M

MACMURRAY, FRED (1907–). American leading man whose casual, easygoing style suited him for a variety of roles. In the early sixties he became a mainstay of the DISNEY Studio and simultaneously found enormous success on television. *The Shaggy Dog*, 1959; *The Absent-Minded Professor*, 1961; *Son of Flubber*, 1963.

MACREADY, GEORGE (1909–73). American character actor whose sinister eyes and set mouth served him well in a variety of villain roles. *The Soul of a Monster*, 1944; *The Monster and the Ape*, 1945; *Down to Earth*, 1947; *Alias Nick Beal*, 1949; *Tarzan's Peril*, 1951; *The Alligator People*, 1959; *Dead Ringer*, 1964; *The Human Duplicators*, 1965; *Count Yorga, Vampire* (narration only), 1970; *The Return of Count Yorga*, 1971.

MADDERN, VICTOR (1926–). British character actor who appears as the twisted and hideously wall-eyed lab assistant in *Blood of the Vampire*, 1958; *The Night My Number Came Up*, 1956; *Circus of Fear*, 1967; *The Lost Continent*, 1968.

MAGEE, PATRICK (1924–). Glowering British character actor, usually a cultured villain infused with maniacal purpose. *Dementia 13*, 1963; *The Masque of the Red Death*, 1964; *Die Monster Die!*, 1965; *A Clockwork Orange* (as Mr. Alexander), 1971; *Asylum*, 1972 (and 1979 rerelease as *House of Crazies*); *Tales from the Crypt*, 1972; *And Now the Screaming Starts*, 1973; others.

MAGUIRE, JOHN (1921–). Diminutive (4 feet 0 inches) British actor who played ventriloquist MICHAEL REDGRAVE's living dummy in the best sequence of *Dead of Night*, 1946. Skillful makeup (Ernest Taylor and Tom Shenton) and Maguire's playing create a truly horrifying image.

MAHONEY, JOCK (1919–). American actor and former stuntman who starred in two particularly eye-filling Tarzan films, *Tarzan Goes to India*, 1962 and *Tarzan's Three Challenges*, 1963. Mahoney's jungle lord is athletic, lean, and bright; it is a shame that he was thought too old to continue in the role. *I've Lived Before*, 1956; *The Land Unknown*, 1957.

MAIBAUM, RICHARD (1909–). American screenwriter, active since the thirties and responsible for many of the James Bond adaptations. *Dr. No* (co-w), 1962; *Goldfinger* (co-w), 1964; *Thunderball* (co-w), 1965; *Chitty Chitty Bang Bang* (co-w; w/ROALD DAHL; b/o the book by IAN FLEMING), 1968; *On Her Majesty's Secret Service* (particularly well-done, as it emphasizes characterization over gadgetry), 1969; *The Man with the Golden Gun* (co-w; w/Tom Mankiewicz), 1974.

Patrick Magee.

MAINWARING, DANIEL. American screenwriter. *Invasion of the Body Snatchers* (co-w; w/(uncredited) Sam Peckinpah; b/o the novel by Jack Finney), 1956; *Atlantis, The Lost Continent*, 1961; *The Minotaur*, 1961; *The Woman Who Wouldn't Die*, 1965; etc.

MALLESON, MILES (1888–1969). Jowly British character actor, playwright, and screenwriter, dramatic or comically eccentric as required. As actor: *The Thief of Bagdad*, 1940; *Dead of Night*, 1946; *The Man in the White Suit*, 1952; *The Horror of Dracula*, 1958; *The Hound of the Baskervilles*, 1959; *Peeping Tom*, 1960; *Brides of Dracula*, 1960; *The Phantom of the Opera*, 1962; *First Men in the Moon*, 1964; etc.

MAMOULIAN, ROUBEN (1897–). American director whose *Dr. Jekyll and Mr. Hyde*, 1932, is among the finest horror films ever, at once graphically shocking and intellectually provocative. FREDRIC MARCH is superb in the demanding Jekyll/Hyde role and won an Oscar for it. Special mention to makeup artist WALLY WESTMORE, who created a brilliant image of Hyde.

Fredric March as Hyde, with Miriam Hopkins in *Dr. Jekyll and Mr. Hyde* (1932).

MANDER, MILES (1888–1946). British character actor in Hollywood. *Tower of London*, 1939; *The House of the Seven Gables*, 1940; *Tarzan's New York Adventure*, 1942; *The Phantom of the Opera*, 1943; *The Return of the Vampire*, 1944; *The Scarlet Claw*, 1944; *Pearl of Death*, 1944; *The Picture of Dorian Gray*, 1945; *The Brighton Strangler*, 1945.

MANNERS, DAVID (1901–). Canadian leading man in Hollywood during the thirties. *Dracula* (as Harker), 1931; *The Death Kiss*, 1932; *The Mummy* (as Whemple), 1932; *The Black Cat*, 1934; *The Mystery of Edwin Drood*, 1935.

MANTEE, PAUL (CA. 1930–). Grim-faced American actor, convincingly lonesome as *Robinson Crusoe on Mars*, 1964. *A Man Called Dagger* (title role), 1967; *The Manitou*, 1978.

MARAIS, JEAN (1913–). Penetrating French star actor, once associated with JEAN COCTEAU, lately in splashy pop melodramas for other directors. *The Eternal Return*, 1943; *Beauty and the Beast* (as the Beast/Avenant), 1946; *Orpheus*, 1950; *Fantomas*, 1964; *Fantomas Strikes Back*, 1965; *Fantomas vs. Scotland Yard*, 1967.

MARCEAU, MARCEL. Famed French mime in occasional films. *Barbarella*, 1968; *Shanks* (as the mad puppeteer), 1974.

MARCH, FREDRIC (1897–1975). American star actor who projected forceful integrity for four decades. *Dr. Jekyll and Mr. Hyde* (title role; Academy Award), 1932; *Death Takes a Holiday* (as Death), 1934; *I Married a Witch*, 1942. See also: SPENCER TRACY.

Hugh Marlowe and Joan Taylor pretend they can see the alien spacecraft in this publicity still from *Earth vs. The Flying Saucers* (1956).

MARGHERITI, ANTONIO. Italian director of heavy-handed science fiction and horror films, usually credited as Anthony Dawson on United States-release prints. *Battle of the Worlds*, 1960; *Assignment—Outer Space*, 1962; *I Lunghi Capelli Della Morte* (*The Long Hair of Death*), 1964; *Killers Are Challenged*, 1965; *Snow Devils*, 1965; *Wild Wild Planet*, 1967; *In the Grip of the Spider*, 1971; others.

MARINS, JOSE MOJICA. Brazilian writer/director/actor whose films are heavy with gore and explicit sadism. The subject of much controversy in his own country, Marins has developed a reputation as one of the wilder auteurs working in the horror genre. *A Meia Noitre Levarei Sua Alma* (*Tonight I Will Steal Your Soul*), ca. 1964; *Esta Noitre Encarnare I Seu Cadaver* (*Tonight I Will Enter Your Corpse*; d only), 1966; *Trilogia de Terror* (d only), 1968; *O Estranho Mundo de Ze O Caixao* (*The Strange World of Ze Do Caixao*), 1969; others.

MARK, MICHAEL (1889–1975). Russian character actor in Hollywood, often cast as a rural European. In *Frankenstein*, 1931, he is the man who carries the body of his drowned daughter through the streets of the village. *The Mummy's Hand*, 1940; *Flash Gordon Conquers the Universe*, 1940; *The Ghost of Frankenstein*, 1942; *House of Frankenstein*, 1945; *Phantom from Space*, 1953; *Attack of the Puppet People*, 1958; *Wasp Woman* (as Dr. Zinthrop), 1959; *Return of the Fly*, 1959.

MARKER, CHRIS (1921–). Progressive French filmmaker whose *La Jetée*, 1962, a short film composed of sequential still photographs, is a disquieting and provocative look at time travel.

MARLOWE, HUGH (1914–). American actor who brought his distinguished radio voice to films. *The Day the Earth Stood Still*, 1951; *World without End*, 1956; *Earth vs. the Flying Saucers*, 1956; *Castle of Evil*, 1966.

MARLY, FLORENCE (1918–78). Interesting French leading lady who did not make it in Hollywood in the late forties but who caused a small stir among horror fans as the sensual and depraved *Queen of Blood*, 1966. *Krakatit* (Czech; as Princess Willy, the Devil's emissary), 1948; *Games*, 1967; *Spaceboy* (and p, w), 1972; *Doctor Death*, 1973.

MARSHALL, HERBERT (1890–1966). British leading man and later character actor, notable as the man who crushes the tormented fly with the human head at the climax of *The Fly*, 1958. *Riders to the Stars*, 1954; *Gog*, 1954; *Five Weeks in a Balloon*, 1962.

MARSHALL, WILLIAM (1924–). American black actor with Shakespearean experience who found modest success as *Blacula*, 1972. Also in *Sabu and the Magic Ring* (as the genie), 1957; *Scream, Blacula, Scream*, 1973; *Abby*, 1974.

Florence Marly *(left)* as Velena, the *Queen of Blood* (1966).

MARTIN, DEAN (1917–). Popular American singer/actor whose carefully cultivated "swinger" image has kept him popular despite some dreadful movie material. Once teamed with JERRY LEWIS, Martin seemed anxious to attempt serious roles in the late fifties but settled a few years later into a succession of leering comedies. His Matt Helm movies, which are takeoffs on the fanciful James Bond series, are awful: how does one spoof a spoof and what is the point? *Scared Stiff*, 1953; *The Silencers*, 1966; *Murderer's Row*, 1966; *The Ambushers*, 1967; *The Wrecking Crew*, 1968.

MARTIN, LOCK (?–CA. 1969). Towering (7 feet 7 inches) American actor, spotted by director ROBERT WISE while doorman at Grauman's Chinese Theater and signed to play the robot Gort in *The Day the Earth Stood Still*, 1951. Not a strong man, Martin had difficulty with the claustrophobic costume, especially during agonizingly long takes in which he was required to stand perfectly still.

MARTIN, ROSS (1920–). American supporting actor, winning as Artemus Gordon on television's the "Wild, Wild West," 1965–69. *Conquest of Space*, 1955; *The Colossus of New York*, 1958; *The Great Race*, 1965.

MARTIN, STROTHER (1920–1980). American character actor who specialized in giggling psychotics. *The Magnetic Monster*, 1953; *The Brotherhood of Satan*, 1971; *Sssssss*, 1973.

MARTON, ANDREW (1904–). American director. *Crack in the World*, 1965; *Around the World under the Sea* (and p), 1966; *Birds Do It*, 1966.

MASON, JAMES (1909–). British star actor of commanding presence, active on both sides of the Atlantic for more than thirty years. *Terror House* aka *The Night Has Eyes* (as the man who believes he is a werewolf), 1942; *Pandora and the Flying Dutchman*, 1951; *20,000 Leagues Under the Sea* (memorable as Captain Nemo), 1954; *Journey To the Center of the Earth*, 1959; *Frankenstein: the True Story* (TV; theatrical release in Britain), 1973; *The Boys From Brazil*, 1978; *Heaven Can Wait* (as Mr. Jordan), 1978; *Salem's Lot* (as Straker; TV; theatrical release in Europe), 1979.

MASSEN, OSA (1915–). Danish actress in Hollywood, remembered as the heroine of KURT NEUMANN's *Rocketship X-M*, 1950. *Cry of the Werewolf*, 1944; *Night unto Night*, 1949.

MASSEY, ANNA (1937–). British character actress usually cast as a plain but good-hearted girl. Her performance as just such a girl in *Peeping Tom*, 1960, is touching and poignant, as she innocently tries to reach romantic resolution with a psychotic young man. Daughter of actor RAYMOND MASSEY. *De Sade*, 1969; *Frenzy* (as Babs), 1972; *The Vault of Horror*, 1973.

Gulliver (Kerwin Mathews) captured by the Lilliputians in *The Three Worlds of Gulliver* (1960).

MASSEY, ILONA (1912–74). Striking Hungarian leading lady in Hollywood. *Invisible Agent*, 1942; *Frankenstein Meets the Wolf Man*, 1943; *Sabu and the Magic Ring*, 1957.

MASSEY, RAYMOND (1896–). Tall, gaunt Canadian character lead who has played villains and benign protagonists for more than forty years. Father of actress ANNA MASSEY. *The Face at the Window*, 1932; *The Old Dark House*, 1932; *Things to Come* (as John Cabal/Oswald Cabal), 1936; *Black Limelight*, 1938; *Arsenic and Old Lace* (as murderous Jonathan Brewster), 1944.

MASSIE, PAUL (1932–). Canadian actor in British films who gives an interesting performance as a particularly beast-like Mr. Hyde in *The Two Faces of Dr. Jekyll*, 1960.

MASTROCINQUE, CAMILLO. Italian director of uneven horror thrillers. *Terror in the Crypt*, 1963; *An Angel for Satan* (which features BARBARA STEELE at her most voluptuous), 1966; others.

MATE, RUDOLPH (1899–1964). Polish cameraman who became a competent Hollywood director. Photographed: *Vampyr*, 1932. As director: *When Worlds Collide*, 1951; *Miracle in the Rain*, 1956.

MATHESON, RICHARD (1926–). Talented and prolific American fictionist and screenwriter, best known for having scripted most of ROGER CORMAN'S EDGAR ALLAN POE films of the sixties. Screenplays: *The Incredible Shrinking Man* (from his novel, *The Shrinking Man*), 1957; *House of Usher*, 1960; *The Pit and the Pendulum*, 1961; *Tales of Terror*, 1962; *Burn Witch Burn* (co-w; w/CHARLES BEAUMONT; b/o the novel *Conjure Wife* by Fritz Leiber), 1962; *The Raven*, 1963; *The Comedy of Terrors* (and associate p), 1963; *Die, Die My Darling* (b/o the novel *Nightmare* by Anne Blaisdell), 1965; *The Devil's Bride*, 1968; *De Sade*, 1969; *Duel* (TV; b/o his short story), 1971; *The Night Stalker* (TV; b/o an unpublished novel by Jeff Rice), 1972; *The Night Strangler* (TV), 1973; *The Legend of Hell House* (b/o his novel *Hell House*), 1973; *Trilogy of Terror* (TV), 1975; *Somewhere in Time* (and cameo role), 1980; others. Curiously, Matheson's straightforward and terrifying 1954 vampire novel *I Am Legend* has been filmed twice (*The Last Man on Earth*, 1964 and *The Omega Man*, 1971), neither time from his own screenplay and both times unsatisfactorily.

MATHEWS, KERWIN (1926–). Athletic and boyish American leading man, a fine swashbuckling Sinbad in *The 7th Voyage of Sinbad*, 1958. Also *The Three Worlds of Gulliver*, 1960; *Jack the Giant Killer*, 1962; *Shadow of Evil*, 1966; *Battle Beneath the Earth*, 1968; *The Boy Who Cried Werewolf*, 1973; *Nightmare in Blood* (cameo), 1976.

MATTEY, ROBERT A. American special-effects technician who designed and built the oversized mechanical sharks used in the most horrifying scenes of *Jaws*, 1975. He also created the impressive giant squid which grips the submarine Nautilus in *20,000 Leagues under the Sea*, 1954.

MATURE, VICTOR (1915–). Husky, sensual-featured American leading man, dubbed "The Hunk" in his heyday during the forties. Often cast in Biblical spectaculars. *One Million B.C.*, 1940; *Samson and Delilah* (as Samson, whose great strength comes from his hair), 1949; *Head*, 1968.

MAXWELL, LOIS (1927–). Canadian leading lady active in Hollywood and later Britain. She is best known as Miss Moneypenny, James Bond's attractive and ever-hopeful coworker in each Bond film since *Dr. No*, 1962. *Corridor of Mirrors*, 1948; *Satellite in the Sky*, 1956; *The Haunting*, 1963; *Operation Kid Brother* (an in-joke: the film stars SEAN (James Bond) CONNERY's younger brother, Neil), 1967.

MCCALLA, IRISH (1929–). Tall (5 feet 9 inches) and tawny American actress, memorable as television's "Sheena, Queen of the Jungle," 1955–56. Before retiring from show business to become a successful painter and art teacher, McCalla lent her striking beauty to a few feature films. *She Demons*, 1958; *Hands of a Stranger*, 1962.

MCCARTHY, KEVIN (1914–). American general purpose actor and sometime leading man, outstanding as Miles Bennell in *Invasion of the Body Snatchers*, 1956, the small-town physician who sees his friends and finally his woman supplanted by an insidious alien presence. McCarthy has a cameo role in the 1978 remake of the same title. *Nightmare*, 1956; *Piranha*, 1978.

MCCORMACK, PATTY (1945–). American child actress of the fifties who repeated her stage role as the murderous little girl in *The Bad Seed*, 1956. *Bug*, 1975.

MCDOWALL, RODDY (1928–). Youthful British actor and onetime child star, active in Hollywood since the second world war. *It!*, 1967; *Planet of the Apes*, 1968; *Beneath the Planet of the Apes*, 1970; *Escape from the Planet of the Apes*, 1971; *The Devil's Widow* (d only), 1972; *Conquest of the Planet of the Apes*, 1972; *Battle for the Planet of the Apes*, 1973; *The Legend of Hell House*, 1973; *Arnold*, 1974; *Embryo*, 1976; *Laserblast*, 1977; *The Martian Chronicles* (TV; theatrical release in Britain), 1980.

MCDOWELL, MALCOLM (1944–). Unorthodox British leading actor of the seventies, usually cast as a confused juvenile. *If . . .*, 1969; *A Clockwork Orange* (a stunning performance as the gang leader Alex), 1971; *O Lucky Man!*, 1973; *Time after Time* (delightful as H.G. WELLS), 1979.

Roddy McDowall in and out of character for his role in *Planet of The Apes* (1968).

Malcolm McDowell *(far right)* toasts us from the hallucinogenic milk bar in Stanley Kubrick's *A Clockwork Orange* (1971).

Steve McQueen *(center)* with Aneta Corsaut and friends in *The Blob* (1958).

McLaren, Norman (1914–). Scottish-born filmmaker, long associated with the National Film Board of Canada. Interested in the physical nature of the film itself, McLaren has painted directly on the celluloid to achieve some of his unique visual effects. His *Neighbors*, 1952, a pixilated fantasy (with stop-motion animation of live actors), is a viciously humorous look at the killer instinct as expressed in suburban violence. *Spook Sport* (animation only), 1941; *Pas de Deux*, 1968; many others.

McClure, Doug (1938–). Husky blond American leading man with television experience who has found recent success in a series of British adaptations of EDGAR RICE BURROUGHS fantasies. *The Land That Time Forgot*, 1975; *At The Earth's Core*, 1976; *The People That Time Forgot*, 1977; *Warlords of Atlantis*, 1978; *Humanoids From the Deep*, 1980.

McQueen, Steve (1930–). Tough American leading man whose first starring role was in *The Blob*, 1958.

Meeker, Ralph (1920–). Somewhat underrated American leading man of the tough-guy school, the quintessential Mike Hammer in ROBERT ALDRICH's *Kiss Me Deadly*, 1955, a brutal detective thriller with marginal but highly disturbing fantastic elements. The scenario concerns a mysterious box full of fissionable material, and its value is such that people kill and torture to get it. At the climax, Gaby Rodgers opens the box and she, and the beach house around her, are immolated. Hammer is also apparently destroyed in this film, which reduces the most terrifying of man's postwar fears to an anonymous box. *The Mind Snatchers*, 1972; *Food of the Gods*, 1976.

Don Megowan is large strong-featured man in shot in *The Werewolf* (1956). Harry Lauter is at far right.

MEGOWAN, DON (CA. 1925–). Giant-sized American actor, often beneath heavy makeup and cast as a monster. *The Creature Walks Among Us* (as the Creature in land sequences only; see also: BEN CHAPMAN), 1956; *The Werewolf* (as the sheriff), 1956; *Creation of the Humanoids* (lead), 1962; *Tarzan and the Valley of Gold* (as Mr. Train), 1966.

MELCHIOR, IB (1917–). Danish writer/director whose projects are imaginatively conceived but usually thwarted by small budgets. *The Angry Red Planet*, 1959; *Journey to the 7th Planet* (w only), 1962; *Reptilicus* (w only), 1963; *The Time Travelers*, 1964; *Robinson Crusoe on Mars* (w only), 1964; *Planet of the Vampires* (w only), 1965; *Death Race 2000* (original story), 1975.

MÉLIÈS, GEORGES (1861–1938). Pioneering French filmmaker whose whimsical trick films were marvels of their day. Fades, wipes, dissolves, superimposition, etc. were applied to fanciful narratives, with magical results. Although Méliès was forgotten long before his death, his contribution to the fantastic cinema is inestimable. *The Haunted Castle*, 1896; *The Artist's Dream*, 1898; *Haggard's "She"—The Pillar of Fire*, 1899; *The Man with the Rubber Head*, 1901; *Voyage to the Moon*, 1902; *The Kingdom of the Fairies*, 1903; *Inventor Crazybrains and His Wonderful Airship*, 1906; *20,000 Leagues under the Sea*, 1907; *In the Bogie Man's Cave*, 1908; *The Conquest of the Pole*, 1912; dozens more.

MENZIES, WILLIAM CAMERON (1896–1957). Accomplished American art director who designed and directed *Things to Come*, 1936. *The Wizard's Apprentice* (silent; p and special effects only), 1930; *The Spider* (co-d; w/Kenneth MacKenna), 1931; *The Maze*, 1953; *Invaders from Mars*, 1953 (and 1976 rerelease; see: WADE WILLIAMS).

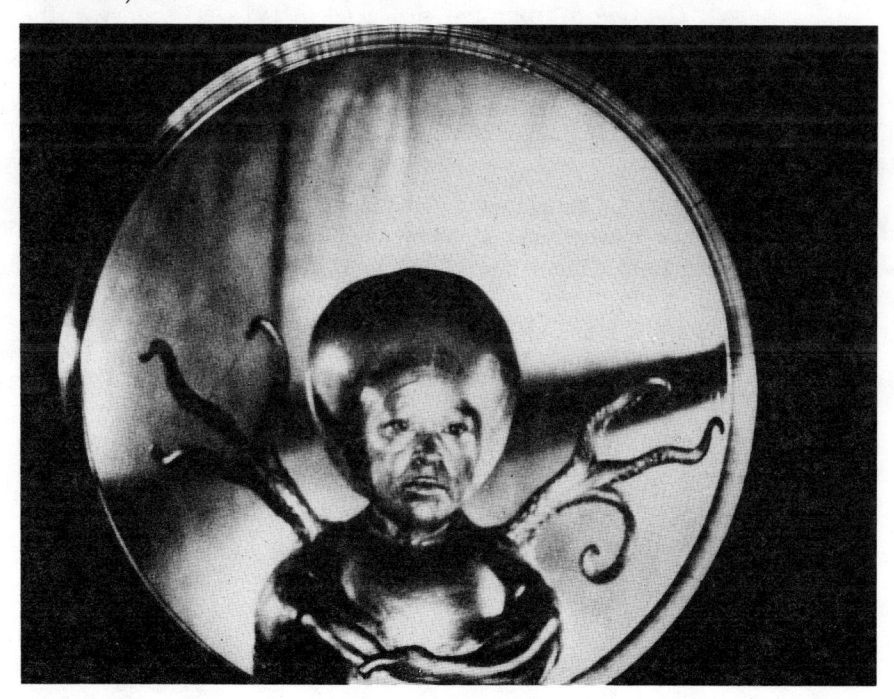

The hideous "rat-bat-crab-spider" that stalks the Martian desert in Ib Melchior's *Angry Red Planet* (1959). Note the support wires visible on the right.

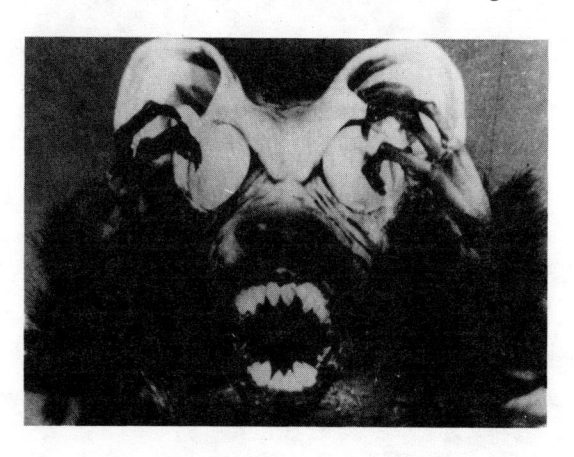

The malevolent leader of the Martians as seen in William Cameron Menzies's *Invaders from Mars* (1954).

Ray Milland ca. 1963.

MEREDITH, BURGESS (1908–). Smiling, uniquely American star character actor, convincing as jovial hayseeds, earnest friends to the hero and, more recently, as anguished old men. *Batman* (as the Penguin), 1966; *Torture Garden* (as the Devil), 1968; *The Sentinel*, 1977; *The Manitou*, 1978; *Magic*, 1978; *Clash of the Titans*, 1981.

MERRILL, FRANK (1894–1966). Muscular American actor of the twenties, a former stuntman and gymnast who appears as a particularly agile Tarzan in *Tarzan the Mighty*, 1928, and *Tarzan the Tiger*, 1929–30, the latter being the first Tarzan film with sound.

MERRILL, GARY (1914–). Dark, beetle-browed American character lead, most popular in urban dramas of the fifties. *The Mysterious Island*, 1961; *The Woman Who Wouldn't Die*, 1965; *Around the World Under the Sea*, 1966; *Destination Inner Space*, 1966; *The Power*, 1968.

MEYER, RUSS (1923–). American independent producer/director who has made a name by specializing in outrageous but good-humored and often imaginative nudie films. His *The Immoral Mr. Teas*, 1959, is the first American skin film to be something more than badly edited shots of embarrassed naked people playing vollyball and is a humorous extrapolation of the X-ray vision theme. Timid Mr. Teas has an uncanny ability to see all women naked, regardless of their clothing. The film is genuinely funny and is a legitimate interpretation of a familiar fantastic film element. (ROGER CORMAN dallies briefly with the sexual aspect of X-ray vision in his otherwise grim *X—The Man with the X-Ray Eyes*, 1963). *Kiss Me Quick* (features Frankenstein's Monster, Dracula, a living mummy, and an extraterrestial), 1963; *Supervixens*, 1975.

MEYRINK, GUSTAV (1868–1932). German author who fashioned a novel, *The Golem*, from Jewish legend in 1916. The story of the hideous artificial man has reached the screen eleven times since 1917, the first being the famous PAUL WEGENER version. *Golem and the Dancer* (a parody), 1917; *The Golem, How He Came into the World*, 1921; *Le Golem*, 1937; *Le Golem*, 1966; *It!*, 1967; others.

MIDDLETON, CHARLES (1879–1949). Acidic American character actor, best remembered as Mongo's Ming the Merciless in *Flash Gordon*, 1936; *Flash Gordon's Trip to Mars*, 1938; and *Flash Gordon Conquers the Universe*, 1940. *Kongo*, 1932; *Daredevils of the Red Circle*, 1939; *Island of Doomed Men*, 1940; *The Mystery of Marie Roget*, 1942; *Perils of Nyoka*, 1942; *Spook Busters*, 1946; *Strangler of the Swamp* (as the Ghost), 1946.

MIFUNE, TOSHIRO (1920–). Japanese star actor, often in medieval costume films as a scowling warrior. *The Drunken Angel*, 1948; *Rashomon*, 1952; *Throne of Blood* (*Macbeth* transplanted to feudal Japan), 1957; *The Lost World of Sinbad*, 1965.

MIKELS, TED V. American cheapie producer/director. *The Astro-Zombies*, 1969; *The Corpse Grinders*, 1971.

MILLAND, RAY (1905–). Accomplished American leading actor who began his career playing light romantic parts and later graduated to heavy drama. He has also directed. *Jungle Princess*, 1936; *The Premature Burial*, 1962; *Panic in Year Zero* (and d), 1962. *X—The Man with the X-Ray Eyes*, 1963; *Frogs*, 1972; *The Thing with Two Heads*, 1972; *The Big Game* (thought control), 1972; *Terror in the Wax Museum*, 1973; *House in Nightmare Park*, 1973.

MILLER, DENNY (1935–). Blond American actor and former U.C.L.A. basketball star who landed the lead in *Tarzan the Ape Man* in 1959. The film is dreadful. Miller's enthusiasm counts for something, but he looks too much like the big, healthy California kid he was at the time. Miller has since been most active on television, *e.g.*, "Mona McCluskey," 1965–66. *The Island at the Top of the World*, 1974.

MILLER, DICK (CA. 1930–). American character actor, the archetypal smart-ass, in many films for ROGER CORMAN. *It Conquered the World*, 1956; *Not of This Earth* (as the obnoxious vacuum cleaner salesman), 1957; *War of the Satellites* (lead), 1958; *A Bucket of Blood* (the lead, as a demented beatnik sculptor who covers bodies in clay), 1959; *The Little Shop of Horrors* (as Fouch, the man who blithely eats flowers for dinner), 1960; *The Terror*, 1963; *X—The Man with the X-Ray Eyes*, 1963; *The Trip*, 1967; *Hollywood Boulevard*, 1976; *Piranha*, 1978.

MILLER, MARVIN (1913–). American character actor who lent his impressive voice to Robby the Robot in *Forbidden Planet*, 1956, and again in 1977 in an amusing television commercial for *Starlog* magazine. *Red Planet Mars*, 1952; *King Dinosaur* (narration), 1955; *Is This Trip Really Necessary?* (sex-horror), 1969; others.

MILLER, PATSY RUTH (1905–). American leading lady of the silent era, a tender and sweet Esmeralda opposite LON CHANEY as *The Hunchback of Notre Dame*, 1923.

MILLIGAN, ANDY. American exploitation writer/producer/director active in England. *The Ghastly Ones*, 1969; *Bloodthirsty Butchers*, 1970; *The Body Beneath* (16mm porno-horror), 1971; *Garu the Mad Monk*, 1971; *The Man with Two Heads*, 1972; *The Rats Are Coming! The Werewolves Are Here!*, 1972; *Blood*, 1973.

MIMIEUX, YVETTE (1939–). Blonde American lady whose first film was *The Time Machine*, 1960, in which she played the innocent Eloi girl Weena. *The Wonderful World of the Brothers Grimm*, 1962; *Black Noon* (TV), 1971; *The Neptune Factor*, 1973; *The Black Hole*, 1979.

Dick Miller.

Sultry as usual: Maria Montez in *Siren of Atlantis* (1948).

MITCHELL, CAMERON (1918–). American tough-guy lead who never attained the importance he deserved. *Flight to Mars*, 1951; *Gorilla at Large*, 1954; *Blood and Black Lace*, 1964; *Island of the Doomed*, 1968; *Nightmare in Wax*, 1969; *The Toolbox Murders*, 1978; *Silent Scream*, 1980; *Supersonic Man*, 1980.

MITCHELL, LAURIE. Leggy American actress in second features of the fifties. *Queen of Outer Space* (title role), 1958; *Missile to the Moon*, 1959.

MOHR, GERALD (1914–68). Dapper American leading man of B-films. *The Monster and the Girl*, 1941; *Jungle Girl*, 1941; *The Catman of Paris*, 1946; *Son of Ali Baba*, 1952; *Invasion U.S.A.*, 1953; *Terror in the Haunted House*, 1958; *Angry Red Planet*, 1959.

MONLAUR, YVONNE (CA. 1938–). French leading lady of the Bardot type, active in Britain during the early sixties. *Brides of Dracula*, 1960; *Circus of Horrors*, 1960.

MONTANA, BULL (1887–1950). Bearlike Italian stuntman and professional wrestler who played apes and villains in Hollywood silents and early talkies. *Go and Get It* (as the gorilla with the brain of a convict), 1920; *The Lost World* (as the primeval apeman), 1925; *The Amazing Exploits of the Clutching Hand*, 1936; others.

MONTEZ, MARIA (1918–51). Exotic leading lady, born in the Dominican Republic and memorable as Hollywood's *Cobra Woman*, 1944. Her premature death robbed the film world of one of its more enjoyable, if artificial, personalities. *The Invisible Woman*, 1940; *The Mystery of Marie Roget*, 1942; *The Arabian Nights*, 1942; *Ali Baba and the Forty Thieves*, 1944; *Siren of Atlantis*, 1948.

Gerald Mohr.

Monty Python. From left: Eric Idle, Graham Chapman, Michael Palin, John Cleese, Terry Jones, and Terry Gilliam.

MONTY PYTHON. A group of talented young British comics, JOHN CLEESE, MICHAEL PALIN, ERIC IDLE, TERRY JONES, GRAHAM CHAPMAN, and an American responsible for clever animations, TERRY GILLIAM. Monty Python's humor is characteristically disjointed and nonsequitur, full of violent slapstick, men in drag, and outrageous nihilism. It is also very, very funny, and the group caught on in America after its successful BBC television series, "Monty Python's Flying Circus," was broadcast over public television. Films: *And Now for Something Completely Different* (reworkings of blackouts and sketches from the BBC series), 1971; *Monty Python and the Holy Grail* (a side-splitting send-up of Arthurian legend), 1975; *Jabberwocky*, 1977; *Life of Brian*, 1979.

MOORE, ALVY. American supporting actor who has produced stylish low-budget thrillers with partner L.Q. JONES since 1963. Moore is probably most familiar as the befuddled county agent on television's "Green Acres," 1965–71. Films as co-producer: *The Devil's Bedroom*, 1963; *The Witchmaker* (actor only), 1969; *The Brotherhood of Satan* (and acts), 1971; *A Boy and His Dog* (and acts; b/o the prize-winning novella by Harlan Ellison), 1976.

Roger Moore as James Bond, ever in control, ever cool. The lady is Maud Adams; the film is *The Man with The Golden Gun* (1974).

MOORE, ROGER (1928–). Handsome British leading man of films and television. Something of a mannequin in his early career, Moore has lately developed a personable good humor. In 1973 he inherited the James Bond role from SEAN CONNERY and has played it aptly. *The Man Who Haunted Himself*, 1971; *Live and Let Die*, 1973; *The Man with the Golden Gun*, 1974; *The Spy Who Loved Me*, 1977; *Moonraker*, 1979.

MOORE, TERRY (1929–). Perky American leading lady of the fifties, charming as the pretty friend of the giant gorilla, *Mighty Joe Young*, 1949. *A Man Called Dagger*, 1967.

Barboura Morris cornered by *The Wasp Woman* (1959), Susan Cabot. Note the cameraman's marks on the carpet.

MOOREHEAD, AGNES (1906–74). Regal, imposing American star character actress who came to Hollywood in association with ORSON WELLES. She is best known to the popular audience as the witch Endora on television's "Bewitched," 1964–72, and is wonderfully seedy as the servant woman in *Hush, Hush Sweet Charlotte*, 1964. *The Story of Mankind*, 1957; *The Bat*, 1958; *What's the Matter with Helen?*, 1971; *Dear, Dead Delilah*, 1972.

MORGAN, FRANK (1890–1949). Winning, apple-cheeked American character actor, much-loved as the "humbug" wizard in *The Wizard of Oz*, 1939. *Secrets of the French Police* (which involves hypnosis and hidden corpses), 1932; *The Cockeyed Miracle* (as a ghost), 1946.

MORGAN, RALPH (1882–1956). American character actor, often cast as an evil schemer. Brother of actor FRANK MORGAN. *Rasputin and the Empress*, 1933; *Condemned to Live*, 1935; *The Mad Doctor*, 1941; *Night Monster*, 1942; *Weird Woman*, 1944; *The Monster Maker* (as a pianist stricken by acromegaly), 1944; *The Creeper*, 1948.

MORLEY, ROBERT (1908–). Fleshy and jovial British character actor who has specialized in blustery nincompoops. *The Ghosts of Berkeley Square*, 1947; *The Old Dark House*, 1963; *A Study in Terror*, 1966; *Theatre of Blood* (as the theater critic who is force-fed his pet poodles), 1973; *Who Is Killing the Great Chefs of Europe?* (black comedy; horror murders), 1978.

MORRIS, BARBOURA AKA BARBOURA O'NEILL (1932–75). Sleepy-eyed American actress, in films for ROGER CORMAN. *A Bucket of Blood* (as the sexy beatnik girl, Carla), 1959; *Wasp Woman*, 1959; *The Haunted Palace*, 1963; *X—The Man with the X-Ray Eyes*, 1963; *The Trip*, 1967, *The Dunwich Horror*, 1970.

Frank Morgan as *The Wizard of Oz* (1939).

MORRIS, CHESTER (1901-70). American character actor, familiar as Boston Blackie. He appears in *The She Creature*, 1956, as the unscrupulous hypnotist who regresses MARLA ENGLISH into a scaly monster. *The Bat Whispers*, 1931.

MORRIS, GLENN (1911-74). American Olympic decathalon champion of 1936 who has the lead role in *Tarzan's Revenge*, 1938. Morris and the film were unsuccessful, and he retired from show business soon after.

MORRIS, KIRK. American bodybuilder who found small success in Italian muscleman epics of the sixties. *Hercules in the Vale of Woe*, 1962; *Hercules of the Desert*, 1964; *Samson vs. the Giant King*, 1965; others.

MORRISSEY, PAUL (1939-). American underground director and disciple of Andy Warhol who found general theatrical release for two horror films, *Blood for Dracula*, 1974, and *Andy Warhol's Frankenstein* (3-D), 1974. Despite their rather nihilistic points of view, the films hint at a genuine directorial talent. *The Hound of the Baskervilles* (parody), 1978.

MORROW, JEFF (1913-). Solid American leading man of second features. *This Island Earth* (as Exeter), 1955; *The Creature Walks among Us*, 1956; *Kronos*, 1957; *The Giant Claw*, 1957; *Legacy of Blood*, 1972.

Jeff Morrow.

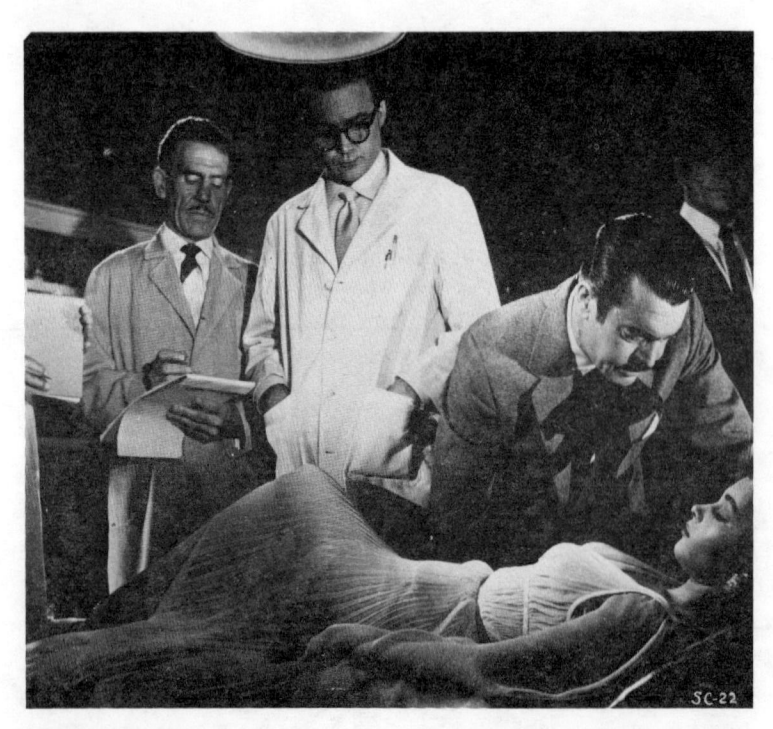

Chester Morris observes Marla English in *The She Creature* (1956). Longtime character player Kenneth McDonald *(second from left)* takes notes.

MORROW, JO (1940–). American juvenile acress of the fifties and later leading lady. *13 Ghosts*, 1960; *The Three Worlds of Gulliver*, 1960; *Doctor Death*, 1973.

MORSE, TERRY (1906–). American programmer director of the forties and fifties who skillfully shot English-language scenes (featuring RAYMOND BURR) for the American release of Japan's *Godzilla*, 1954. *Unknown World*, 1951; *Love Slaves of the Amazon* (associate p and editor only), 1957.

MOXEY, JOHN (1920–). British director whose fog-enshrouded *Horror Hotel*, 1960, is an entertaining and often shockingly effective throwback to horror films of the thirties. Also *Psycho-Circus*, 1967; *A Taste of Evil* (TV), 1971; *The Night Stalker* (TV), 1972.

The residents of Whitewood, Massachusetts, gather to execute a witch in John Moxey's stylish *Horror Hotel* (1960).

Caroline Munro.

Janet Munro.

The delightful "Kinemins" in Michael Myerberg's *Hansel and Gretel* (1954).

MUNRO, CAROLINE (CA. 1950–). British glamour girl in Hammer films of the seventies. *Dracula A.D. 1972*, 1972; *Captain Kronos, Vampire Hunter*, 1972; *The Golden Voyage of Sinbad*, 1973; *Devil within Her*, 1976; *At the Earth's Core*, 1976; *The Spy Who Loved Me*, 1977; *The Adventures of Stella Star* aka *Starcrash*, 1979; *Maniac*, 1980.

MUNRO, JANET (1934–72). British leading lady of the fifties and sixties who could project a pleasant sweetness. *The Crawling Eye*, 1958; *Darby O'Gill and the Little People*, 1958; *The Day the Earth Caught Fire*, 1962; *They All Died Laughing*, 1964.

MURNAU, F. W. (1889–1931). Major German director, active in Hollywood from 1927. *Satanas*, 1919; *Der Januskopf* (b/o *Dr. Jekyll and Mr. Hyde*), 1920; *Nosferatu, the Vampire*, 1922; *Faust*, 1926.

MYERBERG, MICHAEL (1906–74). American trick film producer who called his stop-motion puppets "Kinemins," i.e., kinetic mannequins. At seventy-eight minutes, Myerberg's *Hansel and Gretel*, 1954, is the most ambitious piece of sustained puppet animation ever filmed but was not financially successful enough to allow him to develop other movie projects. He used his Kinemins in television commercials of the early fifties, and eventually became a Broadway producer.

N

NADER, GEORGE (1921–). American action hero of adventure films of the fifties and sixties, now a novelist. *Robot Monster*, 1953; *The Human Duplicators*, 1965; *The Million Eyes of Su-Muru*, 1967; *House of 1,000 Dolls*, 1967.

NAGEL, ANNE (1912–66). American actress whose best-remembered role is opposite LON CHANEY, JR. in *Man Made Monster*, 1941. *Black Friday*, 1940; *The Green Hornet*, 1940; *The Green Hornet Strikes Again*, 1940; *The Invisible Woman*, 1940; *The Secret Code*, 1942; *The Mad Doctor of Market Street*, 1942.

NAISH, J. CARROLL (1900–73). American character actor in some major films of the thirties and forties who overstayed his welcome and finished his career in embarrassingly bad exploitation pictures. *Dr. Renault's Secret* (as the apeman), 1942; *The Man in the Trunk*, 1942; *The Batman*, 1943; *House of Frankenstein* (as Daniel, the sympathetic hunchback), 1945; *The Beast with Five Fingers*, 1946; *Dracula vs. Frankenstein*, 1971; others.

NAKAJIMA, HARUO (CA. 1930–). Japanese special effects technician who on numerous occasions has been the man inside the *Godzilla* (1954 and sequels) costume.

NASCHY, PAUL. Husky Spanish actor and onetime champion weightlifter whose true name is Jacinto Molina, highly popular in Spain and Europe as star of many violent and sexy horror thrillers. *La Marca del Hombre Lobo*, 1969; *La Furia del Hombre Lobo*, 1970; *Dr. Jekyll and the Werewolf*, 1971; *La Orgia de los Muertos* (*The Orgy of The Dead*), 1972; *Dracula's Great Love*, 1972 (1979 rerelease as *Cemetery Girls*); *El Jorobado de le Morgue* (*The Hunchback of the Morgue*), 1972; *La Rebelion de las Muertas* (*The Revolt of the Dead Ones*), 1973; *The Mummy's Vengeance*, 1973; *El Gran Amor del Conde Dracula*, 1973; *The Werewolf vs. the Vampire Woman* (and w), 1974; many others.

NEAL, PATRICIA (1926–). Accomplished American leading actress of unusual appeal, first promoted as a glamour girl. Her talent won out and led to important character roles. Memorable as ally of the alien Klaatu in *The Day the Earth Stood Still*, 1951. Married to writer ROALD DAHL. *Immediate Disaster* aka *Stranger from Venus*, 1954; *The Night Digger*, 1971; *Happy Mother's Day, Love George*, 1973.

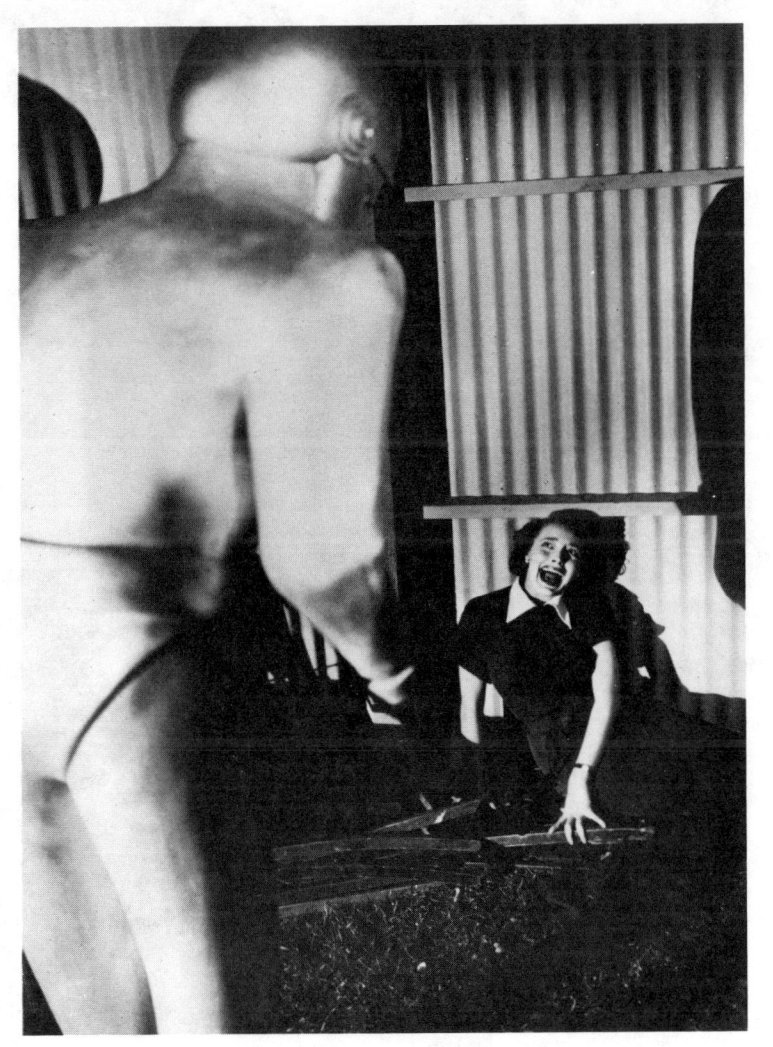

George Nader.

Patricia Neal trapped by the robot Gort in *The Day The Earth Stood Still* (1951).

NEILL, NOEL (CA. 1925–). Red-headed American actress who played snoopy reporter Lois Lane in the serials *Superman*, 1948, and *Atom Man vs. Superman*, 1950, and brought the character to television in the long-running the "Adventures of Superman," 1953–58 (1951–52 Lois was played by PHYLLIS COATES). Neill is also seen in *Invasion U.S.A.*, 1953; *Superman* (as Lois Lane's mother), 1978. In addition, Neill is featured in a series of reedited episodes from the series, released theatrically in 1954: *Superman's Peril*; *Superman Flies Again*; *Superman in Exile*; *Superman and Scotland Yard*; and *Superman and the Jungle Devil*.

NEILL, ROY WILLIAM (1890–1946). Irish-American producer/director who brought verve and atmosphere to many B-films of the forties, notably the BASIL RATHBONE Sherlock Holmes series in 1939–46. *Black Moon*, 1934; *The Black Room*, 1935; *Frankenstein Meets the Wolf Man*, 1943; *Spider Woman*, 1944; *The Scarlet Claw*, 1944; *Pearl of Death*, 1944.

NELSON, ED (1928–). American general-purpose actor who became popular in the sixties as Dr. Rossi on television's "Peyton Place," 1964–69. *Invasion of the Saucer Men*, 1957; *Attack of the Crab Monsters*, 1957; *The Devil's Partner* (lead), 1958; *Night of the Blood Beast*, 1958; *The Brain Eaters* (and p), 1958; *A Bucket of Blood*, 1959.

NELSON, LORI (1933–). Pert American leading lady of the fifties. *Revenge of the Creature*, 1955; *The Day the World Ended*, 1956.

NEUMANN, KURT (1908–58). German director in America from the early thirties. His *The Fly*, 1958, is one of the more notable horror films of the fifties and remains a powerful if vaguely distasteful example of the genre. *Trapped* (and co-w; w/Robert F. Hill), 1931; *Rocketship X-M*, 1950 (and 77 rerelease; see: WADE WILLIAMS); *Kronos*, 1957; *She-Devil*, 1957.

NEWFIELD, SAM (1900–64). Prolific American B-film specialist, active as director during the thirties and forties. *Ghost Patrol*, 1936; *The Mad Monster*, 1942; *Dead Men Walk*, 1943; *The Black Raven*, 1943; *The Monster Maker*, 1944; *Nabonga*, 1944; *White Pongo*, 1945; *Radar Secret Service*, 1950; *Lost Continent*, 1951.

NEWMAN, JOSEPH M. (1909–). Mystifying American director who displayed great talent with *This Island Earth*, 1955, and none at all with *Tarzan the Ape Man*, 1959.

Noel Neill as Lois Lane, in a tight spot with Superman (George Reeves), ca. 1955.

Rex Reason, the $20,000 Metaluna mutant, and Faith Domergue pose in this publicity still from Joseph M. Newman's *This Island Earth* (1955).

This scene from *How to Make a Monster* (1958) sums up much of the ghoulish good humor of films masterminded by James H. Nicholson and released by American-International Pictures during the studio's formative years in the fifties. The mask on the far left is from *Invasion of the Saucermen* (1957), that on the far right from *The She Creature* (1956). The charmer in the middle is unindentified.

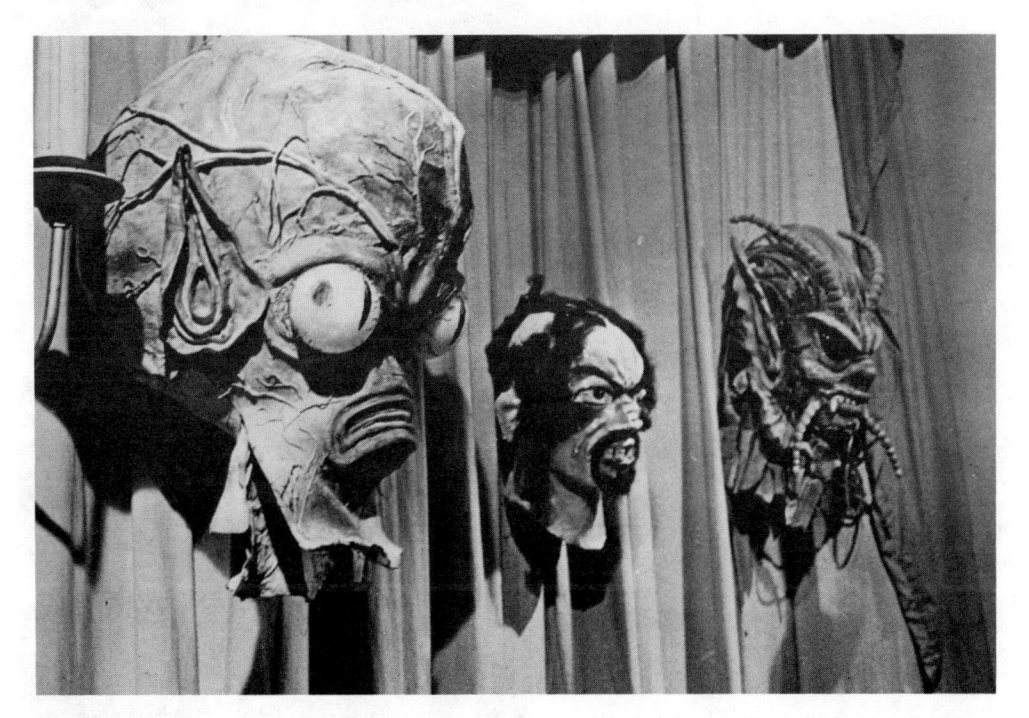

NICHOLSON, JACK (1937–). American star actor of the seventies, a unique personality who often exhibits an eccentric cynicism. Nicholson was associated with ROGER CORMAN during the first half of the sixties and had his wildest role in *The Little Shop of Horrors*, 1960, in which he is marvelously perverse as a masochistic dental patient. *The Terror* (and d; part; uncredited), 1963; *The Raven*, 1963; *The Trip* (w only), 1967; *Head* (and co-w), 1968; *Tommy*, 1976; *The Shining*, 1980.

NICHOLSON, JAMES H. (1916–73). American producer who founded American-International Pictures in 1953 with longtime partner Samuel Z. Arkoff (1918–). Originally called the American Releasing Corporation, AIP grew from a tiny distributor to the only studio in Hollywood to show an annual profit for twenty years. As creative thrust behind the corporation, Nicholson encouraged prolific young mavericks like ROGER CORMAN and HERMAN COHEN and filled the screens of the nation's new drive-ins with furiously fast films appealing to youth. AIP spearheaded the science fiction and teen movie crazes of the fifties, led the way to the domestic resurgence of period horror films, and pioneered the beach party movie, the motorcycle film, and the black action genre. Since the early seventies, American-International has steadily increased its output of "big" films and was, until a corporate takeover in 1980, among the most active studios in Hollywood. Before his death, Nicholson left AIP to form his own production company. His widow is actress SUSAN HART.

Allan Nixon manfully restrains Tarantula Girl Tandra Quinn in 1953's *The Mesa of Lost Women*.

NIELSEN, LESLIE (1925–). Canadian leading man in Hollywood, notable as intrepid Commander J. J. Adams in *Forbidden Planet*, 1956. *Dark Intruder*, 1965; *The Reluctant Astronaut*, 1967; *The Resurrection of Zachary Wheeler*, 1971; *Prom Night*, 1980.

NIGH, JANE (1926–). American actress of the forties, usually in lackluster pretty-girl roles but engagingly sympathetic as the hunchbacked girl in *House of Dracula*, 1945.

NIMOY, LEONARD (1932–). American actor who filled small roles in many bad movies before gaining public acclaim as the logical Mr. Spock in television's "Star Trek," 1966–69. *Zombies of the Stratosphere* (as a thuglike Martian), 1952; *Them!*, 1954; *The Brain Eaters*, 1958; *Invasion of the Body Snatchers*, 1978; *Star Trek: The Motion Picture* (as Spock), 1979.

NIVEN, DAVID (1909–). Dapper British leading man who brings a classy good humor to his roles. A major star in Hollywood since the thirties, he played *Old Dracula* (aka *Vampira*) in 1975. *Stairway to Heaven*, 1946; *Casino Royale* (as James Bond), 1967; *Eye of the Devil*, 1967.

NIXON, ALLAN. American B-picture leading man of the early fifties. *Siren of Atlantis*, 1948; *Prehistoric Women*, 1950; *The Mesa of Lost Women*, 1953; etc.

NOVAK, KIM (1933–). Cool, blonde American leading lady of the fifties and sixties, once considered a successor to Marilyn Monroe. Novak's career was clumsily manipulated, her undeniable talent seldom properly showcased. Often cast in roles beyond her reach, she is just right as a sexy Greenwich Village witch in *Bell, Book and Candle*, 1958. *Son of Sinbad* (bit), 1955; *Vertigo*, 1958; *The Legend of Lylah Clare* (as the girl possessed by the vindictive spirit of a dead actress), 1968; *Tales That Witness Madness*, 1973; *Satan's Triangle* (TV), 1975.

NOZAKI, ALBERT (1912–). Japanese designer active in Hollywood, creator of the elegant Martian war machines for GEORGE PAL's *The War of the Worlds*, 1953. *When Worlds Collide*, 1951.

NYE, BEN. American makeup artist who created a pair of outrageous anthropomorphics, *The Fly*, 1958, and *The Alligator People*, 1959. *The Lost World*, 1960.

Kim Novak, ca. 1957.

The War of the Worlds (1953); Martian war machines designed by Albert Nozaki.

The Alligator People (1959); sinister grin created by Ben Nye.

O

OBOLER, ARCH (1909–). American producer/director/writer who came to films after great success in radio ("Lights Out"). His movie projects have tended to be oddball failures. *Bewitched*, 1945; *Five*, 1951; *The Twonky*, 1953; *The Bubble* (3-D), 1967 (and 1976 rerelease as *The Fantastic Invasion of Planet Earth*).

O'BRIEN, DAVE (1912–69). Handsome American leading man and stunt expert in many B-films of the thirties and forties, best-remembered as star of the Pete Smith Specialties two-reel series, 1942–55. O'Brien retired from acting in the late fifties and won an Emmy in 1961 for comedy writing. *The Devil Bat*, 1940; *The Ghost Creeps*, 1940; *Spooks Run Wild*, 1941; *Captain Midnight* (serial; title role), 1942.

O'BRIEN, EDMOND (1915–). Exciting American character lead of the forties and fifties, at home in crime thrillers and superb as Winston Smith in the 1956 film version of George Orwell's *1984*. *The Hunchback of Notre Dame*, 1939; *Moon Pilot*, 1962; *Fantastic Voyage*, 1966.

O'BRIEN, WILLIS (1886–1962). American stop-motion animator, one of the towering figures of the fantastic film, a pioneer in the articulation and frame-by-frame filming of small, jointed models. O'Brien's work is not flawless (his protégé, RAY HARRYHAUSEN, has surpassed him technically), but his understanding of personality is impeccable. His contribution to *King Kong*, 1933 helped make that film a durable classic, the prototype for all subsequent films of its kind. Kong is more than flashy movement and a loud growl; he is an individual. His brow puckers, his eyes roll, his nostrils quiver. He is an adept fistfighter (his display of poise as he battles a Tyrannosaurus is marvelous), and a sympathetically inept suitor. Like LUGOSI and Monroe, O'Brien's Kong is one of the screen's great originals. *R.F.D. 10,000 B.C.*, 1917; *Prehistoric Poultry*, 1917; *The Ghost of Slumber Mountain*, 1919; *The Lost World*, 1925; *Son of Kong*, 1933; *Mighty Joe Young* (an underrated film, exciting and blessed with honest sentiment), 1949; *The Black Scorpion* (the nighttime scene in which giant scorpions derail a passenger train on the Mexican desert is a classic), 1957; *The Giant Behemoth*, 1959; *It's a Mad, Mad, Mad, Mad World*, 1963.

O'CONNELL, ARTHUR (1908–). Popular American character actor, usually seen as an amiable and supportive friend of the hero. *The Seven Faces of Dr. Lao*, 1964; *The Monkey's Uncle*, 1965; *The Silencers*, 1966; *Fantastic Voyage*, 1966; *The Power*, 1968; *A Taste of Evil* (TV), 1971; *Ben*, 1972.

Arthur O'Connell observes his serpentine double in *The Seven Faces of Dr. Lao* (1964).

Kong picks up a native in a censored scene from the 1933 classic *King Kong*: animation by Willis O'Brien.

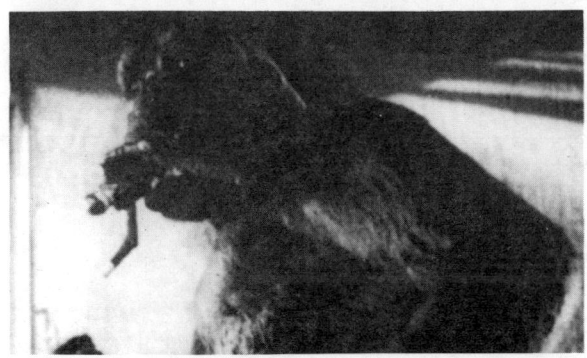

Willis O'Brien's *King Kong* (1933) chews up a New Yorker in a scene cut from many prints of the film.

Another rare censored scene: Kong prepares to devour a helpless villager. Stop-motion animation of *King Kong* (1933) by Willis O'Brien.

Skillful animation by Willis O'Brien brings *Son of Kong* (1933) to life.

O'Connor, Donald (1925–). Energetic, inventive American star dancer and comic actor, at his best in musicals. Throughout the fifties he had the dubious distinction of playing second fiddle to a talking mule in the Francis series. *Francis*, 1949; *Francis Goes to the Races*, 1951; *Francis Goes to West Point*, 1952; *Francis Covers the Big Town*, 1953; *Francis Joins the Wacs*, 1954; *Francis in the Navy*, 1955; *The Wonders of Aladdin*, 1961.

O'Connor, Una (1880–1959). Irish character actress in Hollywood, usually cast as a busybody. *The Invisible Man*, 1933; *Bride of Frankenstein*, 1935; *The Canterville Ghost*, 1944.

Ogilvy, Ian (1943–). Youthful British leading man of the sixties and seventies. *The Sorcerers*, 1967; *The Conquerer Worm*, 1968; *And Now the Screaming Starts*, 1973; *From Beyond the Grave*, 1975.

Ogle, Charles (1865–1940). American actor, the first screen incarnation of Frankenstein's Monster in Edison's *Frankenstein*, 1910. *The Prophecy*, 1913; *The Bribe*, 1915.

Ohmart, Carol (1928–). American leading lady, most active in the fifties. *House on Haunted Hill*, 1958; *Spider Baby or: The Maddest Story Ever Told*, 1970; *The Spectre of Edgar Allan Poe*, 1972.

Inscrutable Warner Oland eyes nemesis Boris Karloff in *Charlie Chan at the Opera* (1936).

Carol Ohmart.

OLAND, WARNER (1880-1938). Swedish character actor who gained public recognition as Charlie Chan. *Charlie Chan in Egypt*, 1935; *Charlie Chan at the Opera*, 1936; *Charlie Chan at the Olympics*, 1937. Also seen in *The Fatal Ring* (a PEARL WHITE serial), 1917; *Lightning Raider*, 1918-19; *The Mysterious Dr. Fu Manchu*, 1929; *Werewolf of London*, 1935.

OLIVIER, SIR LAURENCE (1907-). Acclaimed British stage actor who entered the motion picture mainstream in the nineteen-seventies with leading roles in a number of slick thrillers. *Hamlet*, 1948; *The Boys From Brazil* (as Lieberman), 1978; *Dracula* (as Van Helsing), 1979; *Clash of the Titans* (as Zeus), 1981.

O'MARA, KATE (1939-). Sultry British leading lady of the early seventies. *Corruption*, 1968; *The Horror of Frankenstein*, 1970; *The Vampire Lovers*, 1970; etc.

O'NEAL, PATRICK (1927-). Smooth American actor, skilled at projecting smiling, refined menace. *The Mad Magician*, 1954; *Chamber of Horrors* (lead), 1966; *Matchless*, 1967; *Silent Night, Bloody Night*, 1973; *The Stepford Wives*, 1974.

ORDUNG, WYOTT. American director/screenwriter of grade-Z thrillers in the fifties. *Robot Monster* (w only), 1953; *Monster From the Ocean Floor* (d only; budgeted at $12,000, this was the first science fiction film produced by ROGER CORMAN), 1954; *The Navy vs. The Night Monsters* (asst. d), 1966.*

OSBORN, LYN (1926-58). American actor in American-International films of the fifties, popular as Cadet Happy on television's "Space Patrol," 1950-56. *World Beyond the Moon* (several episodes of "Space Patrol" edited together to make a feature), 1953; *Invasion of the Saucer Men*, 1957; *The Amazing Colossal Man*, 1958; *The Cosmic Man*, 1958.

O'SULLIVAN, MAUREEN (1911-). Pretty and wholesome American leading lady of the thirties and forties, best remembered as Jane to JOHNNY WEISMULLER's Tarzan. *A Connecticut Yankee*, 1931; *Tarzan the Ape Man*, 1932; *Tarzan and His Mate*, 1934; *Tarzan Escapes*, 1936; *The Devil Doll*, 1936; *Tarzan Finds a Son!*, 1939; *Tarzan's Secret Treasure*, 1941; *Tarzan's New York Adventure*, 1942; *The Phynx* (cameo), 1970.

OTTIANO, RAFAELA (1894-1942). Menacing Italian actress in Hollywood. Notable in *The Devil Doll*, 1936. *One Frightened Night*, 1935; *The Florentine Dagger*, 1935; *Topper Returns*, 1941.

OUSPENSKAYA, MARIA (1876-1949). Wizened character actress of Russian origin, remembered as the sage gypsy in *The Wolf Man*, 1941. *The Mystery of Marie Roget*, 1942; *Frankenstein Meets the Wolf Man*, 1943; *Tarzan and the Amazons*, 1945.

P

PAGET, DEBRA (1933–). Pretty American leading lady who started in films while still a teenager; married a Chinese-American oil millionaire and retired to Texas. *From the Earth to the Moon*, 1958; *The Most Dangerous Man Alive*, 1958; *Tales of Terror*, 1962; *The Haunted Palace*, 1963.

PAIVA, NESTOR (1905–66). American character actor, often cast as a superstitious rustic. *Hold That Ghost*, 1941; *A Thousand and One Nights*, 1945; *Mighty Joe Young* (as one of the three men [Paul Guilfoyle and Douglas Fowley are the others] who get Joe drunk), 1949; *Alias Nick Beal*, 1949; *Killer Ape*, 1953; *The Creature from the Black Lagoon*, 1954; *Revenge of the Creature*, 1955; *Tarantula*, 1955; *The Three Stooges in Orbit*, 1962; *Madmen of Mandoras*, 1964; *Jesse James Meets Frankenstein's Daughter*, 1966; others.

PAL, DAVID (CA. 1935–). American stop-motion animator, son of producer GEORGE PAL. *The Time Machine*, 1960; *Jack the Giant Killer*, 1962; *The Wonderful World of the Brothers Grimm*, 1962; *The Power* (notably the hallucinatory sequence in which George Hamilton's head disintegrates), 1968.

Time traveler Rod Taylor *(far right)* observes the hideous Morlocks and captive Eloi in George Pal's *The Time Machine* (1960).

PAL, GEORGE (1908–80). Hungarian producer/director, a trick-film specialist long active in Hollywood. Pal's projects, frequently in collaboration with director BYRON HASKIN, were noted for their opulence and fanciful nature. He enjoyed early Hollywood success with his whimsical Puppetoons films (1943–47), shorts that pioneered stop-motion animation of jointed, cartoonlike dolls. Pal's first feature, *The Great Rupert*, 1949, features what seems to be an amazingly bright squirrel, and was an extension of his Puppetoon technique. *Destination Moon* followed in 1950. Its success ensured Pal's reputation as Hollywood's premier creator of high-quality science fiction. A powerful influence in the fantasy film realm, Pal was highly respected by fans and professionals alike. Two of his films, *The Time Machine*, 1960, and the electrifying *The War of the Worlds*, 1953, are classics. *When Worlds Collide*, 1951; *Conquest of Space*, 1955; *tom thumb*, 1958; *Atlantis, the Lost Continent*, 1961; *The Wonderful World of the Brothers Grimm*, 1962; *The Seven Faces of Dr. Lao*, 1964; *The Power*, 1968; *Doc Savage, the Man of Bronze*, 1975.

The astronauts prepare to explore the lunar surface in Irving Pichel's *Destination Moon* (1950).

PALANCE, JACK (1920–). Skull-faced American character lead, often seen as a soft-spoken villain. A compelling presence, Palance has starred in *Man in the Attic* (as Jack the Ripper), 1953; *Torture Garden*, 1968; *Justine*, 1969; *Dracula* (title role; TV; theatrical release in Britain), 1973; *Craze*, 1974; *The Shape of Things to Come*, 1979.

PALMER, GREGG (1927–). American leading man of low-budget horror films of the fifties. *Son of Ali Baba*, 1952; *The Creature Walks among Us*, 1956; *The Zombies of Mora Tau*, 1957; *From Hell It Came*, 1957; *The Most Dangerous Man Alive*, 1958.

PARK, REG. American muscleman in period fantasy epics made in Italy. *Hercules in the Haunted World*, 1961; *Hercules and the Captive Women*, 1963; *Hercules, Prisoner of Evil*, 1964; *Samson in King Solomon's Mines*, 1964; *La Sfida del Giganti* (*The Challenge of the Giant*), 1965; others.

PARKER, EDDIE (1900–60). American stuntman who doubled for BORIS KARLOFF, BELA LUGOSI, and others, and who played monsters in many films. *Hellzapoppin'* (as Frankenstein's Monster), 1941; *The Ghost of Frankenstein*, 1942; *The Monster and the Ape*, 1945; *The Mummy's Curse*, 1945; *Mighty Joe Young*, 1949; *The Invisible Monster*, 1950; *Abbott and Costello Meet Dr. Jekyll and Mr. Hyde*, 1953; *Abbott and Costello Meet the Mummy*, 1955; *Tarantula*, 1955; *This Island Earth* (as the Metaluna mutant), 1955; *The Mole People*, 1956; *Bride of the Monster*, 1956; *Monster on the Campus*, 1958; *Curse of the Undead*, 1959; others.

PARKIN, DEAN (CA. 1930–). American actor who, disguised beneath a bald dome and heavy facial makeup, played the monster in *War of the Colossal Beast*, 1958. The role is a continuation of one created by GLENN LANGAN in a previous film, *The Amazing Colossal Man*, 1957, and is sometimes erroneously credited to Langan.

PARSONS, MILTON (1904–). Cadaverous, pop-eyed American character actor of the forties, usually seen as a comic undertaker or butler. *Whispering Ghosts*, 1942; *The Hidden Hand*, 1942; *Over My Dead Body*, 1942; *Cry of the Werewolf*, 1944; *Bury Me Dead*, 1947; *The Secret Life of Walter Mitty*, 1947; *Dick Tracy Meets Gruesome*, 1947; *The Monster That Challenged the World*, 1957; *The Haunted Palace*, 1963; *2000 Years Later*, 1969; others.

PATE, MICHAEL (1920–). Australian actor in Hollywood. *The Strange Door*, 1951; *The Black Castle*, 1952; *The Maze*, 1953; *Curse of the Undead* (as the vampire gunslinger), 1959.

PAYTON, BARBARA (1927–67). American leading lady of the fifties who slid from Hollywood Bs to stag movies and alcoholism. *Bride of the Gorilla*, 1952; *The Four-Sided Triangle*, 1953; *Run for the Hills* (A-bomb hysteria), 1953.

PEARCE, JACQUELINE. British actress of the sixties. *The Reptile* (title role: a murderous snake-woman), 1966; *Plague of the Zombies*, 1967; etc.

PECK, GREGORY (1916–). Solid American leading man whose career slipped after having played honorable heroes for thirty years, but who made a big comeback as star of the occult thriller *The Omen*, 1976. *Spellbound*, 1945; *Marooned*, 1969; *The Boys from Brazil* (as Mengele), 1978.

PEEL, DAVID (CA. 1920–). Handsome British actor who took the lead as Baron Meinster in *Brides of Dracula*, 1960, but who went unbilled in most of the film's advertising. *Les Mains d'Orlac* (*The Hands of Orlac*), 1960.

PEREIRA, HAL. Leading American art director, mainly associated with Paramount. *When Worlds Collide*, 1951; *The War of the Worlds*, 1953; *Conquest of Space*, 1955; *The Space Children*, 1958; *I Married a Monster from Outer Space* (particularly moody and disquieting exteriors), 1958; *The Colossus of New York*, 1958; *Robinson Crusoe on Mars*, 1964; *Project X*, 1968; many others.

PERKINS, ANTHONY (1932–). American character lead who began his career in the early fifties by playing skinny boyfriends, but who has been typed as a twitchy nut since a *tour de force* performance as the Oedipal knife murderer Norman Bates in *Psycho*, 1960. *The Fool Killer*, 1965; *Pretty Poison*, 1968; *How Awful about Allan* (TV), 1970; *Winter Kills* (as the insane computer expert who secretly runs the United States), 1979; *The Black Hole*, 1979.

PERRY, ROGER. Bland American actor of the sixties and seventies, from television. *Count Yorga, Vampire*, 1970; *The Return of Count Yorga*, 1971; *The Thing with Two Heads*, 1972.

PERTWEE, JON (1919–). British comic actor who specializes in eccentric nitwits. He appears as a zany vampire in *The House That Dripped Blood*, 1970. *Will Any Gentleman?* (which involves hypnotism), 1953; *Carry on Screaming*, 1966.

PETERS, BROOKE L. American independent producer/director. *The Unearthly*, 1957; *Anatomy of a Psycho*, 1961.

PETRILLO, SAMMY (CA. 1928–). American lowbrow comic who imitated JERRY LEWIS so well that Lewis brought suit in the early fifties. With partner Duke Mitchell (who patterned himself after DEAN MARTIN), Petrillo is featured in *Bela Lugosi Meets a Brooklyn Gorilla*, 1952, a bad film with a gorilla that sings.

PHILBIN, MARY (1903–). American leading lady of silent films. In a scene etched in the memory of all who have seen it, she unmasks Erik (LON CHANEY) in *The Phantom of the Opera*, 1925. *The Man Who Laughs*, 1928.

One of many appealing fellows in Brooke L. Peters' *The Unearthly* (1957).

PICHEL, IRVING (1891-1954). American character actor of the thirties, later director. As actor: *Murder by the Clock*, 1931; *The Return of the Terror*, 1934; *Dracula's Daughter*, 1936; *Torture Ship*, 1939; *Dick Tracy's G-Men* (serial), 1939; *Topper Takes a Trip*, 1939. As director: *The Most Dangerous Game* (co-d; w/ERNEST B. SCHOEDSACK), 1932; *She* (co-d; w/Lansing C. Holden), 1935; *Earthbound*, 1940; *Happy Land*, 1943; *Mr. Peabody and the Mermaid*, 1948; *Destination Moon*, 1950.

PIDGEON, WALTER (1897-). Canadian leading man in Hollywood since the twenties. As he grew older his roles became more forceful. Fantastic film fans will remember him as the tormented Dr. Morbius in *Forbidden Planet*, 1956. *The Gorilla*, 1927; *The Gorilla*, 1930; *The Neptune Factor*, 1973.

PIERCE, JACK (1889-1968). Gifted makeup artist with Universal in the thirties and forties, whose conception of Frankenstein's Monster (*Frankenstein*, 1931) has become one of the screen's most recognizable images. *The Mummy*, 1932; *Bride of Frankenstein*, 1935; *Werewolf of London*, 1935; *The Wolf Man*, 1941; *The Mummy's Tomb*, 1942; *Captive Wild Woman*, 1943; *The Mummy's Ghost*, 1944; *The Mummy's Curse*, 1945; *House of Dracula*, 1945; *House of Frankenstein*, 1945; *Teenage Monster*, 1957; *Giant from the Unknown*, 1958; *The Devil's Hand*, 1958; *Beyond the Time Barrier*, 1960; *Beauty and the Beast*, 1963; many others.

PIERCE, JIM (1900-). Giant-sized American actor and athlete who played Tarzan in *Tarzan and the Golden Lion*, 1927. *Flash Gordon* (as Thun, King of the Lion Men), 1936.

PINK, SIDNEY (1916-). American producer/director/screenwriter active in Scandinavia. *Angry Red Planet*, 1959; *Journey to the 7th Planet*, 1962; *Reptilicus*, 1963; *Pyro* (co-p; w/Richard C. Meyer and co-w; w/Louis De Los Arcos only), 1964; *Operation Atlantis* (p only), 1965; *Sweet Sound of Death* (p only), 1965; *Bang Bang* (p only), 1968.

PITT, INGRID (1944-). Voluptuous Polish leading lady in British horror films of the seventies. She is the object of a cult that, one suspects has arisen as much because of her willingness to disrobe for the camera as for her talent. *Sound of Horror*, 1964; *The Vampire Lovers*, 1970; *The House That Dripped Blood*, 1970; *Countess Dracula*, 1972; *The Wicker Man*, 1973.

PLEASENCE, DONALD (1919-). Balding, mild British star character actor, seen to good advantage when playing neurotic or perverse villains. *Mania*, 1960. *Les Mains d'Orlac* (*The Hands of Orlac*), 1960; *Fantastic Voyage*, 1966; *Eye of the Devil*, 1967; *You Only Live Twice* (as Blofeld), 1967; *Tales That Witness Madness*, 1973; *Tales from beyond the Grave*, 1973; *Raw Meat*, 1973; *The Devil's Men*, 1976; *Oh God!*, 1977; *Land of the Minotaur*, 1977; *Halloween*, 1979; others.

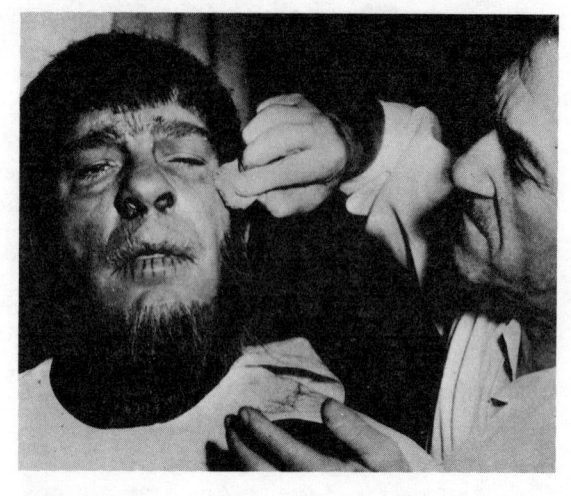

Makeup wizard Jack Pierce transforms Lon Chaney, Jr., into the Wolf Man, ca. 1945.

Reptilicus (1963), toothsome brainchild of Sidney Pink.

Ingrid Pitt *(left)* as *Countess Dracula* (1973).

Donald Pleasence is led away at the conclusion of *Tales That Witness Madness* (1973). Jack Hawkins is at extreme left.

Lon Chaney, Jr., returns from the dead to visit girl friend Marian Carr in Jack Pollexfen's *The Indestructible Man* (1956).

POE, EDGAR ALLAN (1809–49). Popular American poet and short-story writer whose grim and often depraved point of view seems to have been drawn from his wretched life. Several biographical films have been made, the earliest by D.W. GRIFFITH in 1909. ROGER CORMAN made Poe a box office star with a series of often-stylish adaptations in the early sixties. Films from Poe works include *The Raven*, 1912, 1935, 1963; *The Fall of the House of Usher*, 1928, 1928, 1941, 1942 (directed by CURTIS HARRINGTON), 1948, 1955, 1958, and 1960 (entitled *House of Usher*; directed by Roger Corman); *The Pit and the Pendulum*, 1913 and 1961; *The Masque of the Red Death*, 1964 and 1969 (the latter a moody and disturbing Yugoslavian cartoon). Elements from Poe's works, particularly the pendulum and the nasty thrill of walling up one's enemies, have been incorporated into many films, and he appears as a focal character in a number of fictional horror thrillers, among them *The Spectre of Edgar Allan Poe*, 1972 and ANTONIO MARGHERITI's *Castle of Blood*, 1964.

POLANSKI, ROMAN (1933–). Polish-born director of psychological horror thrillers. His turbulent private life has not obscured his considerable talent, but a sensational sex trial in 1977 may have seriously impaired his career. *Two Men and a Wardrobe* (short), 1958; *Knife in the Water*, 1961; *Repulsion*, 1965; *The Fearless Vampire Killers*, 1967; *Rosemary's Baby*, 1968; *Macbeth*, 1971; *Blood for Dracula* (actor only), 1974; *The Tenant* (and title role), 1976.

POLLAR, GENE (1892–). American fireman who was signed to play the jungle lord Tarzan in *The Return of Tarzan*, 1920, but who became disillusioned with filmmaking and returned to firefighting.

POLLEXFEN, JACK. American producer/director whose *The Indestructible Man*, 1956, ranks among the most bluntly savage s.f.-horror films of the fifties (see also: LON CHANEY, JR). *Captive Women* (co-w and p only; w/AUBREY WISBERG), 1952; *Port Sinister* (co-w and p only; w/AUBREY WISBERG), 1953; *Daughter of Dr. Jekyll* (p and w only), 1957; *Monstrosity* (co-p only; w/Dean Dillman, Jr.), 1964.

PORTER, EDWIN S. (1869–1941). Seminal American director whose *The Great Train Robbery*, 1903 is the first important American feature film. He experimented with trick films and, along with GEORGE MÉLIÈS, set down many of the fantastic film's visual ground rules. *An Artist's Dream*, 1900; *The Artist's Dilemma*, 1901; *Another Job for the Undertaker*, 1901; *Dream of a Rarebit Fiend*, 1906; *Rescued from an Eagle's Nest*, 1908; *Faust*, 1909; *Alice's Adventures in Wonderland*, 1910; many more.

Mala Powers eyes a sudsy fungus creature in *The Unknown Terror* (1957).

PORTILLO, RAFAEL LOPEZ. Mexican director responsible for the execrable but enormously popular Aztec Mummy series. *The Aztec Mummy*, 1957; *The Robot vs. the Aztec Mummy*, 1959; *The Curse of the Aztec Mummy*, 1961; *La Isla de los Dinosaurios* (includes stock footage from *One Million B.C.*, 1940), 1967; many others.

POST, DON (1902-79). American makeup artist and maskmaker. *Invasion of the Body Snatchers* (the giant pods), 1956; *Space Master X-7*, 1958; *The Comedy of Terrors*, 1963; *The Haunted Palace*, 1963; *The Time Travelers*, 1964.

POWELL, EDDIE. British stuntman behind the moldy bandages in JOHN GILLING's *The Mummy's Shroud*, 1967. *Daleks—Invasion Earth 2150 A.D.*, 1968.

POWELL, MICHAEL (1905-). British writer/director whose modestly produced *Peeping Tom*, 1960 is a masterful and highly disturbing examination of psychosexual perversion. *A Matter of Life and Death*, 1946.

POWERS, MALA (1931-). American leading lady of the fifties who began her career as a child actress in 1941. *City beneath the Sea*, 1953; *The Unknown Terror*, 1957; *The Colossus of New York*, 1958; *Flight of the Lost Balloon*, 1961; *Doomsday*, 1972.

Vincent Price, most suave of black-hearted villains.

PRICE, VINCENT (1911–). Tall, elegantly sinister American star character actor, adept at conveying smooth, cultured menace. His starring roles in ROGER CORMAN'S impressive series of EDGAR ALLAN POE adaptations seem to have established his screen persona; he is considered one of filmdom's most notable personalities. Something of a Renaissance man, Price is an accomplished gourmet cook, art expert, traveler, and lecturer. At first cast in period costume films after coming to Hollywood from the stage in 1938, Price made a strong impression opposite BORIS KARLOFF and BASIL RATHBONE in *Tower of London*, 1939. In 1953 he starred as the disfigured and insane proprietor of *House of Wax*, and was thereafter typed in horror roles. Price seems proud of his reputation as reigning King of Horror. *The Invisible Man Returns* (as the Invisible Man), 1940; *The House of the Seven Gables*, 1940; *Shock* (as Dr. Corss, the murderous psychiatrist), 1946; *Abbott and Costello Meet Frankenstein* (voice only; as the Invisible Man), 1948; *The Mad Magician*, 1954; *Son of Sinbad*, 1955; *The Story of Mankind* (as the Devil), 1957; *The Fly* (as Francois, not the title role), 1958; *House on Haunted Hill*, 1958; *The Bat*, 1958; *The Tingler*, 1959; *House of Usher* (as Roderick Usher), 1960; *The Pit and the Pendulum*, 1961; *Master of the World* (as Robur), 1961; *Tales of Terror*, 1962; *Confessions of an Opium Eater*, 1962; *Tower of London*, 1962; *The Raven*, 1963; *Diary of a Madman*, 1963; *Twice-Told Tales* ("Dr. Heidegger's Experiment" segment), 1963; *The Comedy of Terrors*, 1963; *The Haunted Palace*, 1963; *The Last Man on Earth*, 1964; *The Masque of the Red Death* (as Prince Prospero), 1964; *The Tomb of Ligeia*, 1965; *War-Gods of the Deep*, 1965; *Dr. Goldfoot and the Bikini Machine* (as Dr. Goldfoot), 1965; *Dr. Goldfoot and the Girl Bombs*, 1966; *House of 1000 Dolls*, 1967; *The Conqueror Worm* (as witchfinder Matthew Hopkins), 1968; *The Oblong Box*, 1969; *Spirits of the Dead* (narration only), 1969; *Cry of the Banshee*, 1970; *Scream and Scream Again*, 1970; *The Abominable Dr. Phibes* (as Dr. Phibes), 1971; *Dr. Phibes Rises Again*, 1972; *Theatre of Blood* (as Shakespearean actor Edward Lionheart), 1973; *Madhouse*, 1973; *The Monster Club*, 1981.

PRINE, ANDREW (1936–). Slender American actor who often plays sneaks. *Simon, King of the Witches*, 1971. *Hannah—Queen of the Vampires*, 1972; *Crypt of the Living Dead*, 1973; *Terror Circus* aka *Barn of the Naked Dead*, 1973; *The Evil*, 1978.

PROHASKA, JANOS (1921–74). Hungarian-born costume maker and actor who specialized in apes. Although most active in television, Prohaska was seen in *Planet of the Apes*, 1968. He died in a plane crash that also claimed the life of his son Robert, also a costume builder.

PROWSE, DAVID (1941–). British weight-lifting champion active in films, usually cast as a brute or monster. *Horror of Frankenstein*, 1970; *A Clockwork Orange* (as Julian), 1971; *Vampire Circus*, 1972; *Frankenstein and the Monster from Hell*, 1973; *Star Wars* (as Darth Vader; voice supplied by James Earl Jones), 1977; *The Empire Strikes Back* (as Darth Vader), 1980.

Vincent Price has it out with unfaithful wife Barbara Steele in Roger Corman's *The Pit and the Pendulum* (1961).

Q

QUARRY, ROBERT (1928–). American character actor and former juvenile performer who achieved minor success as a vampire in *Count Yorga, Vampire*, 1970, and *Return of Count Yorga*, 1971. *Shadow of a Doubt*, 1943; *Dr. Phibes Rises Again*, 1972; *The Deathmaster* (and p), 1972; *The Revenge of Dr. Death*, 1973; *Madhouse*, 1973; *Sugar Hill*, 1974.

QUINN, ANTHONY (1915–). Mexican leading actor in Hollywood from the thirties, an explosive but limited talent who progressed from greasy gigolos to naturalistic heroes. His *Hunchback of Notre Dame*, 1957 is well-played but a little off-the-mark. *Television Spy*, 1939; *The Ghost Breakers*, 1940.

Jack Rabin's awesome *Kronos* (1957), one of the few wholly unanthropomorphized SF film menaces from the fifties.

R

RABIN, JACK (CA. 1910–). American special-effects technician who has achieved impressive illusions on small budgets, often in tandem with IRVING BLOCK. *Rocketship X-M*, 1950; *Unknown World*, 1951; *Captive Women*, 1951; *Flight to Mars*, 1951; *Invasion U.S.A.*, 1953; *Port Sinister*, 1953; *Robot Monster*, 1953; *The Beast of Hollow Mountain*, 1956; *Daughter of Dr. Jekyll*, 1957; *Pharaoh's Curse*, 1957; *The Invisible Boy*, 1957; *Kronos* (and co-p; w/IRVING BLOCK and LOUIS DEWITT), 1957; *The Monster from Green Hell*, 1958; *The Atomic Submarine*, 1960; *Death Race 2000*, 1975; *Hollywood Boulevard*, 1976; others.

RAIN, DOUGLAS. American actor who provided the deceptively rational voice for the computer HAL in STANLEY KUBRICK'S *2001: A Space Odyssey*, 1968.

RAINS, CLAUDE (1889–1967). Distinguished British star character actor in Hollywood, a sophisticated gentleman (or villain) in many films of the thirties and forties. *The Invisible Man* (title role; film debut), 1933; *The Man Who Reclaimed His Head*, 1935; *The Mystery of Edwin Drood*, 1935; *Here Comes Mr. Jordan* (as the Heavenly messenger), 1941; *The Wolf Man*, 1941; *The Phantom of the Opera* (title role), 1943; *Angel on My Shoulder* (as Satan), 1946; *The Lost World* (as Challenger), 1960; *Battle of the Worlds*, 1960.

RAMBALDI, CARLO (1926–). Italian special-effects technician who designed the disappointing forty-foot robot King Kong for the 1976 remake, but who redeemed himself with the beautiful remote-controlled alien seen at the conclusion of *Close Encounters of the Third Kind*, 1977 and the demonic extraterrestrial of *Alien*, 1979. *Nightwing* (radio-controlled mechanical bats), 1979.

RANDALL, TONY (1920–). American actor, often cast as a likeable eccentric and most familiar as fussy Felix on television's "The Odd Couple," 1970–75. In *The Seven Faces of Dr. Lao*, 1964, Randall is in makeup as six of them, the Abominable Snowman being played by Peter Pal. *The Brass Bottle*, 1964.

RATHBONE, BASIL (1892–1967). British star character actor in Hollywood whose cultured manner and distinguished profile served him well when playing suave villains, but who will be remembered as the screen's definitive Sherlock Holmes, 1939–46. Most active throughout the forties, Rathbone remained an elegant figure until his death. *The Hound of the Baskervilles* (as Holmes), 1939; *Tower of London*, 1939; *Son of Frankenstein* (as Baron Wolf von Frankenstein), 1939; *The Mad Doctor*, 1941; *The Black Cat*, 1941; *Fingers at the Window*, 1942; *Spider Woman*, 1944; *The Scarlet Claw*, 1944; *Pearl of Death* (featuring RONDO HATTEN as The Creeper), 1944; *The Adventures of Ichabod and Mr. Toad* (narration only), 1949; *The Black Sleep*, 1956; *The Stingiest Man in Town* (TV; b/o Dickens's *A Christmas Carol*; cast as Scrooge), 1956; *The Magic Sword*, 1962; *Red Hell* (an anti-Communism fantasy-allegory), 1962; *Tales of Terror*, 1962; *The Comedy of Terrors*, 1963; *Voyage to the Prehistoric Planet*, 1965; *Queen of Blood*, 1966; *The Ghost in the Invisible Bikini*, 1966; *Hillbillys [sic] in a Haunted House*, 1967.

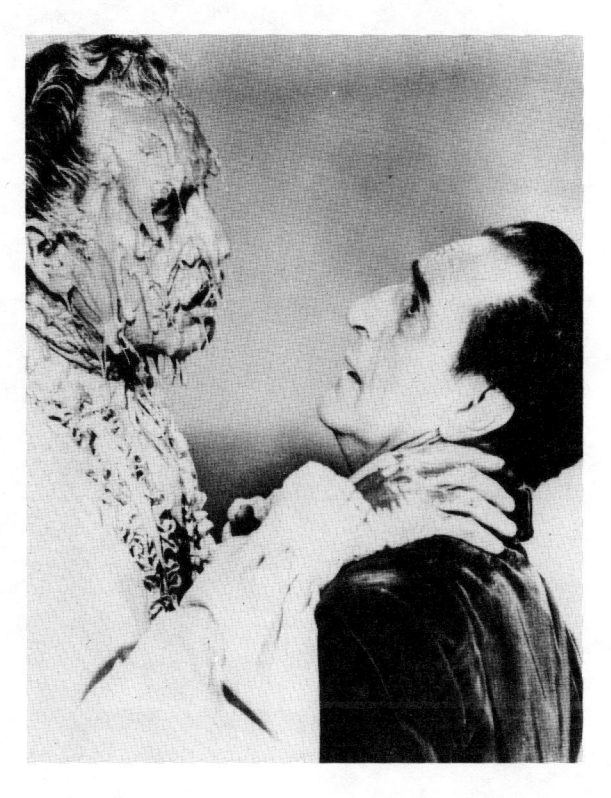

Basil Rathbone *(right)* meets a decaying Vincent Price in *Tales of Terror* (1962).

Tony Randall as Medusa in *The Seven Faces of Dr. Lao* (1964).

Christopher Reeve as the Man of Steel remains unruffled in the face of thugs and crowbars in *Superman* (1978).

RAVEN, MIKE (CA. 1927–). Neatly bearded British actor and former disc jockey, in lurid horror thrillers of the early seventies. *Lust for a Vampire*, 1971; *Crucible of Terror*, 1971; *I, Monster*, 1971; *Disciple of Death* (and w; co-p), 1973.

RAYMOND, PAULA (1923–). Poised American leading lady of the fifties. *The Beast from 20,000 Fathoms*, 1953; *Flight That Disappeared*, 1961; *Hand of Death*, 1961; *Blood of Dracula's Castle*, 1969; *Five Bloody Graves*, 1970.

REASON, REX (1928–). Dark, pleasant American leading man of the fifties. *This Island Earth*, 1955; *The Creature Walks among Us*, 1956.

REDGRAVE, MICHAEL (1908–). Highly respected British leading actor who has brought a forceful dignity to film roles for forty years. He is memorable as the tormented ventriloquist in *Dead of Night*, 1946. *1984*, 1956; *The Innocents*, 1961; *Goodbye Gemini*, 1970.

REED, OLIVER (1938–). Husky British star character actor. *The Two Faces of Dr. Jekyll*, 1960; *Curse of the Werewolf* (as the werewolf), 1961; *These Are the Damned*, 1961; *Night Creatures*, 1962; *Paranoic*, 1963; *The Devils*, 1971; *Z.P.G.*, 1972; *Burnt Offerings*, 1976; *The Brood*, 1978; *Dr. Heckyl and Mr. Hype* (title role), 1980.

George Reeves as *Daily Planet* reporter Clark Kent.

George Reeves, immortal as Superman.

REED, WALTER. American star of serials and B-films. *Daredevils of the Red Circle*, 1939; *Flying Disc Man from Mars*, 1951; *Superman and the Mole Men*, 1951; *Macumba Love*, 1960; others.

REEVE, CHRISTOPHER (1952–). Young American stage actor whose film debut in the title role of *Superman*, 1978 is stunningly good, rich with honest humor and brimming with energy and muscular grace. One of perhaps the most exciting film discoveries of the seventies. *Somewhere in Time*, 1980; *Superman II*, 1981.

REEVES, GEORGE (1914–59). Husky American leading man, television's Superman, 1951–58. After a film debut in *Gone with the Wind* in 1939, Reeves seemed poised on the edge of a promising career. He first played Superman on screen in *Superman and the Mole Men*, 1951; his success in the subsequent television series was immediate and great but typecast him. His suicide in 1959 is generally attributed to his inability to escape his TV image and develop as an actor. In 1954, Twentieth Century-Fox released five Superman features, each composed of three unedited episodes from the television series: *Superman's Peril, Superman Flies Again, Superman in Exile, Superman and Scotland Yard,* and *Superman and the Jungle Devil*. It should be noted that *Superman and the Mole Men* became episodes 25 and 26 of the TV series, and was retitled "The Unknown People."

Steve Reeves as Hercules (1959).

REEVES, MICHAEL (1944–69). British director whose early death put an end to a promising career. *Revenge of the Blood Beast*, 1966; *The Sorcerers*, 1967; *The Conqueror Worm*, 1968.

REEVES, STEVE (1926–). American bodybuilder turned actor, popular in the late fifties and sixties as star of Italian-produced muscleman epics. *Hercules*, 1959; *Hercules Unchained*, 1960; *The Thief of Bagdad*, 1960; *Duel of the Titans*, 1961; others.

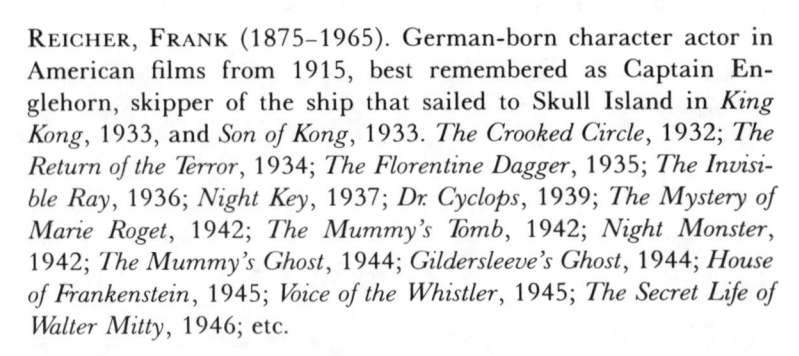

REICHER, FRANK (1875–1965). German-born character actor in American films from 1915, best remembered as Captain Englehorn, skipper of the ship that sailed to Skull Island in *King Kong*, 1933, and *Son of Kong*, 1933. *The Crooked Circle*, 1932; *The Return of the Terror*, 1934; *The Florentine Dagger*, 1935; *The Invisible Ray*, 1936; *Night Key*, 1937; *Dr. Cyclops*, 1939; *The Mystery of Marie Roget*, 1942; *The Mummy's Tomb*, 1942; *Night Monster*, 1942; *The Mummy's Ghost*, 1944; *Gildersleeve's Ghost*, 1944; *House of Frankenstein*, 1945; *Voice of the Whistler*, 1945; *The Secret Life of Walter Mitty*, 1946; etc.

REID, MILTON. Bald, fleshy actor in British thrillers of the sixties and seventies, invariably cast as a brutish thug. *Night Creatures*, 1962; *The Man With the Golden Gun*, 1974; *Arabian Adventure* (as the murderous genie), 1979.

RENARD, MAURICE (1885–1940). French novelist whose *The Hands of Orlac* has inspired three film adaptations, in 1925, 1935 (as *Mad Love*), and 1960 *(Les Mains d'Orlac)*. In addition, there have been numerous uncredited variations on Renard's story of a musician who is surgically given the hands of a murderer after losing his own.

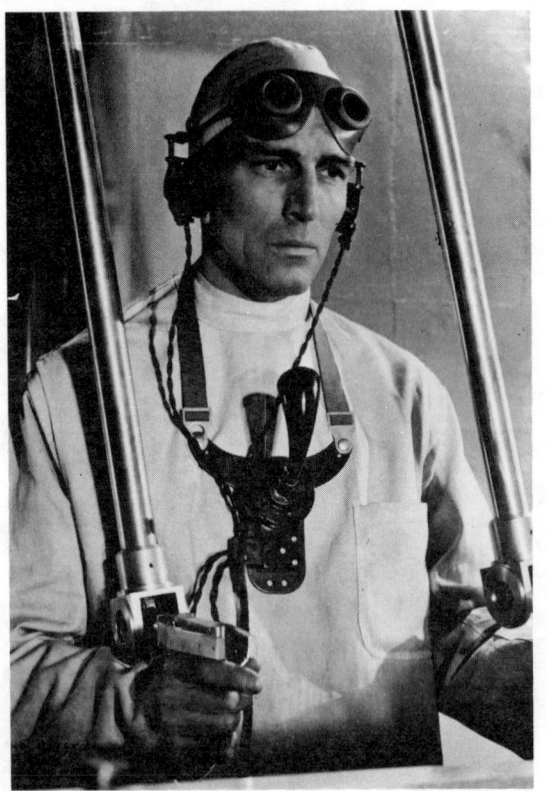

Michael Rennie.

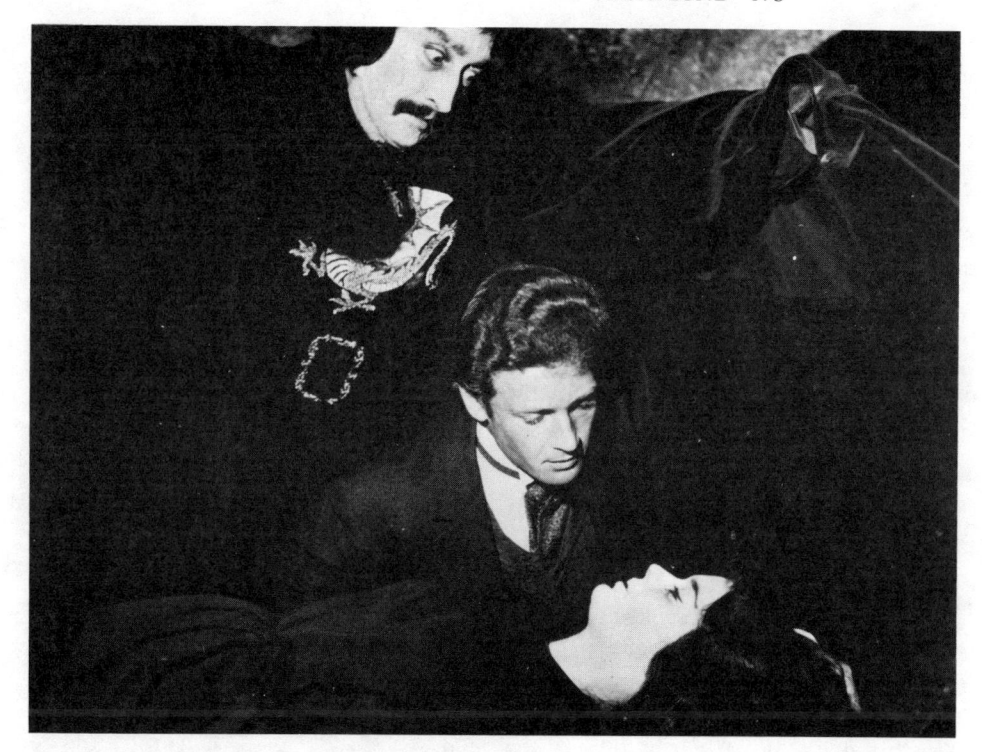

John Richardson bends over Barbara Steele in *Black Sunday* (1960). Ivo Garrani hovers behind.

RENNIE, MICHAEL (1909–71). Distinguished British leading actor who played the benevolent but single-minded extraterrestrial emissary Klaatu in *The Day the Earth Stood Still*, 1951. *Tower of Terror*, 1942; *I'll Never Forget You* (time travel; reincarnation) 1951; *The Lost World*, 1960; *Cyborg 2087*, 1966; *The Power*, 1968; *Krakatoa East of Java*, 1969; *Assignment Terror*, 1970.

REYNOLDS, WILLIAM (CA. 1931–). Youthful-looking American second lead, under contract to Universal Pictures in the fifties, and best known as agent Colby on television's "The FBI" (1965–74). *Cult of the Cobra*, 1955. *The Land Unknown*, 1957. *The Thing That Couldn't Die* (leading role), 1958.

RICHARDSON, JOHN (1936–). Stiff British leading man of the sixties. *Black Sunday*, 1960; *She*, 1965; *One Million Years B.C.*, 1967; *The Vengeance of She*, 1968; *Torso*, 1975.

RICHARDSON, SIR RALPH (1902–). Accomplished British stage and screen actor. *The Ghoul*, 1934; *Things to Come* (as Rudolph), 1936; *The Man Who Could Work Miracles*, 1937; *Whoever Slew Auntie Roo?*, 1971; *Tales from the Crypt* (as the Crypt-Keeper), 1972; *Alice's Adventures in Wonderland* (as the Caterpillar), 1972; *O Lucky Man!*, 1973; *Rollerball*, 1975.

RICHMOND, KANE (1906–73). American leading man of serials and co-features. *The Lost City*, 1935; *Flash Gordon's Trip to Mars*, 1938; *Spy Smasher*, 1942; *Haunted Harbor*, 1944; *Jungle Raiders*, 1945; *Behind the Mask*, 1946; *Brick Bradford*, 1947.

RICKLES, DON (1926–). Bitingly funny American insult comedian who has convincingly handled dramatic roles in a few films. His portrait of the stupid and opportunistic carny barker who exploits RAY MILLAND in *X—The Man with the X-Ray Eyes*, 1963, is outstanding. Also seen in *Pajama Party* (sf-comedy), 1964.

RIGG, DIANA (1938–). Lissome British leading lady and stage star, the object of a worldwide cult for her role as the emancipated Emma Peel on television's "The Avengers," 1965–68. *A Midsummer Night's Dream*, 1969; *On Her Majesty's Secret Service* (as Tracy, the girl who marries super-spy James Bond; she is murdered at the climax by arch-villain Ernst Blofeld), 1969; *Theatre of Blood*, 1973.

RILLA, WOLF (1920–). British director whose generally workmanlike output is led by *Village of the Damned*, 1960, based on JOHN WYNDHAM's brilliant novel *The Midwich Cuckoos*, about an English village that is one day mysteriously stopped dead, its people quietly rendered unconscious, its women impregnated by a sinister alien life-force. Rilla's direction is as cool as the hybrid children who result from the cosmic rape, building with deceptive calm to moments of pure terror, as when the children mentally instruct a man to blow his head off with a shotgun when he has thought of turning the weapon against them. The film's finest moments, however, occur early on, when the town is under the alien influence: a woman sprawls beside her washtub as the water runs over, an iron steadily burns through a dress and, most chillingly, a tractor with an unconscious driver putts round and round until stopping against a tree. While Rilla brings the film to an explosive climax, the tone remains intelligently understated.

Diana Rigg makes it clear why she is the object of a worldwide cult.

Martin Stephens, Barbara Shelley, and George Sanders in a publicity still from Wolf Rilla's disquieting *Village of The Damned* (1960).

Ann Robinson, trying to make the best out of this insipid publicity photo.

RIPPER, MICHAEL (1913-). British character actor, often cast as an eccentric fellow who provides comedy relief. *X—The Unknown*, 1957; *Enemy from Space*, 1957; *The Revenge of Frankenstein*, 1958; *Brides of Dracula*, 1960; *The Anatomist*, 1961; *The Reptile*, 1966; *The Plague of the Zombies*, 1966; *Scars of Dracula*, 1970; many others.

ROBERTSON, CLIFF (1925-). Much-underrated American star actor, an Oscar-winner for his superb performance as *Charly*, 1968, the gentle moron who tastes genius after experimental surgery, and then tragically reverts. *Obsession*, 1976; *Dominique*, 1978.

ROBINSON, ANN (1927-). American leading lady of the early fifties who played the plucky heroine of BYRON HASKIN's *The War of the Worlds*, 1953. She abandoned her career after marrying a bullfighter in the nineteen-sixties, but caused a pleasant stir as an honored guest at a 1977 Hollywood rerelease of *The War of the Worlds*.

ROBINSON, EDWARD G. (1893-1973). Scowling, thickset American star character actor, often cast as a gangster or tough, unorthodox hero. Robinson is probably the most realistically compelling of all the Warner Brothers male stars of the thirties and forties, and remained an important and well-liked figure until his death. *Flesh and Fantasy*, 1943; *Night Has a Thousand Eyes* (as the magician who can foretell the future, and sees his own death), 1948; *Nightmare*, 1956; *Soylent Green* (his last; as the future man with the forbidden love of books), 1973.

ROBLES, GERMAN. Mexican actor long popular in atmospheric horror thrillers, usually cast as a vampire. *The Vampire's Coffin*, 1957; *The Castle of the Monsters*, 1957; *El Vampiro Acecha (The Lucking Vampire*; Argentine), 1959; *The Curse of Nostradamus*, 1961; *Monster Demolisher*, 1962; *Genii of Darkness*, 1962; *Blood of Nostradamus*, 1962; many others.

ROBSON, MARK (1913-). American director who rose from programmers to big commercial films of the sixties and seventies. *The Ghost Ship*, 1943; *Isle of the Dead*, 1945; *Bedlam*, 1946; *Happy Birthday, Wanda June*, 1971.

RODANN, ZIVA (CA. 1933-). Dark and exotic American leading lady of the fifties, usually in films with novel themes. *The Story of Mankind*, 1957; *Pharaoh's Curse*, 1957; *Macumba Love* (voodoo), 1960; *The Giants of Thessaly*, 1960.

ROEG, NICOLAS (1928–). Imaginative British cinematographer and later director. His photography for ROGER CORMAN's *The Masque of the Red Death*, 1964, is lush and splendidly evocative, particularly during a sequence in which the camera tracks VINCENT PRICE as he walks through a succession of differently colored rooms. Roeg brings his keen eye for color and texture to *Don't Look Now*, 1973, probably his best work as director. Set in a decaying Vienna, the film is a nightmarish exercise in the horror of precognition, paranoia, and sudden death. Roeg has thus far demonstrated a knack for fragmented but satisfyingly effective narrative development, and an ability to create startling images without being overwhelmed by them. *The Man Who Fell to Earth*, 1976.

Julie Christie confers with the psychic sisters in Nicolas Roeg's *Don't Look Now* (1973).

ROFFMAN, JULIAN. Canadian independent producer/director responsible for *The Mask*, 1961, a successfully disconcerting low-budget excursion into surreal fantasy concerning an ornate Aztec mask that causes the wearer to hallucinate and commit murder. The mad hallucinatory sequences are in 3-D, and are alternately terrifying and disturbingly sexual. Roffman has been little heard of since *The Mask*, which was given a limited drive-in rerelease in 1977 as *The Eyes of Hell*.

ROGERS, JEAN (1916-). Pretty American leading lady of the thirties, remembered as Dale to BUSTER CRABBE's *Flash Gordon*, 1936. *Night Key*, 1937; *Flash Gordon's Trip to Mars*, 1938.

ROHMER, SAX (1886-1959). British novelist who created the fiendish Oriental mastermind Fu Manchu. The character has come to the screen more than a dozen times since 1923, most notably in the persons of BORIS KARLOFF and CHRISTOPHER LEE. *The Mystery of Dr. Fu Manchu*, 1923; *The Mysterious Dr. Fu Manchu*, 1929; *The Mask of Fu Manchu*, 1932; *Drums of Fu Manchu*, 1940; *El Otro Fu Manchu*, 1940; *The Face of Fu Manchu*, 1965; *The Brides of Fu Manchu*, 1966; others.

Sex and death, disturbingly explored in Julian Roffman's *The Mask* (1961).

ROLFE, GUY (1915–). Gaunt British character actor, suitably grim as *Mr. Sardonicus*, 1961, the man so terrified by the sight of his father's rotted corpse that his face has been frozen into a hideous rictus grin. *Stranglers of Bombay*, 1960; *And Now the Screaming Starts*, 1973.

ROLLIN, JEAN (1940–). French writer/director of cheap, erotic vampire thrillers. *Les Femmes Vampires*, 1967; *La Vampire Nue (The Nude Vampire)*, 1969; *Le Culte du Vampire*, 1971; *Vierges et Vampires (Virgins and the Vampires)*, 1973; many others.

ROMAIN, YVONNE (1938–). French leading lady active in Britain and Hollywood. *Corridors of Blood*, 1958; *Circus of Horrors*, 1960; *Curse of the Werewolf*, 1961; *Night Creatures*, 1962; *Devil Doll*, 1964.

ROMERO, CESAR (1907–). Dashing and good-humored Latin-American leading man of the thirties and forties who was featured as the laughingly psychotic Joker on television's "Batman," 1966–68, and the 1966 theatrical feature *Batman*. *Two on a Guillotine*, 1965; *Latitude Zero*, 1969; *Now You See Him, Now You Don't*, 1972; *The Spectre of Edgar Allan Poe*, 1972; *The Strongest Man in the World*, 1975.

ROMERO, EDDIE. Enterprising producer/director active in the Philippines. *Terror Is a Man* (executive p only), 1959; *Brides of Blood* (co-d; w/Gerardo DeLeon), 1968; *Blood Demon*, 1969; *Mad Doctor of Blood Island*, 1969. *Beast of the Yellow Night* (co-p; w/ JOHN ASHLEY), 1971; *Twilight People* (& co-p; w/JOHN ASHLEY), 1972; *The Womanhunt* (d only), 1972; others.

ROMERO, GEORGE (1940–). Highly talented but much-criticized American director whose *Night of the Living Dead*, 1968, has become one of the big cult films of the seventies. The picture deserves its considerable reputation, combining visceral terror with a shocking nihilism. *The Crazies*, 1973; *Hungry Wives*, 1973; *Martin*, 1978; *Dawn of the Dead*, 1979.

ROONEY, MICKEY (1920–). Dynamic American star actor, known for his short stature, many marriages, and inexhaustible talent. A box-office king as a youngster, Rooney was later effective in a variety of character roles. His career has survived middle age. *A Midsummer Night's Dream* (as Puck), 1935; *Francis in the Haunted House*, 1956; *The Private Lives of Adam and Eve* (& co-d; w/ ALBERT ZUGSMITH; cast as the Devil), 1961; *Everything's Ducky* (which involves a talking duck), 1961; *Pete's Dragon*, 1977.

ROSE, RUTH (CA. 1900–). American screenwriter associated with producer MERIAN C. COOPER, and married to director ERNEST B. SCHOEDSACK. A former actress and explorer. *King Kong* (co-w; w/ James Creelman), 1933; *Son of Kong*, 1933; *She*, 1935; *Mighty Joe Young*, 1949.

Don't trust that smile: Cesar Romero as the Joker in *Batman* (1966).

Katharine Ross in *The Stepford Wives* (1974).

Gene Roth as the sheriff in *Attack of The Giant Leeches* (1959).

Barbara Rush and Richard Carlson. *It Came from Outer Space* (1953).

ROSEN, PHIL (1888–1951). American director of often atmospheric B-films. *Spooks Run Wild*, 1941; *The Man with Two Lives*, 1942; *The Mystery of Marie Roget*, 1942; *Black Magic*, 1944; *Return of the Ape Man*, 1944; *The Jade Mask*, 1945; *The Scarlet Clue*, 1945.

ROSS, KATHARINE (1942–). Doe-eyed American leading lady of the sixties and seventies, one of the few bright elements of *The Stepford Wives*, 1974, as the young wife who suspects that something is amiss with the women in her town. *Games*, 1967; *The Legacy*, 1979; *Murder by Natural Causes* (TV), 1979; *The Final Countdown*, 1980.

ROSSITTO, ANGELO (CA. 1905–). Italian-American dwarf actor active in films for half a century. *Seven Footprints to Satan*, 1929; *Freaks*, 1932; *Spooks Run Wild*, 1941; *The Corpse Vanishes*, 1942; *Scared to Death*, 1947; *The Magic Sword*, 1962; *Dracula vs. Frankenstein*, 1971; *Brain of Blood*, 1971; *Lord of the Rings* (live-action tavern sequence), 1978; *Galaxina* (as an alien), 1980; many others.

ROTH, GENE (1901–76). Bulky American character actor, usually seen as a villain or tough authority figure. He began his career under his real name, Gene Stutenroth. *Captain Video*, 1951; *Red Planet Mars*, 1952; *The Lost Planet*, 1953; *Earth vs. the Spider*, 1958; *She Demons*, 1958; *Tormented*, 1960; *Twice-Told Tales*, 1963.

ROTHMAN, STEPHANIE. American director of the seventies, coming up through the ranks of ROGER CORMAN's New World Pictures. As a woman involved in the creation of blood-and-bosom pictures, Rothman is a rarity. *Voyage to the Prehistoric Planet* (associate p only), 1965; *Blood Bath* (co-d; w/JACK HILL), 1966; *The Velvet Vampire*, 1971; *Terminal Island*, 1973; etc.

ROZSA, MIKLOS (1907–). Hungarian composer in Hollywood who has written lively scores for a few fantasies. *The Thief of Bagdad*, 1940; *The Power*, 1968; *The Golden Voyage of Sinbad*, 1973; *Time after Time* (sweeping and lyrical), 1979.

RUSH, BARBARA (1927–). Beautiful American leading lady who projects a soft-spoken sensitivity. Early in her career she was cast as the heroine in *When Worlds Collide*, 1951 and *It Came From Outer Space*, 1953. Also *The Eyes of Charles Sand* (TV), 1972.

Sabu.

RUSOFF, LOU. American screenwriter associated with American-International during the fifties and sixties. *It Conquered the World*, 1956; *The She Creature*, 1956; *The Day the World Ended*, 1956; *The Phantom from 10,000 Leagues*, 1956; *The Cat Girl* (and p), 1957; *The Ghost of Dragstrip Hollow* (and p), 1959.

RUSSELL, KEN (1927–). British writer/producer/director whose undeniable visual flair has been applied rather hollowly; his loud and colorful films mostly impress the easily impressionable. *The Devils*, 1971; *The Boy Friend*, 1971; *Tommy*, 1976; *Lisztomania*, 1977.

RUSSELL, KURT (1947–). Pleasant American juvenile lead of the sixties and seventies, associated with WALT DISNEY productions. He is usually cast as a bright but normal kid who stumbles upon something with humorous ramifications, *e.g.*, invisibility in *Now You See Him, Now You Don't*, 1972. *The Absent-Minded Professor*, 1961; *The Strongest Man in the World* (title role), 1975.

RUSSELL, RAY (1924–). American screenwriter of the sixties. *Mr. Sardonicus*, 1961; *Zotz!*, 1962; *The Premature Burial* (co-w; w/ CHARLES BEAUMONT), 1962; *X—The Man with the X-Ray Eyes*, 1963; others.

RUVINSKIS, WOLF. European actor in Mexican movies as Neutron, a black-masked wrestler. The films typically feature zombies, mad scientists, and assorted maniacs. *Ladron de Cadavares*, 1956; *Neutron vs. the Maniac*, 1961; *Neutron Against the Death Robots*, 1962; *Neutron and the Black Mask*, 1962; *Neutron Battles the Karate Assassins*, 1962; *Neutron vs. the Amazing Dr. Caronte*, 1964; others.

S

SABU (DASTAGIR) (1924–63). Energetic Indian actor in Hollywood and Britain, boyishly engaging as young hero of *The Thief of Bagdad*, 1940. *The Jungle Book*, 1942; *The Arabian Nights*, 1942; *Cobra Woman*, 1944; *Jungle Hell*, 1956; *Sabu and the Magic Ring*, 1957.

SAHLIN, DON. American stop-motion animator and puppeteer, associated with producer GEORGE PAL in the fifties and sixties and now with Jim Henson and the Muppets. *Hansel and Gretel*, 1954; *tom thumb*, 1958; *The Time Machine* (in addition to his animation work, Sahlin is seen as the fast-moving window dresser in the first time-travel sequence), 1960; *Dinosaurus*, 1960; *The Wonderful World of the Brothers Grimm*, 1962; *The Muppet Movie* (1979).

SAKATA, HAROLD. Burly Japanese wrestler who became world-famous as the awesome villain Odd Job in *Goldfinger*, 1964, the best of the James Bond thrillers. *Dead of Night*, 1974; *Impulse*, 1975.

SALKOW, SIDNEY (1909–). Journeyman American director whose *The Last Man on Earth*, 1964 is a muddled interpretation of RICHARD MATHESON's fine horror novel *I Am Legend*. *Twice-Told Tales*, 1963.

SALTER, HANS J. (1896–). Viennese composer active in Hollywood, notably for Universal during the forties. *Tower of London* (arrangements only; score by Frank Skinner), 1939; *Black Friday*, 1941; *The Wolf Man* (w/Frank Skinner), 1941; *The Black Cat* (w/ Frank Skinner), 1941; *The Ghost of Frankenstein*, 1942; *Invisible Agent*, 1942; *The Mad Doctor of Market Street*, 1942; *The Mystery of Marie Roget*, 1942; *Night Monster*, 1942; *The Strange Case of Dr. Rx*, 1942; *Captive Wild Woman*, 1943; *Frankenstein Meets the Wolf Man* (w/ Frank Skinner), 1943; *Son of Dracula* (w/ Frank Skinner), 1943; *The Mad Ghoul* (w/ Frank Skinner), 1943; *The Scarlet Claw*, 1944; *Weird Woman*, 1944; *Pearl of Death*, 1944; *Jungle Captive*, 1944; *Jungle Woman*, 1944; *The Frozen Ghost*, 1945; *House of Frankenstein*, 1945; *House of Horrors*, 1946; *The Brute Man*, 1946; *Abbott and Costello Meet the Invisible Man*, 1951; *The Black Castle*, 1952; *The 5,000 Fingers of Dr. T* (w/Frederick Hollander and Heinz Roemheld), 1953; *Abbott and Costello Meet Dr. Jekyll and Mr. Hyde*, 1953; *The Mole People* (w/HERMAN STEIN and Heinz Roemheld), 1956; *The Incredible Shrinking Man*, 1957; *The Land Unknown*, 1957; others.

SALTZMAN, HARRY (1915–). Canadian producer active in Britain, most notably in partnership with ALBERT R. BROCCOLI on the James Bond films, from 1962.

SANDERS, GEORGE (1906–72). Smooth British star character actor equally at home as dogged hero or slimy rotter. Brother of actor TOM CONWAY. *The Lodger*, 1944; *The Picture of Dorian Gray*, 1945; *The Ghost and Mrs. Muir*, 1947; *From the Earth to the Moon*, 1958; *Village of the Damned* (as Zellaby), 1960; *Invasion of the Body Stealers* aka *Thin Air*, 1970; *Doomwatch*, 1972; *Psychomania*, 1972.

SANGSTER, JIMMY (1924–). British screenwriter, long associated with Hammer Films. *Spaceways* (assistant d only), 1953; *The Curse of Frankenstein*, 1957; *The Horror of Dracula*, 1958; *The Mummy*, 1959; *Brides of Dracula*, 1960; *Scream of Fear* (and p), 1961; *Nightmare*, 1964; *Hysteria*, 1965; *The Nanny*, 1965; *The Anniversary*, 1968; *The Horror of Frankenstein* (and d), 1970; *Lust for a Vampire* (d only), 1971; *The Legacy*, 1979.

Dracula (Christopher Lee) recoils from the crucifix in Peter Sasdy's *Taste the Blood of Dracula* (1970).

John Saxon in *Planet Earth* (1974).

SANTO. Silver-masked Mexican wrestler(s?) in vulgar film adventures loaded with monsters and senseless violence. The fun, however, is undeniable. *Invasion of the Zombies*, 1961; *Samson vs. the Vampire Women*, 1962; *Samson in the Wax Museum*, 1963; *Santo Ataca las Brujas*, 1964; *Espectro del Estrangulador*, 1965; *Santo Contra Blue Demon en la Atlantida* (see: BLUE DEMON), 1968; *Santo y Blue Demon Contra los Monstruos*, 1970; *Suicide Mission*, 1971; *Santo y Blue Demon Contra Dracula y el Hombre Lobo*, 1973; many others.

SAPERSTEIN, HENRY G. American producer/distributor who has brought many of the Japanese monster epics to the United States. *Monster Zero*, 1965; *Frankenstein Conquers the World*, 1966; *War of the Gargantuas*, 1970; *Godzilla vs. Megalon*, 1973; others.

SARGENT, JOSEPH (1925–). Slick American director whose *Colossus—The Forbin Project*, 1970 is a Hollywood rarity: pure science fiction. Its story of a sentient computer linkage that takes over the world is at once horrifying and plausible. *One Spy Too Many*, 1966.

SASDY, PETER (1934–). Hungarian director active in England. *Caves of Steel* (actor only), 1967. *Taste the Blood of Dracula*, 1970; *Countess Dracula*, 1972; *Hands of the Ripper*, 1972; *Doomwatch*, 1972; *Nothing but the Night*, 1972; *Devil within Her*, 1976.

William Schallert under attack by the renegade robot in *Gog* (1954).

SAVALAS, TELLY (1924–). Bald American character lead, popular on television ("Kojak," 1973–1978) and familiar in aggressive, urban roles. He is miscast as the super-villain Blofeld in the James Bond thriller *On Her Majesty's Secret Service*, 1969. *Horror Express*, 1972; *The House of Exorcism* (as the Devil), 1976.

SAVINI, TOM. Talented American makeup artist whose gruesome designs were first seen in the late seventies. *Dawn of the Dead* (and as actor: leader of the motorcyclists), 1979; *Maniac*, 1980; *Friday the 13th*, 1980; *Midnight*, 1980; *Effects* (and as actor), 1980.

SAXON, JOHN (1935–). American leading man and former model, usually seen as a good-looking but lifeless hero. *The Evil Eye*, 1962; *Blood Beast from Outer Space*, 1965; *Queen of Blood*, 1966; *Planet Earth* (TV), 1974; *Black Christmas*, 1975; *Strange New World* (TV), 1975; *The Bees*, 1978; *Blood Beach*, 1980; *Battle Beyond the Stars*, 1980.

SCHALLERT, WILLIAM. American general-purpose actor, probably most familiar as the harried father on television's "The Patty Duke Show," 1963–66. *Mighty Joe Young*, 1949; *The Man from Planet X*, 1951; *Port Sinister*, 1953; *Commando Cody, Sky Marshal of the Universe*, 1953; *Tobor the Great*, 1954; *Them!*, 1954; *Gog*, 1954; *The Incredible Shrinking Man*, 1957; *Colossus—The Forbin Project*, 1970; many others.

Young Michael Landon modeling Philip Scheer's interesting makeup seen in *I Was a Teenage Werewolf* (1957).

Gordon Scott as Tarzan.

SCHEER, PHILIP. American makeup artist with American-International Pictures during the fifties. His designs are seen in *I Was a Teenage Werewolf*, 1957; *I Was a Teenage Frankenstein*, 1957; *How to Make a Monster*, 1958; *Invisible Invaders*, 1959; others.

SCHEIDER, ROY (1934–). Hard-nosed American star of lively thrillers in the seventies. *The Curse of the Living Corpse* (billed as Roy R. Scheider), 1964; *Jaws*, 1975; *Jaws II*, 1978; *All That Jazz* (heavy fantasy element), 1979.

SCHNEER, CHARLES (1920–). American trick-film producer associated with stop-motion animator RAY HARRYHAUSEN. *Earth vs. the Flying Saucers*, 1956; *Twenty Million Miles to Earth*, 1957; *The 7th Voyage of Sinbad*, 1958; *The Three Worlds of Gulliver*, 1960; *Mysterious Island*, 1961; *Jason and the Argonauts*, 1963; *First Men in the Moon*, 1964; *One Million Years, B.C.*, 1967; *The Valley of Gwangi*, 1969; *The Golden Voyage of Sinbad*, 1973; *Sinbad and the Eye of the Tiger*, 1977; *Clash of the Titans*, 1981.

SCHOEDSACK, ERNEST B. (1893–1979). Ambitious, globe-trotting American director, associated with producer MERIAN C. COOPER and married to screenwriter RUTH ROSE. *The Most Dangerous Game* (co-d; w/IRVING PICHEL), 1932; *King Kong*, 1933; *Son of Kong*, 1933; *Dr. Cyclops*, 1939; *Mighty Joe Young*, 1949.

SCHRECK, MAX (1879–1936). German actor of the silent and early sound eras, effectively nonhuman as *Nosferatu the Vampire*, 1922. *At Edge of World*, 1929; *Rasputins Liebesabenteuer* aka *Rasputin, the Holy Devil*, 1930; *Der Tunnel*, 1933.

SCOB, EDITH. French actress who played the hideously disfigured girl in GEORGES FRANJU's disturbing *Eyes without a Face* aka *The Horror Chamber of Dr. Faustus*, 1959.

SCOTT, GORDON (1927–). Hearty, good-looking American actor and former lifeguard who assumed the Tarzan role after LEX BARKER in 1955, and played it six times until 1960. The Scott films are uniformly of high quality; the actor went on to box-office success in Europe. *Tarzan's Hidden Jungle*, 1955; *Tarzan and the Lost Safari*, 1957; *Tarzan's Fight for Life*, 1958; *Tarzan's Greatest Adventure*, 1959; *Tarzan the Magnificent*, 1960; *Duel of the Titans*, 1961; *Goliath and the Vampires*, 1961; *Samson and the 7 Miracles of the World*, 1963; others.

SCOTT, RIDLEY (1938–). British director who appalled audiences with his second feature film, *Alien*, 1979, a mercilessly manipulative horror/s.f. nightmare that packs a wallop.

SEARS, FRED F. (1913–57). Styleless American director of Columbia second features who also acted in numerous B-westerns. Appeared in *Down to Earth*, 1947; As director: *The Werewolf*, 1956; *Earth vs. the Flying Saucers*, 1956; *The Giant Claw*, 1957; *The Night the World Exploded*, 1957.

SEKELY, STEVE (1899–). Hungarian director who has worked in Hollywood and Britain since 1940. *Revenge of the Zombies*, 1943; *Amazon Quest*, 1949; *The Day of the Triffids* (except the lighthouse sequence, directed without credit by FREDDIE FRANCIS), 1963.

SELANDER, LESLEY (1900–). American B-western director who has directed a few fantastic films. *The Vampire's Ghost*, 1945; *The Catman of Paris*, 1946; *Flight to Mars*, 1951.

SERLING, ROD (1924–75). American television and fiction writer, best known as host of the ground-breaking "Twilight Zone," 1959–63, and of its less interesting successor, "Night Gallery," 1971–73. Serling contributed many scripts to the former, and although his work is sometimes pat, it is more often engaging and provocative. Despite his heavy involvement with science fiction and fantasy, Serling wrote only one screenplay with fantastic content, *Planet of the Apes* (co-w; w/Michael Wilson), 1968.

A saucer crashes the Capitol dome in *Earth vs. The Flying Saucers* (1956), directed by Fred F. Sears.

Rod Serling.

SEWELL, VERNON (1903–). British director of modest thrillers. *The Medium*, 1934; *The Ghosts of Berkeley Square*, 1947; *Ghost Ship* (and w), 1952; *House of Mystery*, 1960; *The Blood Beast Terror*, 1967; *The Crimson Cult*, 1968; *Burke and Hare*, 1971.

SHACKLETON, ALLAN (1937–79). American independent distributor responsible for bringing the Argentine film *Snuff* to the United States in 1976. The subject of much controversy, *Snuff* was touted by Shackleton as showing the *actual* dismemberment and disemboweling of a young woman; this led to rumors about whole colonies of South American killer filmmakers. In reality, *Snuff* is clever fakery—and except for that, quite pointless.

SHAKESPEARE, WILLIAM (1564–1616). English playwright whose imperishable *oeuvre* has inspired filmmakers since film's earliest days. In particular, the fantasy elements of many Shakespearean plays have made for colorful translation to the screen. *Julius Caesar*, 1909, 1950, 1971; *Hamlet*, 1907, 1908, 1910, 1917, 1921, 1927, 1935, 1948 (OLIVIER version), 1953, 1960, 1965 (Ghanian; African setting), 1969, others; *Hamlet at Elsinore*, 1964; *Macbeth*, 1908, 1909, 1911, 1916, 1946 (amateur; costume design by CHARLTON HESTON), 1948 (WELLES version), 1964, 1971 (POLANSKI version), others; *The Tempest*, 1905, 1908, 1911, 1912, 1969, others; *A Midsummer Night's Dream*, 1909, 1913, 1917, 1928, 1935 (the famous Hollywood version, w/James Cagney, Mickey Rooney, et al.), 1958, 1961 (Czech; stop-motion puppets), 1967, 1968 (Royal Shakespeare Company), 1968 (comic homosexual version), others.

Oddities include *Forbidden Planet*, 1956, which is an (uncredited) adaptation of *The Tempest* to a science-fictional milieu, and GEORGES MÉLIÈS's 1907 *Shakespeare Writing Julius Caesar*, in which Shakespeare has a vision of the murder of Caesar. Less successful adaptations of Shakespearean works include Japan's *Throne of Blood* (based on *Macbeth*), 1957, and Germany's *The Rest Is Silence*, 1960, which modernizes *Hamlet* and emphasizes its supernatural elements.

SHANNON, FRANK (1875–1959). American actor, remembered as Dr. Zarkoff, Flash Gordon's faithful but dim-witted associate in *Flash Gordon*, 1936; *Flash Gordon's Trip to Mars*, 1938; *Flash Gordon Conquers the Universe*, 1940.

SHARP, DON (1922–). Australian director active in Britain. *Kiss of the Vampire*, 1963; *Witchcraft*, 1964; *Curse of the Fly*, 1965; *The Face of Fu Manchu*, 1965; *Rasputin—The Mad Monk*, 1966; *The Brides of Fu Manchu*, 1966; *Those Fantastic Flying Fools* aka *Blast Off!*, 1967; *Rocket to the Moon*, 1967; *Psychomania*, 1972.

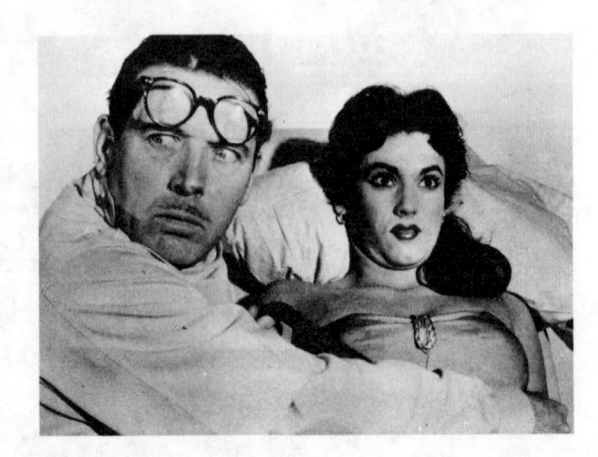

Robert Shayne in *The Neanderthal Man* (1952).

Barbara Shelley is inducted into the ranks of the undead by Christopher Lee in *Dracula, Prince of Darkness,* (1966).

SHARPE, DAVE (1911–80). Athletic American stuntman and actor of the thirties and forties, associated with Republic Pictures. His spectacular flying leaps while doubling for TOM TYLER in *The Adventures of Captain Marvel,* 1941, helped ensure that serial's great success. *Daredevils of the Red Circle* (lead), 1939; *The Mysterious Dr. Satan,* 1940; *Dick Tracy vs. Crime, Inc.,* 1941; *Spy Smasher,* 1942; *Perils of Nyoka,* 1942; *King of the Rocketmen,* 1949; many others.

SHATNER, WILLIAM (1931–). Canadian leading actor in Hollywood, prominent as Captain Kirk on television's "Star Trek," 1966–69, *"The Horror at 37,000 Feet,"* (TV), 1974; *Dead of Night,* 1974; *Impulse,* 1975; *The Devil's Rain,* 1975; *Kingdom of the Spiders,* 1977; *Star Trek: The Motion Picture* (as Kirk), 1979.

SHAYNE, ROBERT (CA. 1905–). American general-purpose actor, well known as Inspector Henderson on television's "The Adventures of Superman," 1951–58. *The Neanderthal Man* (title role), 1952; *Invaders from Mars,* 1953; *Tobor the Great,* 1954; *The Giant Claw,* 1957; *Kronos,* 1957; *Teenage Caveman,* 1958; *How to Make a Monster,* 1958.

SHEFFIELD, JOHNNY (1931–). American boy actor of the thirties and forties, well remembered as Boy in the JOHNNY WEISMULLER Tarzan films, and later familiar as Bomba the Jungle Boy. *Tarzan Finds a Son!,* 1939; *Tarzan Triumphs,* 1943; *Tarzan and the Amazons,* 1945; *Tarzan and the Leopard Woman,* 1946; many others.

SHELLEY, BARBARA (1933–). Poised British leading lady who has worked almost exclusively in horror films. *Cat Girl,* 1957; *Blood of the Vampire,* 1958; *Village of the Damned,* 1960; *The Gorgon,* 1964; *Dracula, Prince of Darkness,* 1965; *Rasputin—The Mad Monk,* 1966; *Five Million Years to Earth,* 1967; others.

210 SHELLEY

The thunderous climax of *Them!* (1954), written by Ted Sherdeman.

Lee Sholem's *Tobor The Great* (1954) cuts through an electrified fence.

SHELLEY, MARY GODWIN WOLLSTONECRAFT (1797–1851). British writer and wife of poet Percy Bysshe Shelley who in her teens composed a novel entitled *Frankenstein or: the Modern Prometheus*. The first film version was seen in 1910; the best known, starring BORIS KARLOFF as the Monster, appeared in 1931. Numerous spinoffs and variations. It should be noted that "Frankenstein" is the doctor, *not* his creation. ELSA LANCHESTER appears as Mary Shelley in the prologue and epilogue to *Bride of Frankenstein*, 1935.

SHERDEMAN, TED. American screenwriter who, with no prior experience in the fantastic, wrote the screenplay for *Them!*, 1954, creating not only outstanding science-horror, but an absorbing crime thriller as well. *Latitude Zero* (co-w; w/Shinichi Sekizawa), 1969.

SHERWOOD, JOHN. American director with Universal during the fifties. *The Creature Walks among Us*, 1956; *The Monolith Monsters*, 1957.

SHIELDS, ARTHUR (1895–1970). Rustic Irish character actor, atypically cast as a bloodthirsty fiend in *Daughter of Dr. Jekyll*, 1957. Brother of actor Barry Fitzgerald. *Tarzan and the Slave Girl*, 1950.

SHOLEM, LEE (CA. 1900–). American programmer director. *Tarzan and the Slave Girl*, 1950; *Superman and the Mole Men*, 1951; *Tobor the Great*, 1954; *Pharaoh's Curse*, 1957; *Doomsday*, 1972; others.

SHONTEFF, LINDSAY. British director with television experience. *Curse of the Voodoo*, 1964; *Devil Doll* (and p), 1964; etc. More recently involved with sexploitation.

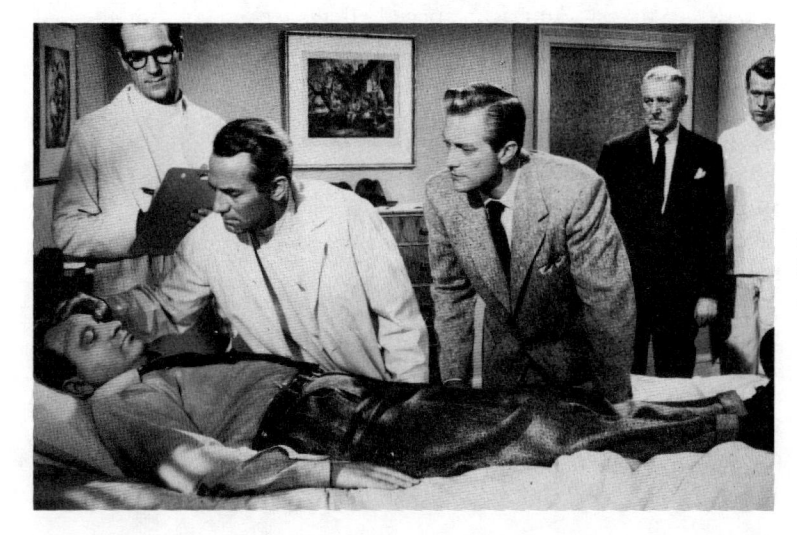

An atomic zombie lies comatose as Richard Denning *(center)* looks on in Curt Siodmak's *Creature with the Atom Brain* (1955).

SIEGEL, DON (1912–). American director who came to prominence in the sixties and seventies with a series of tough and concise crime thrillers. His *Invasion of the Body Snatchers*, 1956, is a science-fiction masterpiece of understatement and finely wrought psychological terror. (See also: KEVIN MCCARTHY). *Night unto Night*, 1947. *The Beguiled* (see also: CLINT EASTWOOD), 1971. *Invasion of the Body Snatchers* (actor only), 1978.

SIMON, SIMONE (1910–). French leading lady in Hollywood who lent a mysterious and decidedly feline presence to *The Cat People*, 1942, and *The Curse of the Cat People*, 1944. *The Devil and Daniel Webster*, 1941.

SIODMAK, CURT (1902–). German writer/director, long active in Hollywood. *The Trans-Atlantic Tunnel* (adaptation only), 1935; *Frankenstein Meets the Wolf Man* (w only), 1943; *Son of Dracula* (w only), 1943; *I Walked with a Zombie* (co-w only; w/Ardel Wray), 1943; *The Beast with Five Fingers* (w only), 1946; *Bride of the Gorilla*, 1951; *The Magnetic Monster* (d only), 1953; *Creature with the Atom Brain* (w only), 1955; *Curucu, Beast of the Amazon*, 1956; *Earth vs. the Flying Saucers* (story only), 1956; *Love Slaves of the Amazon* (and p), 1957; *The Devil's Messenger* (co-d only; w/ HERBERT L. STROCK), 1962.

SIODMAK, ROBERT (1900–1973). American director who won his reputation in the forties with a number of hard-edged crime melodramas. *Son of Dracula*, 1943; *Cobra Woman*, 1944; *The Spiral Staircase*, 1945.

SLAUGHTER, TOD (1885–1956). British star character actor who specialized in sensational melodrama. *Murder in the Red Barn*, 1935; *The Demon Barber of Fleet Street*, 1936; *The Face at the Window*, 1939; *Crimes at the Dark House*, 1940; *The Curse of the Wraydons*, 1946; *Horror Maniacs*, 1948; *A Ghost for Sale*, 1952, others.

Gale Sondergaard.

212 SLOANE

SLOANE, BARTON. American special effects technician who created *The Blob*, 1958, and the wondrous feats of *The 4-D Man*, 1959.

SMIGHT, JACK (1926–). American director who is often done in by overblown screenplays. One would have hoped for more meaningful treatment of RAY BRADBURY's *The Illustrated Man*; Smight's 1969 creation is a rambling mishmash. *The Screaming Woman* (TV), 1972. *Frankenstein: The True Story* (TV; theatrical release in Britain), 1973; *Damnation Alley*, 1977.

SMITH, DICK. Highly talented American makeup artist from television (notably "Way Out," 1961), whose most celebrated work was done for *The Exorcist*, 1973. *House of Dark Shadows*, 1970; *The Stepford Wives* (created KATHARINE ROSS's glittering eyes and enlarged breasts for the climactic sequence), 1974; *Exorcist II: The Heretic*, 1977; *The Sentinel*, 1977; others.

SMITH, DICK. American special-effects technician and prop builder who designed the impressive mechanical ants for *Them!*, 1954. Not to be confused with makeup artist DICK SMITH (above).

SMITH, KENT (1907–). Capable American leading actor and character player, notable as the man involved with *The Cat People*, 1942. *The Curse of the Cat People*, 1944. *The Spiral Staircase*, 1945; *Moon Pilot*, 1962; *Games*, 1967; *Lost Horizon*, 1973; *Die Sister Die!*, 1978.

SMITH, MADELINE (1950–). Dark-eyed, innocent-seeming British actress of the seventies. *The Vampire Lovers*, 1970; *The Devil's Widow*, 1972; *Theatre of Blood*, 1973; *Frankenstein and the Monster from Hell*, 1973.

Joan Weldon is menaced by a giant ant created by Dick Smith for *Them!* (1954).

SMITH, THORNE (1893–1934). American writer of humorous fantasy novels who created Topper, the proper fellow bothered by a pair of light-hearted ghosts. *Topper* (b/o the novel), 1937; *Topper Takes a Trip* (b/o the novel), 1939; *Topper Returns* (b/o characters created by Smith), 1941. Also: *Night Life of the Gods* (b/o the novel), 1935; *Turnabout* (b/o the novel; husband and wife exchange bodies), 1940; *I Married a Witch* (b/o Smith's novel *The Passionate Witch*), 1942.

SNOWDEN, LEIGH (CA. 1933–). American leading lady of the fifties. *The Creature Walks Among Us*, 1956; *I've Lived Before*, 1956.

SOJIN (KAMIYAMA) (1891–1954). Mysterious-seeming Japanese actor, a gaunt menace in numerous Hollywood B's of the twenties. *The Thief of Bagdad*, 1924; *The Bat*, 1926; *The Chinese Parrot* (as Charlie Chan), 1927; *The Unholy Night*, 1929; *Seven Footprints to Satan*, 1929.

SONDERGAARD, GALE (1899–). American character actress of dark and imposing demeanor. *The Cat and the Canary*, 1939; *The Black Cat*, 1941; *Spider Woman* (title role), 1944; *The Invisible Man's Revenge*, 1944; *The Climax*, 1944; *The Spider Woman Strikes Back*, 1946; *The Time of Their Lives*, 1946; *Night in Paradise* (as the witch), 1946; *The Cat Creatures* (TV), 1974; *Hollywood Horror House* aka *A Maniac Is Loose*, 1975.

SPACEK, SISSY (1950–). Unorthodox American leading actress of the seventies who found fame and critical notice as the telekinetic teenager *Carrie*, 1976.

SPELVIN, GEORGINA (1937–). American pornographic film actress who came to prominence as the frustrated spinster who literally goes to Hell in *The Devil in Miss Jones*, 1973. Spelvin (a pseudonym) is unenticing on screen, and has lately taken to personal appearances. *High Priestess of Sexual Witchcraft*, 1973; *In the Beginning*, 1975; *Spikey's Magic Wand*, 1975.

SPIELBERG, STEVEN (1948–). Precocious American writer/director from television, whose awesome and uplifting *Close Encounters of the Third Kind*, 1977, proved that *Jaws*, 1975, was no fluke. *Firelight* (amateur), 1964; *Duel* (TV; theatrical release in Britain), 1971.

STANDING, PERCY DARRELL. British actor who played the Monster in *Life without Soul*, 1915, the second film version of MARY SHELLEY's *Frankenstein*.

A dapper monster from Ray Dennis Steckler's outrageous *The Incredibly Strange Creatures Who Stopped Living and Became Mixed-Up Zombies* (1963).

STECKLER, RAY DENNIS (1939–). American independent producer/director who often stars in his own films under the name Cash Flagg. His *The Incredibly Strange Creatures Who Stopped Living and Became Mixed-Up Zombies*, 1963, is so ludicrously bad as to have become a sort of reverse classic. *Eegah!* (actor only), 1962; *The Thrill Killers*, 1965; *Rat Pfink and Boo Boo* (Batman and Robin parody), 1966; *The Lemon Grove Kids Meet the Monsters* (imitation Bowery Boys; see: LEO GORCEY), 1966; *The Lemon Grove Kids Meet the Green Grasshopper and the Vampire Lady from Outer Space*, ca. 1967; *Sinthia, the Devil's Doll*, 1970; *Blood Monster*, 1972; *The Erotic Adventures of Pinocchio* (ph only), 1976.

STEEL, ALAN. Italian muscleman whose true name is Sergio Ciani, popular in Europe during the early sixties as mesomorphic star of numerous fantasy adventures. *Samson and the Mighty Challenge*, 1964; *Samson and the Slave Queen*, 1964; *Hercules Against the Moon Men*, 1965; etcetera.

STEELE, BARBARA (1938–). British actress of mesmerizing presence, known to her worldwide cult of fans as the Queen of Horror. With her raven hair, prominent cheekbones, full, sensuous mouth, and remarkably large eyes, which can alternately express smoldering desire or evil, Steele is perfect as vampire-woman, ghost, or malevolent temptress. Originally a starlet with the J. Arthur Rank organization in the late fifties, she was first noticed in an impressive dual role in MARIO BAVA's disturbing *Black Sunday*, 1960. Most of her subsequent films have come from the continent, primarily period horror thrillers with farfetched plots. Steele has worked with Fellini (*8½*, 1962), and has done some American television, but is largely unknown outside the horror genre. She has made public her dissatisfaction with her relegation to "the horrors," but emerged from semiretirement in 1976 for a featured role in *They Came from Within*. *The Pit and the Pendulum*, 1961; *The Horrible Dr. Hichcock*, 1962; *Castle of Blood*, 1964; *I Lunghi Capelli Della Morte* (The Long Hair of Death), 1964; *Nightmare Castle* (another dual role, one of them played in a blonde wig), 1965; *Revenge of the Blood Beast*, 1965; *The Ghost*, 1965; *An Angel for Satan*, 1966; *Terror Creatures from the Grave*, 1967; *The Crimson Cult*, 1968; *Piranha*, 1978. *Silent Scream* (as Victoria), 1980.

A rare blonde portrait of the incomparable Barbara Steele.

STEELE, TOM. Good-looking American stuntman and actor associated with Republic Pictures during the forties and fifties. *The Mysterious Dr. Satan* (as the robot), 1940; *The Masked Marvel* (title role), 1943; *Haunted Harbor*, 1944; *The Black Widow*, 1947; *Radar Patrol vs. Spy King*, 1949; *King of the Rocketmen*, 1949; *The Invisible Monster*, 1950; *The Thing* (doubling for JAMES ARNESS as the Thing), 1951; *Radar Men from the Moon*, 1952; *Zombies of the Stratosphere*, 1952; many more.

Sudden inspiration: beautiful Barbara Steele up to no good in *The Pit and The Pendulum* (1961).

STEFANO, JOSEPH. American screen and television writer, best known for the creation of the classic television anthology series, "The Outer Limits," 1963-64. He prepared a faithful and finely convoluted adaptation of the ROBERT BLOCH novel for ALFRED HITCHCOCK's *Psycho*, 1960. *Eye of the Cat*, 1969; *Futz* (co-w; w/ Rochelle Owens; surrealistic fantasy), 1969; *Revenge!* (TV), 1971.

STEIGER, ROD (1925-). Versatile and brilliantly talented American leading actor, convincing as sympathetic protagonist or maniacal heavy. *The Illustrated Man* (title role), 1969; *Happy Birthday Wanda June*, 1971.

STEIN, HERMAN. American composer with Universal during the fifties. *It came from outer Space*, 1953; *The Creature from the Black Lagoon*, 1954; *This Island Earth*, 1955; *Revenge of the Creature*, 1955; others.

STEIN, RONALD. Prolific American film composer, usually of scores for second features. *The Day the World Ended*, 1956; *The She Creature*, 1956; *Attack of the Crab Monsters*, 1957; *Invasion of the Saucermen*, 1957; *The Undead*, 1957; *Attack of the Fifty-Foot Woman*, 1958; *Dinosaurus*, 1960; *The Premature Burial*, 1962; *Dementia 13*, 1963; *Voyage to the Prehistoric Planet*, 1965; *Spider Baby or: The Maddest Story Ever Told*, 1970; many others.

STEINER, MAX (1888–1972). Prolific and original Austrian composer of American film music; his score for *King Kong*, 1933, has become a classic. *The Most Dangerous Game*, 1932; *Son of Kong*, 1933; *She*, 1935.

STEINKE, HANS (1893–1971). German actor and wrestler in Hollywood who played the monkey-man Ouran in *Island of Lost Souls*, 1933.

STENSGAARD, YUTTE (CA. 1948–). Scandinavian leading lady in Britain who bared her fangs and a lot of skin in *Lust for a Vampire*, 1971, and has since dropped from sight. *Zeta One*, 1969.

STEPHENS, MARTIN (1949–). British child actor of the early sixties, memorable as the coolly malevolent leader of the children in *Village of the Damned*, 1960. As he grew up, he became less singular, and his film roles became routine. *The Innocents*, 1961; *The Devil's Own*, 1967.

STEVENS, HARVEY (1971–). British child actor of the seventies who played the Devil's son in *The Omen*, 1976.

STEVENS, LEITH (1909–70). Talented American composer who created a marvelously tense score for GEORGE PAL's *The War of the Worlds*, 1953. *Destination Moon*, 1950; *When Worlds Collide*, 1951; *World Without End*, 1956.

STEVENS, ONSLOW (1902–77). Authoritative American character actor. *The Vanishing Shadow* (lead), 1934; *The Monster and the Girl*, 1941; *House of Dracula* (as the fiendish Dr. Edelmann), 1945; *Angel on My Shoulder*, 1946; *The Creeper*, 1948; *Night Has a Thousand Eyes*, 1948; *Them!* (as General O'Brien), 1954; others.

STEVENS, STELLA (1936–). Blonde American leading lady who has been flirting with a sex-symbol image for twenty years, but who seems better suited for more thoughtful roles. *Li'l Abner* (as the mesmerizing Apassionata von Climax), 1959; *The Nutty Professor*, 1964; *The Secret of My Success*, 1965; *The Silencers*, 1966; *The Mad Room*, 1969; *Arnold*, 1974; *The Manitou*, 1978.

Martin Stephens in *The Innocents* (1961).

STEVENSON, ROBERT (1905–). British director in Hollywood, associated with WALT DISNEY productions since 1957. Most successful with *Mary Poppins*, 1964, Stevenson has since been saddled with gimmicked, rather empty scripts. *Darby O'Gill and the Little People*, 1958; *The Absent-Minded Professor*, 1961; *Son of Flubber*, 1963; *The Misadventures of Merlin Jones*, 1964; *The Monkey's Uncle*, 1965; *The Gnome-Mobile*, 1967; *The Love Bug*, 1969; *Bedknobs and Broomsticks*, 1971; *The Island at the Top of the World*, 1974; *The Shaggy D.A.*, 1977; others.

STEVENSON, ROBERT LOUIS (1850–94). British novelist whose *Dr. Jekyll and Mr. Hyde* is perhaps the most often filmed work of all time, reaching the screen in fifteen versions since 1908, as well as in scores of adaptations, *e.g., Pacto Diabolico*, 1968. Best known film version is ROUBEN MAMOULIAN's 1932 picture starring FREDRIC MARCH as Jekyll. The most curious is ROY WARD BAKER's *Dr. Jekyll and Sister Hyde*, 1972, in which Jekyll (RALPH BATES) becomes a knife-happy female Hyde (MARTINE BESWICK). In addition, Stevenson's short story "The Body Snatcher" came to the screen in 1945, and half a dozen other times in variations like *The Anatomist*, 1961, and *Burke and Hare*, 1971.

STEWART, JAMES (1908–). Lanky, good-humored American leading actor who has brought a folksy drawl and easygoing charm to a variety of film roles since 1935, notably his appearance as tipsy Elwood P. Dowd in *Harvey*, 1950, the man whose best friend is a giant, invisible rabbit. *It's a Wonderful Life* (see: FRANK CAPRA), 1946; *Rear Window*, 1954; *Vertigo*, 1958; *Bell, Book and Candle*, 1958.

James Stewart, obsessed with the dual image of Kim Novak in Alfred Hitchcock's *Vertigo* (1958).

Clifford Stine's clever camera brings *The Monolith Monsters* (1957) to mammoth reality.

STINE, CLIFFORD. American special-effects cinematographer with Universal in the fifties who convinced moviegoers that GRANT WILLIAMS had become *The Incredible Shrinking Man*, 1957. *It Came from Outer Space*, 1953; *This Island Earth*, 1955; *Tarantula*, 1955; *The Creature Walks among Us*, 1956; *The Mole People*, 1956; *The Monolith Monsters*, 1957; *The Deadly Mantis*, 1957; *The Land Unknown*, 1957; *Monster on the Campus*, 1958.

STIRLING, LINDA (1921–). Vivacious American serial queen, Republic Picture's resident heroine in the forties. *The Tiger Woman*, 1944; *Manhunt of Mystery Island*, 1945; *The Purple Monster Strikes*, 1945; *The Crimson Ghost*, 1946. She retired from acting in the fifties to teach college English and drama.

STOKER, BRAM (1847–1912). Irish novelist who wrote *Dracula* in 1897. The flood of filmic vampires inspired by the book shows no sign of drying up. BELA LUGOSI is best known as the vampire count; CHRISTOPHER LEE is the prominent modern incarnation. LON CHANEY, JR. appeared as *Son of Dracula* in 1943, and GLORIA HOLDEN was *Dracula's Daughter* in 1936. The count roamed about contemporary California in the person of FRANCIS LEDERER in 1958's *Return of Dracula*; an actor named Vince Kelley played Dracula as a sex fiend in *Dracula, the Dirty Old Man*, 1969. Variations on Stoker's vampire theme are numerous.

Linda Stirling menaced by thugs (Clayton Moore is at far right) in *The Crimson Ghost* (1946).

Four interpretations of Dracula, inspired by the writings of Bram Stoker. Clockwise from top left they are Max Schreck in *Nosferatu the Vampire* (1922), Bela Lugosi in *Dracula* (1931), Christopher Lee in *The Horror of Dracula* (1958), and Jack Palance in *Dracula* (1973).

Glenn Strange as Frankenstein's Monster, in a publicity shot with comic Ole Olsen.

STONE, LEWIS (1879-1953). Dependable American character lead, popular throughout the forties as MICKEY ROONEY's father in the Andy Hardy series. *The Lost World*, 1925; *The Phantom of Paris*, 1931; *The Mask of Fu Manchu*, 1932; *The Mystery of Mr. X*, 1934; *The Thirteenth Chair*, 1937; *Angels in the Outfield*, 1951.

STONE, MILBURN (1904-80). American supporting actor, long popular as Doc on television's "Gunsmoke," 1955-1975, and familiar in many second features of the thirties and forties as action-filled hero or villain. *Captive Wild Woman*, 1943; *The Mad Ghoul*, 1943; *The Great Alaskan Mystery* (serial; involves a matter transmitter), 1944; *Strange Confession*, 1945; *The Frozen Ghost*, 1945; *The Spider Woman Strikes Back*, 1946; *Invaders from Mars*, 1953.

STOW, PERCY. Pioneering British filmmaker who experimented with fanciful themes and trick visual effects. *When the Man in the Moon Seeks a Wife*, 1908; *The Electric Leg*, 1912; *Electrical Housebuilding*, 1912; many more.

STRANGE, GLENN (1899-1973). Massive and saturnine American character actor, former stuntman, rodeo performer, and professional boxer, cast as a villain in many westerns and horror films of the thirties and forties. He appeared three times as Frankenstein's Monster, in *House of Dracula*, 1945, *House of Frankenstein*, 1945, and *Abbott and Costello Meet Frankenstein*, 1948, the last a genuinely effective film which has belatedly received its due. Strange's interpretation of the Monster is the best after BORIS KARLOFF's, and wholly different: with his heavy eyes, dark gash of a mouth, and rocklike jaw, Strange suggests more than a hint of homicidal dementia. *The Mad Monster*, 1942; *The Mummy's Tomb*, 1942; *The Black Raven*, 1943; *The Monster Maker*, 1944; *Master Minds* (as the apeman), 1949; *The Adventures of the Spirit* (as Frankenstein's Monster; amateur film; see: DON GLUT), 1963.

Teenage high jinks in Herbert L. Strock's *How to Make a Monster* (1958).

STRASBERG, SUSAN (1938–). Pretty American leading lady of the sixties and seventies. *Scream of Fear*, 1961; *The Trip*, 1967; *The Legend of Hillbilly John* (black magic), 1973; *The Manitou*, 1978.

STRIBLING, MELISSA. Seductive British actress of the fifties and sixties. *The Horror of Dracula*, 1958; *Crucible of Terror*, 1971.

STRICKFADEN, KEN (CA. 1900–). American set designer and electrical expert who created the impressive laboratory seen in *Frankenstein*, 1931, and an even more impressive one for *Bride of Frankenstein*, 1935. He was lured from retirement by MEL BROOKS in 1974 to design the lab for *Young Frankenstein*, and contributed greatly to that film's success. *Just Imagine*, 1930; *The Lost City*, 1935; *Werewolf of London*, 1935; *Flash Gordon*, 1936; *Buck Rogers*, 1938; *Monstrosity*, 1964; *Dracula vs. Frankenstein*, 1971.

STRIEPKE, DAN. American television and film makeup artist associated with JOHN CHAMBERS. *The Magic Sword*, 1962; *Planet of the Apes* (and sequels), 1968; *Sssssss* (and p), 1973; *The Island of Dr. Moreau*, 1977; others.

STROCK, HERBERT L. (1918–). American director of B-films. His *How to Make a Monster*, 1958, is a routine film but displays a grisly sense of humor. *Gog*, 1954; *Blood of Dracula*, 1957; *I Was a Teenage Frankenstein*, 1957; *The Devil's Messenger* (co-d; w/CURT SIODMAK), 1962; *The Crawling Hand*, 1963.

STRUSS, KARL (1886–). German cinematographer in Hollywood who devised the startling multiple images of Patricia Owens as seen through the many-faceted eyes of her husband, *The Fly*, 1958. *Dr. Jekyll and Mr. Hyde*, 1932; *Island of Lost Souls*, 1933; *Rocketship X-M*, 1950; *Tarzan and the She-Devil*, 1953; *She Devil*, 1957; *Kronos*, 1957; *The Alligator People*, 1959; others.

STUART, GLORIA (1909–). Blonde American leading lady who retired from films in the middle forties and later became a successful painter. *The Old Dark House*, 1932; *The Invisible Man*, 1933; *The Whistler*, 1944.

SUBOTSKY, MILTON (1921–). American producer/screenwriter active in England as head of Amicus Productions (with partner Max J. Rosenberg), which in the early seventies threatened the supremacy of Hammer Films as Britain's major horror studio. *Horror Hotel* (original story only), 1960; *Dr. Terror's House of Horrors*, 1964; *The Skull*, 1965; *Dr. Who and the Daleks* (p only), 1966; *The Terrornauts* (p only), 1967; *Daleks—Invasion Earth 2150 A.D.* (p only), 1968; *Scream and Scream Again* (p only), 1970; *The House That Dripped Blood* (p only), 1971; *Asylum* (p only), 1972; *Tales from the Crypt*, 1972; *The Vault of Horror*, 1973; *Madhouse* (p only), 1973; *From beyond the Grave* (p only), 1975; *The Monster Club*, 1981; more.

SUCHER, HENRY. American screenwriter of the forties. *The Mummy's Tomb* (co-w; w/GRIFFIN JAY), 1942; *Captive Wild Woman* (co-w; w/GRIFFIN JAY), 1943; *Jungle Woman*, 1944; *The Frozen Ghost* (story only), 1945; others.

SULLIVAN, DON (CA. 1938–). Boyish American actor/singer of the fifties who did a few teenage horror films. *The Giant Gila Monster*, 1959; *The Monster of Piedras Blancas*, 1959; *Teenage Zombies*, 1960.

SUTHERLAND, DONALD (1935–). Tall Canadian actor who progressed from supporting roles in minor European films to stardom in Hollywood. *Castle of the Living Dead*, 1964; *Dr. Terror's House of Horrors*, 1964; *Die Die My Darling*, 1965; *Alex in Wonderland*, 1970; *Don't Look Now*, 1973; *Invasion of the Body Snatchers*, 1978; *Kentucky Fried Movie*, 1978.

SYKES, PETER. British director. *The Legend of Spider Forest*, 1971; *Demons of the Mind*, 1972; *To the Devil ... A Daughter*, 1976.

SZU, SHIH (1953–). Chinese leading lady in violent kung fu fantasies for Hong Kong producer Run Run Shaw. *Supermen Against the Orient*, 1973; *The Legend of the Seven Golden Vampires* (Shaw/Hammer co-production), 1974; others.

SZWARC, JEANNOT. American director with heavy television experience. *Night of Terror* (TV), 1972; *The Devil's Daughter* (TV), 1972; *Bug*, 1975; *Jaws 2*, 1978; *Somewhere in Time*, 1980.

Gloria Talbott *(right)* confronts Coleen Gray in *The Leech Woman* (1960).

Rod Taylor and Yvette Mimieux in a publicity still from *The Time Machine* (1960).

T

TABLER, P. DEMPSEY (1880–1953). American actor and light opera singer who played Tarzan in *The Son of Tarzan*, 1921. Physically unimpressive, Tabler left pictures soon after.

TALBOT, LYLE (1904–). Imposing American character actor whose pleasant features could form a menacing scowl when necessary. *The Thirteenth Guest*, 1932; *Return of the Terror*, 1934; *Trapped by Television*, 1936; *Batman and Robin*, 1949; *Atom Man vs. Superman* (as Luthor), 1950; *Fury of the Congo*, 1951; *Hurricane Island*, 1951; *Untamed Women*, 1952; *Glen or Glenda?* aka *I Changed My Sex*, and *I Led Two Lives*, and *The Transvestite* (magical sex change), 1953; *Commando Cody, Sky Marshal of the Universe*, 1953; *Tobor the Great*, 1954; *Plan 9 from Outer Space*, 1956; many others.

TALBOTT, GLORIA (CA. 1932–). American leading lady of the fifties, her sharp features ideally suited for showing the panic of the young wife in *I Married a Monster from Outer Space*, 1958. *The Cyclops*, 1957; *Daughter of Dr. Jekyll* (title role), 1957; *The Man from 1997*, 1957; *Leech Woman*, 1960.

TAMBLYN, RUSS (1934–). Energetic American acrobatic dancer and actor who ventured into horror and science fiction as the Hollywood musical declined. *tom thumb* (title role), 1958; *The Wonderful World of the Brothers Grimm*, 1962; *The Haunting*, 1963; *War of the Gargantuas*, 1970; *Dracula vs. Frankenstein*, 1971.

TAMIROFF, AKIM (1899–1972). Russian character actor in Hollywood. *Jungle Princess*, 1936; *The Great Gambini*, 1937; *The Black Forest*, 1954; *The Black Sleep*, 1956; *Le Baccanti*, 1960; *Alphaville*, 1965; *The Vulture*, 1966.

TATE, SHARON (1943–69). Blonde American leading lady whose murder made world headlines. Married at the time of her death to director ROMAN POLANSKI. *Eye of the Devil*, 1967; *The Fearless Vampire Killers*, 1967.

TAYLOR, KENT (1907–). Longtime American leading man of second features. *Death Takes a Holiday*, 1934; *The Phantom from 10,000 Leagues*, 1956; *The Day Mars Invaded Earth*, 1963; *The Crawling Hand*, 1963; *Bride of Blood*, 1970; *Brain of Blood*, 1971.

TAYLOR, ROD (1929–). Barrel-chested Australian leading man who almost made it to Hollywood stardom in the sixties. *World without End*, 1956; *Colossus and the Amazons*, 1960; *The Time Machine* (his best role, as the enterprising time traveler), 1960; *The Birds*, 1963.

A sea monster looks for some company in Del Tenney's *Horror of Party Beach* (1964).

Terry-Thomas.

TENNEY, DEL. American independent producer/director. *Psychomania* 1963; *The Horror of Party Beach*, 1964; *I Eat Your Skin* (and w), 1964; *The Curse of the Living Corpse* (and w), 1964.

TERRY-THOMAS (1911–). Gap-toothed British comic actor, familiar as blathering ninny or proper gentleman's gentleman. *tom thumb*, 1958; *The Wonderful World of the Brothers Grimm*, 1962; *Munster Go Home!*, 1966; *Those Fantastic Flying Fools* aka *Blast Off!*; *Rocket to the Moon*, 1967; *The Abominable Dr. Phibes*, 1971; *Dr. Phibes Rises Again*, 1972; *The Vault of Horror*, 1973; etc.

THATCHER, TORIN (1905–). British character actor who played the bullish villain Sokurah in *The 7th Voyage of Sinbad*, 1958, and the evil sorcerer in *Jack the Giant Killer*, 1962. *Case of the Frightened Lady*, 1933.

THESIGER, ERNEST (1879–1961). Eccentric British character actor in Hollywood, whose Dr. Praetorius in *Bride of Frankenstein*, 1935, is among the screen's most outstanding comic grotesques. *The Old Dark House*, 1932; *The Ghoul*, 1934; *The Man Who Could Work Miracles*, 1937; *The Ghosts of Berkeley Square*, 1947; *The Man in the White Suit*, 1952; *Meet Mr. Lucifer*, 1953; *Who Done It?*, 1956. Stills exist of Thesiger in costume as Theotocopulos from *Things to Come*, 1936; although replaced in the role by CEDRIC HARDWICKE, Thesiger is sometimes erroneously credited with it.

Torin Thatcher attempts to bribe Kerwin Mathews in *The Seventh Voyage of Sinbad* (1958), but our hero is clearly not interested. Kathryn Grant looks on.

Ernest Thesiger as the demented Dr. Praetorius shows off his homunculi in *The Bride of Frankenstein* (1935).

THOMPSON, MARSHALL (1926–). American leading man who found some success in sixties television ("Daktari," 1966–69). *The Cockeyed Miracle*, 1946; *Cult of the Cobra*, 1955; *Fiend without a Face*, 1958; *First Man into Space*, 1959; *Flight of the Lost Balloon*, 1961; *Around the World under the Sea*, 1966.

Marshall Thompson with Kim Parker in *Fiend without a Face* (1958).

226 THREE STOOGES

The Three Stooges, ca. 1940. From left: Larry Fine, Jerry (Curly) Howard, Moe Howard.

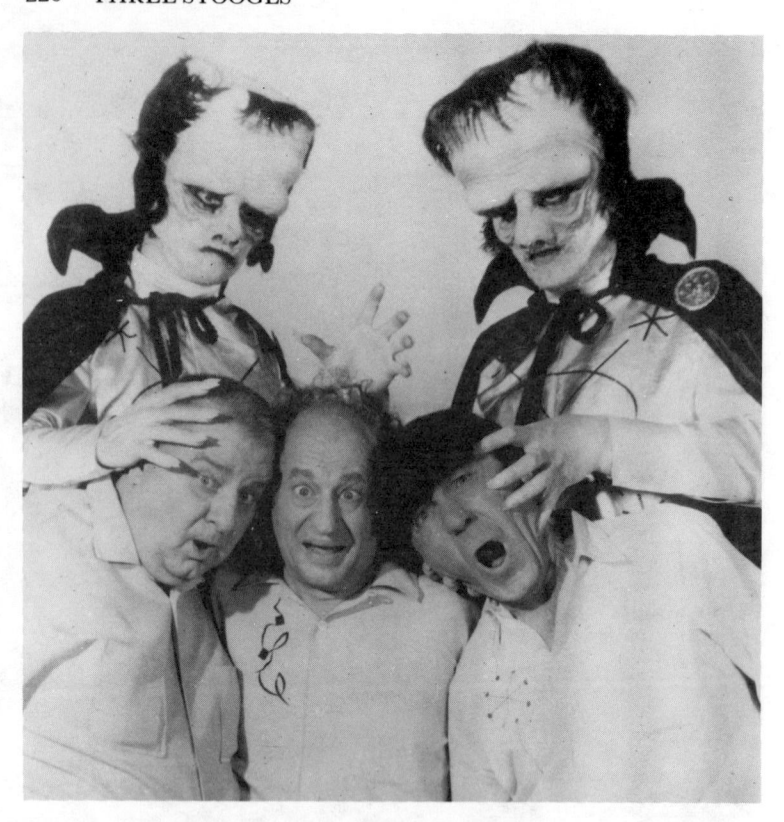

The Three Stooges (Joe DeRita, Larry Fine, Moe Howard) at the mercy of the Martians in *The Three Stooges in Orbit* (1962).

THREE STOOGES, THE: MOE HOWARD (1897–1975), JERRY "CURLY" HOWARD (1903–52), LARRY FINE (1901–75), SAMUEL "SHEMP" HOWARD (1891–1955), JOE BESSER (1907–), JOE DERITA (1909–). American slapstick comics with long vaudeville experience whose mastery of the art of violence delighted two generations. Specialists in two-reelers from 1934, the Stooges suffered a decline in quality of material as the fifties approached, but many of their shorts (especially those with Curly as the third stooge) are true gems. Curly fell victim to a stroke in 1946, and was replaced by brother Shemp, who was in turn replaced by veteran comic Joe Besser in 1955. Besser could not continue with the act when it moved into feature films in the late fifties, and was replaced by Joe DeRita. *We Want Our Mummy*, 1939; *Spook Louder*, 1943; *Idle Roomers* (which involves a werewolf), 1944; *If a Body Meets a Body*, 1945; *A Bird in the Head*, 1946; *Shivering Sherlocks*, 1948; *The Ghost Talks*, 1949; *Cuckoo on a Choo Choo* (their most unusual short; the Stooges do not function as a team, and there is a decidedly surreal tone to the proceedings), 1952; *Spooks* (3-D), 1953; *Stone Age Romeos*, 1955; *Bedlam in Paradise* (Shemp as an angel), 1955; *Space Ship Sappy*, 1957; *Outer Space Jitters*, 1957; *Flying Saucer Daffy*, 1958; others. Features: *Crazy Knights* aka *Ghost Crazy* (Shemp as a solo), 1944; *Space Master X-7* (Moe as a solo), 1958; *Have Rocket, Will Travel*, 1959; *The Three Stooges in Orbit*, 1962; *The Three Stooges Meet Hercules*, 1962; others.

Lovely Greta Thyssen, with Richard Derr and *(back to camera)* Francis Lederer in *Terror Is a Man* (1959).

Ghostly Edna Tichenor *(far right)* with Lon Chaney in *London after Midnight* (1927).

THYSSEN, GRETA (CA. 1935–). Beautiful blonde Danish actress, a onetime Miss Denmark whose first Hollywood job was as foil to THE THREE STOOGES. *Terror Is a Man*, 1959; *Journey to the 7th Planet*, 1961.

TICHENOR, EDNA. Wraithlike American actress of the twenties who, by all evidence, was chilling as the pale and dark-eyed vampire woman in *London after Midnight*, 1927; it is believed that no prints of the film survive.

TIOMKIN, DIMITRI (1899–1979). Russian composer active in Hollywood since the early thirties. His score for *The Thing*, 1951, is rousing and makes good use of the electronic theramin. Other scores: *Alice in Wonderland*, 1933; *Lost Horizon*, 1937; *Shadow of a Doubt*, 1943; *Portrait of Jennie*, 1948; others.

TOBEY, KENNETH (1919–). American actor, a serviceable leading man of science-fiction films of the fifties. *The Thing*, 1951; *The Beast from 20,000 Fathoms*, 1953; *It Came from Beneath the Sea*, 1955; *The Search for Bridey Murphy*, 1956; *The Vampire*, 1957; *Ben*, 1972.

TODD, THELMA (1905–35). American comic actress and two-reel star of the thirties, a beautiful and vivacious blonde whose death by carbon monoxide poisoning in her own garage remains a mystery. *The Haunted House*, 1928; *Vamping Venus*, 1928; *Seven Footprints to Satan*, 1929; *The House of Horror*, 1929; *The Tin Man* (short), 1935; *The Misses Stooge* (short), 1935.

TOLER, SIDNEY (1874–1947). Jowly American character actor, best known as the Oriental sleuth Charlie Chan. *Castle in the Desert*, 1942; *Black Magic*, 1944; *The Jade Mask*, 1945.

TOMLINSON, DAVID (1917–). Likeable British light actor who has brought his placid features to a number of fantasies. *Miranda*, 1948; *Mary Poppins*, 1964; *War-Gods of the Deep*, 1965; *The Love Bug*, 1969; *Bedknobs and Broomsticks*, 1971; *Dominique*, 1978.

TONGE, PHILIP (1898–1959). Mustachioed American character actor of the forties and fifties, sharp or kindly as the script demanded. *Miracle on 34th Street*, 1947; *Hans Christian Andersen*, 1952; *House of Wax*, 1953; *Macabre*, 1958; *Invisible Invaders*, 1959.

TORS, IVAN (1916–). Hungarian writer/producer/director who came to prominence in the sixties as Hollywood's leading purveyor of animal films, *e.g.*, *Flipper*, 1963. *The Magnetic Monster* (co-w: w/CURT SIODMAK and p only), 1953; *Gog* (p only), 1954; *Riders to the Stars* (p only), 1954; *Around the World under the Sea* (executive p only), 1966.

TOTO (true name ANTONIO FURST DE CURTIS-GAGLIARDI) (1897–1967). Italian comic actor, popular in the fifties as star of some broad comedy-fantasies. *Toto the Sheik*, 1950; *Miracle in Milan*, 1951; *Toto in Hell*, 1955; *Toto in the Moon*, 1958, others.

TOURNEUR, JACQUES (1904–78). French director of moody American thrillers, associated with RKO and VAL LEWTON during the forties. Tourneur's *Curse of the Demon*, 1958, is an overambitious but intriguing film that has inspired a cult. *The Cat People*, 1942; *I Walked with a Zombie*, 1943; *The Leopard Man*, 1943; *The Comedy of Terrors*, 1963; *War-Gods of the Deep*, 1965.

Kenneth Tobey and Margaret Sheridan await the arrival of *The Thing* (1951).

Thelma Todd at the peak of her fame in the early 1930s.

Les Tremayne *(far left)* observes a victim of *The Monolith Monsters* (1957).

Tom Tryon is under the control of aliens in *I Married a Monster from Outer Space* (1958). Wife Gloria Talbott looks on.

TOWNE, ROBERT. Major American screenwriter of the seventies (*Chinatown*, 1974, *et al.*) who began his career in association with producer/director ROGER CORMAN. *The Last Woman on Earth*, 1960; *The Tomb of Ligeia*, 1965.

TRACY, SPENCER (1900–67). American leading actor, a respected star for thirty-five years who played *Dr. Jekyll and Mr. Hyde* in 1941. Tracy's performance is a good one, but the film cannot match the 1932 version starring FREDRIC MARCH. Probably sensing as much, MGM bought the rights to the March film from Paramount, and saw to it that all prints were withdrawn from circulation. It did not surface again until the early fifties. *Dante's Inferno*, 1935.

TREMAYNE, LES (1910–). Distinguished-looking American character actor, fine as the dogged Army general in *The War of the Worlds*, 1953. *It Grows on Trees*, 1952; *The Monolith Monsters*, 1957; *The Monster of Piedras Blancas*, 1959; *Angry Red Planet*, 1959; *Creature of Destruction*, 1967; many others.

TRUFFAUT, FRANCOIS (1932–). Influential French director, at the forefront of the "new wave" filmmakers who arose in Europe in the late fifties. *Fahrenheit 451*, 1966; *Close Encounters of the Third Kind* (actor only), 1977.

TRUMBULL, DOUGLAS (CA. 1943–). American special-effects artist who created the wondrous and lyrical visuals for STEVEN SPIELBERG's *Close Encounters of the Third Kind*, 1977. *Cosmos, the Fantastic Journey* (paintings only), 1964; *2001: A Space Odyssey*, 1968; *The Andromeda Strain*, 1971; *Silent Running* (and d), 1972; *Star Trek: The Motion Picture*, 1979.

TRYON, TOM (1926–). American leading man of the fifties and sixties who never quite made the big time. He later turned to writing and became a successful novelist. *I Married a Monster from Outer Space*, 1958; *Moon Pilot*, 1962; *The Other* (original story only, from his novel), 1972; *The Dark Secret of Harvest Home* (TV; original story only, from his novel, *Harvest Home*) 1978.

TSUBURUYA, EIJI (?-1970). Japanese special-effects technician, long with Toho Studios. He is responsible for *Godzilla*, 1954, and numerous other monsters, as well as the miniature cities they systematically destroy. *Rodan*, 1957; *The Mysterians*, 1959; *The H-Man*, 1959; *Mothra*, 1961; *The Last War*, 1961; *King Kong vs. Godzilla*, 1963; *Godzilla vs. the Thing*, 1964; *Ghidrah, the Three-Headed Monster*, 1965; *Godzilla vs. the Sea Monster*, 1966; *Destroy All Monsters*, 1969; *War of the Gargantuas*, 1970; *Godzilla's Revenge*, 1971; many others.

TSUKIJI, YONESABURO. Japanese special-effects expert with Daiei Motion Picture Company who created Gamera, the fanciful giant flying turtle, and the scowling, medieval war god Majin. *Gammera [sic] the Invincible*, 1966; *War of the Monsters*, 1966; *Majin* aka *Majin, the Hideous Idol*, 1966; *The Return of Giant Majin*, 1966; *Majin Strikes Again*, 1966; *Return of the Giant Monsters*, 1967; *Destroy All Planets*, 1968; *Attack of the Monsters*, 1969; *Gamera vs. Monster X*, 1970; *Gamera vs. Zigra* aka *Gamera Tai Shinkai Kaiju Jigura*, 1971; others.

TUCKER, FORREST (1919-). Hearty American character actor, usually cast as a boisterous fellow with a purposeful nature. *The Abominable Snowman of the Himalayas*, 1957; *The Cosmic Monster*, 1958; *The Crawling Eye*, 1958.

Godzilla and Eiji Tsuburuya conspire and Tokyo takes a fall in *Godzilla* (1954).

TUCKER, PHIL (CA. 1927–). American independent producer/director who progressed from innocuous sexploitation films to that nadir of science fiction cinema, *Robot Monster*, 1953. Shot largely in a barren canyon and featuring what looks like a gorilla wearing a diving helmet, the film is so execrable as to have become something of a cult item. *Robot Monster* is the first s-f film shot in 3-D, and incorporates dinosaur footage from *One Million B.C.*, 1940. *The Cape Canaveral Monsters*, 1960.

TUFTS, SONNY (1911–70). Amiable American second lead of the forties who became something of a camp figure late in his life. *Run for the Hills* (A-bomb hysteria), 1953; *Cat Women of the Moon*, 1953; *Serpent Island*, 1954.

TUTTLE, WILLIAM (1911–). American maskmaker and makeup artist associated with MGM in the sixties. *The Time Machine* (the hideous, mush-faced Morlocks), 1960; *Atlantis, the Lost Continent*, 1961; *The Wonderful World of the Brothers Grimm*, 1962; *The Seven Faces of Dr. Lao*, 1964; *The Power*, 1968; *Young Frankenstein*, 1974; *The Fury*, 1978.

TWELVETREES, HELEN (1908–58). American leading lady of the thirties. *The Ghost Talks* (film debut), 1929; *The Cat Creeps*, 1930.

TYLER, TOM (1903–54). Cowboy star and weight-lifting champion best recalled as Captain Marvel in *The Adventures of Captain Marvel*, 1941, a furiously paced and excitingly staged serial that may be the finest ever made. *The Phantom of the Air*, 1933; *The Mummy's Hand* (title role), 1940; *The Phantom* (title role), 1943–44.

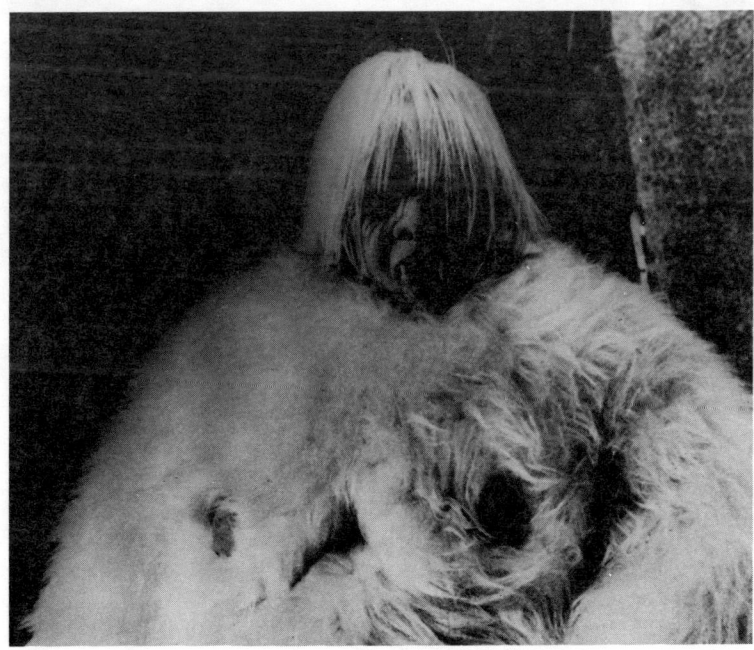

Forrest Tucker *(right)* and Peter Cushing grapple in *The Abominable Snowman of The Himalayas* (1957).

William Tuttle's design for the Abominable Snowman in *The Seven Faces of Dr. Lao* (1964).

Tom Tyler in *The Adventures of Captain Marvel* (1941).

Arthur Shields as the demented killer in Edgar Ulmer's *Daughter of Dr. Jekyll* (1957).

A hirsute Bela Lugosi is comforted by Minerva Urecal in *The Ape Man* (1943).

U

ULMER, EDGAR (1904–72). German-born director who spent most of his career in Hollywood. Prolific and varied (there are Yiddish films in his canon), Ulmer has lately attracted the attention of serious cineasts. *The Black Cat*, 1934; *The Man from Planet X* (an eerie juxtaposition of science fiction and the foggy moors of Scotland), 1951; *Daughter of Dr. Jekyll*, 1957; *The Amazing Transparent Man*, 1960; *Beyond the Time Barrier*, 1960; *L'Atlantide*, 1961.

URECAL, MINERVA (1894–1966). American character actress, often cast as a snoopy spinster. *The Corpse Vanishes*, 1942; *The Living Ghost*, 1942; *The Ape Man*, 1943; *Ghosts On The Loose*, 1943; *Master Minds*, 1949; *The Seven Faces of Dr. Lao*, 1964.

UTSUI, KEN. Japanese actor popular in the fifties as the extraterrestrial hero Super Giant; in most U.S.-release versions the character is called Starman. *Appearance of Super Giant*, 1956; *Rescue from Outer Space*, 1956; *Atomic Rulers of the World*, 1957; *Attack from Space*, 1958; *The Evil Brain from Outer Space*, 1959; *Gamera vs. Zigra* aka *Gamera Tai Shinkai Kaiju Jigura*, 1971; others.

Maila Nurmi, better known as Vampira, in a rare still from *Plan 9 from Outer Space* (1956).

V

VADIM, ROGER (1927–). Ambitious French director whose well-publicized marriages and love affairs have overshadowed his career. His films sum up to less than meets the eye. *Blood and Roses* (and co-w), 1960; *Barbarella* (and co-w), 1968; *Spirits of the Dead* ("Metzengerstein" segment only), 1969; *Night Games*, 1980.

VAMPIRA (1921–). Finnish actress whose true name is Maila Nurmi, a former dancer and onetime protégé of HOWARD HAWKS who achieved popularity on West Coast television in the early fifties as hostess of a Shock Theatre program and was featured in *Plan 9 from Outer Space*, 1956. Cadaverous and wasp-waisted, she cuts a spooky figure. *Night of the Ghouls*, 1959; *Beauty and the Robot* aka *Sex Kittens Go to College*, 1960; *The Magic Sword*, 1962.

Lee Van Cleef meets the Cucumber Creature in Roger Corman's *It Conquered The World* (1956).

VAN CLEEF, LEE (1925–). Lean, slit-eyed American character actor whose Hollywood career went nowhere but who became a major star in Europe after making a few Spanish-Italian westerns in the sixties. *The Beast from 20,000 Fathoms* (as the sharpshooter who kills the beast), 1953; *It Conquered the World* (as the man who is duped by the alien), 1956.

VAN DAMM, ARNOLD. American stuntman and costume maker of the thirties and forties who, like CHARLES GEMORA, specialized in snarly apes. *The Ape Man*, 1943; others, most uncredited.

VAN DOREN, MAMIE (1933–). Chesty blonde American actress of the fifties, one of the more prominent Marilyn Monroe imitators. *Francis Joins the Wacs*, 1954; *Beauty and the Robot* aka *Sex Kittens Go to College*, 1960; *The Private Lives of Adam and Eve* (as a pneumatic Eve), 1961; *The Navy vs. the Night Monsters*, 1966; *Hillbillys* [sic] *in a Haunted House*, 1967; *Voyage to the Planet of Prehistoric Women*, 1968.

Edward Van Sloan confronts Bela Lugosi as *Dracula* (1931).

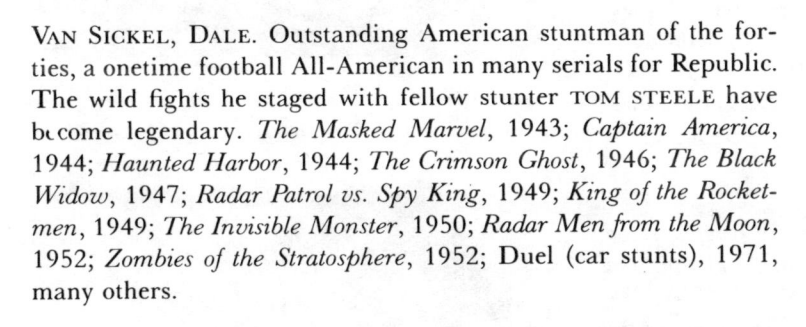

Arnold Van Damm gets fresh with Minerva Urecal in *The Ape Man* (1943).

VAN SICKEL, DALE. Outstanding American stuntman of the forties, a onetime football All-American in many serials for Republic. The wild fights he staged with fellow stunter TOM STEELE have become legendary. *The Masked Marvel*, 1943; *Captain America*, 1944; *Haunted Harbor*, 1944; *The Crimson Ghost*, 1946; *The Black Widow*, 1947; *Radar Patrol vs. Spy King*, 1949; *King of the Rocketmen*, 1949; *The Invisible Monster*, 1950; *Radar Men from the Moon*, 1952; *Zombies of the Stratosphere*, 1952; *Duel* (car stunts), 1971, many others.

VAN SLOAN, EDWARD (1882–1964). Sober-seeming American character actor of the thirties and forties who played the doggedly intrepid Van Helsing in *Dracula*, 1931. Also *Frankenstein*, 1931; *The Mummy*, 1932; *Deluge*, 1933; *Death Takes a Holiday*, 1934; *Dracula's Daughter*, 1936; *The Phantom Creeps*, 1939; *The Masked Marvel*, 1943.

Dale Van Sickel, one of the finest stuntmen in movie history.

VAN VOOREN, MONIQUE (1933–). Belgian nightclub entertainer who has made occasional films in America. *Tarzan and the She-Devil* (as the She-Devil), 1953; *Fearless Frank*, 1969; *Andy Warhol's Frankenstein*, 1974.

VAN ZANDT, PHILIP (1904–58). Smooth-voiced Dutch actor in Hollywood, a familiar nemesis of THE THREE STOOGES. *Tarzan Triumphs*, 1943; *Tarzan's Desert Mystery*, 1943; *The Big Noise*, 1944; *House of Frankenstein*, 1945; *A Thousand and One Nights*, 1945; *Mummy's Dummies* (short), 1948; *Fuelin' Around* (short), 1949; *Ghost Chasers*, 1951; *Son of Ali Baba*, 1952; *Spooks* (short), 1953; *Gog*, 1954; *Bedlam in Paradise* (short; as the Devil), 1955; *Man of a Thousand Faces*, 1957; *Outer Space Jitters* (short), 1957; others.

VAUGHN, ROBERT (1932–). American leading man who took the title role in *Teenage Caveman*, 1958, and later found great popularity as secret agent Napoleon Solo on television's "The Man From U.N.C.L.E.," 1964–68. This fanciful series spawned a number of theatrical features which are in the James Bond mold: *The Spy with My Face*, 1966; *One Spy Too Many*, 1966; *The Venetian Affair*, 1967; *The Helicopter Spies*, 1967. Vaughn has also starred in *The Mind of Mr. Soames*, 1970; *Starship Invasions*, 1977; *Battle Beyond the Stars*, 1980.

VEIDT, CONRAD (1893–1943). Hawklike German character actor who came to Hollywood after much work in German expressionist films and became familiarly cast as ruthless Nazi officers. *Five Sinister Stories*, 1919; *The Cabinet of Dr. Caligari* (as Cesare the somnambulist), 1919; *Der Januskopf* (b/o ROBERT LOUIS STEVENSON's *Dr. Jekyll and Mr. Hyde*), 1920; *Three Wax Men*, 1924; *The Hands of Orlac*, 1925; *The Man Who Laughs*, 1927; *F.P.1* aka *Floating Platform 1 Does Not Answer* (English-language version only), 1933.

VERNE, JULES (1828–1905). Imaginative French novelist whose fanciful works have been adapted for the screen many times. *20,000 Leagues under the Sea*, 1907; 1917; 1954; *Journey to the Center of the Earth*, 1909; 1959; *The Mysterious Island*, 1929; 1941; 1951; 1961; 1972; *From the Earth to the Moon* (with Carl Esmond as Verne), 1958; *Master of the World*, 1961; *Voyages Extraordinaires de Jules Verne*, 1952; others.

VESOTA, BRUNO (1922–76). Heavyset American character actor of the fifties, usually cast as a greasy, nasty villain. *Dementia* aka *Daughter of Horror* (and associate p), 1953; *The Undead*, 1957; *The Brain Eaters* (d only), 1958; *War of the Satellites*, 1958; *Attack of the Giant Leeches*, 1959; *A Bucket of Blood*, 1959; *Wasp Woman*, 1959; *Invasion of the Star Creatures* (d only), 1962; *Night Tide*, 1963; *Attack of the Mayan Mummy*, 1963; *The Haunted Palace*, 1963; *Curse of the Stone Hand* (narrator), 1965; *Creature of the Walking Dead*, 1966; *The Wild World of Batwoman* aka *She Was a Hippy Vampire*, 1966.

VETRI, VICTORIA (1944–). Australian model who made a few films in Britain and the United States after being featured in *Playboy* magazine. *Rosemary's Baby* (billed as Angela Dorian), 1968; *When Dinosaurs Ruled the Earth*, 1971; *Invasion of the Bee Girls*, 1973.

Robert Vaughn, ca. 1966, in character as superspy Napoleon Solo, the Man from U.N.C.L.E.

Conrad Veidt.

Yvette Vickers being forced into the swamp by Bruno Ve Sota in *Attack of The Giant Leeches* (1959).

Bruno Ve Sota as the bitter cuckold in *Attack of The Giant Leeches* (1959).

VICKERS, YVETTE (CA. 1938–). Vivacious blonde actress of the fifties, convincing as the Bad Girl in lurid melodramas and science-horror films. *Attack of the Fifty-Foot Woman*, 1958; *Attack of the Giant Leeches*, 1959.

VICTOR, HENRY (1898–1945). British character actor in Hollywood from the early thirties, memorable as the dim-witted and cruel carnival strongman in *Freaks*, 1932. *The Picture of Dorian Gray*, 1916; *She*, 1916; *The White Shadow*, 1924; *The Mummy*, 1932; *The Living Dead*, 1936; *King of the Zombies*, 1941.

Katherine Victor *(far left)* observes the *Teenage Zombies* (1960).

VICTOR, KATHERINE (1928–). Dark and statuesque American leading lady, a villainess in many low-budget thrillers for producer/director JERRY WARREN. *Mesa of Lost Women* (billed as Katena Vea), 1953; *Teenage Zombies*, 1960; *The Cape Canaveral Monsters*, 1960; *Curse of the Stone Hand*, 1965; *House of the Black Death*, 1965; *Creature Of the Walking Dead*, 1966; *The Wild World of Batwoman* aka *She Was a Hippy Vampire*, 1966; *Fear No Evil* (TV), 1969; *Captain Mom* (short), 1970.

VILLAR, CARLOS VILLARIAS. Spanish actor with Universal Pictures in 1931 who played *Dracula* in a Spanish-language version shot simultaneously with the BELA LUGOSI version.

VILLECHAIZE, HERVE (1943–). Latin midget actor in Hollywood. *Malatesta's Carnival*, 1973; *Seizure*, 1974; *The Man with the Golden Gun*, 1974. TV series: "Fantasy Island," 1977.

VITTES, LOUIS. American screenwriter whose *I Married a Monster from Outer Space*, 1958, is a harrowing exercise in paranoiac terror, as well as a rare instance of nineteen-fifties role reversal: the "hero" who saves the world is a woman. *The Monster from Green Hell*, 1958; *The Eyes of Annie Jones*, 1964.

Jock Mahoney and Shawn Smith meet a dinosaur in *The Land Unknown* (1957), directed by Virgil Vogel.

VITTI, MONICA (1933–). Italian leading lady in international films of the sixties, the screen personification of Peter O'Donnell's comic strip heroine *Modesty Blaise*, 1966. *Il Disco Volante (The Flying Disc)*, 1964.

VOGEL, VIRGIL. American director and former editor, active in television. *The Mole People*, 1956; *The Land Unknown*, 1957; *Invasion of the Animal People* (English-language version only; co-d; w/ JERRY WARREN), 1962; *The Sword of Ali Baba*, 1964.

VON HARBOU, THEA (1888–1954). German novelist and screenwriter of the twenties and thirties, frequently in collaboration with director FRITZ LANG. *Destiny*, 1921; *The Phantom*, 1922; *Dr. Mabuse, the Gambler*, 1922; *Siegfried*, 1925; *The Chronicles of the Gray House*, 1925; *Metropolis* (b/o her novel), 1926; *The Girl in the Moon*, 1929; *M*, 1931; *The Testament of Dr. Mabuse*, 1933; *The Testament of Dr. Mabuse* (original story only), 1962.

VONNEGUT, KURT (1922–). Leading American writer whose determinist fantasy-satires have been welcomed by the young but not by Hollywood. *Happy Birthday Wanda June* (w), 1971; *Slaughterhouse-Five* (original story only, from his novel *Slaughterhouse-Five or The Children's Crusade*), 1972; *Between Time and Timbuktu* (TV), 1972.

240 VON STROHEIM

Von Stroheim, Erich (1885–1957). Austrian actor/director who inspired the Hollywood caricature of the overbearing Prussian director with riding crop, jodhpurs, and monocle. Gifted but undisciplined, von Stroheim was notorious for his overlong films and lapses into fury. As actor: *Macbeth*, 1916; *The Great Gabbo* (one of the more notable films to find horror in the relationship between ventriloquist and dummy), 1930; *The Crime of Dr. Crespi*, 1935; *The Lady and the Monster*, 1944; *Unnatural*, 1952.

Von Sydow, Max (1929–). Intense Swedish leading actor, long associated with director INGMAR BERGMAN. *The Seventh Seal*, 1956; *The Magician*, 1958; *Hour of the Wolf*, 1968; *Shame*, 1968; *The Night Visitor*, 1971; *The Exorcist* (as Father Merrin), 1973; *The Ultimate Warrior*, 1975; *Exorcist II: The Heretic*, 1977.

Vorkov, Zandor. Lean American actor, vaguely reminiscent of CHRISTOPHER LEE, and the object of much nonsensical ballyhoo when he played Dracula in *Dracula vs. Frankenstein*, a minor cheapie from 1971.

Erich von Stroheim, in a publicity still that illustrates his penchant for overlong films.

W

WAGGNER, GEORGE (1894–). American director whose generally undistinguished output is enlivened by a number of entertaining horror films, notably *The Wolf Man*, 1941. *Man Made Monster*, 1941; *Horror Island*, 1941; *Frankenstein Meets the Wolf Man* (p only), 1943.

WALLACE, EDGAR (1875–1932). British author whose crime and mystery novels have provided the ground for many lurid films. *The Terror*, 1928; *King Kong* (treatment), 1933; *Return of the Terror*, 1934; *Chamber of Horrors* (b/o the the novel *The Door With Seven Locks*), 1940; *The Human Monster* (b/o the novel *The Dark Eyes of London*), 1940; *The Avenger*, 1960; *Dead Eyes of London* (b/o the novel *The Dark Eyes of London*), 1961; *The Door with Seven Locks*, 1962; *The Secret of the Black Trunk*, 1962; *The Indian Scarf* (b/o the novel *The Frightened Lady*), 1963; *The Mysterious Magician* (b/o the novel *The Ringer*), 1965; others.

WALTER, WILFRED (1882–1958). British actor of the thirties, memorable as the pathetically blind "monster" in *The Human Monster*, 1940.

WALTERS, THORLEY (1913–). British comic actor. *Dracula, Prince of Darkness*, 1966; *Frankenstein Must Be Destroyed*, 1970; *Vampire Circus*, 1972.

WALTHALL, HENRY B. (1878–1936). American character actor from 1909, in fine form as the demented scientist in *Devil Doll*, 1936, who discovers how to make big people small. *The Avenging Conscience* (b/o "The Tell-Tale Heart" and "Annabel Lee" by EDGAR ALLAN POE), 1914; *The Raven* (as Poe), 1915; *The Unknown Purple*, 1923; *London after Midnight*, 1927; *The Whispering Shadow*, 1933; *Dante's Inferno*, 1935.

WARD, BURT (1945–). American juvenile actor of the sixties who played a rather dim Robin to ADAM WEST's Batman in the popular television series, 1966–68, and in the 1966 theatrical feature *Batman*.

WARD, SIMON (1941–). Slender and intense British leading actor. *If . . .*, 1967; *Frankenstein Must Be Destroyed*, 1970; *The Chosen*, 1978; *Dominique*, 1978.

WARNER, DAVID (1941–). British stage and film actor of understated, forthright appeal. *A Midsummer Night's Dream*, 1968; *Tales from the Crypt*, 1972; *From Beyond the Grave*, 1975; *The Omen*, 1976; *Nightwing*, 1979; *Time After Time* (marvelous as Jack the Ripper), 1979.

Hysteria in Jerry Warren's *Creature of The Walking Dead* (1966).

WARREN, CHARLES MARQUIS (1912–). American director, responsible for *The Unknown Terror*, 1957, and its sudsy fungus men. *Back from the Dead*, 1957.

WARREN, GENE. American special-effects technician who began his career with the GEORGE PAL Puppetoons, 1943–47. Warren is now active in television. *tom thumb*, 1958; *The Time Machine* (Academy Award), 1960; *Dinosaurus*, 1960; *The Wonderful World of the Brothers Grimm*, 1962; *The Seven Faces of Dr. Lao*, 1964; *The Power*, 1968; *The Tool Box* (short), 1972; *The Legend of Hillbilly John*, 1973; others.

WARREN, JERRY. American independent producer of low-budgeters. *Man Beast*, 1955; *The Incredible Petrified World*, 1959; *Teenage Zombies*, 1960; *Invasion of the Animal People* (English-language version only; co-d; w/VIRGIL VOGEL), 1962; *Attack of the Mayan Mummy* (includes much footage from Mexican films; see: RAFAEL PORTILLO), 1963; *Curse of the Stone Hand*, 1965; *The Wild World of Batwoman* aka *She Was a Hippy Vampire*, 1966; *Creature of the Walking Dead*, 1966.

WATERS, JOHN (CA. 1945–). American exploitation filmmaker with a penchant for violence, outrageous characterizations, scatological humor, and scatter-shot satire. His *Pink Flamingos*, 1974, has achieved modest cult status and, like all his films, is mad and inexplicably compelling. *Female Trouble*, 1975; *Desperate Living*, 1977.

WATKIN, PIERRE (?-1960). American actor, notable as *Daily Planet* editor Perry White in the serials *Superman*, 1948, and *Atom Man vs. Superman*, 1950. *Dead Man's Eyes*, 1944; *The Phantom Speaks*, 1945; *Shock*, 1946; *Radar Secret Service*, 1950; *Two Lost Worlds*, 1950; *The Lost Planet*, 1953; *Creature with the Atom Brain*, 1955; *Beginning of the End*, 1957; *Spook Chasers*, 1957.

WATKINS, PETER (1937-). British director whose *The War Game*, 1966, a documentary-style look at the fate of Britain after a nuclear attack, is surely one of the most harrowing films of the sixties. *Privilege*, 1967; *Punishment Park*, 1970; *The Gladiators*, 1971.

WAYNE, JOHN (1907-79). Durable American star actor whose controversial politics did not diminish his great appeal. Known primarily as the rugged hero of innumerable westerns, Wayne starred in a couple of fantastic films early in his career. *Shadow of the Eagle* (serial; science fiction), 1932; *Haunted Gold* (involves phantoms who guard a mine), 1933.

WAYNE, PATRICK (1939-). Athletic American leading man, son of JOHN WAYNE. *Beyond Atlantis*, 1975; *The People That Time Forgot*, 1977; *Sinbad and the Eye of the Tiger* (as Sinbad), 1977.

WEAVER, SIGOURNEY (1949-). Forceful American stage actress who made a smashing film debut as the gutsy heroine of *Alien*, 1979.

John Wayne *(right)* in *Haunted Gold* (1933).

Pierre Watkin *(left)* as *Daily Planet* editor Perry White confers with Superman (Kirk Alyn), Lois Lane (Noel Neill), and Jimmy Olsen (Tommy Bond) in *Superman* (1948).

Wegener, Paul (1874–1948). German writer/actor/director who brought to the screen the Jewish legend of *The Golem*, 1917, *The Golem, How He Came into the World*, 1921, and a parody, *Golem and the Dancer*, 1917; *The Lost Shadow* (actor and d only), 1921; (*The Magician* actor only), 1926; *Svengali* (actor only), 1927; *The Living Dead* (actor only), 1933; others.

Paul Wegener as *The Golem* (1917), the Jewish man of clay who comes to malevolent if brief life.

WEINTRAUB, SY (1922–). American independent producer who picked up the film rights to Tarzan from SOL LESSER in 1959, and found commercial and critical success with GORDON SCOTT, JOCK MAHONEY, and MIKE HENRY as the jungle lord in successive films. Weintraub also produced the Tarzan television series (1966–69) that starred RON ELY. *Tarzan's Greatest Adventure*, 1959; *Tarzan Goes to India*, 1962; *Tarzan's Three Challenges*, 1963; *Tarzan and the Great River*, 1967; many others.

WEISBERG, BRENDA. American screenwriter of the forties. *The Scarlet Claw* (story only), 1944; *Weird Woman*, 1944; *The Mummy's Ghost* (co-w; w/GRIFFIN JAY and HENRY SUCHER), 1944.

WEISMULLER, JOHNNY (1904–). American actor and Olympic swimming champion, best known as Tarzan in *Tarzan of the Apes*, 1932, and sequels to 1948. His conception of the jungle lord remains the most popular, but gives no hint of the character's keen mind and cultured background. When Weismuller grew too old for the role, he slipped comfortably into *Jungle Jim*, 1950 and sequels. *Tarzan and His Mate*, 1934; *Tarzan Escapes*, 1936; *Tarzan Finds a Son!*, 1939; *Tarzan's Secret Treasure*, 1941; *Tarzan's New York Adventure*, 1942; *Tarzan and the Leopard Woman*, 1946; *Tarzan and the Mermaids*, 1948; *Jungle Jim in the Forbidden Land*, 1952; *Voodoo Tiger*, 1952; *Killer Ape*, 1953; *Jungle Moon Men*, 1955; *The Phynx* (cameo), 1970; others.

WELCH, RAQUEL (1940–). Busty, artificial American sex symbol of the sixties and seventies who contributed her figure and little else to *Fantastic Voyage*, 1966; *One Million Years B.C.*, 1967, and *Bedazzled* (as Lust), 1967.

Johnny Weismuller as Tarzan, with Maureen O' Sullivan and Johnny Sheffield.

246 WELDON

WELDON, JOAN (1933–). American leading lady who had a brief film career in the fifties. Her pictures are routine with the exception of *Them!*, 1954, in which she is convincing as the take-charge entomologist.

WELLES, MEL (CA. 1930–). American character actor in Hollywood B's of the fifties, later a low-budget director active in Europe. He is highly amusing as harried florist Gravis Mushnik in ROGER CORMAN's *The Little Shop of Horrors*, 1960. *Abbott and Costello Meet the Mummy*, 1955; *The Undead*, 1957; *Attack of the Crab Monsters*, 1957; *The She-Beast*, 1966; *Island of the Doomed* (d only), 1968; *Lady Frankenstein* (d only), 1973; *Dr. Heckyl and Mr. Hype*, 1980.

WELLES, ORSON (1915–). Virtuoso American filmmaker and actor who has battled studio interference and his sometimes questionable artistic judgment for thirty-five years. His *Citizen Kane*, 1941, is a contemporary masterpiece, a thrillingly modern film which set many of the visual ground rules still in effect. *Hearts of Age* (amateur; experimental surrealism), 1934; *Macbeth*, 1948; *Black Magic* (actor only; as Cagliostro), 1949; *Desodre* (*Disorder*; actor only; fantasy tour of Paris), 1950; *Necromancy* (actor only), 1973.

Mel Welles *(right)* confronts the bungling burglar in Roger Corman's *The Little Shop of Horrors* (1960).

Joan Weldon is about to meet one of *Them!* (1954).

WELLS, H. G. (1866-1946). Gifted and imaginative British novelist, essayist, and historian whose works have been dramatized many times. He wrote the screenplay for *Things to Come*, 1936, adapting his novel *The Shape of Things to Come*, and wrote *The Man Who Could Work Miracles* (from his short story), 1937. Film adaptations by other writers include *Island of Lost Souls* (b/o the novel *The Island of Dr. Moreau*), 1933; *The Invisible Man*, 1933; *The Invisible Man Returns*, 1940; *The Invisible Man's Revenge*, 1944; *The War of the Worlds*, 1953; *The Time Machine*, 1960; *The Island of Dr. Moreau*, 1977; *Time after Time* (a charming novelty, since Wells himself is the focal character); 1979; more. Wells's notion of invisibility has inspired scores of broader (and usually uncredited) adaptations, *e.g.*, *The Amazing Transparent Man*, 1960; his *The Island of Dr. Moreau* has been used as the springboard for minor but interesting variations like *Terror Is a Man*, 1959. It may be argued that Wells's *The War of the Worlds* inspired the entire "invasion picture" sub-genre.

WERKER, ALFRED LOUIS (1896-). American director of the forties who demonstrated a flair for mild horror-comedies. *The Reluctant Dragon* (co-d; w/Hamilton Luske), 1941; *Whispering Ghosts*, 1942; *A-Haunting We Will Go*, 1942; *Shock*, 1946.

WEST, ADAM (1929-). American television actor who found transient fame as Batman, 1966-68, and who played the role in *Batman*, a 1966 theatrical feature. The character has not lived down West's campy, paunchy image. *The Eyes of Charles Sand* (TV), 1972.

WEST, ROLAND (1887-1952). American writer/director, responsible for a pair of fine films with the classic masked killer theme, *The Bat* (and p), 1926, and *The Bat Whispers*, 1931. *The Unknown Purple* (b/o the play by West and Carlyle Moore), 1923; *The Monster*, 1925.

WESTMORE, BUD (1916-73). American makeup artist associated with Universal Pictures who created *The Creature from the Black Lagoon*, 1954. *Abbott and Costello Meet Frankenstein*, 1948; *It Came from Outer Space* (the Xenomorph), 1953; *This Island Earth*, 1955; *Revenge of the Creature*, 1955; *Tarantula*, 1955; *The Mole People*, 1956; *Man of a Thousand Faces* (the LON CHANEY story), 1957; *Monster on the Campus*, 1958; *Munster Go Home!*, 1966; *Soylent Green*, 1973; numerous others. Brother of makeup artist WALLY WESTMORE.

WESTMORE, WALLY (1906-73). American makeup artist who helped FREDRIC MARCH to an Academy Award as *Dr. Jekyll and Mr. Hyde*, 1932. Brother of makeup artist BUD WESTMORE. *Island of Lost Souls* (the Manimals), 1933; *Murders in the Zoo*, 1933; *Death Takes a Holiday*, 1934; *Conquest of Space* (notably the G-force facial effect), 1955; *The Colossus of New York*, 1958; *Project X*, 1968; etc.

The Creature From The Black Lagoon (1954); makeup created by Bud Westmore.

Wally Westmore's impressive design for *The Colossus of New York* (1958).

Judith Evelyn is driven to the brink of insanity in William Castle's *The Tingler* (1959), written by Robb White.

WETHERELL, VIRGINIA (CA. 1948–). British leading lady, wife of actor RALPH BATES. *The Crimson Cult*, 1968; *A Clockwork Orange*, 1971; *Dr. Jekyll and Sister Hyde*, 1972; *Demons of the Mind*, 1972; *Disciple of Death*, 1973; *Dracula* (TV; theatrical release in Britain), 1973.

WHALE, JAMES (1886–1957). British director in Hollywood, whose *Frankenstein*, 1931, got Universal rolling on the road to horror. At his best, Whale was able to mix expressionism and dark humor deftly, as in *Bride of Frankenstein*, 1935. But his stage background restricted his artistic vision, and he remains important more for his influence than for his actual output. *The Old Dark House*, 1932; *The Invisible Man*, 1933.

WHITE, JULES (1900–). American producer/director of two-reelers, associated with Columbia and THE THREE STOOGES from 1938. Fanciful Stooges shorts supervised by White include *Dizzy Detectives*, 1943; *If a Body Meets a Body*, 1945; *A Bird in the Head*, 1946; *All Gummed Up*, 1947; *Shivering Sherlocks*, 1948; *Heavenly Daze*, 1948; *The Ghost Talks*, 1949; *Three Arabian Nuts*, 1951; *Scrambled Brains*, 1951; *Cuckoo on a Choo Choo*, 1952; *Spooks* (3-D), 1953; *Bedlam in Paradise*, 1955; *Space Ship Sappy*, 1957; *Outer Space Jitters*, 1957; *Flying Saucer Daffy*, 1958; others.

WHITE, PEARL (1889–1938). American stuntwoman who became the screen's first (and quintessential) serial heroine. Her films are characteristically full of death rays, ghosts, and cliff-hanging thrills. *The Exploits of Elaine*, 1914; *The Perils of Pauline*, 1914 (this inspired a limp 1967 version of the same title starring pretty Pamela Austin); *The New Exploits of Elaine*, 1915; *The Romance of Elaine*, 1915; *The Iron Claw*, 1916; *The Fatal Ring*, 1917; *Lightning Raider*, 1918–19; *Plunder*, 1922–23; *The Perils of Paris*, 1924.

WHITE, ROBB (1909–). American screenwriter, associated chiefly with producer/director WILLIAM CASTLE. Facile and gimmicky, White's scripts succeed on the strength of their verve and humor. *Macabre*, 1958; *House on Haunted Hill*, 1958; *The Tingler*, 1959; *13 Ghosts*, 1960; *Homicidal*, 1961.

WHITMORE, JAMES (1921–). American leading actor of determined nature and down-to-earth appeal. Lately noted for impersonations of Harry Truman and Will Rogers, Whitmore will be remembered by thriller fans as the brave and self-sacrificing state trooper who battles the giant ants in *Them!*, 1954. *The Next Voice You Hear* (in which God speaks over the radio), 1950; *Planet of the Apes*, 1968.

James Whitmore *(far right)* with James Arness and Edmund Gwenn in *Them!* (1954).

WIENE, ROBERT (1881–1938). German director of the silent era whose *The Cabinet of Dr. Caligari*, 1919, is perhaps the cinema's most fully realized expressionist exercise. With its odd angles and twisted perspectives, interplay of light and shadow, and deft exploration of the dark tricks of the mind, the film remains as immediately disturbing as last night's bad dream. *The Hands of Orlac*, 1925.

Robert Wiene explored the twisted torments of the human soul in his 1919 expressionist masterpiece *The Cabinet of Dr. Caligari*. The mesmerized prowler is Conrad Veidt.

Myopia from Mars or *Killers from Space* (1954), directed by W. Lee Wilder.

WILCOX, FRED McLEOD (CA. 1905-64). American director of innocuous Lassie movies who unexpectedly guided *Forbidden Planet*, 1956, to dazzling success.

WILDE, OSCAR (1856-1900). Iconoclastic and brilliantly talented British playwright, poet and novelist whose *The Picture of Dorian Gray* has inspired nine film versions since 1910, and numerous uncredited variations. *The Picture of Dorian Gray*, 1910; *Portret Doriana Greya* (Soviet), 1915; *The Picture of Dorian Gray*, 1916; *Das Bildnis des Dorian Gray* (German), 1917; *The Picture of Dorian Gray* (the famous Hollywood version with HURD HATFIELD as Gray), 1945; *The Secret of Dorian Gray*, 1971; others. *The Canterville Ghost* (b/o Wilde's short story), 1944.

WILDER, W. LEE (1904-). Austrian producer/director in Hollywood, brother of writer/director Billy Wilder. *Phantom from Space*, 1953; *Killers from Space*, 1954; *The Snow Creature*, 1954; *Manfish*, 1956; *The Man without a Body* (co-d; w/Charles Saunders), 1958.

WILLIAMS, GRANT (1930-). American leading man who gave a sensitive performance as *The Incredible Shrinking Man*, 1957, but who was subsequently (pardon the joke) little seen. Other films with fantastic content: *The Monolith Monsters*, 1957; *Leech Woman*, 1960; *Brain of Blood*, 1971; *Doomsday*, 1972.

WILLIAMS, GUY (1924-). Handsome American leading man, popular as television's Zorro, 1957-59, and as Professor Robinson on "Lost in Space," 1965-68. *I Was a Teenage Werewolf*, 1957; *Captain Sinbad* (title role), 1963.

WILLIAMS, JOHN. American film composer who came to sudden prominence with fine back-to-back scores for *Star Wars* (Academy Award), 1977, and *Close Encounters of the Third Kind*, 1977. *Jaws*, 1975; *Superman*, 1978. *The Empire Strikes Back*, 1980.

WILLIAMS, WADE (1942-). American film fan and promoter based in Missouri who rereleased *Invaders from Mars*, 1953, in 1976 and *Rocketship X-M*, 1950, in 1977, and put together a fine soundtrack album from the latter. Directed *Sherry's House of Nudes* (sex-fantasy), 1964.

WILLIAMSON, MALCOLM (1931-). Australian composer active in England for Hammer Films. *Brides of Dracula*, 1960; *Crescendo*, 1969; *The Horror of Frankenstein*, 1970; *Nothing but the Night*, 1972.

WILLIS, MATT. American actor of the forties, featured as the tormented werewolf Andreas in *The Return of the Vampire*, 1944. *Mark of the Whistler*, 1944.

WILSON, LEWIS. American actor who took the title role in *The Batman*, a 1943 serial based on Bob Kane's comic-book hero.

Grant Williams, in peril as *The Incredible Shrinking Man* (1957).

WINTERS, SHELLEY (1922–). Popular American star character actress who began her career in the late forties as a glamour girl. Since the sixties she has played a variety of pushy and sometimes homicidal matrons. *Wild in the Streets*, 1968; *The Mad Room*, 1969; *What's the Matter with Helen?*, 1971; *Whoever Slew Auntie Roo?*, 1971; *Revenge!* (TV), 1971; *The Devil's Daughter* (TV), 1972; *The Tenant*, 1976; *Tentacles*, 1977; *The Visitor*, 1980.

WISBAR, FRANK. German director associated with Hollywood's poverty-row PRC studio during the war. His atmospheric *Strangler of the Swamp*, 1946, is a modest success and is a remake of a film Wisbar had directed in Germany eleven years before, *Fahrmann Maria (Ferryboat Woman Maria)*, 1935 (a stunningly visual, virtually silent study of ghostly love and the supernatural, and one of the few bright spots of Nazi-controlled German cinema); *Der Werwolf* (incomplete), 1934; *The Devil Bat's Daughter*, 1946.

3000 A.D.: New York City is destroyed in *Captive Women* (1952), co-written by Aubrey Wisberg and Jack Pollexfen.

WISBERG, AUBREY (1909–). British writer/producer active in Hollywood. *The Power of the Whistler* (w only), 1945; *Escape in the Fog* (w only), 1945; *The Man from Planet X* (p; co-w; w/JACK POLLEXFEN), 1951; *Captive Women* (co-w only; w/JACK POLLEXFEN), 1952; *Port Sinister* (co-w only; w/JACK POLLEXFEN), 1953; *The Neanderthal Man*, 1953; *Son of Sinbad*, 1955; others.

WISE, ROBERT (1914–). American director whose *The Day the Earth Stood Still* (1951) is a triumph of provocative and cerebral science fiction. His considerable talent has been squandered lately on overblown projects. *The Devil and Daniel Webster* (editor only), 1941; *The Curse of the Cat People* (co-d; w/Gunther V. Fritsch), 1944; *The Body Snatcher*, 1945; *A Game of Death*, 1945; *The Haunting*, 1963; *The Andromeda Strain*, 1971; *Audrey Rose*, 1977; *Star Trek: The Motion Picture*, 1979.

WITNEY, WILLIAM (CA. 1910–). American serial and B-western director with Republic, often teamed with JOHN ENGLISH. *Dick Tracy's G-Men* (co-d; w/John English), 1939; *Daredevils of the Red Circle* (co-d; w/English), 1939; *Drums of Fu Manchu* (co-d; w/English), 1940; *The Mysterious Dr. Satan* (co-d; w/English), 1940; *Dick Tracy vs. Crime, Inc.* (co-d; w/English), 1941; *The Adventures of Captain Marvel* (co-d; w/English), 1941; *Spy Smasher*, 1942; *The Crimson Ghost* (co-d; w/FRED C. BRANNON), 1946; *Master of the World*, 1961; others.

WOLFIT, SIR DONALD (1902–68). Respected British stage and film actor. *Svengali* (title role), 1955; *Satellite in the Sky*, 1956; *Blood of the Vampire* (as Callistratus), 1958; *Les Mains D'Orlac* (*The Hands of Orlac*), 1960; *Dr. Crippen*, 1963.

Tor Johnson proves himself more than a match for hero Tony McCoy in Edward D. Wood's infamous *Bride of The Monster* (1956). Note the painted "masonry" walls.

WOOD, JR., EDWARD D. (1922–78). Poverty-row American producer/director/screenwriter of the fifties who gave an aging BELA LUGOSI the actor's final contracts. *Glen or Glenda?* aka *I Changed My Sex* and *I Led Two Lives* and *The Transvestite* (magical sex change), 1953; *Bride of the Monster*, 1956; *Plan 9 from Outer Space* aka *Graverobbers from Outer Space*, 1956; *The Bride and the Beast* (w only), 1958; *Night of the Ghouls*, 1959; *Orgy of the Dead* (w only), 1966. In his later years, Wood wrote pornographic horror stories for limited-circulation sex magazines.

WORDSWORTH, RICHARD. British actor of the fifties who gave a notable peformance in *The Creeping Unknown*, 1956, as the pathetic astronaut infected with alien spores. *Curse of the Werewolf*, 1961 (as the bestial beggar who commits rape and fathers a lycanthrope).

WORONOV, MARY (1946–). Dark and sultry American leading lady of the seventies, bidding fair to become queen of the drive-in pictures. *Silent Night, Bloody Night*, 1974; *Seizure*, 1974; *Death Race 2000*, 1975; *Hollywood Boulevard*, 1976; others.

WRAY, FAY (1907–). American leading lady of the thirties, unforgettable as the blonde maiden cherished by *King Kong*, 1933. She puts her famous scream to even better use in *The Mystery of the Wax Museum*, 1933, when she strikes the mask from the scarred face of LIONEL ATWILL. *Dr. X*, 1931; *The Most Dangerous Game*, 1932; *The Vampire Bat*, 1933; *Black Moon*, 1934.

Fay Wray with Bruce Cabot in a publicity still from *King Kong* (1933).

WYNDHAM, JOHN (1903–69). British science-fiction novelist (true name John Benyon Harris) whose intelligent prose has lent itself to film adaptation. *The Midwich Cuckoos* came to the screen in 1960 as *Village of the Damned*, and is excellent (see: WOLF RILLA). Wyndham's *The Day of the Triffids* is one of the most frightening sf novels ever written, but the 1963 movie version aims for the book's more obvious aspects, and is rather ho-hum. *Children of the Damned* (b/o a concept in his novel, *The Midwich Cuckoos*), 1963.

WYNGARDE, PETER. Versatile, sensually-featured British character actor, mostly on television. *The Innocents* (as a ghost), 1961; *Burn, Witch, Burn*, 1962.

Y

YARBROUGH, JEAN (1900–). Workmanlike American director, a mainstay of Monogram Pictures during the thirties and forties. *The Devil Bat*, 1941; *King of the Zombies*, 1941; *House of Horrors*, 1946; *The Brute Man*, 1946; *She-Wolf of London*, 1946; *The Creeper*, 1948; *Master Minds*, 1949; *Hillbillys* [sic] *in a Haunted House*, 1967.

YATES, GEORGE WORTHING. American screenwriter, most active during the science-fiction boom of the fifties. *Sinbad the Sailor* (story only), 1947; *Them!* (story only), 1954; *Conquest of Space* (co-w; w/Phillip Yordan and BARRE LYNDON), 1955; *It Came from Beneath the Sea* (co-w; w/Hal Smith), 1955; *Earth vs. the Flying Saucers*, 1956; *Frankenstein—1970* (co-w; w/Richard Landau), 1958; *War of the Colossal Beast*, 1958; *The Flame Barrier* (co-w; w/ Pat Fiedler), 1958; others.

YATES, HERBERT (1880–1966). American studio executive who ran Republic Pictures virtually unassisted. The studio became Hollywood's leading producer of entertaining B-westerns and vivid serials in the forties, and is remembered with fondness by grown-up children everywhere. For partial list of Republic serials see: DAVE SHARPE, TOM STEELE, DALE VAN SICKEL.

YEAWORTH, JR., IRVIN S. American director associated with producer JACK H. HARRIS in the late fifties. Yeaworth's films display a sense of humor and a knack for coaxing smoothly underplayed performances from his players; *The Blob*, 1958, in particular, has fine moments of perversely funny horror, as when the blob slithers under a car to gobble up the mechanic working beneath it. *The 4-D Man*, 1959; *Dinosaurus*, 1960.

YORK, DUKE (1902–52). American actor/stuntman of the thirties and forties who often played brutes or monsters. *Island of Lost Souls* (as one of the Manimals), 1933; *Flash Gordon* (as King Kala), 1936; *Topper Takes a Trip*, 1938; *Idle Roomers* (THREE STOOGES short; as a comic werewolf), 1944; *Shivering Sherlocks*, 1948; others.

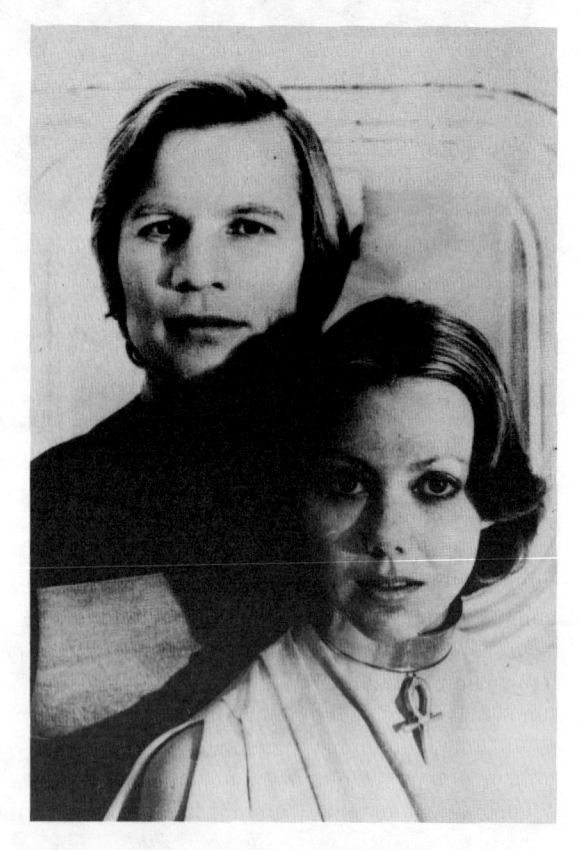

Michael York with Jenny Agutter in *Logan's Run* (1976).

Roland Young toasts comely ghost Constance Bennett in *Topper Takes a Trip* (1939).

YORK, FRANCINE (CA. 1935–). Pretty American leading lady of second features and television. *Space Monster*, 1965; *Curse of the Swamp Creature*, 1967.

YORK, MICHAEL (1942–). Athletic British leading man of the seventies. *Lost Horizon*, 1973; *Logan's Run*, 1976; *The Island of Dr. Moreau*, 1977.

YORK, SUSANNAH (1942–). Blonde British leading lady of the sixties and seventies, often cast as a beautiful but emotionally fragile woman. *Happy Birthday Wanda June*, 1971; *Images*, 1972; *Superman* (as Lara, Superman's mother), 1978. *Superman II*, 1981.

YOUNG, ALAN (1919–). British-Canadian light actor in America, familiar as star of television's "Mr. Ed," 1960–66 and fondly remembered as the gentle friend of the hero in *The Time Machine*, 1960. *tom thumb*, 1958.

YOUNG, HAROLD (1897–). American programmer director of the forties. *The Mummy's Tomb*, 1942; *Jungle Captive*, 1945; *The Frozen Ghost*, 1945.

YOUNG, ROLAND (1887–1953). British star character actor of the thirties and forties, most active in Hollywood, and adept at portraying good-humored, upper-class ninnies. He is a delight as *Topper*, 1937, the man pestered by a pair of whimsical ghosts, and most memorable as *The Man Who Could Work Miracles*, 1937, a meek fellow who is given the power to stop the Earth's rotation—and does. *The Unholy Night*, 1929; *Ali Baba Goes to Town*, 1937; *Topper Takes a Trip*, 1939; *Topper Returns*, 1941.

YOUNG, TERENCE (1915–). British director who has guided some of the James Bond fantasies. *Corridor of Mirrors*, 1948; *Dr. No* (first of the Bond series), 1962; *Thunderball*, 1965.

YURICICH, MATTHEW (1923–). Talented American matte painter and special-effects technician. *The Day the Earth Stood Still*, 1951; *Forbidden Planet*, 1956; *Soylent Green*, 1973; *Young Frankenstein* (notably the fine matte painting of Frankenstein's castle), 1974; *Death Race 2000*, 1975; *Logan's Run*, 1976; *Close Encounters of the Third Kind*, 1977; *The China Syndrome*, 1979; *Star Trek: The Motion Picture*, 1979; more.

Z

ZEMAN, KAREL (1910–). Czechoslovakian producer/director of colorful fantasies that sometimes incorporate cartoon or stop-motion animation. *Journey to the Beginning of Time* (and co-w; w/ J.A. Novotny), 1954; *The Fabulous World of Jules Verne* aka *Weapons of Destruction* and *The Diabolic Invention* and *The Deadly Invention* (and art directed; and co-w; w/Frantisek Hrubin), 1958; *Baron Munchausen* (and art directed; and co-w; w/Joseph Kainar), 1961; others.

ZIMBALIST, AL. American producer of low-budget science fiction. *Robot Monster* (the first science-fiction film shot in 3-D), 1953; *Cat Women of the Moon*, 1953; *The Monster from Green Hell*, 1958; *Valley of the Dragons*, 1962.

ZUCCO, GEORGE (1886–1960). British character actor in Hollywood films from 1931, usually cast as a cultured and imposing villain. *The Man Who Could Work Miracles*, 1937; *The Cat and the Canary*, 1939; *The Hunchback of Notre Dame*, 1939; *The Mummy's Hand*, 1940; *The Monster and the Girl*, 1941; *Topper Returns*, 1941; *Dr. Renault's Secret*, 1942; *The Mad Monster*, 1942; *The Mummy's Tomb*, 1942; *The Black Raven*, 1943; *Dead Men Walk*, 1943; *The Mad Ghoul*, 1943; *Return of the Ape Man* (as the ape man in some scenes; played by Frank Moran in others), 1944; *Voodoo Man*, 1944; *The Mummy's Ghost*, 1944; *Shadows in the Night*, 1944; *House of Frankenstein*, 1945; *The Flying Serpent*, 1946; *Scared to Death*, 1947; *Tarzan and the Mermaids*, 1948.

ZUGSMITH, ALBERT (1910–). American producer of lurid exploitation films. *Captive Women* (associate p), 1952; *Invasion U.S.A.* (co-p; w/Robert Smith), 1953; *Port Sinister* (associate p), 1953; *The Incredible Shrinking Man*, 1957; *The Girl in the Kremlin*, 1957; *The Private Lives of Adam and Eve* (and co-d; w/MICKEY ROONEY), 1960; *Confessions of an Opium Eater*, 1962; *Movie Star American Style or LSD I Hate You* (as actor and d only), 1966.

George Zucco.

Index

Films are listed chronologically.
Italics indicate photographs.

1896
The Haunted Castle, 161

1897
Faust, 96
Faust and Marguerite, 96

1898
The Artist's Dream, 161

1899
Haggard's "She" — The Pillar of Fire, 161
Upside Down or The Human Flies, 30

1900
An Artist's Dream, 186

1901
Another Job for the Undertaker, 186
The Artist's Dilemma, 186
The Famous Illusion of de Kolta, 30
The Haunted Curiosity Shop, 30
The Man with the Rubber Head, 161

1902
Voyage to the Moon, 161

1903
The Kingdom of the Fairies, 161

1904
The Haunted Scene Painter, 30
Tropical Tricks, 30

1905
The Tempest, 208

1906
Dream of a Rarebit Fiend, 186
Faust, 96
Inventor Crazybrains and His Wonderful Airship, 161

1907
Hamlet, 208
The £1000 Spook, 30
The Quick Change Mesmerist, 30
Shakespeare Writing "Julius Caesar," 208
20,000 Leagues Under the Sea, 161, 236

1908
Hamlet, 208
In the Bogie Man's Cave, 161
Macbeth, 208
Rescued From an Eagle's Nest, 100, 186
The Tempest, 208
When the Man in the Moon Seeks a Wife, 220

1909
Edgar Allan Poe, 100, 186
Faust, 96, 186
Journey to the Center of the Earth, 236
Julius Caesar, 208
Macbeth, 208
A Midsummer Night's Dream, 208
The Sealed Room, 100

1910
Alice's Adventures in Wonderland, 186
The Bewitched Boxing Gloves, 30
Faust, 96
Frankenstein, 178, 210
Hamlet, 208
The Picture of Dorian Gray, 250

1911
The Cap of Invisibility, 30
Macbeth, 208
Notre Dame de Paris, 118
The Tempest, 208

1912
The Conquest of the Pole, 161
Electrical Housebuilding, 220
The Electric Leg, 220
In Gollywog Land, 30
Man's Genesis, 100
The Raven, 186
The Tempest, 208

1913
Faust and the Lily, 96
A Midsummer Night's Dream, 208
Notre Dame, 118
The Pit and the Pendulum, 186
The Prophecy, 178

1914
The Avenging Conscience, 100, 241

258 INDEX

The Exploits of Elaine, 248
The Magical Mystic, 30
The Perils of Pauline, 248

1915

The Bribe, 178
Faust, 96
Life Without Soul, 213
The New Exploits of Elaine, 248
Portret Doriane Greya, 250
The Raven, 241
The Romance of Elaine, 248

1916

The Darling of Paris, 118
Dr. Jekyll and Mr. Hyde, 146
Hilda Warren and Death, 140
Intolerance, 100
The Iron Claw, 146, 248
Macbeth (D.W. Griffith version), 100, 208, 240
Macbeth (French), 208
Nacht des Grauens, 135
The Picture of Dorian Gray, 237, 250
The Portrait of Dolly Gray, 30
She, 237

1917

Das Bildnis des Dorian Gray, 250
Az Elet Kuralya, 150
The Fatal Ring, 179, 248
The Golem, 162, *244*
Golem and the Dancer, 162, 244
Hamlet, 208
The Hidden Hand, 146
A Midsummer Night's Dream, 208
Prehistoric Poultry, 176
R.F.D. 10,000 B.B., 176
20,000 Leagues Under the Sea, 236

1918

Alraune, 61
The Eyes of the Mummy, 121
Lightning Raider, 179, 248
The Romance of Tarzan, 146
Tarzan of the Apes, 120, 146

1919

The Cabinet of Dr. Caligari, 62, *135*, 236, *249*
The Fall of Babylon, 100
Five Sinister Stories, 236
The Ghost of Slumber Mountain, 176
Die Goldene See, 62, 140
The Master Mystery, 118

The Miracle Man, 45
Satanis, 170

1920

The Devil's Garden, 21
Dr. Jekyll and Mr. Hyde, 21
The Flaming Disk, 146
Go and Get It, 164
Der Januskopf, 150, 170, 236
Leaves From Satan's Book, 72
The Penalty, 45
The Return of Tarzan, 186
Terror Island, 118
Witch Woman, 72

1921

The Adventures of Tarzan, 146
Destiny, 62, 140, 239
Dream Street, 100
Faust, 96
Fountain of Youth, 96
The Golem, How He Came Into the World, 162, 244
Hamlet, 208
The Lost Shadow, 244
The Son of Tarzan, 223

1922

A Blind Bargain, 45
Dr. Mabuse, the Gambler, 52, 134, 140, 239
The Man From Beyond, 118
Nosferatu, the Vampire, 170, 206, *219*
The Phantom, 62, 239
Plunder, 248

1923

The Hunchback of Notre Dame, 44, 118, 146, 163
The Mystery of Dr. Fu Manchu, 199
Soul of the Beast, 66
The Unknown Purple, 241, 247

1924

The Perils of Paris, 248
The Thief of Bagdad, 123, 213
Three Wax Men, 68, 144, 236
Waxworks, 121, 135
The White Shadow, 237

1925

The Chronicles of the Gray House, 62, 239
The Hands of Orlac, 194, 236, 249
The Lost World, 24, 71, 164, 176, 220
The Monster, 45, 247

Phantom of the Opera, 44, 183
Secrets of a Soul, 135
Siegfried, 140, 239
The Unholy Three, 35, 45, 75
The Wizard of Oz, 104

1926

The Bat, 213, 247
The Bells, 21, 129
Faust, 68, 96, 121, 170
The Lodger, 115
The Magician, 244
Metropolis, 89, 113, 134, 140, 239
The Sorrows of Satan, 100
The Student of Prague, 135

1927

The Chinese Parrot, 144, 213
Flying Elephants, 141
The Gorilla, 184
Hamlet, 208
King of the Jungle, 146
London After Midnight, 35, *44*, *227*, 241
The Man Who Laughs, 236
Mockery, 45
Mr. Wu, 45
Svengali, 244
Tarzan and the Golden Lion, 129, 184
The Unknown, 59
The Wizard, 119

1928

Alraune, 113
The Cat and the Canary, 141, 144
The Fall of the House of Usher, 186
Habeas Corpus, 141
The Haunted House, 228
The Life and Death of 9413 — A Hollywood Extra, 82
The Loves of Zero, 82
The Man Who Laughs, 19, 144, 183
A Midsummer Night's Dream, 208
Tarzan the Mighty, 162
The Terror, 66, 114, 117, 241
Vamping Venus, 228

1929

At Edge of World, 68, 113, 206
Un Chien Andalou, 36, 63
Die Frau im Mond, 140, 239
The Ghost Talks, 231
House of Horror, 102, 228
The Last Warning, 141, 144
The Mysterious Dr. Fu Manchu, 112, 143, 179, 199
Mysterious Island, 21, 236

Seven Footprints to Satan, 146, 201, 213, 228
Tarzan the Tiger, 162
The Unholy Night, 21, 129, 213, 255

1930

Brats, 141
The Cat Creeps, 231
Daughter of Evil, 113, 135
The Gorilla, 184
The Great Gabbo, 240
Ingagi, 92
Just Imagine, 18, 221
L'Age D'or, 36, 63
The Laurel and Hardy Murder Case, 141
Rasputins Liebesabenteuer, 206
The Return of Dr. Fu Manchu, 122, 135, 143
The Unholy Three, 35, *45*, 75
The Wizard's Apprentice, 161

1931

The Bat Whispers, 168, 247
A Connecticut Yankee, 179
Daughter of the Dragon, 82, 114, 135
Dracula, 35, 43, 90, *91*, 150, 154, *219*, *235*
Dracula (Spanish-language version), 238
Drums of Jeopardy, 18
Frankenstein, v, 48, 49, 90, *107*, 127, 155, 184, 210, 221, 235, 248
King of the Wild, 129
L'Atlantide, 113
M, 140, 147, 239
The Mad Genius, 21, 61, 129
Murder by the Clock, 184
The Phantom of Paris, 119, 220
The Spider, 161
Svengali, 21, 82
Trapped, 172

1932

Chandu the Magician, 150
The Crooked Circle, 119, 194
The Death Kiss, 154
Dr. Jekyll and Mr. Hyde, 153, *154*, 217, 221, 229, 247
Dr. X, 18, 61, 84, 253
The Face at the Window, 157
Freaks, 19, *35*, *74*, 75, 84, 119, 201, 237
Jungle Mystery, 137
Kongo, 162
The Lodger, 111
The Mask of Fu Manchu, 129, 199, 220
The Midnight Warning, 24
The Monster Walks, 18, 26, 146
The Most Dangerous Game, 19, 54, 123, 184, 206, 216, 253
The Mummy, 82, 89, 122, 123, *128*, 129, 154, 184, 235, 237

Murders in the Rue Morgue, 82, 123
The Old Dark House, 129, 141, 157, 222, 224, 248
Secrets of the French Police, 167
Shadow of the Eagle, 23, 243
Sinister Hands, 18
Strange Adventure, 90
Tarzan the Ape Man, 179, 245
The Thirteenth Guest, 223
Vampyr, 72, 157
White Zombie, *102*, 150

1933

Alice in Wonderland, 16, 98, 113, 117, 228
Case of the Frightened Lady, 224
Deluge, 27, 78, 235
F.P. 1, 110, 147, 236
Haunted Gold, *243*
International House, 150
The Invisible Man, 90, 114, 178, 190, 222, 247, 248
Island of Lost Souls, 16, 37, 77, 119, 131, 135, 138, *140*, 141, 150, 216, 221, 247, 254
King Kong, v, 16, 39, 54, 66, 123, 176, *177*, 194, 200, 206, 216, 241, *253*
King of the Jungle, 102
The Living Dead, 244
The Mystery of the Wax Museum, 18, 61, 114, 253
Murders in the Zoo, 37, 102, 247
Nature in the Wrong, 47
Night of Terror, 150
Now We'll Tell One, 47
The Phantom of the Air, 231
Rasputin and the Empress, 18, 21, 113, 167
Son of Kong, 16, 54, 66, 123, 176, *177*, 194, 200, 206, 216
Supernatural, 102
Tarzan the Fearless, 18, 58, 124, 137
Techno-Crazy, 138
The Testament of Dr. Mabuse, 134, 140, 239
Der Tunnel, 206
The Vampire Bat, 18, 90, 253
The Whispering Shadow, 150, 241

1934

Another Wild Idea, 47
Babes in Toyland, 33, *113*, *141*
The Black Cat, 129, 150, 154, 232
Black Moon, 172, 253
Death Takes a Holiday, 154, 223, 235, 247
The Ghoul, 104, 129, 195, 224
Gold, 110, 113
Hearts of Age, 246
The Lost Jungle, 23
The Medium, 208
The Mystery of Mr. X, 220
The Return of Chandu, 150
The Return of the Terror, 184, 194, 223, 241

Tarzan and His Mate, 42, 92, 179, 245
The Vanishing Shadow, 216
Der Werwolf, 251

1935

The Black Room, 129, 172
Bride of Frankenstein, 41, *49*, 90, 98, *112*, 116, 127, 138, *139*, 178, 184, 210, 221, 224, *225*, 248
Charlie Chan in Egypt, 179
Condemned to Live, 18, 167
The Crime of Dr. Crespi, 90, 240
Dante's Inferno, 57, 137, 229, 241
Fahrmann Maria, 251
Faust Fantasy, 96
The Florentine Dagger, 82, 179, 194
Hamlet, 208
Life Hesitates at 40, 47
The Lost City, 195, 221
Mad Love, 49, 89, 147, 194
The Man Who Reclaimed His Head, 18, 62, 84, 190
Mark of the Vampire, 18, 21, *31*, 35, 114, 150
A Midsummer Night's Dream, 39, 65, 68, 114, 200, 208
The Misses Stooge, 228
Murder By Television, 150
Murder in the Red Barn, 116, 211
The Mysterious Mr. Wong, 84, 150
The Mystery of Edwin Drood, 116, 154, 190
The New Adventures of Tarzan, 24
Night Life of the Gods, 213
Okay, Toots!, 47
One Frightened Night, 179
Public Ghost No. 1, 47
The Raven, 62, 127, 138, 150, 186
She, 35, 54, 71, 123, 184, 200, 216
Superspeed, 115
The Tin Man, 228
The Trans-Atlantic Tunnel, 19, 70, 211
Werewolf of London, 62, 116, 118, 179, 184, 221

1936

The Amazing Exploits of the Clutching Hand, 101, 164
El Baul Macabro, 40
Charlie Chan at the Opera, 119, 129, *178*, 179
Darkest Africa, 23
The Demon Barber of Fleet Street, 211
The Devil Doll, 21, 35, 65, 84, 92, 179, 241
Dracula's Daughter, 62, 115, 116, 135, 184, 218, 235
Flash Gordon, 58, 162, 184, 199, 208, 221, 254
The Ghost Goes West, 138
Ghost Patrol, 172
Green Pastures, 120
House of Secrets, 27, 114
The Invisible Ray, 115, 129, 150, 194
Jungle Princess, 119, 163, 223
The Living Dead, 237

The Man Who Lived Again, 129
The Man Who Lived Twice, 137
Mummy's Boys, 138
Revolt of the Zombies, 102, 121
Shadow of Chinatown, 24, 150
Tarzan Escapes, 119, 124, 179, 245
Things to Come, 76, 104, 157, 161, 195, 224, 247
Trapped By Television, 142, 223
Undersea Kingdom, 57
The Walking Dead, 61, 101, 127

1937

Ali Baba Goes to Town, 255
Charlie Chan at the Olympics, 119, 179
Dick Tracy, 38, 84, 151
Le Golem, 22, 110, 162
The Great Gambini, 223
Lost Horizon, 39, 121, 228
The Man Who Could Work Miracles, 195, 224, 247, 255, 256
Night Key, 129, 194, 199
The Phantom Ship, 150
The Thirteenth Chair, 63, 220
Topper, 37, 98, 213, 255

1938

Black Limelight, 157
Flash Gordon's Trip to Mars, 23, 58, 73, 162, 195, 199, 208
Sh! the Octopus, 114
Snow White and the Seven Dwarfs, 69
Tarzan's Revenge, 168
The Terror, 143

1939

Beware, Spooks, 142
Buck Rogers, 33, 58, 73, 221
The Cat and the Canary, 23, 90, 96, 117, 213, 256
Daredevils of the Red Circle, 24, 162, 193, 209, 252
Dick Tracy's G-Men, 38, 125, 184, 252
Dr. Cyclops, *65*, 75, 194, 206
The Face at the Window, 211
The Gorilla, 73, 92, 150
The Hound of the Baskervilles, 35, 71, 98, 191
The Hunchback of Notre Dame, 29, 68, 104, 110, 118, 141, 176, 256
The Man They Could Not Hang, 71, 84, 100, 129
Miracles for Sale, 35, 116, 118
The Phantom Creeps, 150, 235
Raspoutine, 22
The Return of Dr. X, 29, 101, 117, 118, 140
Son of Frankenstein, 18, 127, 143, 150, *151*, 191
Tarzan Finds a Son!, 119, 120, 179, 209, 245
Television Spy, 66, 84, 189
Topper Takes a Trip, 37, 184, 213, 254, *255*
Torture Ship, 102, 184

Tower of London, 127, 143, 154, 188, 191, 203
We Want Our Mummy, 226
The Wizard of Oz, 16, *28*, 29, *37*, 60, 64, *65*, *80*, *92*, *93*, 94, *101*, *103*, 104, 132, *138*, *167*

1940

The Ape, 129
Before I Hang, 24, 65, 100, 129
Black Friday, 101, 127, 148, 150, 170, 203
The Blue Bird, 35
Chamber of Horrors, 19, 241
Charlie Chan at the Wax Museum, 142
A Chump at Oxford, *105*, 141
Crimes at the Dark House, 211
The Devil Bat, 150, 176, 254
Dreams, 78
Drums of Fu Manchu, 33, 90, 199, 252
Earthbound, 65, 184
Fantasia, 69
Flash Gordon Conquers the Universe, 23, 58, 101, 155, 162, 208
The Ghost Breakers, 26, 65, 96, 117, 123, 189
The Ghost Creeps, 176
The Green Hornet, 71, 138, 170
The Green Hornet Strikes Again, 170
The House of the Seven Gables, 154, 188
The Human Monster, 150, 241
The Invisible Man Returns, 90 104, 188, 247
The Invisible Woman, 21, 98, 164, 170
Island of Doomed Men, 147, 162
The Man With Nine Lives, 84, 100, 129
The Mummy's Hand, 82, 84, 121, 138, 155, 231, 256
The Mysterious Dr. Satan, 209, 214, 252
One Million B.C., 46, 100, 158, 187, 231
El Otro Fu Manchu, 199
Pinocchio, *69*
The Shadow, 30, 126
Stranger on the Third Floor, 54, 147
The Thief of Bagdad, 76, *120*, 153, 201, 202
Turnabout, 213
You'll Find Out, 129, 147

1941

The Adventures of Captain Marvel, 73, 135, 151, 209, *231*, 252
Among the Living, 65
The Black Cat, 101, 114, 138, 150, 191, 203, 213
The Body Disappears, 26, 35, 47, 117
The Devil and Daniel Webster, 114, 211, 252
The Devil Commands, 129
Dick Tracy vs. Crime Inc., 38, 209, 252
Dr. Jckyll and Mr. Hyde, 80, 92, 229
The Face Behind the Mask, 82, 147
The Fall of the House of Usher, 186
Here Comes Mr. Jordan, 34, 117, 190
Hold That Ghost, 15, 18, 40, 57, 142, 148, 180

262   INDEX

Horror Island, 82, 241
The Invisible Ghost, 146, 150
Jungle Girl, 164
King of the Zombies, 237, 254
The Mad Doctor, 122, 135, 167, 191
Man Made Monster, 18, 46, 77, 84, 170, 241
The Monster and the Girl, 142, 164, 216, 256
The Mysterious Island, 236
Old Mother Riley's Ghosts, 149
Peer Gynt, 32, 38, 115
The Reluctant Dragon, 138, 247
The Smiling Ghost, 26
Spook Sport, 160
Spooks Run Wild, 96, 125, 150, 176, 201
Tarzan's Secret Treasure, 53, 179, 245
Topper Returns, 37, 66, 179, 213, 255, 256
The Wolf Man, *15*, 46, 134, 150, 179, 184, 190, 203, 241

1942

A-Haunting We Will Go, 26, 141, 247
The Arabian Nights, 9, 101, 164, 202
Black Dragons, 150
The Boogie Man Will Get You, 129, 138, 147
Bowery at Midnight, 85, 150
Captain Midnight, 176
Castle in the Desert, 63, 67, 137, 228
The Cat People, 53, 62, 146, 211, 212, 228
The Corpse Vanishes, 51, 85, 150, 201, 232
Dr. Renault's Secret, 137, 170, 256
The Fall of the House of Usher, 186
Fingers at the Window, 191
The Ghost of Frankenstein, 15, 18, 23, 46, 90, 104, 114, *131*, 134, 150, 155, 182, 203
Hellzapoppin', 18, 114, 182
The Hidden Hand, 182
I Married an Angel, 117
I Married a Witch, 138, 154, 213
Invisible Agent, 90, 101, 104, 147, 157, 203
The Jungle Book, 38, 123, 202
The Living Ghost, 23, 232
The Loves of Edgar Allan Poe, 137
The Mad Doctor of Market Street, 18, 123, 146, 170, 203
The Mad Monster, 172, 220, 256
The Man in the Trunk, 170
The Man Who Wouldn't Die, 67, 118
The Man With Two Lives, 73, 201
The Mummy's Tomb, 26, *46*, 82, 84, 98, 121, 184, 194, 220, 222, 255, 256
The Mystery of Marie Roget, 73, 162, 164, 179, 194, 201, 203
Night Monster, 18, 23, 150, 167, 194, 203
Over My Dead Body, 182
Perils of Nyoka, 162, 209
The Secret Code, 170
Spy Smasher, 24, 47, 51, 151, 195, 209, 252
The Strange Case of Dr. Rx, 42, 101, 203
Tarzan's New York Adventure, 154, 179, 245

Terror House, 156
Tower of Terror, 195
The Undying Monster, 82
Whispering Ghosts, 41, 182, 247

1943

The Ape Man, 84, 151, *232*, 234, *235*
The Batman, 59, 170, 250
The Black Room, 172
The Black Raven, 172, 220, 256
Cabin in the Sky, 16, 104, 120
Calling Dr. Death, 46, 65, 114, 142
Captive Wild Woman, 9, 15, 121, 184, 203, 220, 222
Dead Men Walk, 90, 172, 256
Dizzy Detectives, 248
The Eternal Return, 154
Flesh and Fantasy, 197
Frankenstein Meets the Wolf Man, 18, 46, 90, 116, 134, 150, 157, 172, 179, 203, 211, 241
The Ghost Ship, 70, 134, 138, 197
Ghosts on the Loose, 48, 125, 151, 232
Happy Land, 184
Heaven Can Wait, 59
I Walked With a Zombie, 53, 62, 124, 138, 211, 228
The Leopard Man, 146, 228
The Mad Ghoul, 15, 16, 26, *35*, 203, 220, 256
The Masked Marvel, 24, 214, 235
Meshes of the Afternoon, 67
The Phantom, 231
The Phantom of the Opera, 148, 154, 190
Revenge of the Zombies, 30, 148, 207
Shadow of a Doubt, 57, 84, 115, 189, 228
The Song of Bernadette, 125
Son of Dracula, 46, 90, 203, 211, 218
Spook Louder, 224
Tarzan's Desert Mystery, 135, 148, 236
Tarzan Triumphs, 65, 209, 236

1944

Ali Baba and the Forty Thieves, 101, 148, 164
Arsenic and Old Lace, 39, 98, 117, 147, 157
At Land, 67
Between Two Worlds, 101
The Big Noise, 30, 236
Black Magic, 201, 228
Bluebeard, 18, 41
The Canterville Ghost, 124, 141, 178, 250
Captain America, 77, 151, 235
The Climax, 129, 213
Cobra Woman, 46, 101, 164, 202, 211
Crazy Knights, 226
Cry of the Werewolf, 82, 121, 144, 156, 182
Curse of the Cat People, 62, 138, 146, 211, 212, 252
Dead Man's Eyes, 9, 243
The Ghost Catchers, 124

Gildersleeve's Ghost, 71, 194
The Girl Who Dared, 12, 30
The Great Alaskan Mystery, 135, 220
Haunted Harbor, 19, 73, 151, 195, 214, 235
Idle Roomers, 66, 226, 254
The Invisible Man's Revenge, 23, 41, 90, 101, 213, 247
Jungle Woman, 9, 65, 203, 222
The Lady and the Monster, 16, 27, 240
The Lodger, 59, 104, 151, 203
The Man in Half Moon Street, 18, 42, 151
Mark of the Whistler, 42, 70, 250
The Monster Maker, 95, 167, 172, 220
The Mummy's Curse, 46, 114, 135, 182, 184
The Mummy's Ghost, 121, 142, 148, 184, 194, 245, 256
Murder in the Blue Room, 101
Nabonga, 172
Pearl of Death, 35, 71, 98, 110, 116, 154, 172, 191, 203
The Phantom Speaks, 16, 243
Pillow of Death, 85
Return of the Ape Man, 151, 201, 256
Return of the Vampire, 82, 121, 138, 151, 154, 250
The Scarlet Claw, 35, 42, 71, 154, 172, 191, 203, 245
Shadows in the Night, 256
Soul of a Monster, 65, 152
Spider Woman, 35, 71, 98, 116, 172, 191, 213
The Tiger Woman, 218
Voodoo Man, 23, 130, 151, 256
Weird Woman, 15, 46, 101, 142, 167, 203, 245
The Whistler, 42, 70, 84, 222
Wonder Man, 119, 135

1945

Bewitched, 101, 176
The Body Snatcher, 62, *63*, 98, 127, 146, 151, 217, 252
The Brighton Strangler, 154
The Enchanted Forest, 138
Escape in the Fog, 82, 135, 252
The Frozen Ghost, 15, 46, 135, 203, 220, 222, 255
A Game of Death, 252
Hangover Square, 59, 114
House of Dracula, 18, 41, 46, 131, 134, 174, 184, 216, 220
House of Frankenstein, 18, 41, 46, 101, 129, 131, 155, 170, 184, 194, 203, 220, 236, 256
If a Body Meets a Body, 226, 248
Isle of the Dead, 62, 129, 134, 146, 197
The Jade Mask, 201, 228
Jungle Captive, 110, 135, 140, 203, 255
Jungle Raiders, 195
Manhunt of Mystery Island, 218
The Monster and the Ape, 57, 148, 152, 182
The Picture of Dorian Gray, 65, 104, 110, 132, 154, 203, 250
The Power of the Whistler, 70, 138, 252
The Purple Monster Strikes, *18*, 19, 24, 73, 151, 218
The Scarlet Clue, 201
Shadow of Terror, 138
Spellbound, 63, 115, 183

The Spiral Staircase, 19, 62, 211, 212
Strange Confession, 34, 220
Tarzan and the Amazons, 179, 209
A Thousand and One Nights, 116, 120, 180, 236
The Vampire's Ghost, 19, 207
Voice of the Whistler, 19, 42, 70, 194
White Pongo, 172
The Woman Who Came Back, 135
Zombies on Broadway, 71, 124, 151

1946

Angel on My Shoulder, 190, 216
The Beast With Five Fingers, 65, 82, 147, 170, 211
The Beauty and the Beast, *50*, 65, 154
Bedlam, 48, 129, 146, 197
Behind the Mask, 195
A Bird in the Head, 66, 138, 226, 248
The Brute Man, *110*, 203, 254
The Cat Creeps, 65, 131
The Catman of Paris, 18, 164, 207
The Cockeyed Miracle, 167, 224
The Crimson Ghost, 34, 73, *218*, 235, 252
The Curse of the Wraydons, 211
Dead of Night, 65, 152, 153, 192
The Devil Bat's Daughter, 251
Face of Marble, 26
The Flying Serpent, 256
Genius at Work, 151
House of Horrors, 110, 135, 148, 203, 254
It's a Wonderful Life, 39, 98, 217
Macbeth, 208
A Matter of Life and Death, 187
Mr. Hex, 96, 100, 125
The Mysterious Intruder, 42, 70
Night in Paradise, 213
Ritual in Transfigured Time, 67
She-Wolf of London, 116, 254
Shock, 188, 243, 247
Song of the South, 69
The Spider Woman Strikes Back, 110, 148, 213, 220
Spook Busters, 96, 100, 125, 162
Stairway to Heaven, 174
Strangler of the Swamp, 162, 251
Tarzan and the Leopard Woman, *9*, 116, 209, 245
The Time of Their Lives, 21, 57, 65, 92, 213

1947

All Gummed Up, 248
The Black Widow, 214, 235
Brick Bradford, 40, 195
Bury Me Dead, 182
Day of Wrath, 72
Dick Tracy Meets Gruesome, 38, 101, 129, 134, 182
Down to Earth, 117, 152, 206
Dream Girl, 134

264   INDEX

Fear in the Night, 71
The Ghost and Mrs. Muir, 114, 203
The Ghost Goes Wild, 27, 101
The Ghosts of Berkeley Square, 167, 207, 224
Miracle on 34th Street, 101, 113, 228
Night Unto Night, 156, 211
Scared to Death, 151, 201, 256
The Secret Life of Walter Mitty, 129, 182, 194
The Secret of the Whistler, 19, 70
Sinbad the Sailor, 254
The 13th Hour, 70

1948

Abbott and Costello Meet Frankenstein, 9, 18, *21*, 46, *56*, 57, 150, 188, 220, 247
Corridor of Mirrors, 74, 143, 158, 256
The Creeper, 167, 216, 254
The Drunken Angel, 162
Tha Fall of the House of Usher, 186
Hamlet, 179, 208
Horror Maniacs, 94, 211
Krakatit, 155
Macbeth, 208, 246
Miranda, 123, 228
Mr. Peabody and the Mermaid, 184
Mummy's Dummies, 66, 236
Night Has a Thousand Eyes, 216
Portrait of Jennie, 57, 68, 85, *125*, 228
Return of the Whistler, 118
Le Sang des Betes, 87
Shivering Sherlocks, 226, 248, 254
Siren of Atlantis, 63, *164*, 174
Superman, *12*, 24, 40, 172, *243*
Tarzan and the Mermaids, 245, 256

1949

Abbott and Costello Meet the Killer, Boris Karloff, 18, 21, 57, 113, 129
The Adventures of Ichabod and Mr. Toad, 191
Africa Screams, 21, 23
Alias Nick Beal, 152, 180
Amazon Quest, 207
Batman and Robin, 24, 73, 148, 223
Black Magic, 246
Francis, 148, 178
Fuelin' Around, 66, 236
The Ghost Talks, 226, 248
The Great Rupert, 181
Heavenly Daze, 66, 248
King of the Rocketmen, 34, *48*, 51, 151, 209, 214, 235
The Lost Tribe, 130
Master Minds, 96, 134, 220, 232, 254
Mighty Joe Young, 16, 40, 54, 66, 108, 137, 166, 176, 180, 182, 200, 205, 206
Samson and Delilah, 158

Tarzan's Magic Fountain, 20, 65, 137
Zamba the Gorilla, 101, 124, 142

1950

April 1, 2000, 126
Atom Man vs. Superman, 12, 19, 24, 172, 223, 243
Cinderella, 69
Destination Moon, 29 112, *181*, 184, 216
Disorder, 50, 246
Faust and the Devil, 96
Flying Disc Man From Mars, 19, 34, 142, 151, 193
Harvey, 84, 217
The Invisible Monster, 34, 182, 214, 235
Julius Caesar, 32, 208
Jungle Jim, 245
The Next Voice You Hear, 248
Los Olidados, 36
Orpheus, 50, 154
Prehistoric Women, 174
Radar Patrol vs. Spy King, 12, 34, 214, 235
Radar Secret Service, 38, 51, 73, 146, 172, 243
Rocketship X-M, 28, 34, 95, 146, 156, 172, 190, 221, 250
Room to Let, 74, 142
Tarzan and the Slave Girl, 20, 110, 210
Toto the Shiek, 228
Two Lost Worlds, 16, 243

1951

Abbott and Costello Meet the Invisible Man 57, 87, 138, 203
Alice in Wonderland, 69
Angels in the Outfield, 71, 220
Atoll K, 141
Captain Video, 116, 201
The Day the Earth Stood Still, 114, 121, 130, 142, 155, 156, *171*, 195, 252, 256
Five, 176
Flight to Mars, 28, 47, 164 190, 207
Francis Goes to the Races, 148, 178
Fury of the Congo, 130, 223
Ghost Chasers, 23, 96, 100, 236
Highly Dangerous, 146
Hurricane Island, 138, 223
I'll Never Forget You, 195
Jungle Treasure, 149
Lost Continent, 9, 26, 73, 118, 146, 172
The Man From Planet X, 48, 205, 232, 252
Miracle in Milan, 228
Mysterious Island, 58, 236
Pandora and the Flying Dutchman, 156
Scrambled Brains, 66, 248
Son of Dr. Jekyll, 112
The Strange Door, 129, 141, 182
Superman and the Mole Men, 49, 146, 193, 210
Tarzan's Peril, 20, 110, 152
The Thing, 16, 55, 60, 62, 88, 99, 111, 214, *228*

Three Arabian Nuts, 66, 248
Unknown World, 28, 146, 169, 190
Der Verlorene, 147
When Worlds Collide, 29, 67, 118, 122, 157, 174, 181, 183, 201, 216

1952

Aladdin and His Lamp, 138
Bela Lugosi Meets a Brooklyn Gorilla, 23, 151, 183
The Black Castle, 11, 46, 126, 129, 182, 203
Blackhawk, 12
Bride of the Gorilla, 37, 46, 53, 182, 211
Captive Women, 28, 48, 186, 190, *252*, 256
Cuckoo on a Choo Choo, 226, 248
Francis Goes to West Point, 148, 178
A Ghost For Sale, 94, 211
Hans Christian Andersen, 228
It Grows on Trees, 67, 121, 148, 229
Jack and the Beanstalk, 57
Jungle Jim in the Forbidden Land, 130, 245
The Man in the White Suit, 101, 153, 224
Neighbors, 160
Old Mother Riley Meets the Vampire, 94, 149, 151
Radar Men From the Moon, 19, *34*, 151, 214, 235
Rashomon, 162
Red Planet Mars, 98, 163, 201
Son of Ali Baba, 142, 164, 182, 236
Tarzan's Savage Fury, 20, 76, 119
Ulysses, 66
Unnatural, 240
Untamed Women, 223
Voodoo Tiger, 245
Voyages Extraordinaires de Jules Verne, 236
Zombies of the Stratosphere, 34, 116, 151, 174, 214, 235

1953

Abbott and Costello Go to Mars, 28, 57, 119, 138
Abbott and Costello Meet Dr. Jekyll and Mr. Hyde, 57, 129, 132, 138, 182, 203
Badshah Dampati, 118
The Beast From 20,000 Fathoms, 32, 71, 108, 148, 192, 228, 234
Cat Women of the Moon, 126, 231, 256
City Beneath the Sea, 187
Commando Cody, Sky Marshal of the Universe, 116, 151, 205, 223
Dementia, 236
Donovan's Brain, *78*
The 5000 Fingers of Dr. T, 53, 135, 137, 203
Forbidden Moon, 58
The Four-Sided Triangle, 182
Francis Covers the Big Town, 178
Ghost Ship, 57, 146, 208
Glen or Glenda?, 151, 223, 253
Gypsy Moon, 58

Hamlet, 208
The Hindu, 129
House of Wax, 34, 42, 99, 124, 188, 228
Invaders From Mars, 15, 60, 87, *161*, 209, 220, 250
Invasion U.S.A, 41, 164, 172, 190, 256
It Came From Outer Space, 11, 17, 32, 40, 77, 124, *201*, 215, 218, 247
Killer Ape, 57, 130, 180, 245
The Lost Planet, 116, 201, 243
The Magnetic Monster, 38, 71, 84, 110, 156, 211, 228
Man in the Attic, 151, 182
The Maze, 40, 161, 182
Meet Mr. Lucifer, 224
The Mesa of Lost Women, *174*, 238
The Neanderthal Man, 58, *208*, 209, 252
Peter Pan, 69
Phantom From Space, 155, 250
Port Sinister, 42, 95, 186, 190, 205, 252, 256
Project Moonbase, 112, 146
Robot Monster, 170, 179, 190, 231, 256
Run for the Hills, 182, 231
Scared Stiff, 33, 113, *145*, 156
Spaceways, 203
Spooks, 226, 236, 248
The Twonky, 53, 176
The War of the Worlds, v, 20, 26, 29, 55, 88, 92, 104, 110, 122, *123*, 124, 151, 174, *175*, 181, 183, 197, 216, 229, 247
Will Any Gentleman?, 13, 183
World Beyond the Moon, 130, 179

1954

The Atomic Kid, 26
Bait, 104
Beyond the Moon, 58
The Black Forest, 223
Blast Off, 58
The Bowery Boys Meet the Monsters, 25, *96*
The Cold Sun, 58
Crash of Moons, 58
The Creature From the Black Lagoon, *10*, 11, 17, 35, 40, 66, 77, 132, 180, 215, *247*
Devil Girl From Mars, *56*, 57
Duel in Space, 58
Francis Joins the WACS, 178, 234
Godzilla, 37, 117, 120, 169, 170, *230*
Gog, 155, *205*, 221, 228, 236
Gorilla at Large, 37, 164
Hansel and Gretel, *170*, 202
Immediate Disaster, 171
Inferno in Space, 58
Journey to the Beginning of Time, 256
Killers From Space, 98, *250*
Man About Men, 123
The Mad Magician, 179, 188
The Magnetic Moon, 58
Manhunt in Space, 58

266   INDEX

Menace for Outer Space, 58
Monster From the Ocean Floor, 55, 60, 179
Out of This World, 58
Phantom of the Rue Morgue, 66, 92
Rear Window, 37, 115, 217
Riders to the Stars, 40, 119, 155, 228
Robot of Regalio, 58
The Rocket Man, 11, 35, 48, 85, 91
Serpent Island, 97, 231
Silver Needle in the Sky, 58
The Snow Creature, 250
Superman and Scotland Yard, 172, 193
Superman and the Jungle Devil, 172, 193
Superman Flies Again, 172, 193
Superman in Exile, 172, 193
Superman's Peril, 172, 193
Target — Earth, 26, 66, 73
Tarzan and the She-Devil, 20, 37, 53, 221, 235
Them!, v, 16, *17*, 67, *70*, 71, 101, 118, 174, 205, *210, 212*, 216, *246, 248*, 254
Tobor the Great, 137, 151, 205, 209, 210, 223
20,000 Leagues Under the Sea, 69, 76, 79, 113, 121, 147, 156, 158, 236

1955

Abbott and Costello Meet the Mummy, 57, 138, 182, 246
The Beast With 1,000,000 Eyes, 26, 55
Bedlam in Paradise, 66, 226, 236, 248
The Bespoke Overcoat, 48
Bowery to Bagdad, 96
Conquest of Space, 29, 48, 79, 90, 110, 117, 151, 156, 181, 183, 247, 254
Creature With the Atom Brain, 19, 39, *51*, 66, *211*, 243
Cult of the Cobra, 70, 92, 146, 151, 195, 224
Les Diaboliques, 49
The Fall of the House of Usher, 186
Francis in the Navy, 148, 178
Half Human, 15, 41
It Came From Beneath the Sea, 19, 70, 108, 142, 228, 254
It's a Dog's Life, 101, 121
Jungle Moon Men, 38, 130, 245
King Dinosaur, 97, 146, 163
Kiss Me Deadly, 160
Man Beast, 242
Panther Girl of the Kongo, 49
Reflections in Black, 33
Revenge of the Creature, 11, 17, 35, 75, 172, 180, 215, 247
Son of Sinbad, 28, 174, 188, 252
Stone Age Romeos, 226
Svengali, 252
Tarantula, 11, 17, *41*, 54, 75, 180, 182, 218, 247
Tarzan's Hidden Jungle, 120, 206
This Island Earth, 11, 17, 70, 124, 168, *172*, 182, 192, 215, 218, 247
Toto in Hell, 228
The Way to Shadow Garden, 33

The Wormwood Star, 104

1956

The Animal World, 12, 108
Appearance of Super Giant, 232
The Atomic Man, 70
The Bad Seed, 117, 158
The Beast of Hollow Mountain, 68, 190
The Black Sleep, 46, 124, 142, 151, 191, 223
Bride of the Monster, 96, 124, 151, 182, *253*
The Creature Walks Among Us, 11, 47, 92, 161, 168, 182, 192, 210, 213, 218
The Creeping Unknown, 25, 32, 70, 84, 100, 134, 142, 253
Curucu, Beast of the Amazon, 91, 211
The Day the World Ended, 26, 28, 36, 53, 55, 66, 73, 112, 172, 202, 216
Dig That Uranium, 48
Earth vs. the Flying Saucers, 15, 19, 88, 108, 114, 130, 142, 154, 155, 206, *207*, 211, 254
Faustina, 96
Fire Maidens of Outer Space, 68
Forbidden Planet, 14, 20, 28, *84*, 85, 92, 94, 119, 163, 174, 184, 208, 250, 256
Francis in the Haunted House, 42, 138, 200
The Gamma People, 94
The Indestructible Man, *46*, 95, *186*
Invasion of the Body Snatchers, 71, 99, 124, 153, 158, 187, 211
It Conquered the World, 24, 28, 36, 55, 91, 98, 100, 112, 163, 202, *234*
I've Lived Before, 152, 213
Jungle Hell, 35, 202
Ladron de Cadavares, 202
Manfish, 250
Meet Mr. Kringle, 67
Miracle in the Rain, 157
The Mole People, 92, 182, 203, 218, 239, 247
Nightmare, 158, 197
The Night My Number Came Up, 152
1984, *13*, 176, 192
The Phantom From 10,000 Leagues, 202, 223
Plan 9 From Outer Space, 124, 151, 223, *233*, 253
Rescue From Outer Space, 232
Satellite in the Sky, 84, 158, 252
The Search For Bridey Murphy, 112, 228
The Seventh Seal, *25*, 75, 240
The She Creature, *28*, 36, 39, 53, 77, 96, 120, *168*, 173, 202, 216
The Stingiest Man in Town, 191
The Ten Commandments, 90
The Werewolf, 19, 130, *160*, 161, 206
Who Done It?, 224
World Without End, 25, 155, 216, 223
Yambao, 92

1957

The Abominable Snowman of the Himalayas, 134, 230, *231*

The Amazing Colossal Man, 24, 95, 97, 104, 116, *140*, 179, 182
Atomic Rulers of the World, 232
Attack of the Crab Monsters, *54*, 55, 60, 68, 73, *92*, 100, 124, 172, 216, 246
The Aztec Mummy, 92, 187
Back From the Dead, *41*, 87, 102, 242
Beginning of the End, 41, 95, 97, 98, *99*, 114, 243
The Black Scorpion, *54*, 66, 73, 176
Blood of Dracula, 51, 67, 107, 114, 221
Castle of the Monsters, 197
The Cat Girl, 202, 209
Curse of Frankenstein, 25, 41, *57*, 61, 79, 92, 115, *142*, 143, 203
The Cyclops, 46, 88, 97, 223
Daughter of Dr. Jekyll, 11, 186, 190, 210, 223, *232*
The Deadly Mantis, 11, 92, 117, 126, 218
The Disembodied, 111
Enemy From Space, 70, 84, 100, 134, 197
Frankenstein Meets Dracula, 95
Fright, 79
From Hell It Came, 28, 182
The Giant Claw, 15, 19, 54, 130, 168, 206, 209
The Girl in the Kremlin, 91, 256
The Hunchback of Notre Dame, 118, 189
The Incredible Shrinking Man, 17, 157, 203, 205, 218, 250, *251*, 256
Invasion of the Saucermen, 24, 28, 36, 39, 98, 172, 173, 179, 216
The Invisible Boy, 28, 68, *76*, 77, 107, 119, 190
I Vampiri, 88
I Was a Teenage Frankenstein, 26, 49, 51, 53, 73, 206, 221
I Was a Teenage Werewolf, 26, *51*, 73, 85, 139, *206*, 250
Kronos, 15, 28, 68, 168, 172, *190*, 209, 221
The Land Unknown, 11, 33, 92, 152, 195, 203, 218, *239*
The Living Idol, 40
Love Slaves of the Amazon, 169, 211
The Man From 1997, 223
Man of a Thousand Faces, 39, 45, 132, 236, 247
The Man Who Turned to Stone, 42, 71, *126*, 130
The Monolith Monsters, 17, 92, 210, *218*, *229*, 250
The Monster That Challenged the World, *53*, 182
The Night the World Exploded, 51, 98, 130, 206
Not of This Earth, 26, 39, *55*, *91*, 100, 104, 112, 163
Outer Space Jitters, 226, 236, 248
Pharaoh's Curse, 190, 197, 210
Return of the Wolf Man, 95
Rodan, *116*, 117, 230
Sabu and the Magic Ring, 27, 155, 157, 202
The Saga of the Viking Women and Their Voyage to the Waters of the Great Sea Serpent, 28, 39, 53, 55, *67*, 112, 125, 131
She-Devil, 28, 65, 172, 221
Space Ship Sappy, 226, 248
Spook Chasers, 48, 113, 243
The Story of Mankind, 12, 38, 63, 68, 104, 117, 147, 167, 188, 197
Tales of Frankenstein, 69
Tarzan and the Lost Safari, 119, 206
Teenage Monster, 101, 184

Throne of Blood, 162, 208
Twenty Million Miles to Earth, 19, 108, *109*, 114, 117, 126, 206
The 27th Day, 19, *20*, 26
The Undead, 55, 67, *73*, 92, 100, 104, 216, 236, 246
The Unearthly, 41, *111*, *124*, *183*
The Unknown Terror, iv, 138, *187*, 241
Up in Smoke, 48, 84
The Vampire, 22, 23, 99, 139, 228
The Vampire's Coffin, 197
Voodoo Island, 129, 142
Voodoo Woman, 39, 53, 73, 77, *97*
Womaneater, 57
X — The Unknown, 121, 126, 197
Zombies of Mora Tau, 39, 111, *130*, 182

1958

The Astounding She-Monster, 73
Attack From Space, 232
Attack of the 50-Foot Woman, 104, 111, *126*, 216, 237
Attack of the Puppet People, *11*, 95, 118, 131, 155
The Bat, 167, 188
Bell, Book and Candle, 138, 174, 217
The Blob, 106, *118*, *160*, 212, 254
Blood of the Vampire, 152, 209, 252
The Brain Eaters, 172, 174, 236
The Brain From Planet Arous, 11, *114*
The Bride and the Beast, 23, 253
The Colossus of New York, 48, 90, 135, 148, 156, 183, 187, *247*
Corridors of Blood, 56, 99, 129, 143, 200
The Cosmic Monster, 230
The Crawling Eye, 32, 121, 170, 230
Curse of the Demon, 14, 228
Curse of the Faceless Man, 14, 27, 39
Darby O'Gill and the Little People, 52, *69*, 76, 170, 217
The Devil's Hand, 117, 184
The Devil's Partner, 58, 84, 102, 172
Earth vs. the Spider, 95, 97, 130, 131, 201
The Fabulous World of Jules Verne, 256
The Fall of the House of Usher, 186
Fiend Without a Face, *58*, *224*, *225*
The Flame Barrier, 139, 254
The Fly, 112, 155, 172, 174, 188, 221
Flying Saucer Daffy, 226, 248
Frankenstein — 1970, 73, 129, 254
The Frankenstein Story, 95
From the Earth to the Moon, 57, 63, 110, 180, 203, 236
Giant from the Unknown, *15*, 60, 95, 130, 184
The Haunted Strangler, 129
Horror of Dracula, 25, 61, 79, 92, 98, 115, 142, *143*, 153, 203, *219*, 221
House on Haunted Hill, *13*, *42*, 54, 68, 146, 178, 188, 248
How to Make a Monster, 15, 17, 28, *48*, 51, 53, 73, *107*, *173*, 206, 209, *221*
I Bury the Living, 24
I Married a Monster From Outer Space, v, *85*, 90, 92, *93*, 183, 223, *229*, 238

Invisible Avenger, 67
It! — The Terror From Beyond Space, *27*, 28, 39, 57, 71, 99
Macabre, 23, 28, 68, 228, 248
The Magician, 25, 240
The Man Without a Body, 119, 250
A Midsummer Night's Dream, 208
The Monster From Green Hell, 47, *68*, 190, 238, 256
Monster on the Campus, 17, 73, 87, 92, 132, 182, 218, 247
The Most Dangerous Man Alive, 15, 73, 180, 182
Night of the Blood Beast, 54, 55, 102, 135, 172
Queen of Outer Space, 23, 25, 26, *79*, 91, 164
Return of Dracula, 139, *142*, 218
Revenge of Frankenstein, 101, 122, 142, 197
The 7th Voyage of Sinbad, 77, 98, *108*, 114, 126, 157, 206, *224*
She Demons, 60, 158, 201
The Space Children, 17, 48, 67, 75, 124, 183
Space Master, X-7, 25, 88, 114, 187, 226
Tarzan's Fight For Life, 142, 206
Teenage Caveman, 68, 95, 209, 236
Terror From the Year 5000, 104
Terror in the Haunted House, 164
The Thing That Couldn't Die, 73, 92, 195
tom thumb, 47, 181, 202, 223, 224, 242, 255
Toto in the Moon, 228
Two Men and a Wardrobe, 186
Varan the Unbelievable, 120
Vertigo, 115, 174, *217*
War of the Colossal Beast, 24, 95, *97*, 182, 254
War of the Satellites, 28, 39, 55, 60, 67, 68, 163, 236

1959

The Alligator People, 24, 46, *58*, 66, 91, 120, 152, 174, *175*, 221
Angry Red Planet, *161*, 164, 184, 229
Attack of the Giant Leeches, 54, 97, *134*, 135, *201*, 236, *237*
A Bucket of Blood, 40, 55, 100, 102, 129, 163, 167, 172, 236
Beast From Haunted Cave, 54, 100
La Casa del Terror, *46*
The Cosmic Man, 24, *41*, 179
Curse of the Undead, 79, 182
Dog-Star Man, 33
The Evil Brain from Outer Space, 232
Eyes in Outer Space, 88
Eyes Without a Face, 87, 206
First Man Into Space, 224
The 4-D Man, *106*, 212, 254
The Four Skulls of Jonathan Drake, 42, 63, 73
Frankenstein's Daughter, 17, *60*, *134*
The Ghost of Dragstrip Hollow, 24, 28, 102, 117, 202
The Giant Behemoth, 148, 176
The Giant Gila Monster, 61, 130, 222
Gigantis the Fire Monster, 100
Have Rocket, Will Travel, 19, 226
Hercules, *194*
The Hideous Sun Demon, 48, *49*
The H-Man, 88, 117, 230
Horrors of the Black Museum, 51, 58, 78, *98*

The Hound of the Baskervilles, 25, 61, 71, 143, 153
The Immoral Mr. Teas, 162
The Incredible Petrified World, 48, 49, 242
Invisible Invaders, 11, 38, *39*, 41, 119, 206, 228
Journey to the Center of the Earth, 114, 144, 156, 236
The Killer Shrews, 61, *130*
Li'l Abner, 216
The Man Who Could Cheat Death, 17, 69, 143, 151
Missile to the Moon, 48, 60, 164
The Monster of Piedras Blancas, *132*, 222, 229
The Mummy, 17, 61, 90, 143, 203
The Mysterians, 117, 120, 230
Night of the Ghouls, 73, 124, 233, 253
On the Beach, 135
Return of the Fly, *25*, 102, 155
The Robot vs. the Aztec Mummy, 92, 187
The Shaggy Dog, 21, 134, 152
Sleeping Beauty, 69
Tarzan's Greatest Adventure, 52, 206, 245
Tarzan the Ape Man, 163, 172
The Teenage Werewolf, 95
Terror is a Man, 67, 142, 200, *227*, 247
The 30-Foot Bride of Candy Rock, 57
The Tingler, *42*, 68, 188, *248*
El Vampiro Acecha, 197
The Very Eye of the Night, 20, 67
Wasp Woman, 39, *55*, 75, 97, 129, 155, *167*, 236

1960

The Amazing Transparent Man, *47*, 232, 247
Atom Age Vampire, *151*
The Atomic Submarine, *24*, 53, 68, 73, 82, 87, 96, 102, 103, 141, 190
The Avenger, 72, 241
La Baccanti, 151, 223
Battle of the Worlds, 155, 190
Beauty and the Robot, 233, 234
Beyond the Time Barrier, 48, 184, 232
Black Sunday, *22*, *195*, 214
Blood and Roses, 233
The Boy and the Pirates, 97, 102
Brides of Dracula, 17, 61, 79, 115, 121, 153, 164, 183, 197, 203, 250
The Cape Canaveral Monsters, 231, 238
Circus of Horrors, 23, *68*, 69, 164, 200
Colossus and the Amazons, 223
The Curse of the Doll People, 92
Dinosaurus, 47, 106, 202, 216, 242, 254
A Dog, a Mouse, and a Sputnik, 18
Faust, 96
The Giants of Thessaly, 197
Goliath and the Dragon, 84
Hamlet, 208
Hercules Unchained, 40, 194
Horror Hotel, 23, 74, 122, *123*, 143, *169*, 222
House of Mystery, 208
House of Usher, 23, 55, 60, 63, 77, 102, 157, 186, 188
The Hypnotic Eye, 13, *27*, 111

Il Ladro di Bagdad, 148
The Last Woman on Earth, *40*, 55, 125, 229
The Leech Woman, 65, 73, 92, 99, *222*, 223, 250
The Little Shop of Horrors, 55, 100, 102, *112*, 129, 163, 173, *246*
The Lost World, 12, 71, 112, 174, 190, 195
Macumba Love, 193, 197
Les Mains d'Orlac, 143, 183, 184, 194, 252
Mania, 94, 184
Peeping Tom, 28, 78, 153, 156, 187
Psycho, 35, 114, 115, 144, *145*, 183, 215
The Rest is Silence, 208
Son of Sampson, 84
Spotlight on a Murderer, 87
Stranglers of Bombay, 200
Tarzan the Magnificent, 206
Teenage Zombies, 222, *238*, 242
The Tell-Tale Heart, 56
The Testament of Orpheus, 36, 50
The Thief of Bagdad, 194
13 Ghosts, 42, 68, 103, 169, 248
The Thousand Eyes of Dr. Mabuse, 140
The Three Worlds of Gulliver, 108, 114, *157*, 169, 206
The Time Machine, 20, 26, 47, 73, 88, 163, *180*, 181, 202, *222*, 223, 231, 242, 247, 255
Tormented, 40, 97, 201
12 to the Moon, 32, 38, 53, 68
The Two Faces of Dr. Jekyll, 11, 79, 143, 157, 192
Uncle Was a Vampire, 143
Village of the Damned, 101, *196*, 203, 209, 216, 254
Visit to a Small Planet, 145
The Witch's Curse, 88

1961

The Absent-Minded Professor, 69, 121, 151, 202, 217
The Anatomist, 56, 197, 217
Anatomy of a Psycho, 183
Atlantis, the Lost Continent, 20, 88, 94, 153, 181, 231
Babes in Toyland, 69, 134
Bar on Munchausen, 256
The Beast of Yucca Flats, 124
Bloodlust, 60, 131
Caltiki, the Immortal Monster, 22, *88*
Creature From the Haunted Sea, 40, 55, 68, 100, 125, 129
Curse of Nostradamus, 60, 197
Curse of the Aztec Mummy, 92, 187
Curse of the Werewolf, *17*, 32, 115, 192, 200, 253
The Day the Earth Caught Fire, 32, 100, 126, 170
Dead Eyes of London, *25*, 241
The Devil's Eye, 25
Dr. Blood's Coffin, 57, 90
Duel of the Titans, 194, 206
Everything's Ducky, 200
Flight of the Lost Balloon, 126, 187, 224
Flight That Disappeared, 192
Goliath and the Vampires, 206
Gorgo, *148*
Hand of Death, 11, 192
The Hellfire Club, 56
Hercules in the Haunted World, 143, 182
Homicidal, *16*, 42, 140, 248
The Innocents, 48, 86, 87, 131, 192, *216*, 254

Invasion of the Zombies, 204
Knife in the Water, 186
Konga, 51, 98
The Last War, 230
L'Atlantide, 232
The Magic Fountain, 104
The Man in the Moon, 65, 78, 84, 99
The Mask, *199*
Master of the World, 34, 118, 188, 236, 252
A Midsummer Night's Dream, 208
The Minotaur, 153
Molemen vs. the Son of Hercules, 84
Mothra, 117, 230
Mr. Sardonicus, 68, 117, 140, 200, 202
Mysterious Island, 76, 99, 108, 114, 146, 162, 206, 236
Neutron vs. the Maniac, 202
The Night Walker, 42
An Occurance at Owl Creek Bridge, 77
The Pit and the Pendulum, 13, 23, 40, 55, 60, 102, 157, 186, 188, *189*, 214, *215*
The Private Lives of Adam and Eve, 200, 234, 256
Scream of Fear, 117, 143, 203, 221
Shadow of the Cat, 23, 94, 121
The Snake Woman, 90
These Are the Damned, 78, 192
20,000 Eyes, 13
Voyage to the Bottom of the Sea, 12, 18, 63, 82, 147
The Wonders of Aladdin, 178

1962

Assignment Outer Space, 155
Attack of the Robots, 53
The Blood of Nostradamus, 60, 197
Burn Witch Burn, 23, 157, 254
The Cabinet of Caligari, 28, 123
Carnival of Souls, 110
The Cliff Monster, 28
Confessions of an Opium Eater, 95, 188, 256
Creation of the Humanoids, 161
Death in the Arena, 84
The Devil's Messenger, 211, 221
The Door With Seven Locks, 72, 241
Dr. No, 14, 52, 80, *81*, 119, 143, 152, 158, 256
Eegah!, 133, 214
8½, iv, 214
The Evil Eye, 22, 205
Five Weeks in a Balloon, 12, 104, 147, 155
Genii of Darkness, 60, 197
Hands of a Stranger, 158
Hercules in the Vale of Woe, 168
The Horrible Dr. Hichcock, 82, 88, 214
Invasion of the Animal People, 41, 239, 242
Invasion of the Star Creatures, 112, 236
Jack the Giant Killer, 63, 92, 126, 157, 180, 224
La Jetee, 55
Journey to the 7th Planet, 11, 63, 161, 184, 227
The Magic Sword, 97, 133, 146, 191, 201, 221, 233
The Manchurian Candidate, 87

Monster Demolisher, 60, 197
Moon Pilot, 134, 176, 212, 229
Neutron Against the Death Robots, 60, 202
Neutron and the Black Mask, 60, 202
Neutron Battles the Karate Assassins, 202
Night Creatures, 192, 194, 200
Panic in Year Zero, 18, 23, 24, 92, 163
The Phantom of the Opera, 79, 146, 153
Phantom Planet, 38, 68, 133
The Premature Burial, 55, 57, 60, 102, 163, 202, 216
Red Hell, 191
RoGoPag, 95
Samson vs. the Vampire Women, 204
The Secret of the Black Trunk, 241
Tales of Terror, 23, 55, 60, 102, 147, 157, 180, 188, *191*
Tarzan Goes to India, 97, 152, 245
The Testament of Dr. Mabuse, 90, 239
The Three Stooges in Orbit, 25, 180, *226*
The Three Stooges Meet Hercules, 25, 73, 226
Tower of London, 55, 60, 97, 102, 188
Underwater City, 11, 73, 96, 138
Valley of the Dragons, 256
Whatever Happened to Baby Jane?, 11, 36, 59, 64, 102
The Wonderful World of the Brothers Grimm, 20, 28, 47, 63, 135, 144, 163, 180, 181, 202, 223, 224, 231, 242
Zotz!, 202

1963

The Adventures of the Spirit, 95, 220
Attack of the Mayan Mummy, 236, 242
Beauty and the Beast, 13, 184
The Birds, 114, 115, 121, 223
Black Sabbath, 22, 63, 129
The Black Zoo, 51, 60, 73, 98
Blood Feast, 90, *145*
Captain Sinbad, 110, 250
Children of the Damned, 254
The Comedy of Terrors, 102, 129, 147, 157, 187, 188, 191, 228
The Crawling Hand, 16, 111, 221, 223
The Day Mars Invaded Earth, 68, 223
The Day of the Triffids, 86, 207, 254
Dementia 13, 13, 39, 54, 55, 152, 216
El Demonio Azul, 28
The Devil's Bedroom, 125, 165
Diary of a Madman, 135, 142, 188
Dr. Crippen, 252
The Exterminating Angel, 36
From Russia with Love, *81*
The Haunted Palace, 23, 46, 55, 60, 97, 102, 148, 167, 180, 182, 187, 188, 236
The Haunting, 28, 54, 74, 106, 158, 223, 253
Hercules and the Captive Women, 182
House of the Damned, 13, 58, 68, 133
The Incredibly Strange Creatures Who Stopped Living and Became Mixed-Up Zombies, 34, *214*
The Indian Scarf, 72, 241

It's a Mad, Mad, Mad, Mad World, 176
Jason and the Argonauts, 27, *43*, 99, 108, *109*, 114, 135, 206
King Kong vs. Godzilla, 103, 117, 230
Kiss Me Quick, 162
Kiss of the Vampire, 32, 115, 208
Maniac, 41
The Mind Benders, 65
Night Tide, 13, 104, 236
The Old Dark House, 11, 42, 167
Paranoic, *86*, 192
Psychomania, 223
The Raven, 23, 55, 57, 60, 102, 127, 147, 157, 173, 186, 188
Reptilicus, 161, *184*
Samson and the Seven Miracles of the World, 206
Samson in the Wax Museum, 204
Santo Contra el Ray de Crimen, 60
The Slime People, 110, 119
Son of Flubber, 69, 121, 152, 217
Tarzan's Three Challenges, 152, 245
Terrified, 138
The Terror, 54, 55, 97, 102, 112, 115, 129, 134, 163, 173
Terror in the Crypt, 143, 157
Twice-Told Tales, 28, 66, 91, 102, 188, 201, 203
X — The Man With the X-Ray Eyes, 15, 23, 55, 60, 102, 112, 118, 162, 163, 167, 196, 202

1964

Blood and Black Lace, 22, 164
Blue Demon Contra el Poder Satanico, 28
The Brass Bottle, 190
Castle of Blood, 186, 214
Castle of the Living Dead, 143, 222
Cosmos, the Fantastic Journey, 229
The Curse of the Living Corpse, 206, 223
The Curse of the Mummy's Tomb, 41
Curse of the Voodoo, 102, 210
Dead Ringer, 64, 102, 152
Devil Doll, 102, 200, 210
Il Disco Volante, 239
Doctor of Doom, 40
Dr. Strangelove or: How I Learned to Stop Worrying and Love the Bomb, 10, 88, 136
Dr. Terror's House of Horrors, 121, 143, 222
The Earth Dies Screaming, *78*
The Evil of Frankenstein, 17, 86, 115, 134
The Eyes of Annie Jones, 142, 238
Fantomas, 154
Firelight, 213
First Men in the Moon, 108, *119*, *122*, 126, 134, 153, 206
The Flesh Eaters, 135
Godzilla vs. the Thing, 117, 120, 230
Goldfinger, 10, 20, *27*, 52, 80, *81*, 90, 103, 119, 152, 203
Goliath and the Sins of Babylon, 84
The Gorgon, 17, 143, 209
Hamlet at Elsinore, 208
Hercules of the Desert, 168

Hercules, Prisoner of Evil, 182
The Horror if it All, 74
The Horror of Party Beach, *223*
Hush, Hush Sweet Charlotte, 11, 36, 39, 57, *64*, 65, 67, 113, 167
I Eat Your Skin, 223
The Incredible Mr. Limpet, 134, 148
The Last Man on Earth, 157, 188, 203
I Lunghi Capelli Della Morte, 155, 214
Macbeth, 208
Maciste, Spartan Gladiator, 84
Madmen of Mandoras, 32, 180
Mary Poppins, 76, 217, 228
The Masque of the Red Death, 23, 55, 57, 99, 186, 198
A Meia Noitre Levarei Sua Alma, 155
The Misadventures of Merlin Jones, 134, 217
Monstrosity, 186, 221
Neutron vs. the Amazing Dr. Caronte, 202
Nightmare, 203
Night Must Fall, 86
The Nutty Professor, 145, 216
Pajama Party, 134, 138, 196
Pyro, 119, 184
Robinson Crusoe on Mars, 110, 154, 161, 183
Samson and the Mightly Challenges, 214
Samson and the Slave Queen, 214
Samson in King Solomon's Mines, 182
Santo Ataca las Brujas, 204
Seance on a Wet Afternoon, 84
The Seven Faces of Dr. Lao, 23, 47, 63, 77, *176*, 181, *191*, *231*, 232, 242
Sherry's House of Nudes, 250
Sound of Horror, 184
Spy Smasher vs. the Purple Monster, 95
Strait-Jacket, 28, 42, *59*
The Strangler, 36
The Sword of Ali Baba, 239
They All Died Laughing, 122, 170
The Time Travelers, 9, 84, 161, 187
Two Thousand Maniacs, 90, 145
Witchcraft, 46, 208

1965

Alphaville, 53, *95*, 223
The Beach Girls and the Monster, 101
Blood Beast From Outer Space, 205
Color Me Blood Red, 145
Crack in the World, 14, 156
Curse of the Fly, 70, 98, 208
Curse of the Stone Hand, 236, 238, 242
Dark Intruder, 151, 174
Die, Die My Darling!, 19, 129, 148, 157, 222
Die Monster Die!, 11, 102, 121, 152
Dr. Goldfoot and the Bikini Machine, 110, 188
Espectro del Estrangulador, 204
The Exterminators, 88
The Face of Fu Manchu, 99, 143, 199, 208

Fantomas Strikes Back, 154
The Fool Killer, 183
Ghidrah, the Three-Headed Monster, 117, 120, 230
The Ghost, 88, 214
The Great Race, 156
Hamlet, 208
Hercules Against the Moon Men, 214
Horror Castle, 143
House of the Black Death, 41, 46, 142, 238
The Human Duplicators, 16, 100, 133, 152, 170
Hysteria, 96, 121, 134, 203
I Saw What You Did, 42, 59
Killers Are Challenged, 155
The Lost World of Sinbad, 162
The Monkey's Uncle, 134, 176, 217
Monster A Go-Go, 145
Monster Zero, 11, 120, 204
Mutiny in Outer Space, 92, 100, 140
The Mysterious Magician, 72, 241
The Nanny, 64, 70, 87, 117, 203
Nightmare Castle, 214
Night of Violence, 151
The Night Walker, 28, 42, 135
Operation Atlantis, 77, 184
Planet of the Vampires, 22, 161
Raiders From Beneath the Sea, 68
Repulsion, 66, 90, 186
Samson vs. the Giant King, 168
The Satan Bug, 14, 21, 24, 85
The Secret of My Success, 27, 216
La Sfida del Giganti, 182
She, 14, 25, 143, 195
The Skull, 57, 61, 86, 99, 143, 222
Snow Devils, 155
Spaceflight IC-1, 144
Space Monster, 24, 255
Superman vs. the Gorilla Gang, 19, 73, 95
Sweet Sound of Death, 184
The Tenth Victim, 14
The Thrill Killers, 34, 214
Thunderball, 10, 20, 26, 52, 80, *81*, 119, 152, 256
The Tomb of Ligeia, 55, 188, 229
Two on a Guillotine, 118, 124, 200
Village of the Giants, 97, 134
Voyage to the Prehistoric Planet, 70, 104, 191, 201, 216
War Gods of the Deep, 102, 110, 188, 228
What!, 22, 143
The Witches, 75
The Woman Who Wouldn't Die, 153, 162
Woman of the Prehistoric Planet, 13
Wrestling Women vs. the Aztec Mummy, 40

1966

An Angel for Satan, 157, 214
Around the World Under the Sea, 34, 156, 162, 224, 228
Batman, *98*, 162, *200*, 241, 247

Billy the Kid vs. Dracula, 19, 23, 41
Birds Do It, 10, 156
Blood Bath, 39, 115, 134, 201
The Brides of Fu Manchu, 72, 98, 143, 199, 208
Carry On Screaming, 183
Chamber of Horrors, 179
The Christmas That Almost Wasn't, 18
Creature of the Walking Dead, 236, 238, *242*
Les Creatures, 66
Cyborg 2087, 195
Death Curse of Tartu, 100
Destination Inner Space, 19, 32, 151, 162
Devils of Darkness, 98
Dracula, Prince of Darkness, 17, 32, 130, 143, *209*, 241
Dr. Goldfoot and the Girl Bombs, 22, 188
Dr. Who and the Daleks, 82, 222
Esta Noitra Encarnare I Sea Cadaver, 155
Fahrenheit 451, 32, 47, 69, 114, 229
Fantastic Voyage, 27, 73, 79, 113, 176, 184, 245
Faust XX, 96
Frankenstein Conquers the World, *10*, 11, 117, 204
Gammera the Invincible, 65, 70, 230
The Ghost and Mr. Chicken, 134
The Ghost in the Inyisible Bikini, 18, 38, 110, 129, 191
Godzilla vs. the Sea Monster, 90, 230
Le Golem, 162
Island of Terror, 79, 98, 126
Jesse James Meets Frankenstein's Daughter, 23, 180
The Lemon Grove Kids Meet the Monsters, 214
Majin, 230
Majin Strikes Again, 230
Modesty Blaise, 239
Movie Star American Style or LSD I Hate You, 256
Munster Go Home!, 65, 224, 247
Murderer's Row, 10, 144, 156
The Navy vs. the Night Monsters, 24, 75, 179, 234
One Spy Too Many, 41, 204, 236
Orgy of the Dead, 253
Picture Mommy Dead, 91, 97, 119
Plague of the Zombies, *94*, 183, 197
The Psychopath, 28
Queen of Blood, 9, 104, *155*, 191, 205
Rasputin, the Mad Monk, 143, 208, 209
Rat Pfink and Boo Boo, 34, 214
The Reptile, 94, 183, 197
The Return of Giant Majin, 230
Revenge of the Blood Beast, 194, 214
Rocketman Flies Again, 95
Seconds, 14, 87
Shadow of Evil, 157
The She-Beast, 246
She Freak, 90
The Silencers, 10, 67, 129, 135, 156, 176, 216
Spy in Your Eye, 14, 102
The Spy With My Face, 41, 236
A Study in Terror, 56, 167

Tarzan and the Valley of Gold, 113, 135, 161
The War Game, 243
War of the Monsters, 230
Way . . . Way Out, 71
The Wild World of Batwoman, 236, 238, 242

1967

The Ambushers, 10, 144, 156
Bedazzled, 96, 245
The Blood Beast Terror, 82, 208
The Blood Demon, 20, 143, 200
The Bubble, 176
Casino Royale, 14, 174
Caves of Steel, 204
Circus of Fear, 152
Creature of Destruction, 36, 229
Curse of the Swamp Creature, 11, 255
The Destructors, 73, 77, 151
The Devil's Own, 82, 134, 216
Dr. Dolittle, 70
Dr. Terror's Gallery of Horrors, 46
Eye of the Devil, 131, 174, 184, 223
Fantomas vs. Scotland Yard, 154
The Fearless Vampire Killers, 186, 223
Les Femmes Vampires, 200
Five Million Years to Earth, 19, 130, 134, 209
Frankenstein Created Woman, 25, 66
The Frozen Dead, 14
Games, 104, 155, 201, 212
The Gnome-Mobile, 76, 84, 217
The Gruesome Twosome, 145
The Helicopter Spies, 41, 236
Hillbillys (sic) in a Haunted House, 46, 141, 191, 234, 254
Hour of the Wolf, 25, 240
House of 1000 Dolls, 119, 170, 188
La Isla de los Dinosaurios, 187
Island of the Burning Damned, 143
It!, 158, 162
Kill Baby Kill, 22
King of Hearts, 36
The Lemon Grove Kids Meet the Green Grasshopper and the Vampire Lady From Outer Space, 34, 214
A Man Called Dagger, 133, 154, 166
Matchless, 179
A Midsummer Night's Dream, 208
The Million Eyes of Su Muru, 170
Las Mujeres Panteras, 40
The Mummy's Shroud, 94, 187
One Million Years B.C., 26, 32, 43, 108, 195, 206, 245
Operation Kid Brother, 158
Our Mother's House, 48, 87, 144
The Perils of Pauline, 248
Privilege, 243
The Projected Man, 102
Psycho-Circus, 143, 169

The Reluctant Astronaut, 134, 174
Return of the Giant Monsters, 230
Rocket to the Moon, 208
The Sorcerers, 129, 178, 194
Sting of Death, 100
Tarzan and the Great River, 113, 245
Tarzan's Jungle Rebellion, 76
A Taste of Blood, 145
Terror Creatures From the Grave, 214
The Terrornauts, 222
They Came From Beyond Space, 119, 121
Those Fantastic Flying Fools, 90, 122, 208, 224
The Trip, 55, 67, 163, 167, 173, 221
The Undertaker and His Pals, 148
The Venetian Affair, 41, 129, 236
The Vulture, 119, 223
Wild Wild Planet, 155
You Only Live Twice, 10, 20, 52, 63, 80, *81*, 94, 103, 119, 184

1968

The Anniversary, 19, 64, 203
The Bamboo Saucer, 77, 90
Bang Bang, 184
Barbarella, 66, 82, *83*, 92, 142, 154, 233
Battle Beneath the Earth, 157
Beserk!, 51, 59, 71, 92, 98
Blood Fiend, 96, 143
Blue Demon vs. Cerebros, 28
Blue Demon vs. Las Diobolicas, 28
Brides of Blood, 200
The Castle of Fu Manchu, 143
Castle of Evil, 32, 73, 151, 155
Cauldron of Blood, 129
Chitty Chitty Bang Bang, 10, 34, 63, 80, 90, 122, 152
Charly, 28, 197
The Conquerer Worm, 178, 188, 194
Corruption, 61, 179
Countdown, 12
The Crimson Cult, 129, 143, 208, 214, 248
Daleks — Invasion Earth 2150 A.D., 82, 130, 187, 222
Danger: Diabolik, 142
Destroy All Planets, 230
The Devil's Bride, 25, 99, 143, 157
Dracula Has Risen From the Grave, 40, 86, 143, *144*
The Eye Creatures, 17, *36*
The Fear Chamber, 115, 129
Head, 113, 158, 173
House of Evil, 115, 129
The Incredible Invasion, 129
In the Year 2889, 36
Island of the Doomed, 164, 246
It's Alive!, 36, 134
Journey to the Center of Time, 75
King Kong Escapes, 103, 117, 120
The Legend of Lylah Clare, 11, 31, 174

The Lost Continent, 41, 152
A Midsummer Night's Dream (Royal Shakespeare Company), 196, 208, 241
A Midsummer Night's Dream (homosexual version), 208
Mission Mars, 11
Night of the Living Dead, 124, *125*, 200
The Oldest Profession, 106
One Hour to Doomsday, 12, 21
Pacto Diaboloco, 217
Pas de Deux, 160
Planet of the Apes, 32, *43*, *114*, 115, 158, *159*, 188, 207, 221, 248
The Power, 40, 47, 65, 110, 162, 176, 180, 181, 195, 201, 231, 242
Prehistoric Women, 41
Pretty Poison, 91, 183
Project X, 48, 183, 247
Rosemary's Baby, 24, 27, 42, 54, 77, 98, 145, 186, 236
Santo Conta Blue Demon en la Atlantida, 204
Shame, 25, 240
She-Devils on Wheels, 145
Slave Girls, 26
Something Weird, 145
Son of Godzilla, 90
Space Thing, 90
Targets, 29, 127
Tarzan and the Jungle Boy, 113
Torture Garden, 10, 25, 28, 86, 162, 182
Trilogia de Terror, 155
2001: A Space Odyssey, 48, 73, 88, 136, *137*, 146, 190, 229
Las Vampiras, 60
Vengeance of Fu Manchu, 143
Vengeance of She, 26, 195
Voyage to the Planet of Prehistoric Women, 29, 234
Wild in the Streets, 251
The Wrecking Crew, 99, 129, 156
Zontar: The Thing From Venus, 11, 36

1969

Angel, Angel Down We Go, 125
The Astro-Zombies, 41, 163
Attack of the Monsters, 230
The Bed Sitting Room, 78
Blood of Dracula's Castle, 11, 192
Crescendo, 94, 250
De Sade, 55, 73, 76, 156, 157
Destroy All Monsters, 120, 230
Dionysus in 69, 67
Dracula, the Dirty Old Man, 218
O Estranho Mundo de Ze O Caixao, 155
Eye of the Cat, 119, 215
Fearless Frank, 235
Fear No Evil, 238
Frankenstein Must Be Destroyed, 40, 61, 124, 241
Futz, 215
The Ghastly Ones, 163

Hamlet, 208
If..., 158, 241
The Illustrated Man, 22, 28, 32, 212, 215
Is This Trip Really Necessary?, 163
Journey to the Far Side of the Sun, 146
Justine, 182
Kiss and Kill, 143
Krakatoa, East of Java, 142, 195
Latitude Zero, 57, 200, 210
The Love Bug, 76, 124, 217, 228
Las Luchadoras Contra el Robot Asesino, 40
Mad Doctor of Blood Island, 200
The Mad Room, 91, 216, 251
La Marca del Hombre Lobo, 171
Marooned, 87, 135, 183
The Masque of the Red Death, 186
The Milky Way, 36
Moon Zero Two, 19, 56
Nightmare in Wax, 32, 164
Night of Bloody Horror, 118
The Oblong Box, 115, 143, 188
On Her Majesty's Secret Service, 20, 80, *81*, 119, 142, 152, 196, 205
Santo en la Vengaza de las Mujeres Vampire, 60
Simon of the Desert, 36
Spirits of the Dead, 82, 188, 233
Stereo, 60
The Tempest, 208
Twisted Nerve, 84, 114
2000 Years Later, 182
The Valley of Gwangi, 40, 87, 108, 121, 206
La Vampire Nue, 200
El Vampiro y el Sexo, 40
Whatever Happened to Aunt Alice?, 98
What's Up, Tiger Lily?, 12
The Witchmaker, 75, 125, 165
Zeta One, 216

1970

Alex in Wonderland, 222
Assignment Terror, 195
Beast of Blood, 17
Beneath the Planet of the Apes, 32, 36, 43, 87, 115, 158
The Bird With the Crystal Plumage, 15
Bloodthirsty Butchers, 163
Bride of Blood, 223
Captain Mom, 238
Colossus — The Forbin Project, 204, 205
El Conde Dracula, 87
Count Dracula, 143, 146
Count Yorga, Vampire, 130, 152, 183, 189
Crimes of the Future, 60
Cry of the Banshee, 23, 115, 119, 188
Dinosaurs, the Terrible Lizards, 47
The Dunwich Horror, 102, 121, 148, 167

Eugenie — The Story of Her Journey Into Perversion, 87, 143, 146
Every Home Should Have One, 78
Five Bloody Graves, 192
Flesh Feast, 138
La Furia del Hombre Lobo, 171
Gamera vs. Monster X, 230
Gas-s-s-s, 55
Goodbye Gemini, 92, 94, 192
A Hatchet for the Honeymoon, 22
Horror House, 18
The Horror of Frankenstein, 22, 40, 78, 179, 183, 188, 203, 250
House of Dark Shadows, 61, *89*, 212
The House That Dripped Blood, 28, 87, 143, 184, 222
How Awful About Allan, 104, 106, 183
The Incredible Two-Headed Transplant, 67
Invasion of the Body Stealers, 82, 203
The Love War, 34
The Mind of Mr. Soames, 236
La Noche de Walpurgys, 134
Peau D'Ane, 66
The Phynx, 96, 179, 245
Punishment Park, 243
Santo y Blue Demon Contra los Monstruos, 28, 204
Scars of Dracula, 19, 101, 115, 143, 197
Scream and Scream Again, 115, 143, 188
Scrooge, 101
The Secret Cinema, 21
Sinthia, the Devil's Doll, 214
Skullduggery, 71
Spider Baby or: The Maddest Story Ever Told, 46, 115, 178, 216
Tarzan's Deadly Silence, 76
Taste the Blood of Dracula, 25, 111, 143, *204*
Trog, 51, 59, 87, 98
The Vampire Lovers, 11, 19, 78, 92, 179, 184, 212
Vampyr, 146
Vampyros Lesbos, 87
Venus in Furs, 87
War of the Gargantuas, 117, 204, 223, 230

1971

The Abominable Dr. Phibes, 57, 90, 188, 224
And Now for Something Completely Different, 165
The Andromeda Strain, 59, 229, 252
Asylum of Satan, 94
Beast of the Yellow Night, 17, 200
Bedknobs and Broomsticks, 77, 217, 228
The Beguiled, 75, 211
Bigfoot, 141
Black Noon, 163
Blood and Lace, 98
Blood From the Mummy's Tomb, 41, 57, 117, 130
Blood of Ghastly Horror, 11, 134
Blood on Satan's Claw, 111

The Body Beneath, 163
The Boy Friend, 202
Brain of Blood, 201, 223, 250
Brewster McCloud, 12, 103
The Brotherhood of Satan, 125, 156, 165
Burke and Hare, 208, 217
City Beneath the Sea, 12
A Clockwork Orange, 56, *136*, 152, 158, *159*, 188, 248
The Corpse Grinders, 163
Creatures the World Forgot, 43, 75
Crucible of Terror, 192, 221
Le Culte du Vampire, 200
The Devils, 192, 202
Diamonds Are Forever, 20, 52, 80, 99, 103, 142
Dracula vs. Frankenstein, 9, 11, 46, 75, 170, 201, 221, 223, 240
Dr. Jekyll and the Werewolf, 171
El Dr. Mabuse, 87
Duel, 157, 213, 235
Equinox, 12, 106
Escape From the Planet of the Apes, 32, 43, 158
Fragment of Fear, 119
Fright, 27
From Ear to Ear, 100
Gamera vs. Zigra, 230, 232
Garu the Mad Monk, 163
The Gladiators, 243
Godzilla's Revenge, 117, 230
Godzilla Tai Giagan, 90
Grimm's Fairy Tales for Adults, 146
Happy Birthday, Wanda June, 197, 215, 239, 255
Horror of the Blood Monsters, 11
I Drink Your Blood, 100
I, Monster, 87, 143, 192
In Search of Dracula, 143
In the Grip of the Spider, 155
Julius Caesar, 208
The Legend of Spider Forest, 222
Lust for a Vampire, 22, 92, 192, 203, 216
Macbeth, 186, 208
The Man Who Haunted Himself, 65, 166
Million Dollar Duck, 124
Murders in the Rue Morgue, 73, 115, 146
Necromancy, 87, 97, 246
The Nightcomers, 23
The Night Digger, 63, 114, 171
Night Hair Child, 76, 144
Night of Dark Shadows, 61
The Night Visitor, 240
The Octoman, 19
The Omega Man, 115, 157
Play Misty for Me, 75
The Resurrection of Zachary Wheeler, 51, 174
The Return of Count Yorga, 130, 152, 183, 189
Revenge!, 215, 251
The Secret of Dorian Gray, 146, 250
See No Evil, 48, 77, 79

Simon, King of the Witches, 188
Suicide Mission, 204
A Taste of Evil, 169, 176
The Tell-Tale Heart, 121
THX 1138, 149
El Topo, 122
Twins of Evil, 52, 92, 118
The Velvet Vampire, 201
What's the Matter With Helen?, 104, 167, 251
When Dinosaurs Ruled the Earth, 12, *62*, 63, 100, 236
Whoever Slew Auntie Roo?, 87, 104, 122, 144, 195, 251
Willie Wonka and the Chocolate Factory, 63
Willard, 31, 138
The Wizard of Gore, 145

1972

Alice's Adventures in Wonderland, 195
The Amazing Mr. Blunden, 71, 122
Asylum, 17, 28, 76, 146, 152, 222
Baron Blood, 57
Ben, 129, 176, 228
Between Time and Timbuktu, 239
Beware! the Blob, 106
The Big Game, 163
Blacula, 54, 155
Blood Demon, 17
Blood Monster, 34, 214
Capulina Contra los Vampiros, 40
The Champions of Justice Return, 60
Conquest of the Planet of the Apes, 32, 43, 158
Countess Dracula, 99, 184, *185*, 204
The Creeping Flesh, *61*, 143
The Cremators, 77
The Crypt, 119
Dear Dead Delilah, 167
The Deathmaster, 63, 189
Demons of the Mind, 34, 222, 248
The Devil's Daughter, 222, 251
The Devil's Widow, 23, 158, 212
Doomsday, 187, 210, 250
Doomwatch, 92, 203, 204
Dracula A.D. 1972, 23, 32, 94, 143, 170
Dracula's Great Love, 171
Dr. Jekyll and Sister Hyde, 19, 22, 26, 48, 217, 248
Dr. Phibes Rises Again, 90, 188, 189, 224
Everything You Always Wanted to Know About Sex But Were Afraid to Ask, 12, 41
The Eyes of Charles Sand, 201, 247
Fear in the Night, 52, 92
Flesh Gordon, 12, 63, 118
Four Flies on Grey Velvet, 15
Frenzy, 78, 84, 115, 156
Frogs, 23, 163
The Gore-Gore Girls, 145
Hands of the Ripper, 204

Hannah, Queen of the Vampires, 63, 188
Haunts of the Very Rich, 34, 85
La Hua de Dracula, 87
The Hunchback of the Morgue, 118, 171
Horror Express, 143, 205
Horror on Snape Island, 23, 57, 102
Images, 12, 255
Legacy of Blood, 13, 70, 168
The Mad Butcher, 36
The Man With Two Heads, 163
Mark of the Devil, 133
The Mind Snatchers, 160
Moonchild, 36
The Mysterious Island, 236
Night of 1000 Cats, 40
Night of Terror, 222
Night of the Blood Monster, 143
Night of the Lepus, 144
The Night Stalker, 61, 157, 169
Nothing But the Night, 71, 143, 204, 250
Now You See Him, Now You Don't, 200, 202
La Orgia de los Muertos, 171
The Other, 229
Private Parts, 21
Psychomania, 203, 208
The Rats Are Coming! The Werewolves Are Here, 163
Revolt of the Dead Ones, 134, 171
The Screaming Woman, 65, 212
Silent Running, 67, 229
Slaughterhouse-Five, 239
Spaceboy, 20, 155
The Spectre of Edgar Allan Poe, 178, 186, 200
Stanley, 100
Tales From the Crypt, 17, 52, 61, 78, 87, 91, 152, 195, 222, 241
The Thing With Two Heads, 163, 183
The Tool Box, 242
Twilight People, 17, 200
Vampire Circus, 56, 188, 241
The Womanhunt, 17, 200
ZPG, 192

1973

And Now the Screaming Starts, 23, 146, 152, 178, 200
Battle for the Planet of the Apes, 32, 43, 158
Blood, 163
The Boy Who Cried Werewolf, 126, 157
Captain Kronos, Vampire Hunter, 34, 48, 170
The Crazies, 200
Crypt of the Living Dead, 63, 188
The Devil in Miss Jones, 213
The Devil's Wedding Night, 23, 63
Disciple of Death, 192, 248
Doctor Death, 155, 169
Don't Look Now, 47, *198*, 222
Dracula, 61, 182, *219*, 248
Dr. Maniac, 78

The Exorcist, 19, 27, 90, 212, 240
The Final Program, 78
Frankenstein and the Monster From Hell, 32, 34, 61, 79, 115, 143, 188, 212
Frankenstein: The True Story, 156, 212
Ganja and Hess, 124
Godzilla vs. Megalon, 90, 204
The Golden Voyage of Sinbad, 48, 108, 115, 142, 170, 201, 206
El Gran Amor del Conde Dracula, 171
Happy Mother's Day, Love George, 171
High Plains Drifter, 60, 75
High Priestess of Sexual Witchcraft, 213
Horror Hospital, 98
House in Nightmare Park, 163
House of Freaks, 73
The House of the Seven Corpses, 41, 70
Hungry Wives, 200
Invasion of the Bee Girls, 236
The Island at the Top of the World, 76, 163, 217
The Killing Kind, 13, 104
Lady Frankenstein, 23, 57, 246
The Last House on the Left, 60
The Legend of Hell House, 87, 118, 119, 157, 158
The Legend of Hillbilly John, 106, 221, 242
Live and Let Die, 10, 80, *81*, 103, 112, 166
Lost Horizon, 212, 255
The Love Bug Rides Again, 101
Madhouse, 56, 111, 188, 189, 222
Malatesta's Carnival, 238
The Mummy's Vengeance, 171
The Mutation, 73, 75
The Neptune Factor, 31, 163, 184
The Night Strangler, 61, 157
Night Watch, 111
O Lucky Man!, 158, 195
Poor Devil, 143
Quest for Love, 52
Raw Meat, 143, 184
The Revenge of Dr. Death, 189
Santo y Blue Demon Contra y el Hombre Lobo, 28, 204
Schlock, 9, 19, 139
Scream, Blacula, Scream, 130, 155
Sisters, 67, 114, 132
Sleeper, 12, 113
Soylent Green, 26, 57, 79, 113, 115, 197, 247, 256
Sssssss, 135, 156, 221
Superman Against the Orient, 222
Tales From Beyond the Grave, 184
Tales That Witness Madness, 52, 86, 111, 174, 184, *185*
Terminal Island, 201
Terror Circus, 188
Terror in the Wax Museum, 112, 134, 138, 163
Theatre of Blood, 71, 111, 167, 188, 196, 212
Three on a Meathook, 94
The Vault of Horror, 11, 17, 19, 78, 91, 123, 126, 156, 222, 224
Vierges et Vampires, 200
The Werewolf of Washington, 73

Westworld, *36*, 59
The Wicker Man, 76, 143, 184

1974

Abby, 94, 155
Andy Warhol's Frankenstein, 63, 133, 168, 235
Antichristo, 57
Arnold, 158, 216
The Beast Must Die, 69, 99
Blood For Dracula, 63, *133*, 168, 186
The Cat Creatures, 213
Craze, 75, 182
Curse of the Lviing Dead, 22
Dark Star, 40
Dead of Night, 203, 209
The Holy Mountain, 122
The Horror at 37,000 Feet, 209
It's Alive, 19, 51, 114
The Last Days of Man on Earth, 75, 78, 90
The Legend of the Seven Golden Vampires, 19, 25, 75, 222
Legend of the Werewolf, 87
The Man With the Golden Gun, 76, 80, *81*, 103, 142, 143, 152, *166*, 194, 238
Persecution, 87
Pink Flamingos, 242
Planet Earth, *204*, 205
The Satanic Rites of Dracula, 94, 124, 143
Seizure, 26, 89, 238, 253
Shanks, 42, 154
Silent Night, Bloody Night, 179, 253
The Stepford Wives, 84, 145, 179, *200*, 201, 212
Sugar Hill, 189
The Terminal Man, 59
The Terror of Sheba, 87
The Texas Chain Saw Massacre, 104, 117
The Vampires' Night Orgy, 134
The Werewolf vs. the Vampire Woman, 134, 171
Young Frankenstein, 32, *33*, 35, 78, 113, 221, 231, 256
Zardoz, *30*, 52

1975

Beyond Atlantis, 243
Black Christmas, 73, 205
Black Moon, 63
Bug, 158, 222
Death Race 2000, *20*, 21, 100, 161, 190, 253, 256
The Devil's Rain, 31, 90, 151, 209
Doc Savage, Man of Bronze, 13, 76, 181
Eaten Alive, 117
Escape to Witch Mountain, 118
Fear in the Night, 22
Female Trouble, 242
From Beyond the Grave, 52, 71, 178, 222, 241
Hollywood Horror House, 213
Impulse, 100, 203, 209
In the Beginning, 213

Jaws, 72, 158, 206, 213 250
The Land That Time Forgot, *52*, 160
Love and Death, 12
Monty Python and the Holy Grail, 165
Night of the Strangler, 118
Old Dracula, 40, 111, 142, 174
Phantom of the Paradise, 67
The Reincarnation of Peter Proud, 132
The Rocky Horror Picture Show, 99
Rollerball, 195
Satan's Triangle, 174
Spikey's Magic Wand, 213
Star Maidens, 11, 92
Strange New World, 205
The Strongest Man in the World, 200, 202
Supervixens, 162
Torso, 195
Trilogy of Terror, 61, 157
The Ultimate Warrior, 36, 240
Vengeance of the Zombies, 134

1976

At the Earth's Core, 52, 160, 170
The Big Bus, 98
The Blue Bird, 82
A Boy and His Dog, 125, 165
Burnt Offerings, 61, 64, 192
Carrie, 121, 133, 142, 213
Crash!, 77
The Creature From Black Lake, 118
Deep Red, 15
Demon, 51
The Demon Lover, 104
The Devil's Men, 184
Devil Within Her, 22, 52, 170, 204
Embryo, 158
The Erotic Adventures of Pinocchio, 214
Family Plot, 67, 115
Food of the Gods, 87, 97, 151, 160
Futureworld, 36
Grizzly, 94
Gus, 134
Hollywood Boulevard, 21, 100, 163, 190, 253
The House of Exorcism, 22, 205
King Kong, 11, 19, 20, 32, 66, 190
Logan's Run, 13, *254*, 255, 256
Mansion of the Doomed, 21, 98
The Man Who Fell to Earth, 32, 198
Mr. Superinvisible, 124
Murder By Death, 11
Nightmare in Blood, 157
Obsession 36, 67, 114, 197
The Omen, 71, 88, 183, 216, 241
The Pink Panther Strikes Again, 146
Psychic Killer, 11, 26, 63
Satan's Cheerleaders, 41

278 INDEX

Shadowman, 87
The Shaggy D.A., 53, 217
The Slipper and the Rose, 74, 84
Snuff, 208
Starlight Slaughter, 117
Taxi Driver, 84
The Tenant, 186, 251
They Came From Within, 60, 214
Tommy, 173, 202
To the Devil . . . a Daughter, 27, 143, 222

1977

Audrey Rose, 252
The Car, 34
Cinderella 2000, 11
Close Encounters of the Third Kind, 72, 101, 190, 213, 229, 250, 256
The Crater Lake Monster, 12
Damnation Alley, 212
Demon Seed, 47
Desperate Living, 242
Empire of the Ants, 52, 97
End of the World, 121, 143
Exorcist II: The Heretic, 27, 30, 212, 240
Freaky Friday, 84
Herbie Goes to Monte Carlo, 124
Hollywood Meatcleaver Massacre, 143
The Island of Dr. Moreau, 21, 43, 138, 221, 247, 255
Jabberwocky, 165
Kingdom of the Spiders, 209
Land of the Minotaur, 61, 184
Laserblast, 12 158
The Last Remake of Beau Geste, 78
Lisztomania, 202
The Little Girl Who Lived Down the Lane, 84
Oh, God!, 37, 184
The People That Time Forgot, 160, 243
Pete's Dragon, 200
Rabid, 60
Ruby, 104, 142
The Sentinel, 41, 162, 212
Sinbad and the Eye of the Tiger, 108, 206, 243
The Spy Who Loved Me, 80, *81*, 94, 126, 133, 166, 170
Starship Invasions, 143, 236
Star Wars, 19, 32, 61, 74, 76, 79, 88, 101, 104, *149*, 188, 250
Telefon, 34
Tentacles, 251

1978

Battlestar Galactica, 74
The Bees, 205
The Boys From Brazil, 111, 145, 156, 179, 183
The Brood, 60, 192
Capricorn One, 34
The Cat From Outer Space, 53, 76

The Chosen, 241
Coma, 36, 59
The Dark Secret of Harvest Home, 64, 229
Die Sister Die!, 212
Dominique, 13, 92, 197, 228, 241
The Evil, 36, 188
Eyes of Laura Mars, 40, 106
The Fury, 19, 32, 67, 121, 231
Heaven Can Wait, 156
High Anxiety, *34*, 35
The Hound of the Baskervilles, 168
The Incredible Melting Man, 19, 32
Invasion of the Body Snatchers, 96, 158, 174, 211, 222
It Lives Again, 51, 53, 114
Jaws 2, 206, 222
Kentucky Fried Movie, 9, 139, 142, 222
Lord of the Rings, 201
Magic, 162
The Manitou, 94, 154, 162, 216, 221
Martin, 200
Piranha, 21, 32, 158, 163, 214
Return From Witch Mountain, 64, 76, 143
Superman, 12, 33, 71, 132, 172, *192*, 193, 250, 255
Suspiria, 15, 133
The Swarm, 12
The Toolbox Murders, 164
Warlords of Atlantis, 52, 160
Who is Killing the Great Chefs of Europe?, 167

1979

The Adventures of Stella Star, 170
Alien, 190, 206, 243
All That Jazz, 206
The Amityville Horror, 34
Arabian Adventure, 52, 143, 194
Beyond the Door II, 22
The Black Hole, 20, 31, 76, 163, 183
Buck Rogers in the 25th Century, 102
The China Syndrome, 82, 256
Dawn of the Dead, 200, 205
Dracula, 179
Halloween, 40, 61, 147, 184
The Humanoid, 133
The Legacy, 99, 201, 203
Life of Brian, 165
Meteor, 52
Moonraker, 10, 20, 80, 94, 133, 166
The Muppet Movie, 35, 117, 202
Murder by Natural Causes, 201
Nightwing, 190, 241
Parts—The Clonus Horror, 98
Phantasm, 57, 99
The Phoenix, 133
Prophecy, 87
Quintet, 12
Salem's Lot, 117, 133, 156

The Shape of Things To Come, 182
Star Trek: The Motion Picture, 74, 174, 209, 229, 252, 256
Time After Time, 158, 201, 241, 247
Winter Kills, 183

1980

Battle Beyond the Stars, 205
Blood Beach, 205
Brave New World, 73
The Coming, 97
The Curse of King Tut, 37
Death Ship, 115
Dressed to Kill, 67
Dr. Heckyl and Mr. Hype, 100, 192, 246
Effects, 205
The Empire Strikes Back, 76, 79, 88, 104, 149, 188, 250
The Final Countdown, 201
Flash Gordon, 66
The Fog, 32, 40, 61, 144, 147
Friday the 13th, 60, 205
Fun House, 117
Galaxina, 201
The Hearse, 57

Humanoids From the Deep, 32, 160
The Incredible Shrinking Woman, 139
Maniac, 170, 205
The Martian Chronicles, 32, 119, 158
Midnight, 205
Night Games, 20, 233
Popeye, 12
Prom Night, 61, 174
Scanners, 60
The Shining, 133, 136, 173
Silent Scream, 65, 164, 214
Somewhere in Time, 157, 193, 222
Supersonic Man, 164
Tanya's Island, 19, 32
The Visitor, 251
The Watcher in the Woods, 48, 64
When Time Ran Out, 12, 31, 87
Witches Brew, 12

1981

Clash of the Titans, 14, 28, 108, 162, 174, 206
The Monster Club, 188
Superman II, 193, 255